HOLT Science Spectr...

Physical Science

Interactive Reader

HOLT, RINEHART AND WINSTON

A Harcourt Education Company

Orlando • **Austin** • New York • San Diego • London

ISBN-13: 978-0-030-93638-8
ISBN-10: 0-03-093638-1

25 26 27 28 29 30   0982   20 19 18
4500696314

Contents

PHYSICS

CHAPTER 16 Sound and Light

CHAPTER 17 Electricity

CHAPTER 18 Magnetism

CHAPTER 1 | Introduction to Science

SECTION 1 # The Nature of Science

KEY IDEAS

As you read this section, keep these questions in mind:

• What processes do scientists use to answer questions?

• How is a scientific theory supported by evidence?

• How do scientists use math and models to represent ideas?

What Is Science?

When you have a question about how something works, how do you find the answer? People from all parts of the world use science to answer questions. **Science** is the different processes that people use to discover how things work in the natural world. Science is also the knowledge that people gain about the natural world by using scientific processes. Some examples of scientific processes are shown in the table below.

Scientific Process	Examples
Investigating	learning about an object or event by watching, measuring, testing, or reading other scientists' work
Experimenting	setting up a planned, controlled test to find out how something reacts to a change
Observing	carefully watching, measuring, and writing down information about an object or an event
Confirming results	repeating observations and experiments to see whether the results are the same

People who do science are called *scientists*. Many scientists perform experiments. An *experiment* is a careful test of the way something reacts to a change. A scientist may perform experiments to describe a newly discovered feature of the natural world. Some scientists perform experiments to help explain a natural event. Scientists also perform experiments to check the results of other experiments. ☑

Scientists who do experiments to learn more about the world are doing *pure science*. However, many people use science in other ways. **Technology** is the application of science for practical uses. Advances in science and technology depend on one another.

READING TOOLBOX

Summarize As you read, underline important ideas about scientific theories. When you are finished reading, write a short summary of scientific theories using the underlined ideas.

Talk About It
Brainstorm In a small group, talk about ways that you use scientific processes in your everyday life.

✓ READING CHECK

1. Identify What are three reasons scientists carry out experiments?

_____

_____

_____

_____

_____

_____

SECTION 1 The Nature of Science *continued*

How Do Scientists Learn About the World?

Many scientists use experiments to learn about the natural world. For example, in 1895 a German scientist named Wilhelm Roentgen experimented with a newly discovered form of energy. At that time, scientists were learning about this new form of energy. Scientists first discovered this kind of ray when they passed electricity through tubes like the one shown below.

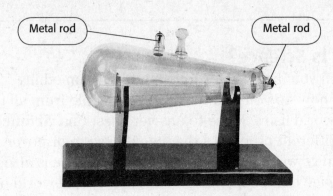

Metal rod   Metal rod

Talk About It

Research Learn more about cathode rays, Roentgen, or another historic scientific discovery. Share what you learn with a partner or a small group.

The tube contained two metal rods that were separated from each other. Scientists removed all of the air from the tube. Then, they connected the rods to an electrical source. Electric charges flowed through the empty space between the rods and produced the rays. Scientists called these rays *cathode rays*.

Roentgen learned about cathode rays from the work of other scientists. He knew that cathode rays could make certain minerals glow. Scientists used pieces of cardboard coated with powder made from these minerals to *detect*, or find, the rays.

Some scientists had carried out experiments to learn whether cathode rays could pass through different materials. They learned that cathode rays could pass through thin metal foil. They also learned that cathode rays could travel only a few centimeters through the air.

Scientists had also tried to find out whether cathode rays could travel through glass. They tried to detect the rays outside of the tube using the mineral-coated cardboard. They did not see the cardboard glow. However, Roentgen thought that bright light from inside the tube might have kept them from seeing the cardboard glow. He decided to carry out an experiment to test this idea. ☑

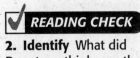

READING CHECK

2. Identify What did Roentgen think was the reason that other scientists did not see the cardboard glowing?

_____

_____

_____

_____

SECTION 1 The Nature of Science *continued*

EXPERIMENTING AND CONFIRMING RESULTS

Roentgen planned his experiment carefully. First, he covered the tube with heavy black paper. He thought that the paper would block any light from inside the tube. Next, he turned off the lights in the room and turned on the electricity in the tube. He did this to check that no light was passing through the paper. ☑

When Roentgen turned on the tube, he noticed something he didn't expect. The cardboard detector was glowing. However, the cardboard was more than 1 m away from the tube. Roentgen knew that cathode rays could not travel that far through the air. He hypothesized that the tube was producing rays other than cathode rays. He thought these were a new kind of ray that no one had seen before. ☑

Roentgen's results were unexpected. He repeated his experiment to find out whether he would get the same results. He set up the experiment exactly as before, and held the cardboard detector 1 m away from the tube. Again, the cardboard glowed. His results were confirmed.

Roentgen's results helped him to think of new questions. He carried out more experiments to find answers to these questions. For example, he tried holding his hand in the path of the rays. The bones in his hand made shadows on the cardboard detector. The rays could pass through his skin, but not through the bones.

Roentgen called the new rays *X rays*. He found that X rays passed through almost everything. Roentgen included an X ray of his wife's hand in one of the first papers that he published on X rays. That image is shown below.

✔ **READING CHECK**

3. Explain Why did Roentgen cover the tube with heavy paper?

_____

_____

✔ **READING CHECK**

4. Describe What made Roentgen think that the tube was producing rays other than cathode rays?

_____

_____

_____

_____

_____

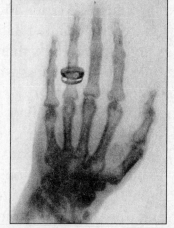

X rays pass through skin and muscle, but not through bone or metal. The dark object on the second finger of Roentgen's wife's hand is her wedding ring.

LOOKING CLOSER

5. Infer What do you think is the reason Roentgen's wife's wedding ring appears on the X ray, but her fingernails do not?

_____

_____

What Is a Scientific Law?

Scientists like Roentgen may carry out experiments to learn how things behave. In some cases, scientists can use the results of experiments to predict what will happen in other situations. In those cases, the result of an experiment may be considered a scientific law.

A scientific **law** is a statement or equation that accurately describes a natural process. For example, one scientific law states that warm objects become cooler when they are placed in cooler surroundings. An example of this is shown below. ☑

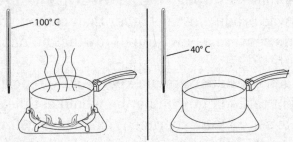

A hot cooking pot always cools when it is moved from a hot stove to a cooler counter top.

Scientists can use scientific laws to make predictions. A *prediction* is an idea about what will happen in the future. However, a law does not explain how a process takes place. For example, the law that states that warm objects cool off does not explain why they cool off. To explain why an event happens, scientists use scientific theories.

What Is a Scientific Theory?

In everyday speech, people often use the word *theory* to mean "guess." However, in science, a theory is much more than a guess. A scientific **theory** is a system of ideas that explains many related observations. Scientific theories are supported by many observations.

The theory that explains why warm objects cool down is called the *kinetic theory of energy.* This theory states that the particles in an object *vibrate*, or move quickly from side-to-side. The energy of the vibrating particles is heat. The faster the vibrations, the hotter the object. This theory explains that warm objects cool down because they lose energy. The energy moves into the surroundings. As a result, the particles in the object move more slowly.

✓ **READING CHECK**

6. Define What is a scientific law?

_____

_____

_____

Critical Thinking

7. Compare What is the main difference between a scientific theory and a scientific law?

_____

_____

_____

_____

_____

TESTING SCIENTIFIC THEORIES

Scientific theories are always being questioned and examined. A theory must continue to pass several tests in order to be accepted. These tests are shown in the table below.

Test of Scientific Theories	Example
A theory must clearly explain all available observations.	The kinetic theory explains why the hot cooking pot gets cooler when it is placed on the cooler counter. It also explains why a hot cup of tea gets cooler when it is placed in a cooler room. In fact, it explains why any hot object cools off in cooler surroundings.
Experiments that support the theory must be repeatable.	A hot cooking pot always gets cooler when placed in cooler surroundings. No matter how many times you do this test, the pot will always cool off.
You must be able to predict results from the theory.	Based on the kinetic theory, you can predict that any hot object placed in cool surroundings will cool down. You can also predict that adding energy to a cool object will make the particles in it vibrate faster. This should cause the object to heat up. Many experiments have shown that these predictions are true.

LOOKING CLOSER
8. Apply Concepts A scientist adds energy to a block of metal. According to the kinetic theory, what should the scientist predict will happen to the metal?

Scientific theories must explain all of the available information that scientists have. Sometimes, scientists change or replace theories when new discoveries are made. For example, more than 200 years ago, scientists used the *caloric theory* to explain how objects become warmer and cooler. This theory stated that heat was an invisible fluid, called *caloric*, that flowed from warm objects to cool ones.

Later, scientists began to realize that caloric theory could not explain some of their observations. After doing many experiments, some scientists presented a new theory of heat—the kinetic theory. At first, people criticized the new theory. However, the kinetic theory was eventually accepted because it explained both old and new observations. ☑

READING CHECK
9. Explain Why did scientists accept the kinetic theory in place of the caloric theory?

How Do Scientists Describe Physical Events?

There are many ways to describe scientific theories and laws. For example, the *law of universal gravitation* describes the gravitational force between two objects. The law states that gravitational force depends on the masses of the objects and the distance between them. This is a qualitative statement of the law of universal gravitation. *Qualitative* statements describe processes or events using words. They are not very precise.☑

Many times, scientists need to describe things precisely. In those cases, they use quantitative statements. A *quantitative* statement is a statement that describes something precisely. Most quantitative statements use numbers or equations to describe things.

For example, scientists use an equation to exactly describe the relationship between mass, distance, and gravitational force. This equation describes exactly how large the gravitational force between any two objects will be. By using this equation, scientists can make quantitative statements about the effects of gravity. ☑

Qualitative Statement	Quantitative Statement
The gravitational force between two objects depends on their masses and on the distance between them.	$F = G\dfrac{m_1 m_2}{d_2}$ *F* is gravitational force, *G* is a constant, m_1 and m_2 are the masses of the objects, and *d* is the distance between the objects.

Scientists may also use models to represent physical events. A scientific *model* is something scientists use to represent an object or event in order to make it easier to study. In many cases, models represent things that are too small, too big, or too complex to study easily. ☑

Models can take many forms. Drawings on paper can be models. Real objects can also be used as models to help us picture things we cannot see. For example, a spring can be used as a model of a sound wave. A model can also be a mental "picture" or set of rules that describes how something works.

Models have uses in our everyday lives. Computer models help forecast the weather. For example, scientists use models like those at the top of the next page to predict how hurricanes will move.

READING CHECK

10. Define What is a qualitative statement?

_____

_____

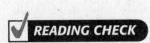

READING CHECK

11. Identify Why do scientists often use quantitative statements instead of qualitative statements?

_____

_____

READING CHECK

12. Describe Why do scientists use models?

_____

_____

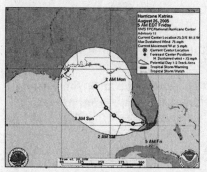 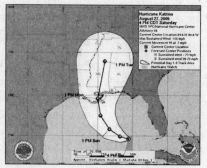

Models like these help scientists predict the paths of hurricanes. By collecting more data, scientists were able to make the right-hand model more accurate than the left-hand model.

What Are the Branches of Science?

Scientists study everything from ants and people to planets and stars. You can think of science as having two main groups, or branches: social science and natural science. *Social science* deals with human behavior. *Natural science* deals with how "nature," or the whole universe, behaves. ☑

Today, natural science has many branches and specialties, as shown in the figure below. The branches of science sometimes mix. For example, *geophysics* is the study of forces that affect Earth. It is both an Earth science and a physical science.

LOOKING CLOSER

13. Explain The model in the right image is more accurate than the model in the left image. How did scientists make the model more accurate?

_____

_____

_____

✓ READING CHECK

14. List What are the two main branches of science?

_____

_____

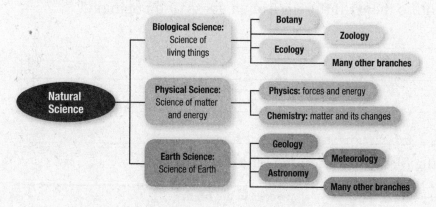

The natural sciences include many different types of science.

LOOKING CLOSER

15. Identify Name two branches of physical science.

_____

_____

Section 1 Review

SECTION VOCABULARY

law a descriptive statement or equation that reliably predicts events under certain conditions **science** the knowledge obtained by observing natural events and conditions in order to discover facts and formulate laws or principles that can be verified or tested	**technology** the application of science for practical purposes; the use of tools, machines, materials, and processes to meet human needs **theory** a system of ideas that explains many related observations and is supported by a large body of evidence acquired through scientific investigation

1. Describe Relationships How are science and technology related?

_____

_____

_____

2. Explain Why did Wilhelm Roentgen repeat his experiment before describing his results to others?

_____

_____

3. Compare How are scientific theories and laws similar?

_____

_____

4. Describe How is a scientific theory different from a guess or an opinion?

_____

_____

_____

_____

5. Apply Concepts Fill in the blank spaces in the table below.

A scientist who studies...	...works in the branch of...
...how plants and animals interact...	...life science.
...how two chemicals react with each other...	
...what causes earthquakes...	
...how objects move...	

CHAPTER 1 | Introduction to Science

SECTION 2 The Way Science Works

As you read this section, keep these questions in mind:

• How can you use critical thinking to solve problems?

• What are scientific methods?

• What is the SI system of units?

What Skills Are Important in Science?

When you think about science skills, you might think of mixing chemicals or pouring liquid into a test tube. These skills may be useful in a lab, but other skills are more important in science. Important science skills include identifying problems, planning experiments, recording observations, and correctly reporting data. The most important science skill, though, is learning to think creatively and critically.

SOLVING PROBLEMS WITH CRITICAL THINKING

Imagine that you and a friend want to buy some popcorn at a movie. You are trying to decide whether to share one large container or buy two small containers. The pictures below show the size and price of each container.

Logical decision-making is important in scientific processes and in everyday life.

$4.50 (160 oz.) $2.00 (80 oz.)

Which size popcorn should you buy in order to get the most popcorn for your money? If you try to solve the problem by asking more questions, making observations, and using logic, you are using **critical thinking**. For example, notice that two small containers cost less than one large container. However, two small containers hold the same amount of popcorn as one large container. Therefore, it is a better deal to buy two small containers.

READING TOOLBOX

Summarize After you read this section, create a Spider Map for scientific methods. Label the center "Scientific methods," and create a branch for each step.

Math *Skills*

1. Calculate How much money would you save by buying four small containers instead of two large containers? Show your work.

What Are Scientific Methods?

Recall that science is a process used to answer questions about the natural world. **Scientific methods** are general processes that scientists use to help organize their thinking about the questions they want to answer. The flow chart below shows some of the steps that make up scientific methods. Note that the exact steps can vary.

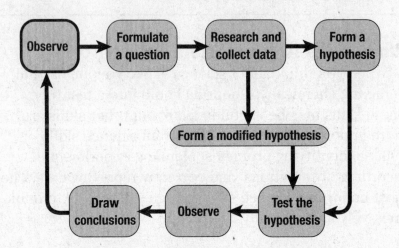

LOOKING CLOSER

2. Identify When may a scientist change a hypothesis?

_____

_____

_____

Many scientific investigations begin with observations. For example, you may notice that when you open a door, you hear a squeak. You may ask the question, "Why does this door squeak?" Then, you may form a *hypothesis*, or a possible answer that you can test. For example, you may think that the doorknob is causing the squeak.

Every investigation has factors, or **variables**, that can affect the outcome. For example, variables that could make the door squeak include the doorknob and how fast you open the door. ☑

3. Define What is a variable?

_____

_____

_____

In many cases, scientists test hypotheses by doing controlled experiments. In a *controlled experiment*, only one variable changes at a time. The other variables are kept constant. In this way, scientists can determine how each variable affects the result of the experiment. If many variables changed at a time, it would be hard to determine the effects of only one of them.

Some scientists test hypotheses without doing experiments. Instead, they collect data by measuring and observing the natural world. Then, they use the data to test their hypotheses.

SECTION 2 The Way Science Works *continued*

SHOWING THAT A HYPOTHESIS IS FALSE

If you removed the doorknob and the door still squeaked, your experiment would not be a failure. Experiments that show a hypothesis is false may be just as helpful as experiments that support a hypothesis. Either way, the outcome of the experiment can lead to new hypotheses. For example, you might hypothesize that oiling the hinges would stop the squeak.

Why Do Scientists Use Tools?

Scientists have developed tools to make observations that they cannot make with only their senses. Modern science depends upon the use of tools to make exact measurements. Scientists must know how to use these tools, what the limits of the tools are, and how to interpret data from them. Some common tools are shown in the chart below.

Tool	Measurement
Stopwatch 	time
Meter Stick 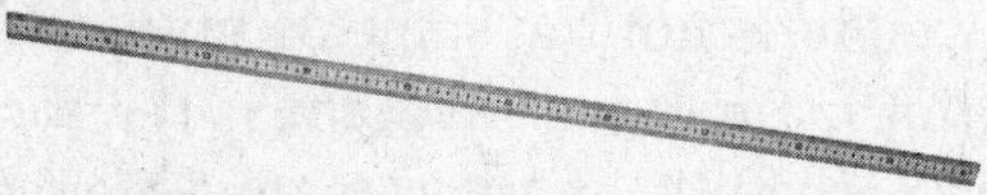	length
Triple-Beam Balance 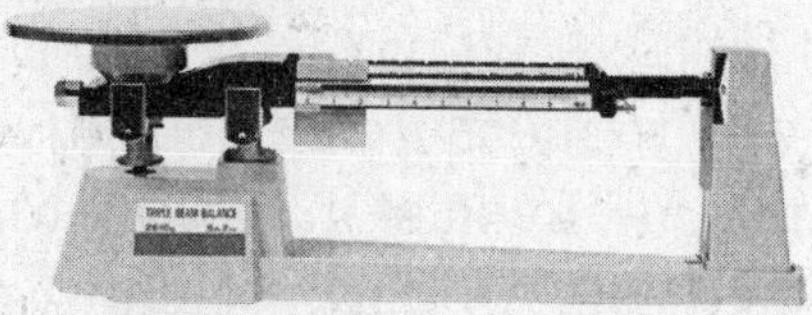	mass
Graduated Cylinder 	volume

Critical Thinking

4. Apply Concepts A scientist carries out an experiment. The results do not support the scientist's hypothesis. How can thinking critically be helpful to the scientist?

_____

_____

_____

_____

_____

_____

_____

Talk About It

Discuss In a small group, talk about different tools that you use every day. How does each tool help you in your life?

LOOKING CLOSER

5. Identify A student needs to measure the volume of a liquid. What tool could the student use?

_____

What Units of Measurement Do Scientists Use?

Scientists from all around the world work together and share data. However, different units of measurement are commonly used in different countries. For example, people in the United States measure car trips in miles. However, people in most other countries use kilometers. To avoid confusion, scientists use standard units of measurement. These standard units together form the *International System of Units*, or *SI*. ☑

SI is based on the metric system. Common SI base units are listed in the table below. The base units can be combined to describe area, volume, pressure, weight, force, speed, and other familiar quantities.

✓ **READING CHECK**

6. Explain Why do scientists use SI units?

_____

_____

Common SI Base Units		
Quantity	**Unit**	**Abbreviation**
Length	meter	m
Mass	kilogram	kg
Time	second	s
Temperature	kelvin	K

In your science class, you will probably measure time, length, volume, and mass. **Length** is the distance between two points, measured in a straight line. **Volume** is a measure of the size of an object or fluid in three-dimensional space. **Mass** is a measure of the amount of matter in an object.

You may hear people say they are "weighing" objects with a balance, but weight is not the same as mass. Mass is the amount of matter in an object. **Weight** is the force with which Earth's gravity pulls on that amount of matter.

USING PREFIXES IN SI

Scientists must have a way to measure objects at very different scales. For example, a biologist may want to measure the length of a bird's egg. An Earth scientist may want to measure the length of a river. The egg may be 5/100 m, or 0.05 m, long. The river may be 800,000 m long. The SI system uses prefixes so scientists do not have to write a lot of decimal places and zeros. The table at the top of the next page gives some common SI prefixes.

Critical Thinking

7. Infer A student uses a triple-beam balance to measure an object. What SI base unit could the student use to describe the measurement?

_____

SI Prefixes			
Prefix	Symbol	Meaning	Multiple of Base Unit
giga-	G	billion	1,000,000,000
mega-	M	million	1,000,000
kilo-	k	thousand	1,000
centi-	c	hundredth	0.01
milli-	m	thousandth	0.001
micro-	μ	millionth	0.000001
nano-	n	billionth	0.000000001

LOOKING CLOSER
8. Identify How many meters are in one gigameter?

Using SI prefixes, the length of the bird's egg is 5 cm (1 *centi*meter equals 0.01 m). The length of the river is 800 km (1 *kilo*meter equals 1,000 m).

It is easy to *convert*, or change, SI units to smaller or larger units. To convert a large unit to a small unit, multiply by the ratio of the small unit to the large unit. For example, if a person's height is 1.85 m, he is 185 cm tall.

$$1.85 \text{ m} \times \frac{100 \text{ cm}}{1 \text{ m}} = 185 \text{ cm}$$

To convert a small unit to a large unit, multiply by the ratio of the large unit to the small unit. For example, if a book has a mass of 1,500 g, its mass is 1.5 kg.

$$1,500 \text{ g} \times \frac{1 \text{ kg}}{1,000 \text{ g}} = 1.5 \text{ kg}$$

Math Skills
9. Calculate The height of a building is 31.0 m. How tall is the building in kilometers? Show your work.

How Do Scientists Draw Conclusions?

After scientists collect data, they use the data to draw conclusions about the hypothesis they were testing. To keep from making false conclusions, they must carefully search for bias. *Bias* causes people to make judgments that may not be based on evidence. Scientists must also guard against *conflict of interest*. This can occur when groups that pay for experiments want to see specific conclusions.

Scientists who work together may have similar biases. Therefore, it is important for scientists to share their work with scientists they do not work with. The other scientists may be better able to identify biases or errors. ☑

READING CHECK
10. Explain What is one reason that scientists should share their work?

Name _____ Class _____ Date _____

Section 2 Review

SECTION VOCABULARY

critical thinking the ability and willingness to assess claims critically and to make judgments on the basis of objective and supported reasons	**scientific methods** a series of steps followed to solve problems, including collecting data, formulating a hypothesis, testing the hypothesis, and stating conclusions
length a measure of the straight-line distance between two points	**variable** a factor that changes in an experiment in order to test a hypothesis
mass a measure of the amount of matter in an object; a fundamental property of an object that is not affected by the forces that act on the object, such as the gravitational force	**volume** a measure of the size of a body or region in three-dimensional space
	weight a measure of the gravitational force exerted on an object; its value can change with the location of the object in the universe

1. Compare How is mass different from weight?

_____

_____

_____

2. Apply Concepts A student plans an experiment to find out if house plants will grow faster when they are watered more. Describe two variables that the student should keep constant.

_____

_____

3. Calculate The width of a soccer goal is 7 m. How wide is the goal in centimeters? Show your work.

4. Calculate The mass of an object is 100 mg. What is the object's mass in kg? Show your work.

5. Infer A student needs to calculate the density of some liquid. The student knows that density is equal to mass divided by volume. Name two tools the student could use to measure the liquid in order to calculate its density. Explain what the student should measure with each tool.

_____

_____

CHAPTER 1	Introduction to Science

SECTION 3 **Organizing Data**

> **KEY IDEAS**
>
> **As you read this section, keep these questions in mind:**
> - What is scientific notation?
> - How are precision and accuracy different?
> - How do scientists use graphs to show data?

How Do Scientists Write Numbers?

When scientists conduct an experiment, they must carefully record the data. In most cases, the first step in recording data is writing down measurements. Scientists need to record their measurements carefully.

Sometimes, the value of a measurement is very large or very small. This results in long numbers with many zeros or decimal places. It is easy to make mistakes when writing and copying long numbers. Recall that you can use SI prefixes to reduce the number of zeros. Another way to reduce the number of zeros is to use scientific notation.

In **scientific notation**, you express a value as a number multiplied by a power of 10. A power of 10 is written as a small number above the 10 called an *exponent*. The exponent shows how many times 10 is multiplied by itself. For example, $10^2 = 10 \times 10$. Negative exponents show how many times to divide by 10. For example, $10^{-2} = 1 \div (10 \times 10)$. The table shows some other powers of 10.

Decimal Number	Equivalent Power of 10	Example
1,000,000	10^6	$5,000,000 = 5 \times 10^6$
1,000	10^3	$3,000 = 3 \times 10^3$
100	10^2	$150 = 1.5 \times 10^2$
10	10^1	$20 = 2 \times 10^1$
0.1	10^{-1}	$0.6 = 6 \times 10^{-1}$
0.001	10^{-3}	$0.009 = 9 \times 10^{-3}$
0.000001	10^{-6}	$0.000004 = 4 \times 10^{-6}$

To determine the power of ten for a number, count the number of zeroes in the number. For example, 800,000 m is written 8×10^5 m. If the number is less than one, count the number of decimal places. For example, 0.00004 cm is written as 4×10^{-5} cm. ☑

> **READING TOOLBOX**
>
> **Apply Concepts** After you read this section, create a table showing the heights of five of your friends. Then, use the data to make a bar graph.

Critical Thinking

1. Infer When may it be a good idea to use scientific notation or SI prefixes?

_____

_____

> **✓ READING CHECK**
>
> **2. Apply Concepts** What exponent should you use to represent one hundred thousand?
>
> _____

SECTION 3 Organizing Data *continued*

MAKING CALCULATIONS USING SCIENTIFIC NOTATION

When you use scientific notation in calculations, follow the math rules for powers of 10. For example, when you multiply two values, you add the powers of 10. When you divide two values, you subtract the powers of 10.

Suppose you want to find out how long it takes for light to travel from Neptune to Earth. Light travels at a speed of about 3.0×10^8 m/s. The distance between Neptune and Earth is about 4.5×10^{12} m. To calculate the time it takes light to travel this distance, use the process below.

$$t = \frac{\text{distance from Earth to Neptune (m)}}{\text{speed of light (m/s)}}$$

$$t = \frac{4.5 \times 10^{12} \text{ m}}{3.0 \times 10^8 \text{ m/s}}$$

$$t = \left(\frac{4.5}{3.0} \times \frac{10^{12}}{10^8}\right) \frac{\text{m}}{\text{m/s}}$$

$$t = (1.5 \times 10^{(12-8)}) \text{ s}$$

$$t = 1.5 \times 10^4 \text{ s}$$

Math Skills

3. Convert What is the distance between Neptune and Earth in kilometers? Give your answer in scientific notation.

_____

_____

PRECISION AND ACCURACY OF MEASUREMENTS

Imagine that you are measuring how far a long jumper jumped. If you use a tape measure that is marked every 0.1 m, you could report that the jump was 4.1 m. If you used a tape measure that was marked every 0.01 m, you could report a more exact value—4.11 m. The second measurement has greater **precision**, or exactness.

Scientists use **significant figures** to show the precision of a measurement. The distance of 4.1 m has two significant figures because the measured value has two digits. The distance of 4.11 m has three significant figures.

Suppose that the tape measure had a mistake in it. Instead of the marks being 0.01 m apart, they were actually 0.02 m apart. Your measurements would be far from their true value. In other words, they would not be very accurate. **Accuracy** describes how close a measurement is to the true value of the quantity being measured. The figures at the top of the next page give other examples of accuracy and precision.

Critical Thinking

4. Apply Concepts A student has two rulers. One is marked in centimeters. The other is marked in millimeters. Which ruler should the student use to make the most precise measurements?

_____

_____

SECTION 3 Organizing Data *continued*

_____ precision,
_____ accuracy

_____ precision,
_____ accuracy

Good precision,
poor accuracy

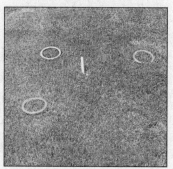

_____ precision,
_____ accuracy

LOOKING CLOSER

5. Identify Fill in the blanks to describe the precision and accuracy shown in each picture.

SIGNIFICANT FIGURES IN CALCULATIONS

When you use measurements in calculations, you must give your answer with the correct number of significant figures. The answer can be only as precise as the least precise measurement used in the calculation. The least precise measurement is the one with the fewest significant figures. ☑

When you multiply or divide measurements, round the answer to the number of significant figures of the least precise measurement. For example, imagine that you need to calculate the area of a wall. The wall is 8.871 m long and 9.14 m high. To calculate the area, you multiply 8.871 m by 9.14 m. The result is 81.08094 m². The least precise value, 9.14 m, has three significant figures. The correctly rounded answer is therefore 81.1 m².

Whenever you add or subtract measurements, round the answer to the same number of decimal places as the least precise measurement. For example, if you add 6.3421 to 12.1, your answer should have only one decimal place. This is because the least precise value, 12.1, has one decimal place. Therefore, the correctly rounded answer is 18.4. ☑

☑ READING CHECK

6. Describe A student takes several measurements. How can the student determine which measurement is the least precise?

_____

_____

_____

☑ READING CHECK

7. Identify A student adds two numbers together. How can the student determine the number of significant figures in the answer?

_____

_____

MORE CALCULATIONS WITH SIGNIFICANT FIGURES

Suppose you want to find the volume of a book that is 24.8 cm long, 19 cm wide, and 6.2 cm high. The equation for finding volume is shown below.

$$volume = length \times width \times height$$

Substitute your book measurements into the equation.

$$volume = 24.8 \text{ cm} \times 19 \text{ cm} \times 6.2 \text{ cm}$$

If you use a calculator to solve the problem, you will get the answer shown below.

$$volume = 2,921.44 \text{ cm}^3$$

Is this the correct answer? Not yet. Remember, the answer can only be as precise as the least precise measurement. In this case, both the width and height were measured to two significant digits. Therefore, you must also round your answer to two significant digits. Rounding 2,921.44 cm³ gives you the correct answer: 2,900 cm³.

How Do Scientists Present Data?

Measurements, calculations, and other results of experiments may lead to new questions that can be tested by different scientists. Therefore, scientists must present their data clearly. Otherwise, other scientists may not be able to understand or use the data easily. The best way to present data depends on the situation. ☑

Suppose you want to find the speed of a certain chemical reaction that makes a gas. You mix two chemicals in a flask attached to one end of a rubber hose. You place the other end of the hose in a graduated cylinder full of water. As the reaction proceeds, the gas travels through the hose and into the graduated cylinder. The gas bubbles push the water out of the graduated cylinder, as shown in the figure below.

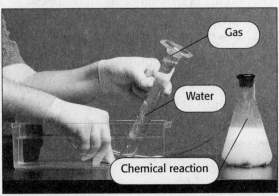

Gas

Water

Chemical reaction

You can measure the volume of the gas in the graduated cylinder and record your results in a data table.

Math *Skills*

8. Identify Which measurement of the book is most precise?

_____

_____

✓ **READING CHECK**

9. Explain Why should scientists present their data clearly?

_____

_____

LOOKING CLOSER

10. Infer How could the person determine the volume of gas produced in the reaction?

_____

_____

_____

Name _____ Class _____ Date _____

USING LINE GRAPHS TO SHOW CHANGE

You can read the volume of gas in the cylinder every 20 s from the start of the reaction until there is no change in volume. Then, you can make a table like the one below to organize the data that you collect in the experiment.

Time (s)	Volume of Gas (mL)
0	0
20	6
40	25
60	58
80	100
100	140
120	152
140	156
160	156
180	156

The table of numbers is the best way to record your data accurately. However, a table can be difficult to read and interpret. You can help people more easily see how the volume changed by making a graph. There are many types of graphs that you could use. A *line graph* is a good choice for displaying data that change over time.

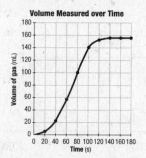

Volume Measured over Time

This graph makes it easier to see how the volume of gas changed over time.

The line graph above shows the same information as the data table. It shows two variables, time and volume. Time is the *independent variable*. In other words, it is the variable you could control in the experiment. The volume of gas is the *dependent variable* because it depends on the independent variable.

Line graphs clearly show changes during an experiment. The graph shows that gas was produced slowly during the first 20 s. From 40 s to 100 s, the gas was produced at a rate of about 40 mL every 20 s. The reaction then slowed down and stopped after about 140 s.

Math *Skills*

11. Calculate How many milliliters of gas were produced between 40 s and 100 s? Show your work.

_____

_____

LOOKING CLOSER

12. Read a Graph When did the reaction stop producing gas? Explain how you know.

_____

_____

_____

_____

SECTION 3 Organizing Data *continued*

USING BAR GRAPHS TO SHOW THE VALUE OF ITEMS

Suppose a scientist measured the melting temperatures of some metals. The scientist could show her data in a table, like the one below. However, a list of numbers in a table does not easily show the relationship between the values. Suppose you want to know which metal has the highest melting temperature. To find out, you must read through all of the entries in the temperature column.

Element	Melting temperature (K)
Aluminum	933
Gold	1,337
Iron	1,808
Lead	601
Silver	1,235

LOOKING CLOSER

13. Compare Which has the higher melting temperature, gold or silver?

_____

_____

To more easily compare the data, you could show the data in a graph. A *bar graph* shows the values of several different items. Bar graphs can be useful when you want to compare data for several individual items or events. By comparing the sizes of the bars in the graph, you can determine which value is largest or smallest. The graph below is a bar graph of the melting temperatures in the table. ☑

✓ **READING CHECK**

14. Identify When should you use a bar graph to display your data?

_____

_____

_____

Melting Points of Some Common Metals

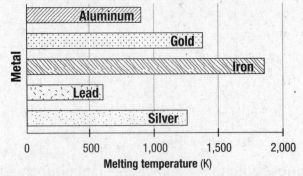

This bar graph shows the relative melting points of different metals. It is easier to read than the data table.

Compare the table of melting temperatures to the bar graph. The bar graph contains the same data as the table. However, the differences in melting temperature between the metals are easier to see in the bar graph. You can easily tell that iron has the highest melting temperature. You can also see that the melting temperature of aluminum is about half the melting temperature of iron.

USING PIE GRAPHS TO SHOW THE PARTS OF A WHOLE

Sometimes, you need to use a graph to show the amounts of different parts of a whole. For example, suppose a clothing company is making a new kind of winter coat. The new coat is made from three different materials. Each material gives the coat different properties. The company wants to show how much of each material is in the new coat.

The company could make a data table that shows the different materials in the coat. The table may look like the one below. From the table, you can see that the coat is made from three different materials: nylon, polyester, and spandex. You can also see how much of each material is in the coat.

Type of Fabric	Percentage of Fabric in the Coat
Nylon	66
Polyester	30
Spandex	4

The company could also use a pie graph to show the materials in the coat. In a *pie graph*, the different parts of a whole are shown as "slices" of a pie. The size of each slice shows how much of the whole is made up of that part. For example, the pie graph below shows the composition of the winter coat. In this case, the "pie" represents the coat. Each slice represents a different material in the coat. ☑

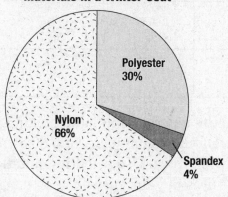

Materials in a Winter Coat

Polyester 30%
Nylon 66%
Spandex 4%

The graph shows the same information as the data table. However, the graph makes it easier to see that most of the coat is nylon. Only a small fraction of the coat is spandex.

Talk About It

Brainstorm Think of some other examples that you have seen of people displaying data. What kind of data were being displayed? How were they displayed? Share your list with a small group.

LOOKING CLOSER

15. Identify Which material makes up the smallest fraction of the coat?

_____

_____

READING CHECK

16. Describe What do the different slices in a pie graph represent?

_____

_____

Section 3 Review

SECTION VOCABULARY

accuracy a description of how close a measurement is to the true value of the quantity measured **precision** the exactness of a measurement **scientific notation** a method of expressing a quantity as a number multiplied by 10 to the appropriate power	**significant figure** a prescribed decimal place that determines the amount of rounding off to be done based on the precision of the measurement

1. **Evaluate** A student measures her height with a meter stick and finds that she is about 1.5 m tall. How can she measure her height with greater accuracy and precision?

   _____

   _____

   _____

   _____

2. **Compare** Fill in the blank spaces in the table below.

Example of Data to Be Displayed	Best Type of Graph to Use
changes in the mass of a rock over time	
the fractions of different gases in the atmosphere	
the maximum speed of several different cars	
how the height of a rocket changes with time	
the relative amounts of different minerals in a rock	

3. **Apply Concepts** A student measures the length, width, and height of a fish tank. She finds that the fish tank is 105 cm long, 75 cm wide, and 80.5 cm high. What is the volume of the fish tank? Show your work. Use scientific notation and show the correct number of significant figures in your answer.

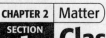

CHAPTER 2 | Matter

SECTION 1

Classifying Matter

KEY IDEAS

As you read this section, keep these questions in mind:

• How can matter be classified?

• Why are elements and compounds considered pure substances?

• How are elements and compounds different from mixtures?

What Is Matter?

This book, a pencil, a piece of paper, and even you are made of matter. In fact, anything that you can hold or touch is made of matter. **Matter** is anything that has both mass and volume. *Mass* consists of all the particles that make up an object. *Volume* is how much space the object occupies. ☑

Some things you cannot see are matter. For example, you cannot see air, but because it has both mass and volume, it is matter. Some things you can see, however, are not matter. For example, light is not matter even though you can see it. Why isn't light matter? It does not have mass or volume.

MATTER AND CHEMISTRY

Chemistry is the branch of science that studies matter and its changes. Chemists study the particles that make up matter. They also study what happens to these particles as they interact with one another. Chemists often use the knowledge they gain to develop new products for consumers such as you. Almost everything that you use in daily life involves chemistry. This includes foods, soaps, clothing, and compact discs (CDs).

READING TOOLBOX

Compare After you read this section, make a Venn diagram to show the similarities and differences between elements, compounds, and mixtures.

✓ READING CHECK

1. Identify What two properties does all matter have?

_____

_____

LOOKING CLOSER

2. Explain What can you see in this picture that is not matter? Explain your answer.

_____

_____

_____

_____

CLASSIFYING MATTER

To *classify* something is to place it into a specific group. All members in the group share certain features. For example, the CDs in a music store are classified into groups such as rock, classical, and jazz. Like CDs, matter is classified into different groups.

Matter can be classified in several ways. One of the most common ways scientists group matter is based on what makes it up. Every sample of matter is either an element, a compound, or a mixture. Gold and oxygen are examples of elements. Water and sugar are examples of compounds. Vinegar and brass are examples of mixtures.

```
          ┌──────────┐
          │  Matter  │
          └──────────┘
   ┌──────────┼──────────┐
   ▼          ▼          ▼
┌──────┐  ┌──────┐  ┌──────┐
│      │  │      │  │      │
└──────┘  └──────┘  └──────┘
```

LOOKING CLOSER

3. Complete Fill in the graphic organizer to show the three main groups of matter.

What Is an Element?

Gold and oxygen are classified as elements. An **element** is a substance that cannot be separated or broken down into simpler substances. An element is made of only one kind of atom. An **atom** is the smallest unit of an element that has the chemical properties of that element.

Some elements exist as single atoms. Helium, an element often used to fill balloons, exists as a single atom. Other elements exist as combinations of more than one atom known as molecules. A **molecule** is a combination of two or more atoms that are combined in a definite ratio. For example, a molecule of water has two hydrogen atoms and one oxygen atom. The ratio of hydrogen atoms to oxygen atoms in water is always 2:1.

Critical Thinking

4. Identify Relationships How are atoms and molecules related?

_____

_____

_____

Each of these molecules is made up of atoms of the same element. Many molecules are made of two or more different elements.

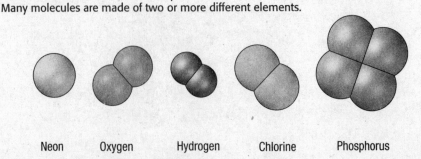

Neon   Oxygen   Hydrogen   Chlorine   Phosphorus

ELEMENT SYMBOLS

Each element is represented by a one- or two-letter symbol. The symbol is either a single capital letter or a capital letter and a lowercase letter. For example, the symbol for carbon is C and the symbol for copper is Cu. All the elements and their symbols are listed in the periodic table.

What Is a Compound?

Water and sugar are examples of compounds. A **compound** is a substance made up of atoms of different elements that are chemically combined. When elements combine to form a compound, they always combine in the same ratio. For example, a water molecule is always made of two hydrogen atoms and one oxygen atom.

Water is a compound. Each water molecule is made up of two hydrogen atoms and one oxygen atom.

Oxygen atom

Hydrogen atoms

Critical Thinking

5. Explain A particular molecule has two hydrogen atoms and two oxygen atoms. How do you know that this is not a molecule of water?

_____

_____

_____

_____

_____

_____

UNIQUE PROPERTIES

The properties of a compound are different from the properties of the elements that make up the compound. For example, both hydrogen and oxygen are gases at room temperature. However, hydrogen and oxygen combine chemically to form the compound water, which is liquid at room temperature.

CHEMICAL FORMULAS

A *chemical formula* shows how many atoms of each element are in a unit of a substance. The number of atoms of each element appears as a *subscript* after the symbol. For example, a molecule of O_2 has two oxygen atoms.

Numbers placed in front of a chemical formula show how many molecules of a substance that you have. One molecule of table sugar is written as $C_{12}H_{22}O_{11}$. Therefore, three molecules of sugar are written as $3C_{12}H_{22}O_{11}$.

Math *Skills*

6. Calculate How many total atoms are in three molecules of table sugar?

_____

$$C_{16}H_{10}N_2O_2$$

Indigo is a dye that was once used to make jeans blue. Four different elements make up a molecule of this compound.

LOOKING CLOSER

7. Label Use the periodic table in the back of the book to label the elements in a molecule of indigo.

What Are Pure Substances?

All elements and compounds are considered pure substances. In chemistry, a **pure substance** is matter that has a fixed composition and definite properties. Consider a pot of water. The water will boil at 100 °C, no matter how much water is in the pot. ☑

When boiling water to cook pasta, some people add salt. Like water, salt is a compound and therefore a pure substance. However, when salt and water are mixed, the combination is no longer a pure substance. Instead, the combination of salt and water is classified as a third type of matter called a mixture.

☑ **READING CHECK**

8. Identify What two kinds of matter are pure substances?

_____

_____

What Is a Mixture?

A **mixture** is a combination of two or more pure substances that are not chemically combined. The chart below shows how mixtures differ from elements and compounds. ☑

☑ **READING CHECK**

9. Explain How are mixtures and pure substances related?

_____

_____

_____

Pure substance (element or compound)	Mixture
Has a fixed composition	Does not have a fixed composition
Properties of components change when their elements combine	Components keep their original properties when combined
Components cannot be separated physically	Components can be separated physically

HETEROGENEOUS AND HOMOGENEOUS

Mixtures can be classified into two main groups. These groups are based on how well the components of the mixture are *distributed*, or spread out.

Name _____ Class _____ Date _____

SECTION 1 Classifying Matter *continued*

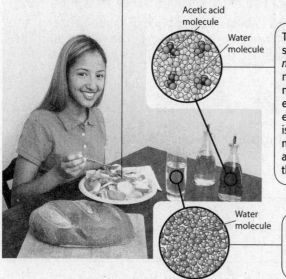

A tossed salad is an example of a *heterogeneous mixture*. The substances in a heterogeneous mixture are not distributed, or spread, evenly throughout the mixture. Different parts of the mixture may not be the same. Some parts of the salad, for example, may have more tomatoes or carrots than other parts of the salad.

Acetic acid molecule

Water molecule

The vinegar used on a salad is a *homogeneous mixture*. The components of a homogeneous mixture are distributed evenly. This means that every part of the mixture is the same. In vinegar, molecules of acetic acid are spread evenly among the molecules of water

Water molecule

Water is a *pure substance*. It has a fixed composition and definite properties.

LOOKING CLOSER
10. Compare How do homogeneous and heterogeneous mixtures differ?

_____

_____

_____

_____

MISCIBLE AND IMMISCIBLE

Gasoline is a homogeneous mixture made up of many different liquids. The liquids in gasoline are *miscible*, which means that they can be mixed and will stay mixed.

If you shake up a mixture of oil and water, they will not mix well. The oil will rise to the top of the container and the water will stay at the bottom. Oil and water are *immiscible*, which means they do not mix or will not stay mixed.

Critical Thinking
11. Apply Concepts Generally, you must stir a can of paint before you use it. Is paint miscible or immiscible? Explain your answer.

_____

_____

_____

MAKING MIXTURES

A mixture can be made up of solids, liquids, or gases. It can even be made up of all three. For example, a carbonated drink is a homogeneous mixture made up of water, sugar, flavorings, and carbon dioxide gas. Some other examples of mixtures are shown below.

Example	A mixture of...
Air	gases
Sand	solids
Gasoline	liquids
Fog	gases and liquid
Seawater	solids, liquids, and gases

Section 1 Review

SECTION VOCABULARY

atom the smallest unit of an element that maintains the chemical properties of that element

compound a substance made up of atoms of two or more different elements joined by chemical bonds

element a substance that cannot be separated or broken down into simpler substances by chemical means; all atoms of an element have the same atomic number

matter anything that has mass and takes up space

mixture a combination of two or more substances that are not chemically combined

molecule the smallest particle of a substance that has all of the chemical properties of that substance; a molecule is made up of one atom or two or more atoms bonded together

pure substance a sample of matter, either a single element or a single compound, that has definite chemical and physical properties

1. Explain Why is Co an element, but CO a compound? (Hint: Use the periodic table in the back of the book to help you.)

_____

_____

_____

2. Compare How are compounds and mixtures alike? How are they different?

_____

_____

_____

3. Complete Fill in the concept map below to show the relationship between the following: compound, element, matter, mixture, pure substance.

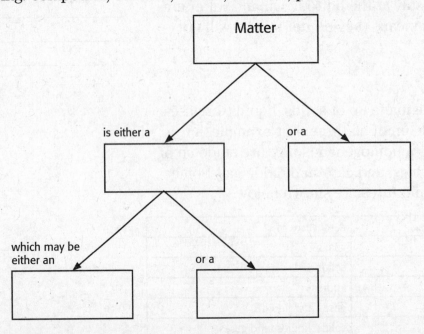

CHAPTER 2 | Matter

SECTION 2 Properties of Matter

As you read this section, keep these questions in mind:

• Why are color, volume, and density physical properties?

• Why are flammability and reactivity chemical properties?

What Are Physical Properties?

Each of the balls in the figure below is used in a different sport because it has certain properties.

When you play football, you want a ball that is light and will spin easily through the air.

Tennis players need a small ball that can bounce.

If you bowl, you need a heavy ball that will roll smoothly down the lane to knock over the pins.

A *physical property* is a characteristic that can be observed without changing the identity of the substance. Some of the properties of an object are easy to observe. For example, you can observe an object's color, texture, shape, odor, or weight. In general, the properties of an object are determined by the properties of the materials the object is made of. ☑

Many of the physical properties of materials that make up objects can be measured. These properties include strength, hardness, magnetism, and the ability to conduct heat and electricity.

Some physical properties depend on how much of a material you have. In other words, a large amount of a material may have different properties than a smaller amount of the material. Other physical properties do not depend on how much of the material is present. This means that no matter how large or small a sample of material is, the particular property is always the same.

READING TOOLBOX

Underline As you read, use a red pen or colored pencil to underline physical properties of matter. Use a blue pen or colored pencil to underline chemical properties of matter.

LOOKING CLOSER

1. Identify List three properties of objects that you can observe in this picture.

_____

_____

_____

READING CHECK

2. Identify What determines the properties of an object?

_____

_____

_____

Which Physical Properties Depend on Amount?

Some physical properties of a material depend on how much of the material you have. For example, two objects made of the same material may have different masses and volumes. ☑

READING CHECK

3. Identify Give two physical properties of an object that depend on the amount of material you have.

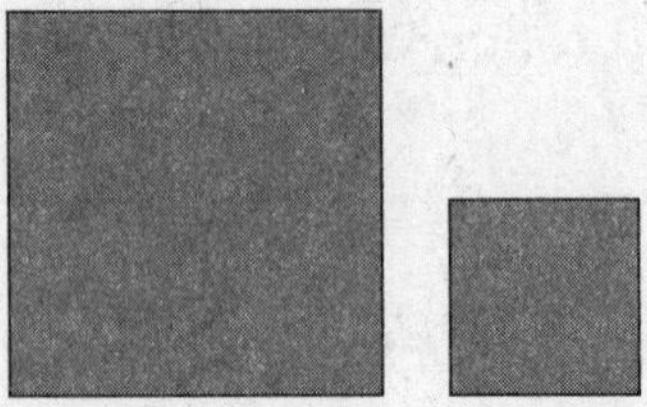

These two objects are made of the same material. However, the objects have different volumes.

Which Physical Properties Do Not Depend on Amount?

Many physical properties of a substance do not depend on how much of the substance you have. In other words, some physical properties stay the same no matter how small or large a sample is. These properties depend on what the substance is made of. They include:

- state
- melting point
- boiling point
- density

MELTING POINT AND BOILING POINT

State is the physical form of a substance. Solid, liquid, and gas are three common states of matter. For example, water can be in the form of solid ice, liquid water, or water vapor. ☑

READING CHECK

4. Define What is state?

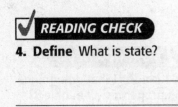

When ice melts, water is changing from one state to another. The temperature at which a substance changes from a solid to a liquid is called the **melting point**. When water boils, it is also changing from one state to another. The temperature at which a substance changes from a liquid to a gas is called the **boiling point**.

Melting point and boiling point do not depend on how much of a substance is present. For example, a small sample of water has the same boiling point as a much larger sample of water.

SECTION 2 Properties of Matter *continued*

DENSITY

Density is a measure of how much matter is in a certain volume of a substance. This physical property of a substance does not depend on how much of the substance you have.

All of these objects are made of the same material. The mass and volume of the objects differ. However, the density of the material making up the objects is the same. Density is a physical property of a substance that does not depend on the size of the sample.

CALCULATING DENSITY

The density of a liquid or solid is usually expressed in grams per cubic centimeter (g/cm³). A cubic centimeter has the same volume as a millimeter (mL).

> **Density equation:**
>
> $$density = \frac{mass}{volume}$$
>
> $$D = \frac{m}{V}$$

If 10.0 cm³ of ice has a mass of 9.17 g, what is the density of ice?

Step 1: List the given and unknown values.	Given: mass, $m = 9.17$ g volume, $V = 10.0$ cm³	Unknown: density, D
Step 2: Write the equation.	$D = \dfrac{m}{V}$	
Step 3: Insert the known values and solve for the unknown value.	$D = \dfrac{9.17 \text{ g}}{10.0 \text{ cm}^3}$ $D = 0.917$ g/cm³	

Critical Thinking

5. Apply Concepts A 1 kg mass of water has a density of 1 g/cm³. What is the density of a 10 kg mass of water?

_____

Math Skills

6. Write an Equation Rearrange the density equation to show how to find the mass of a substance if you know the volume and density.

_____

Math Skills

7. Calculate A piece of metal has a density of 11.3 g/cm³ and a volume of 6.7 cm³. What is the mass of the piece of metal?

_____

SECTION 2 Properties of Matter *continued*

DENSITY VERSUS WEIGHT

(More mass) (Denser)   (Less mass) (Less dense)

Both of these objects have the same volume, but the brick has a larger mass. Therefore, the density of the brick is greater than the density of the sponge.

Critical Thinking

8. Apply Concepts If the brick and sponge had the same mass, which one would have a greater volume?

_____

_____

Because many dense materials feel heavy, people sometimes confuse density and weight. However, density and weight are not the same thing.

How Can Physical Properties Affect the Use of Substances?

DETERMINING USES

People often choose a material for a particular use because of its physical properties. For example, helium gas is often used to fill balloons. The density of helium is lower than the density of air. As a result, a balloon filled with helium can float in the sky.

People choose to use some substances because of their ability to conduct electricity. For example, metals are good conductors of electricity. Thus, metals such as copper are used in power lines and electric motors.

Sometimes people need a substance that does not conduct electricity or heat. For example, plastic foam does not conduct heat well. Thus, plastic foam can be used to make cups for hot liquids.

Talk About It

Describe Choose an object in your classroom. Identify and describe to the class some of the physical properties of the whole object. Also, identify and describe the substances it is made of. Explain why you think the particular substances are useful for the object.

LOOKING CLOSER

9. Predict Would aluminum be as useful as a food wrapping if it had a much lower melting point? Explain your answer.

_____

_____

_____

_____

Some metals can be rolled into thin, flexible sheets. This physical property makes aluminum a good choice for food wrappings.

SECTION 2 Properties of Matter *continued*

IDENTIFYING SUBSTANCES

Because many physical properties stay constant, you can use them to identify a material. For example, all samples of pure water are colorless liquids at room temperature and atmospheric pressure. Pure water is never a powdery green solid.

You can often identify a substance by comparing the properties you observe with known properties of a substance. For example, if you know the density of substance, you can do research to find what substance has that density. Many reference books list properties of different substances.

What Are Chemical Properties?

A *chemical property* describes how a substance changes into a new substance. A substance may change into a new substance by combining with another substance or by breaking apart. In general, chemical properties are not as easy to observe as physical properties. ☑

FLAMMABILITY

One example of a chemical property is *flammability*, or the ability to burn. Wood is an example of a flammable substance. When wood burns, it produces different substances. A substance that does not burn has the chemical property of *nonflammability*.

A substance always has both its physical and chemical properties, even when you cannot observe them. For example, wood has the chemical property of flammability even if the wood is not burning.

Because of its chemical property of flammability, wood makes a good fuel.

✓ **READING CHECK**

10. Identify Give two ways that a substance can change into a new substance.

_____

_____

_____

Critical Thinking

11. Infer How does wood that is not burning differ from a nonflammable material?

_____

_____

_____

_____

_____

SECTION 2 Properties of Matter *continued*

REACTIVITY

The ability of a substance to react with another substance is called **reactivity**. Reactivity is another example of a chemical property.

Some elements react very easily with other elements. For example, if you drop a piece of aluminum foil into vinegar, tiny gas bubbles form. However, if you drop a piece of copper wire into vinegar, no gas bubbles will form. Bubbles are one clue that a chemical reaction is taking place. In nature, reactive elements are usually found as compounds. Less-reactive elements are more likely to be uncombined. ☑

How Can Chemical Properties Determine Uses?

In some cases, a chemical property can cause problems. Iron is an element that has many useful physical and chemical properties. However, iron reacts readily with oxygen. This chemical property can be undesirable in some situations.

Iron reacts with oxygen in the air to form *rust*. Cars are made mostly of steel, which is a mixture of iron and other metals. The paint on a car can prevent the iron from reacting with oxygen. However, over time, the iron may become exposed to the air and the reaction between iron and oxygen can occur.

✔ READING CHECK

12. Identify In nature, what kind of elements are likely to be found as compounds?

_____

_____

This hole started as a chip in the paint. The chip exposed the iron in the car to oxygen. The iron rusted and crumbled away.

Steel contains iron. Paint on the steel keeps the iron from rusting. This is because paint does not react with oxygen.

The bumper does not have any rust because it is covered with chromium. Chromium does not react with oxygen.

LOOKING CLOSER

13. Identify Which of the following reacts most easily with oxygen—iron, paint, or chromium?

_____

_____

Name _____ Class _____ Date _____

SECTION 2 Properties of Matter *continued*

PHYSICAL VERSUS CHEMICAL PROPERTIES

It is important to remember the differences between physical and chemical properties. You can observe physical properties without changing the identity of the substance. You can observe chemical properties only when the identity of the substance changes. The table below describes some physical and chemical properties of a few common substances.

Comparison of Physical and Chemical Properties			
Substance	Wood	Iron	Fabric dye
		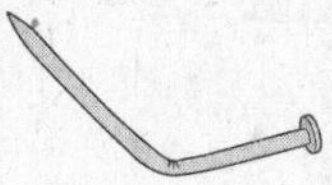	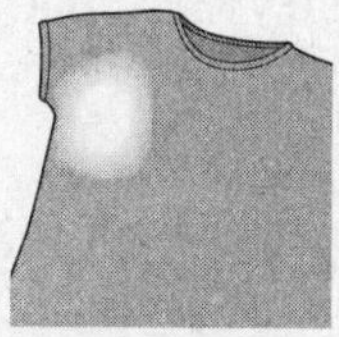
Physical property	has a grainy texture	bends without breaking	has a dark color
Chemical property	is flammable	reacts with oxygen to form rust	reacts with bleach; loses color

Material or object	Observation	Physical or chemical property?
Chalk	forms bubbles when put into vinegar	
Ice cream	melts in the sun	
Tin	bends easily	
Paper	burns quickly	
Liquid water	evaporates	
Car door	starts to rust	
Helium balloon	floats in air	

LOOKING CLOSER

14. Infer When bleach reacts with fabric dye, there is a chemical change. What kind of change happens to the fabric? Explain your answer.

_____
_____
_____

LOOKING CLOSER

15. Identify Complete the table to identify each example as a physical property or a chemical property.

Section 2 Review

SECTION VOCABULARY

boiling point the temperature at which a liquid becomes a gas	**melting point** the temperature and pressure at which a solid becomes a liquid
density the ratio of the mass of a substance to the volume of the substance; commonly expressed as grams per cubic centimeter for solids and liquids and grams per liter for gases	**reactivity** the capacity of a substance to combine chemically with another substance

1. List List five physical properties.

_____

_____

2. Calculate What is the density of a rock that has a mass of 454 g and a volume of 100.0 cm^3?

3. Infer Brand X aluminum foil is thicker than Brand Y. Is thickness a physical property or chemical property? Explain your answer.

_____

_____

_____

4. Apply Concepts How could you use the physical properties of melting point and boiling point to identify a substance?

_____

_____

_____

5. Explain Iron is much denser than a feather. Yet, a particular sample of feathers weighs more than a sample of iron. Explain how this is possible.

_____

_____

_____

6. Identify Give two examples of chemical properties.

_____

CHAPTER 2 Matter

SECTION 3 Changes of Matter

As you read this section, keep these questions in mind:
- What is a physical change?
- What is a chemical change?
- How can the parts of a mixture and a compound be separated?

What Is a Physical Change?

Suppose you break a piece of chalk in half. You have changed some of its physical properties. The two pieces of chalk have a different size and shape than the original piece. However, you have not changed the chemical properties of the chalk. For example, each piece of chalk would produce bubbles if you placed it in vinegar.

Breaking chalk is an example of a physical change. A **physical change** affects one or more physical properties of a substance without changing the identity of the substance. No matter how small the pieces of chalk are, each piece still has the same chemical properties. ☑

Examples of physical changes include boiling water, sanding a piece of wood, and mixing sand and water. The figure below shows other examples of physical changes.

Cutting changes the size of an object or substance.

Crushing changes the shape of an object or substance.

DISSOLVING SUBSTANCES

People often add sugar to tea. As you stir the tea, the sugar seems to disappear. However, just one taste will tell you that the sugar is still there. What happened to it?

The sugar *dissolved* in the tea. When sugar dissolves, the sugar molecules spread out among the water molecules in the tea.

Organize After you read this section, prepare two-column notes. Place the three Key Ideas in the left column. Add details and examples in the right column for each Key Idea. Then reread the section to see if you can add more details and examples.

1. Explain How does a physical change affect the identity of a substance?

_____

_____

_____

LOOKING CLOSER

2. Identify Give two properties of an object that can be affected by a physical change.

_____

_____

_____

SECTION 3 Changes of Matter *continued*

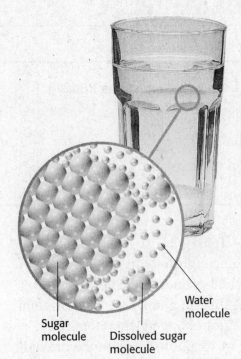

Water molecules attract the sugar molecules and pull them apart. As a result, the sugar molecules spread out, or dissolve, in the water.

Water molecule

Sugar molecule

Dissolved sugar molecule

LOOKING CLOSER

3. Analyze Do the molecules of water and sugar change as sugar dissolves?

_____

_____

When sugar dissolves in water or tea, the molecules do not change. In other words, the components of the mixture keep their identities. Because no atoms recombine when one substance dissolves in another, dissolving is a physical change.

MELTING AND FREEZING

Melting and freezing are also examples of physical changes. Consider what happens when a gold nugget is melted to form a gold ring. The gold changes from solid to liquid and then back to solid again. The shape of the gold also changes, but the atoms of gold do not change.

Critical Thinking

4. Infer Why is melting a physical change and not a chemical change?

_____

_____

_____

_____

One way to form gold rings is to melt the gold and then pour it into a mold.

Gold nugget

Molten gold

Gold rings

SECTION 3 Changes of Matter *continued*

What Is a Chemical Change?

Some materials are useful because they can change and combine to form new substances. For example, gasoline is flammable. When it burns, it produces CO_2 and H_2O and releases a great deal of energy. Because of this property, people use gasoline to power machines. Burning compounds is an example of a chemical change. A **chemical change** happens when one or more substances change into new substances that have different properties. ☑

Chemical changes take place constantly both around you and inside you. For example, chemical changes occur when fruits ripen and when leaves change color. The oxygen we breathe undergoes several chemical changes inside your body. These chemical changes supply the energy your body needs.

REARRANGEMENT OF ATOMS

Recall that atoms are not rearranged during a physical change. During a chemical change, however, atoms re-arrange to form new substances. For example, when you bake bread, you combine water, flour, and yeast. Each ingredient has its own properties. The heat of the oven and interactions among the ingredients cause chemical changes. These changes produce a new substance—bread.

EVIDENCE OF CHEMICAL CHANGE

Certain clues can tell you that a chemical change has happened. These may include:
- Production of gas bubbles
- Change in color or odor
- Release of light, sound, or heat

✓ **READING CHECK**

5. Describe What happens during a chemical change?

_____

_____

_____

_____

Critical Thinking

6. Compare How does a chemical change differ from a physical change?

_____

_____

_____

_____

When you add effervescent tablets to water, a chemical reaction takes place. The citric acid and baking soda in the tablets react to form carbon dioxide. This causes bubbles to form.

The Statue of Liberty is made of copper. Copper is a shiny, orange-brown metal. However, when copper reacts with water and compounds in the air, green compounds form.

LOOKING CLOSER

7. Identify What two clues that a chemical change has happened are shown in this figure?

_____

_____

Name _____ Class _____ Date _____

SECTION 3 Changes of Matter *continued*

REVERSING CHEMICAL CHANGES

Most chemical changes that you observe in your daily life cannot be reversed. For example, bread baking, milk turning sour, and iron rusting are examples of chemical changes that cannot be reversed. However, under the right conditions, some chemical changes can be reversed by another chemical change. To reverse a chemical change, the atoms in the new substance must recombine again. ☑

How Can a Mixture Be Separated?

Recall that a mixture is a combination of substances that are not chemically combined. Each component of a mixture has the same chemical identity that it had before the mixture was made. Therefore, separating a mixture does not involve recombining atoms. In other words, the components of a mixture can be separated by physical changes.

Some mixtures can be separated easily. For example, pizza is a mixture that has components you can see. If you don't like one of the toppings on a pizza, you can take it off. Removing a component of a mixture is a physical change. ☑

Other mixtures are more difficult to separate. For example, you cannot pick salt out of saltwater. However, you can separate the components of saltwater by heating the mixture. When the water evaporates, the salt remains.

Sea water is a mixture. Its components can be separated by physical changes. In a saltwater pond such as this one, sea water evaporates and salt is left behind.

Some other methods of separating mixtures are described below:
- During *distillation*, a mixture is heated and each component boils and evaporates at a different time.
- In *filtration*, a liquid component passes through a filter and solid components stay in or on the filter.
- Spinning some mixtures in a *centrifuge* causes components to separate.

READING CHECK

8. Explain How can a chemical change be reversed?

_____

_____

_____

READING CHECK

9. Identify What kind of change is used to separate components of a mixture?

_____

Talk About It

Find Examples With a partner, think of some types of mixtures that could be separated with each of these methods: evaporation, distillation, filtration, by centrifuge. Discuss whether each method would be better for separating mixtures of solids, mixtures of liquids, or mixtures of both.

A centrifuge is used to separate substances that have different densities. The centrifuge spins rapidly and denser substances collect at the bottom of the tube.

LOOKING CLOSER

10. Identify What property of a substance is important for separating a mixture with a centrifuge?

_____

_____

How Can a Compound Be Separated?

Recall that a compound is made up of atoms that are chemically combined. As a result, a compound can be broken apart only by rearranging atoms. In other words, the elements that make up a compound can be separated only by chemical changes. For example, when the compound mercury (II) oxide is heated, it breaks down into the elements mercury and oxygen. ☑

A compound, such as mercury (II) oxide, can be separated into elements only by chemical changes.

READING CHECK

11. Identify What kind of change is needed to separate a compound—physical or chemical?

_____

_____

Some compounds can be separated with electrical currents. For example, scientists can pass current through table salt when the compound is in a liquid state. This causes the compound to separate into its elements— sodium and chlorine.

Some compounds undergo chemical changes to form simpler compounds. Gasoline in a car engine reacts with oxygen to produce carbon dioxide and water. Additional changes can break down carbon dioxide and water into the elements carbon, oxygen, and hydrogen.

Section 3 Review

SECTION VOCABULARY

chemical change a change that occurs when one or more substances change into entirely new substances with different properties	**physical change** a change of matter from one form to another without a change in chemical properties

1. Classify For each example, place a mark in the correct column to indicate whether it is a physical change or a chemical change.

Example	Chemical change	Physical change
Ice cream melting		
Fruit rotting		
Paint peeling		
An egg frying		
Plants changing carbon dioxide and water into sugar and oxygen		
Salt dissolving in water		

2. Infer Can a physical change reverse a chemical change? Explain your answer.

_____

_____

3. Compare How do the general methods for separating mixtures and compounds differ?

_____

_____

4. Apply Concepts Suppose your teacher asks you to separate a mixture of sand and water. Which of the following methods would you use: distillation, filtration, or evaporation? Explain your answer.

_____

_____

5. Compare Does a physical change affect the identity of a substance? Does a chemical change affect the identity of a substance?

_____

_____

CHAPTER 3 States of Matter

SECTION 1 # Matter and Energy

KEY IDEAS

As you read this section, keep these questions in mind:

• What makes up matter?

• What is the difference between a solid, a liquid, and a gas?

• What kind of energy do all particles of matter have?

What Makes Up Matter?

Recall that matter is anything that has mass and takes up space. This textbook is made of matter. Trees, cars, food, air, and you are all made of matter. What is matter made of?

All matter is made of atoms. The atoms in many forms of matter are joined in molecules. All of these particles move constantly. They may move in all directions or vibrate in place. These motions explain many of our observations of how matter behaves. ☑

If you leave a bottle of perfume open, eventually you will be able to smell the perfume from across the room. Why? Like the particles of all matter, the particles in the perfume move constantly. When the bottle is open, some perfume particles can leave the bottle and enter the air. They can move through the air and reach your nose.

Scientists have made many observations about the movement of particles. These observations helped scientists develop the *kinetic theory of matter*. This theory has three main parts:

1. All matter is made of particles that are in constant motion.

2. The faster particles move, the higher the temperature of the substance.

3. At the same temperature, more massive particles move more slowly than less massive ones.

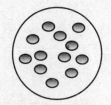 

READING TOOLBOX

Summarize As you read, make a table that compares the three common states of matter.

✓ READING CHECK

1. Identify What makes up all matter?

_____

_____

LOOKING CLOSER

2. Explain Both of these samples of matter are at the same temperature. Which particles are moving more slowly? Explain your answer.

_____

_____

_____

SECTION 1 Matter and Energy *continued*

What Are the Common States of Matter?

The kinetic theory can help you understand the differences between the three common states of matter: solid, liquid, and gas. The figure below shows models for each of these three states.

Particles in a gas, such as carbon dioxide, move very fast. The particles are usually far apart.

Gas

Particles in a liquid move quickly, but they are fairly close together. The particles in a liquid can move past each other. This allows a liquid to flow.

Liquid

Solid

Particles in a solid, such as ice, do not move fast enough to slide past one another. However, they do vibrate in place.

LOOKING CLOSER

3. Compare How does the movement of particles in a liquid differ from the movement of particles in a solid?

_____

_____

_____

_____

You can classify matter as a solid, liquid, or gas by determining whether the shape and volume are definite or variable. *Definite* means something does not change. *Variable* means something can change.

SOLIDS

The particles in a solid cannot change position easily. Strong attractions hold them close together. The particles can only vibrate in place. These strong attractions give a solid a rigid structure. As a result of its rigid structure, a solid has a definite volume and a definite shape. ☑

READING CHECK

4. Identify What causes a solid to have a definite volume and shape?

_____

_____

Solids
☑ Definite volume
☑ Definite shape

LIQUIDS

The particles that make up a liquid move more quickly than those in a solid. Because the particles move more quickly, they can overcome some of the forces of attraction between them. Thus, liquids can flow freely. ☑

Liquids take the shape of the container they are in. In other words, a liquid has a variable shape. For example, if you pour water into a glass, the water will take the shape of the glass. However, the volume of that water does not change even if you use a different glass.

> **Liquids**
> ☑ Definite volume
> ☑ Variable shape

☑ **READING CHECK**

5. Explain Why can the particles in a liquid overcome some forces of attraction?

_____

_____

_____

_____

GASES

The particles in a gas move more quickly than the particles in solids and liquids do. Like liquids, gases can change shape. However, gases can also change volume. The particles in a gas are generally far apart from one another. They can move to fill up the entire space inside a closed container. However, if you apply pressure to the gas, the particles can move closer together.

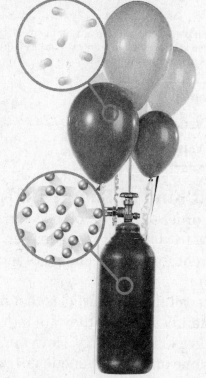

The shape and volume of a gas are variable. The helium atoms in the cylinder have been *compressed*, or forced close together. The atoms in the balloon have more space, so they spread out.

> **Gases**
> ☑ Variable volume
> ☑ Variable shape

LOOKING CLOSER

6. Compare How does the amount of space between particles differ in the balloon and helium cylinder?

_____

_____

_____

What Is a Fluid?

Recall that both liquids and gases have variable shapes. The particles in these states of matter are not held rigidly in place. Instead, the particles can move past each other. A state of matter in which the particles are free to move past each other is called a **fluid**. ☑

What Is a Plasma?

Most matter on Earth is either a solid, liquid, or gas. However, most of the other matter in the universe, including the stars, is made of plasma. A **plasma** is made up of electrically charged, or *ionized*, particles. Like gases, plasmas have variable shape and volume. However, unlike gases, plasmas conduct electricity. Lightning is an example of plasma.

At certain places on Earth, streams or bands of light sometimes appear in the night sky. These lights are called auroras. Auroras form when plasma collides with gas particles in the upper atmosphere.

Plasmas

☑ Variable volume

☑ Variable shape

What Kind of Energy Do All Particles Have?

In order to move, you need energy. **Energy** is the ability to change or move matter. Energy can take many different forms. The energy of motion is called *kinetic energy*.

Recall that the particles that make up all matter move constantly. Because they are moving, all particles of matter have kinetic energy. However, not all particles have the same amount of kinetic energy. ☑

Compared to the particles in liquids and gases, the particles in a solid move very slowly. Particles in a solid have the least kinetic energy.

Particles in a liquid have more kinetic energy than particles in a solid, but less than particles in a gas.

Compared to the particles in solids and liquids, particles in a gas have the most kinetic energy.

LOOKING CLOSER
10. Identify Which of the three common states of matter has particles with the most kinetic energy?

_____

TEMPERATURE

Particles of matter are always moving, but all particles in a material do not move at exactly the same speed. Thus, some particles have more kinetic energy than others. Because particles in a substance have different amounts of kinetic energy, scientists usually measure only the *average* kinetic energy of particles.

Many people think of temperature as a measure of how hot or cold something feels. In fact, **temperature** is a measure of the average kinetic energy of the particles in an object. When you measure an object's temperature, you are measuring the average kinetic energy of its particles. The higher the average kinetic energy of the particles in a substance, the higher its temperature. ☑

THERMAL ENERGY

The temperature of a substance is not affected by how much of the substance you have. For example, imagine that you have just poured a cup of hot tea. The average kinetic energy of tea particles is the same in the teacup and the teapot.

Although the average kinetic energy of the particles in the cup and pot are the same, the *total* kinetic energy in each container is different. Why? The teapot holds more particles than the cup does. The total kinetic energy of all the particles in a substance is called **thermal energy**. Thus, when two samples of the same substance have the same temperature, the larger sample will have more thermal energy.

✓ READING CHECK
11. Identify What does temperature measure?

_____

_____

_____

Name _____ Class _____ Date _____

Section 1 Review

SECTION VOCABULARY

<table>
<tr><td>

energy the capacity to do work

fluid a nonsolid state of matter in which the atoms or molecules are free to move past each other, as in a gas or liquid

plasma in physical science, the state of matter that consists of free-moving ions and electrons; a plasma's properties differ from the properties of a solid, liquid, or gas

</td><td>

temperature a measure of how hot (or cold) something is; specifically a measure of the average kinetic energy of the particles in an object

thermal energy the total kinetic energy of a substance's atoms

</td></tr>
</table>

1. List List three states of matter that are fluids.

_____

2. Describe Complete the table below to describe four states of matter.

State of matter	Is shape definite or variable?	Is volume definite or variable?	Is it a fluid?	How do the particles move?	Are the particles electrically charged?
Solid		definite			
Liquid				move past each other	
Gas					no
Plasma	variable				

3. Infer Which is easier to compress, a gas or a solid? Explain your answer.

_____

_____

4. Identify Relationships Which particles have more kinetic energy—those in a substance with a high temperature or those in a substance with a low temperature?

_____

5. Compare A scientist has two samples of a substance. Both samples have the same temperature. One sample has a mass of 10 g. The other sample has a mass of 20 g. Compare the average kinetic energy and total kinetic energy of the particles in each sample.

_____

_____

_____

CHAPTER 3 States of Matter
SECTION 2 **Changes of State**

KEY IDEAS

As you read this section, keep these questions in mind:

• What happens when a substance changes from one state of matter to another?

• What happens to mass and energy during physical and chemical changes?

What Causes Matter to Change States?

Imagine that you have a glass of ice water. You leave it on a table to answer the phone. When you come back, what do you find? The ice has melted and the outside of the glass is wet. You are observing two changes of state. During a *change of state*, matter changes from one physical form to another. In your glass, solid ice became a liquid. Water vapor in the air around the glass cooled and became liquid water.

Changes of state are caused by a transfer of energy. Thus, during a change of state, the energy of a substance changes. However, the identity of a substance does not change during a change of state. For example, ice and liquid water are the same substance. ☑

ADDING AND REMOVING ENERGY

You can change the state of a substance by adding or removing energy. For example, you can add energy to a substance by heating it. Adding energy causes the particles of a substance to move more quickly. Removing energy causes the particles of a substance to move more slowly. If enough energy is added to or removed from a substance, the substance will change state.

READING TOOLBOX

Compare As you read this section, make a table that compares the five changes of state of water. In your table, include information about the states of matter at each change and the direction of energy transfer.

READING CHECK

1. Identify During a change of state, what stays the same?

_____

_____

This figure shows five changes of state that water can undergo. The dotted arrows represent changes that require energy. The dark colored solid arrows represent changes that release energy.

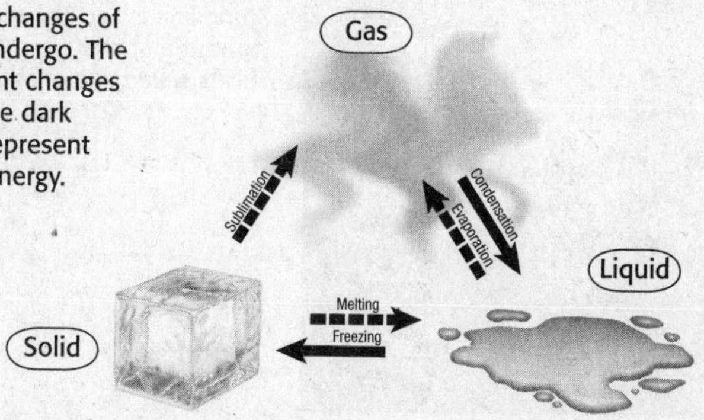

LOOKING CLOSER
2. List What three changes of state require energy?

_____

_____

_____

TEMPERATURE AND ENERGY

In most cases, when you add energy to a substance, the particles in the substance move more quickly. In other words, adding energy can increase the kinetic energy of the particles. Recall that temperature is a measure of the average kinetic energy of particles in a substance. ☑

When you remove energy from a substance, the particles in the substance usually move more slowly. Removing energy can decrease the kinetic energy of the particles. Thus, as you remove energy from a substance, its temperature usually decreases.

CHANGES OF STATE THAT REQUIRE ENERGY

Some changes of state can happen only if energy is added. *Melting* is the change in state from a solid to a liquid. When you heat a solid, you transfer energy to the substance's particles. As the particles gain energy, they vibrate faster. When the particles have enough energy to break from their rigid positions, the substance melts. The melting point is the temperature at which a substance changes from a solid to a liquid. The *melting point* of a substance can change if pressure changes. ☑

Evaporation is the change in state from a liquid to a gas. *Boiling* is evaporation that happens throughout a liquid at a specific temperature and pressure. The temperature at which a liquid boils is its *boiling point*.

Sublimation is the change in state from a solid to a gas. For example, solid carbon dioxide, or *dry ice*, changes to a gas at room temperature.

Some solids can change to a gas without first changing to a liquid. This is called sublimation.

READING CHECK

3. Explain Why may the temperature of a substance change when energy is added?

_____

_____

_____

READING CHECK

4. Define What is melting?

_____

_____

_____

Critical Thinking

5. Compare How does melting differ from sublimation?

_____

_____

_____

_____

_____

CHANGES OF STATE THAT RELEASE ENERGY

Some changes of state release energy. For example, when water vapor in the air becomes a liquid, energy is released. This process is an example of condensation. **Condensation** is the change in state from a gas to a liquid. The *condensation point* is the temperature at which a gas becomes a liquid. Condensation often happens when a gas touches a cool surface. For instance, drops of water may form on a glass of ice water as air touches the cool glass.

Water vapor can change to drops of water when it touches a cool surface, such as grass or dragonfly wings.

LOOKING CLOSER
6. Identify What change of state does this figure show?
_____
_____

FREEZING POINT

Freezing is the change in state from a liquid to a solid. The temperature at which a substance freezes is its *freezing point*. The freezing point of a substance is the same as its melting point. Recall that energy must be added for a substance to melt. When a substance freezes, energy is released.

What Happens to Temperature During Changes of State?

When a substance loses or gains energy, either its temperature changes or its state changes. In other words, these two changes do not happen at the same time. The temperature of a substance does not change during a change of state. ☑

For example, if you heat a pot of water on a stove, the temperature of the water increases. When the water's temperature reaches the boiling point, adding more energy will not increase the temperature further. Instead, adding energy causes the water to change state. The temperature of the water will stay the same until all of the water has changed to water vapor.

☑ **READING CHECK**
7. Describe What happens to the temperature of a substance during a change of state?
_____
_____

Graphing *Skills*

8. Label On the graph, label each of the four arrows with one of the following: melting, freezing, boiling, condensing.

9. Identify What is the melting point of water? What is the boiling point?

_____

_____

10. Identify Put boxes around the parts of the graph where energy is being added but the state is not changing.

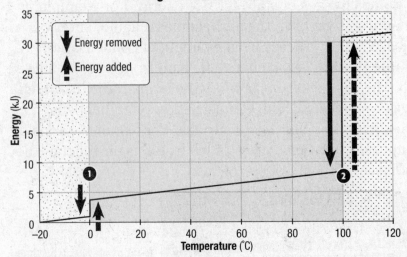

Changes of State for Water

❶ When water freezes, energy is released, or removed. When ice melts, energy is absorbed, or added.

❷ When water vapor condenses, energy is released. When liquid water becomes a gas, or *vaporizes*, energy is absorbed.

Solid ice

Liquid water

Water vapor

Critical Thinking

11. Describe In a chemical change, how does the mass of the reactants compare to the mass of the products?

_____

_____

What Happens to Mass During Physical and Chemical Changes?

Imagine weighing an ice cube. After the ice cube melts, you weigh the liquid that formed. Which state weighed more—the solid or the liquid? Neither—they have the same mass. During a chemical or physical change, mass cannot be created or destroyed. This is the *law of conservation of mass. Conserve* means "to keep the same." When the ice melts and becomes liquid water, no mass is lost.

Law of Conservation of Mass:
Mass cannot be created or destroyed.

SECTION 2 Changes of State *continued*

What Happens to Energy During Chemical and Physical Changes?

Just like mass, energy cannot be created or destroyed during a physical or chemical change. This is known as the *law of conservation of energy*. Energy can be changed to another form of energy. However, the total amount of energy before the change must equal the total amount of energy after the change.

> **Law of Conservation of Energy:**
> Energy cannot be created or destroyed.

For example, when a lawn mower burns gasoline for energy, a chemical change takes place. The lawn mower uses some of the energy stored in the gasoline. Some of the energy is transferred to the environment as heat. Thus, the total amount of energy released equals the energy used by the lawn mower, plus heat energy. No energy is created or destroyed.

Critical Thinking

12. Infer In a chemical change, how does the total energy of the reactants compare to the total energy of the products?

_____

_____

When a lawn mower burns gasoline, the forms of energy change. However, the total amount of energy stays the same.

Name _____ Class _____ Date _____

Section 2 Review

SECTION VOCABULARY

condensation the change of state from a gas to a liquid **evaporation** the change of state from a liquid to a gas	**sublimation** the process in which a solid changes directly into a gas (the term is sometimes also used for the reverse process)

1. Define What is a change of state?

_____

_____

2. Identify What causes a change of state?

_____

3. Describe Relationships What two things can happen to a substance when energy is added?

_____

_____

_____

4. Describe Identify and describe two changes of state that release energy.

_____

_____

5. Compare Identify two ways condensation differs from boiling. Identify one way they are similar.

_____

_____

_____

_____

6. State In your own words, what is the *law of conservation of mass*?

_____

_____

7. Describe What would happen to the temperature of boiling water if you added energy?

_____

54

CHAPTER 3 States of Matter
SECTION 3 **Fluids**

KEY IDEAS

As you read this section, keep these questions in mind:
- How do fluids exert pressure?
- What causes objects to float?
- What happens when pressure in a fluid changes?
- What affects the speed of a fluid?

What Are Fluids?

Recall that liquids and gases are examples of fluids. The particles in a fluid can move past each other. Fluids exert pressure, or push, evenly in all directions. The properties of fluids allow ships to float, divers to explore the ocean, and jets to soar across the sky.

What Is Pressure?

Pressure is the amount of force exerted on a given area of surface. For example, when you add air to a bicycle tire, you push air into the tire. Inside the tire, the air molecules push against each other and also against the walls of the tire. As you pump more air into the tire, the pressure inside the tire increases. Why? More air particles are pushing against the inside of the tire and against each other.

READING TOOLBOX

Summarize As you read, write down each scientific law or principle described in this section. Write each one in your own words. Include a diagram or equation that describes the principle or law.

The force of air particles inside the tire creates pressure. Pressure keeps the tire firm.

LOOKING CLOSER

1. Predict What would happen to pressure in the tire if some of the air were removed? Explain your answer.

_____
_____
_____
_____
_____

CALCULATING PRESSURE

You can calculate pressure by dividing the force by the area over which the force acts. The equation for calculating pressure is on the next page.

SECTION 3 Fluids *continued*

Pressure

$$pressure = \frac{force}{area} \qquad P = \frac{F}{A}$$

The SI unit of pressure is the **pascal**. One pascal (1 Pa) is the force of one newton exerted over an area of one square meter (1 N/m²). The newton is the SI unit of force. ☑

What Causes an Object to Float?

What happens if you push a rubber duck to the bottom of a tub and release it? It does not sink to the bottom of the tub. It pops up to the surface. Why does this happen? A force called the **buoyant force** pushes the rubber duck upward. All fluids exert an upward buoyant force on matter. You may feel this force when you float on your back in a pool or lake.

DETERMINING BUOYANT FORCE

A Greek mathematician named Archimedes discovered a method to determine buoyant force.

> **Archimedes' Principle**
>
> The buoyant force on an object equals the weight of the fluid that the object displaces.

The figure below shows how to find the buoyant force on an object.

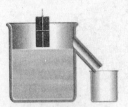 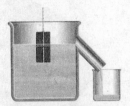 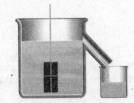

Lower an object into a container of water.

The object displaces water. The displaced water flows into a smaller container.

When water covers the object completely, you can measure the volume of the displaced water. The volume of the water equals the volume of the object.

Once you have collected the displaced water, you can find its weight. The weight of the displaced water equals the buoyant force.

READING CHECK

2. Identify What is the SI unit of pressure?

_____

Talk About It

Discuss According to legend, Archimedes helped a king determine if his crown was made of pure gold or of silver. With a partner, discuss ways to use Archimedes' principle to help the king learn if his crown was made of gold. (Hint: The density of silver is less than the density of gold.)

LOOKING CLOSER

3. Identify Relationships What does the volume of displaced water equal?

_____

_____

DETERMINING IF AN OBJECT WILL SINK OR FLOAT

You can predict if an object will sink or float by comparing its weight with the buoyant force on it. An object floats when the buoyant force is greater than or equal to the object's weight.

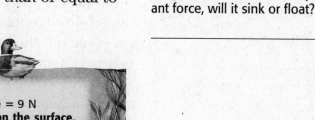

Weight = 12 N
Buoyant force = 12 N
Fish floats and is suspended in the water.

Weight = 9 N
Buoyant force = 9 N
Duck floats on the surface.

Weight = 75 N
Buoyant force = 50 N
Rock sinks.

You can also compare the densities of a fluid and an object to predict if the object will float. If the object is denser than the fluid, it will sink. For example, the density of a brick is 2 g/cm³. The density of water is 1.00 g/cm³. The brick is denser than water and thus will sink in water.

Steel is almost eight times denser than water. However, large ships made of steel can float in the ocean. Why? The shape of the boat allows it to float. Because a large part of the boat is hollow, the same mass of steel takes up a larger volume. Increasing volume decreases overall density and the boat floats.

Critical Thinking

4. Analyze If an object's weight is less than the buoyant force, will it sink or float?

_____

_____

A large part of the boat is hollow. Although shape does not change the mass of the boat, the volume of the hollow boat is larger. A larger volume for a particular mass reduces the density of the boat.

A block of steel is denser than water, so the block sinks.

LOOKING CLOSER

5. Explain Why does a block of steel have a larger density than a boat made of steel?

_____

_____

_____

_____

What Happens When Pressure Changes in a Fluid?

What happens when you squeeze one end of a tube of toothpaste? The pressure you apply at one end is passed along throughout the entire tube. This causes toothpaste to come out the other end. In the 17th century, a French scientist named Blaise Pascal explained this kind of observation.

> **Pascal's Principle**
>
> If the pressure in a container is increased at any point, the pressure increases at all points by the same amount.

Critical Thinking

6. Identify What do the variables *P*, *F*, and *A* represent?

_____

_____

_____

Pascal's principle can be stated by the following equations:

Pascal's Principle

$$P_1 = P_2$$

$$P = \frac{F}{A}$$

Therefore, $\dfrac{F_1}{A_1} = \dfrac{F_2}{A_2}$

HYDRAULIC DEVICES

Hydraulic devices are based on Pascal's principle. Hydraulic devices use liquids to transmit, or pass, pressure from one point to another. They can be used to multiply force.

Math Skills

7. Calculate A hydraulic lift uses Pascal's principle to lift a 19,000 N car. The area of the small piston equals 10.5 cm² and the area of the large piston equals 400 cm². What force must you exert on the small piston to lift the car?

_____

A small downward force is applied to a small area. This force exerts pressure on the fluid in the device.

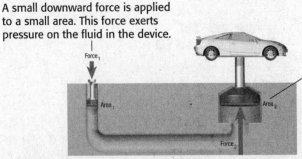

Force₁

Area₁   Area₂

Force₂

The pressure is transmitted to a larger area, where the pressure creates a larger force.

According to Pascal's principle, the pressure is the same on both sides of the fluid in the device. Therefore, a small force on a smaller area produces a larger force on the larger area.

What Are the Properties of Fluids in Motion?

Examples of moving fluids include liquds flowing through pipes, air moving as wind, and honey dripping. Fluids can flow at different rates. However, fluids in motion have some properties in common.

SECTION 3 Fluids *continued*

FLUIDS AND AREA

If the flow rate stays the same, fluids move faster through small areas than through large areas. For example, if you place your thumb over the end of a garden hose, your thumb blocks part of the opening. The water must flow through a small area. Because the area is small, the water leaves the hose at a faster speed. ☑

FLUID PRESSURE AND SPEED

Imagine water carrying a leaf through a pipe. The water moves faster through the narrow part of the pipe than through the wider part. Therefore, the leaf carried by the water moves more quickly in the narrow part of the pipe. The water pressure behind the leaf is greater than the pressure in front of the leaf. The pressure difference causes the leaf to speed up, or accelerate, as it enters the narrow tube.

More pressure

Less pressure

Pressure is lower in the narrow part of the pipe than in the wide part. As the leaf enters the narrow part, the pressure in front of the leaf is less than the pressure behind it. Thus, the leaf speeds up when it enters the narrow part of the pipe.

A Swiss mathematician named Daniel Bernoulli described this property of a moving fluid.

Bernoulli's Principle

As the speed of a moving fluid increases, the pressure of the moving fluid decreases.

VISCOSITY

Some fluids move much more slowly than others. For example, it would take you longer to pour a cup of honey than a cup of water. Another way to say this is that different fluids have different viscosities. **Viscosity** is a fluid's resistance to flow. A viscous fluid does not flow as easily as a less viscous fluid. In general, the stronger the attraction between the particles of a fluid, the more viscous the fluid is.

✓ READING CHECK

8. Describe How does area affect the speed of a fluid?

_____

_____

_____

LOOKING CLOSER

9. Identify On the diagram, write the words *slower* and *faster* to show how speed differs in different parts of the tube.

Section 3 Review

SECTION VOCABULARY

buoyant force the upward force that keeps an object immersed in or floating on a fluid	**pressure** the amount of force exerted per unit area of a surface
pascal the SI unit of pressure; equal to the force of 1 N exerted over an area of 1 m² (symbol, Pa)	**viscosity** the resistance of a gas or liquid to flow

1. Describe How can you use density to determine if an object will sink or float in a fluid?

_____

_____

_____

2. Analyze You put a small object into a cup of water and weigh the displaced water. The displaced water weighs 235 N. What is the buoyant force on the object? Explain your answer.

_____

_____

_____

3. Explain How does a hydraulic device multiply force?

_____

_____

4. Infer A balloon filled with helium floats in the air. What does this tell you about the density of helium?

_____

5. Explain How are speed and pressure of a fluid related?

_____

_____

_____

6. Explain How do the attractions between particles in a fluid determine viscosity?

_____

_____

CHAPTER 3 States of Matter
SECTION 4 # Behavior of Gases

As you read this section, keep these questions in mind:
- What are some properties of gases?
- How do changes of pressure, temperature, or volume affect a gas?

What Are Some Properties of Gases?

Particles in a gas move rapidly in all directions. Some of the unique properties of gases are listed below:
- expand to fill their containers
- easily mix with one another
- have low densities
- can be compressed
- are mostly empty space

Organize As you read, make a table that lists all of the gas laws discussed in the section. For each law, identify which factor must stay constant, which variables change, and the relationship between the variables.

GASES AND THEIR CONTAINERS

Gases exert pressure on their containers. For example, as helium molecules inside a balloon move, they bump into each other and the walls of the balloon. One molecule alone does not have a large effect. However, millions of molecules create a steady force. If too many gas molecules are in the balloon, the total pressure they exert can cause the balloon to break.

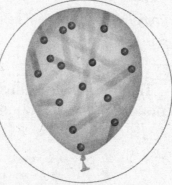

Gas particles exert pressure on the walls of a balloon.

LOOKING CLOSER
1. Predict What would happen to pressure if you removed some of the gas particles from the balloon?

_____

_____

A gas under pressure will escape its container if possible. For example, if you open the end of a balloon, gas will rush out of the balloon. For this reason, gases in pressurized containers, such as propane tanks or helium tanks, can be very dangerous.

What Are the Gas Laws?

Gases behave differently than solids or liquids do. For example, the volume of a gas can change due to pressure, but the volume of a solid or liquid generally cannot. The **gas laws** describe how variables such as pressure, volume, and temperature affect the behavior of gases. The gas laws will help you understand and predict the behavior of gases in specific situations.

PRESSURE AND VOLUME

A diver is swimming at a depth of 10 m below sea level. An air bubble escapes from her mouthpiece. As the bubble rises to the surface, it gets bigger. When the bubble reaches the water's surface, its volume is double its original size.

This example shows the relationship between the volume and pressure of a gas, also known as Boyle's law.

Boyle's law is true for almost any gas, if temperature and amount of gas are constant, or unchanged. ☑

READING CHECK

2. Identify Boyle's law describes the relationship between which two variables?

____

____

Boyle's Law

For a certain amount of gas at a constant temperature, the volume of a gas decreases as the gas's pressure increases. Likewise, the volume of a gas increases as the gas's pressure decreases.

In mathematical terms:

Boyle's Law

(initial pressure)(initial volume) = (final pressure)(final volume)

$P_1V_1 = P_2V_2$

The figure below illustrates Boyle's law. Both pistons contain the same amount of gas at the same temperature.

LOOKING CLOSER

3. Identify What happens to volume as pressure decreases?

____

____

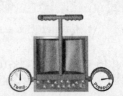

If you lift the piston, pressure decreases. The gas particles spread farther apart, and the volume increases.

If you push the piston, pressure increases. The gas particles are pushed closer together, and the volume decreases.

SECTION 4 Behavior of Gases *continued*

APPLYING BOYLE'S LAW

You can use Boyle's law to predict changes in the pressure or volume of a gas. Remember that Boyle's law is true only when the temperature and amount of gas do not change. ☑

A balloon has a volume of 7.5 L at 100.0 kPa. As the balloon rises in the atmosphere, the gas inside expands to a volume of 11 L. Assume the balloon is at a constant temperature and the amount of gas does not change. What is the pressure when the volume is 11 L?

READING CHECK

4. Identify Under what conditions does Boyle's law apply?

_____

_____

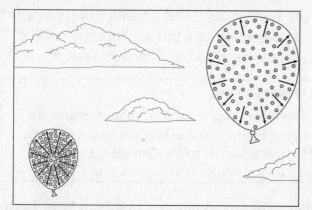

The ballon on the left has a volume of 7.5 L and a pressure of 100 kPa. As the balloon rises, it becomes larger. The balloon's new volume is 11 L. The temperature and number of molecules inside the balloon stay the same.

Step 1: List the given and unknown values.	Given: $V_1 = 7.5$ L $P_1 = 100.0$ kPa $V_2 = 11$ L	Unknown: P_2
Step 2: Write the equation and rearrange to solve for the unknown.	$P_1V_1 = P_2V_2$ $P_2 = \dfrac{P_1V_1}{V_2}$	
Step 3: Insert the known values and solve for the unknown value.	$P_2 = \dfrac{(100.0 \text{ kPa})(7.5 \text{ L})}{11 \text{ L}}$ $P_2 = 68$ kPa	

Math *Skills*

5. Calculate A 300 mL sample of hydrogen gas is at a pressure of 0.500 kPa. If the pressure increases to 0.750 kPa, what will be the final volume of the sample? Assume that temperature stays constant.

_____

PRESSURE AND TEMPERATURE

Recall that temperature is a measure of the average kinetic energy of particles. As the particles of a substance move faster, the substance's temperature increases. The particles bump into each other and the sides of the container more often, which increases pressure. Thus, as temperature increases, pressure increases. This is known as Gay-Lussac's law.

SECTION 4 Behavior of Gases *continued*

> **Gay-Lussac's Law**
>
> When volume is constant, the pressure of a gas increases as temperature increases. Pressure decreases as temperature decreases.

In other words, the pressure and temperature of a gas are directly related. As one changes, the other changes in the same direction.

TEMPERATURE AND VOLUME

Like the temperature and pressure of a gas, the temperature and volume of a gas are directly related. This relationship is described in Charles's Law.

> **Charles's Law**
>
> When the amount of a gas and pressure are constant, the volume of a gas increases as its temperature increases. Likewise, as volume decreases, temperature decreases.

The figure below illustrates Charles's Law. Both pistons have the same amount of gas at the same pressure.

Critical Thinking

6. Compare How are the relationships between variables described in Gay-Lussac's law and Charles's law similar?

_____

_____

_____

_____

_____

When temperature decreases, the gas particles move more slowly and volume decreases.

When temperature increases, the gas particles move faster and volume increases.

The following experiment also illustrates Charles's law.

Air-filled balloons are put into liquid nitrogen.

The low temperature of the liquid nitrogen makes the volumes of the air in the balloons smaller."

When the balloons are removed from the liquid nitrogen, their temperature increases. The volume of each balloon increases to its original volume.

LOOKING CLOSER

7. Identify What two factors did not change during the experiment?

_____

_____

SECTION 4 Behavior of Gases *continued*

How Can Graphs Illustrate the Gas Laws?

You can use graphs to show how temperature, pressure, and volume affect gases. A graph can show the relationship between two factors. For example, the graph can show if a relationship is direct or inverse. In a *direct relationship*, the two variables change in the same direction. In an *inverse relationship*, the variables change in opposite directions. In the graph below, temperature and volume have a direct relationship.

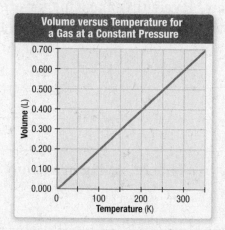

The shape of the line in a graph also describes the relationship. If a graph is a straight line, such as the graph above, one variable is directly or inversely *proportional* to the other. In a proportional relationship, the variables stay in the same ratio to each other as their values change. If a graph is a curve, one variable is not proportional to the other. This means that the variables do not stay in the same ratio to each other as their values change.

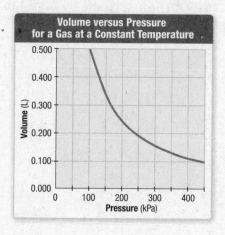

Graphing *Skills*

8. Analyze Is the relationship shown in this graph direct or inverse? How do you know?

_____

_____

_____

9. Analyze Is this relationship proportional? Explain your answer.

_____

_____

_____

LOOKING CLOSER

10. Identify Which gas law does this graph represent?

_____

11. Infer Is the relationship between the variables direct or inverse? Explain your answer.

_____

_____

_____

Section 4 Review

SECTION VOCABULARY

gas laws the laws that state the mathematical relationships between the volume, temperature, pressure, and quantity of a gas	

1. Identify How do gas particles exert pressure on their container?

_____

_____

2. Apply Concepts Chandra notices that her bicycle tires have higher pressure during the hot summer than during the cold winter. Which gas law explains her observation? Explain your answer.

_____

_____

_____

3. Predict What would happen eventually to a balloon sitting in a sunny window? Which gas law predicts this?

_____

_____

_____

4. Describe In Boyle's law, what is the relationship between pressure and volume?

_____

_____

5. Graph Relationships In the space below, create a graph showing the proportional relationship between temperature and pressure described by Gay-Lussac's law. Be sure to label the axes of your graph and give your graph a title.

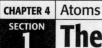

SECTION
1 **The Development of Atomic Theory**

KEY IDEAS

As you read this section, keep these questions in mind:

• What scientists helped to develop atomic theory?

• What part of atoms did Thomson discover?

• What part of atoms did Rutherford discover?

Who Proposed the First Atomic Theory?

You may know what atoms are: they are the tiny particles that make up all matter. Today, we know a great deal about the structure and behavior of atoms. However, scientists have not always known about atoms.

ORIGINS OF ATOMIC THEORY

The things we know about atoms today were discovered by many scientists over a long period of time. In fact, the first person to hypothesize that atoms exist was Democritus. Democritus was a Greek philosopher who lived in the fourth century BCE. He suggested that everything in the universe was made of tiny, indivisible units. He called these units atoms. The word *atom* comes from the Greek word *atomos*. *Atomos* means "unable to be cut or divided." ☑

Scientists Who Helped Develop Atomic Theory	
Scientist	**Contribution**
Democritus	first proposed that the universe is made up of tiny, indivisible units called atoms

Democritus made many observations of how matter changes. He thought that the movements of atoms caused the changes he observed. However, Democritus did not have any evidence to show that his theory was correct. Although some people agreed with Democritus's theory, others thought that different theories were correct. ☑

As the science of chemistry was developing in the 1700s, scientists began to focus on making careful measurements in experiments. Therefore, scientists began to collect more accurate and precise data about matter. Just as scientists do today, scientists in the past used data to decide which theories were most correct.

READING TOOLBOX

Compare After you read this section, write a paragraph or two comparing Dalton's, Thomson's, and Rutherford's models of the atom.

✔ READING CHECK

1. Identify Where does the word *atom* come from?

_____

_____

_____

✔ READING CHECK

2. Explain What do you think is the reason that not everyone agreed with Democritus's theory?

_____

_____

SECTION 1 The Development of Atomic Theory *continued*

How Did Dalton Contribute to Atomic Theory?

In 1808, an English schoolteacher named John Dalton proposed a different atomic theory. Like Democritus, Dalton proposed that atoms could not be divided into smaller parts. However, unlike Democritus, Dalton performed scientific experiments to find data to support his theory. ☑

Dalton's experiments showed that atoms of different elements could combine in certain ways to form compounds. This is known as the "law of definite proportions."

The law of definite proportions states that a chemical compound always contains the same proportion of a particular element. For example, in any sample of water, hydrogen will make up 11% of the mass of the sample. In other words, in 100 g of water, there will be 11 g of hydrogen and 89 g of oxygen.

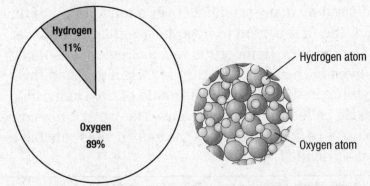

Water Composition by Mass

Hydrogen 11%

Oxygen 89%

Hydrogen atom

Oxygen atom

For any sample of water, 11% of its mass is hydrogen and 89% is oxygen. This suggests that hydrogen and oxygen atoms combine in specific ratios to form water molecules.

Some parts of Dalton's atomic theory are still accepted by scientists today. In fact, Dalton's explanation of how atoms combine to form substances is considered the foundation of modern atomic theory. However, as scientists continued to carry out experiments, they made new observations that did not fit Dalton's theory. New theories were developed that better explained the new observations. ☑

READING CHECK

3. Describe How was Dalton's theory different from Democritus's?

_____

_____

_____

Critical Thinking

4. Apply Concepts Carbon makes up 27% of the mass of carbon dioxide. How many grams of carbon are there in 88 g of carbon dioxide?

_____

_____

READING CHECK

5. Explain Why did scientists have to develop new atomic theories that were different from Dalton's theory?

_____

_____

_____

Scientists Who Helped Develop Atomic Theory	
Scientist	**Contribution**
Democritus	first proposed that the universe is made up of tiny, indivisible units called atoms
John Dalton	carried out scientific experiments that showed that atoms exist

SECTION 1 | The Development of Atomic Theory *continued*

How Did Thomson Contribute to Atomic Theory?

In 1897, a British scientist named J. J. Thomson was working with *cathode rays*, mysterious rays in vacuum tubes. His experiments helped scientists better understand the structure of atoms.

In his experiments, Thomson used a vacuum tube that contained two electrodes. One electrode, called the *cathode*, was negatively charged. The other, called the *anode*, was positively charged. When electricity was sent through the tube, a glowing beam appeared inside the tube. Other scientists had shown that this beam came from the cathode. However, they had not been able to determine what the beam was made of. ☑

When Thomson placed a magnet near the tube, the beam was *deflected*, or bent, as shown in the figure below. Only streams of charged particles can be bent by a magnet. Light rays cannot. Therefore, Thomson's experiment suggested that cathode rays were actually streams of tiny, charged particles.

READING CHECK

6. **Identify** Which electrode in Thomson's vacuum tube was positively charged?

_____

_____

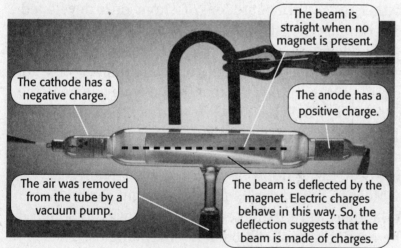

The beam is straight when no magnet is present.

The cathode has a negative charge.

The anode has a positive charge.

The air was removed from the tube by a vacuum pump.

The beam is deflected by the magnet. Electric charges behave in this way. So, the deflection suggests that the beam is made of charges.

LOOKING CLOSER

7. **Explain** Why did the deflection of the beam by a magnet suggest that the cathode ray contained charged particles?

_____

_____

_____

Based on the direction the beam bent, Thomson determined that the particles in the beam were negatively charged. His experiments also showed that, no matter what substance the cathode was made of, the beam was always the same.

Based on his results, Thomson concluded that the particles in the beam came from atoms. He also concluded that the particles were the same in atoms of different elements. This is how Thomson discovered **electrons**, the negatively charged particles inside an atom.

Critical Thinking

8. Compare How was Thomson's model of the atom different from Dalton's model?

_____

_____

_____

_____

THOMSON'S MODEL OF THE ATOM

Thomson's experiment showed that atoms contained even smaller particles. He proposed a new model of the atom based on his discovery. According to Thomson's model, electrons were spread randomly throughout an atom. The rest of the atom was a positively charged material. The electrons floated in the positively charged material.

Scientists Who Helped Develop Atomic Theory	
Scientist	**Contribution**
Democritus	first proposed that the universe is made up of tiny, indivisible units called atoms
John Dalton	carried out scientific experiments that showed that atoms exist
J. J. Thomson	showed that atoms contain smaller particles called electrons

How Did Rutherford Contribute to Atomic Theory?

According to Thomson's atomic theory, the mass of an atom was spread evenly throughout its volume. Ernest Rutherford, a former student of Thomson's, developed experiments to test this idea.

In one experiment, Rutherford's students aimed a beam of positively charged particles at a very thin sheet of gold foil. Rutherford predicted that the positive charge in the gold atoms would be too weak to affect the positively charged particles. Therefore, the particles would either pass straight through the foil or be deflected slightly. However, this is not what the experiment showed. ☑

Most of the particles passed straight through the foil. Some were deflected slightly. However, some of the particles bounced back at sharp angles. These results are shown in the figure below.

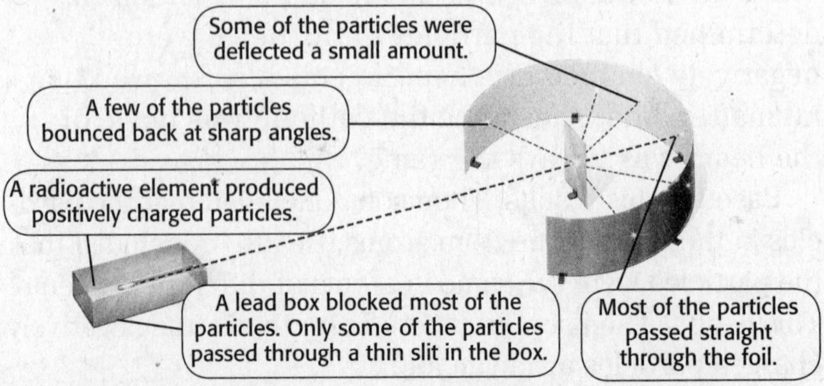

READING CHECK

9. Describe What did Rutherford predict would happen to the positively charged particles when they hit the foil?

_____

_____

_____

Some of the particles were deflected a small amount.

A few of the particles bounced back at sharp angles.

A radioactive element produced positively charged particles.

A lead box blocked most of the particles. Only some of the particles passed through a thin slit in the box.

Most of the particles passed straight through the foil.

SECTION 1 The Development of Atomic Theory *continued*

RUTHERFORD'S MODEL OF THE ATOM

The results of Rutherford's experiment were very surprising. In his notebook, Rutherford wrote, "It was almost as incredible as if you fired a 15-inch shell at a piece of tissue paper and it came back and hit you." However, further experiments produced the same results. Therefore, Rutherford's results were confirmed. ☑

Rutherford concluded that the sharply reflected particles collided with dense parts of the atoms in the gold foil. The particles bounced back because they had the same charge as the dense parts of the atom. Because so few particles bounced back at sharp angles, Rutherford concluded that these dense parts must be very tiny.

Based on his results, Rutherford concluded that an atom's positive charge is concentrated at the center of the atom. This positively charged, dense core of the atom is called the **nucleus** (plural, *nuclei*). Data from the experiments showed that the nucleus must be very tiny. If an atom were the size of a football stadium, its nucleus would be only as big as a marble.

Rutherford's results led to a new model of the atom. In the Rutherford model, negatively charged electrons orbit the positively charged nucleus, as shown below. This is similar to the way that the planets orbit the sun.

☑ **READING CHECK**

10. Describe How did Rutherford confirm the results of the gold-foil experiment?

_____

_____

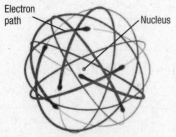

Electron path   Nucleus

The Rutherford model of the atom

In the Rutherford model of the atom, electrons orbit the nucleus. This drawing does not accurately show the sizes and distances of the parts of the atom.

LOOKING CLOSER

11. Identify On the figure, label the part of the atom that has a positive charge and the part that has a negative charge.

Scientists Who Helped Develop Atomic Theory	
Scientist	**Contribution**
Democritus	first proposed that the universe is made up of tiny, indivisible units called atoms
John Dalton	carried out scientific experiments that showed that atoms exist
J. J. Thomson	showed that atoms contain smaller particles called electrons
Ernest Rutherford	showed that the positive charge in an atom is concentrated in a nucleus at its center

Section 1 Review

SECTION VOCABULARY

electron a subatomic particle that has a negative charge	**nucleus** in physical science, an atom's central region, which is made up of protons and neutrons

1. **Describe** What did Rutherford's gold-foil experiment suggest about the structure of an atom?

   _____

   _____

2. **Define** State the law of definite proportions in your own words.

   _____

   _____

   _____

3. **Compare** How was Dalton's atomic theory similar to Democritus's atomic theory?

   _____

   _____

4. **Compare** How was Thomson's atomic theory different from Rutherford's atomic theory?

   _____

   _____

   _____

5. **Describe** What did Thomson conclude about the particles in cathode rays?

   _____

   _____

   _____

6. **Apply Concepts** Nitrogen makes up 82% of the mass of ammonia. How many grams of nitrogen are there in 200 g of ammonia?

   _____

7. **Calculate** The compound ammonia contains nitrogen and hydrogen atoms. How many grams of hydrogen are there in 150 g of ammonia? (Hint: What percentage of the mass of ammonia is hydrogen?)

   _____

SECTION 2 The Structure of Atoms

KEY IDEAS

As you read this section, keep these questions in mind:

• What do atoms of the same element have in common?

• What are isotopes?

• How is an element's average atomic mass calculated?

• How is Avogadro's number used?

What Is Inside an Atom?

Democritus and John Dalton thought that atoms could not be divided into smaller parts. J. J. Thomson and Ernest Rutherford discovered that atoms are not indivisible, but contain electrons and nuclei. Later, other scientists discovered that the nucleus of an atom contains smaller particles called protons and neutrons. Each of these *subatomic particles*—protons, neutrons, and electrons—has different properties, as shown in the table below.

Particle	Charge	Mass (kg)	Location
Proton	+1	1.67×10^{-27}	inside the nucleus
Neutron	0	1.67×10^{-27}	inside the nucleus
Electron	−1	9.11×10^{-31}	outside the nucleus

As you can see from the table, the nucleus of an atom contains protons and neutrons. **Protons** have a positive charge. **Neutrons** do not have a charge. Protons and neutrons are almost identical in size and mass.

Outside the nucleus is a cloud of negatively charged *electrons*. Electrons have a negative charge. The mass of an electron is much smaller than the mass of a proton or a neutron. ☑

What Do Atoms of the Same Element Have in Common?

All of the atoms of a given element have one thing in common: they have the same number of protons. In fact, you can use the number of protons in an atom to determine which element the atom comes from. For example, all atoms with one proton are atoms of the element hydrogen. Atoms with two protons are helium atoms, as shown in the figure at the top of the next page.

READING TOOLBOX

Compare After you read this section, make a chart comparing atomic number, mass number, atomic mass, and average atomic mass.

LOOKING CLOSER

1. Identify Which two types of subatomic particles are located in the nucleus?

_____

_____

READING CHECK

2. Compare How does the mass of an electron compare with the mass of a proton?

_____

_____

_____

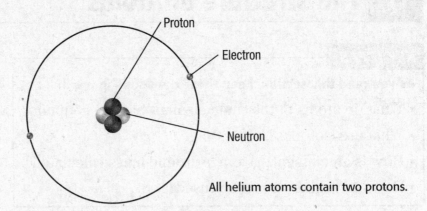

Proton

Electron

Neutron

All helium atoms contain two protons.

LOOKING CLOSER

3. Infer The nucleus of a helium atom contains four subatomic particles. How many neutrons does the helium atom have?

_____

BALANCING CHARGE WITH ELECTRONS

Protons and electrons have electric charges. However, atoms are *neutral*—that is, they do not have an electric charge. The reason for this is that atoms have the same number of electrons as protons. The negative charges of the electrons cancel out the positive charges of the protons. (Remember that neutrons, which are also found in atoms, have no electric charge.) ☑

4. Describe Why are atoms neutral?

_____

_____

_____

For example, a helium atom contains two protons in its nucleus. Therefore, the nucleus of a helium atom has a charge of +2. However, a helium atom also has two electrons. The electrons have a charge of −2. The −2 charge of the electrons balances out the +2 charge of the nucleus. As a result, the helium atom is neutral.

Sometimes, atoms can gain or lose electrons. When this happens, an ion forms. An *ion* is an atom that has gained or lost electrons and thus has an electric charge.

THE ELECTRIC FORCE

Positive and negative charges attract each other with a force called the *electric force*. The negatively charged electrons and the positively charged protons in an atom attract each other with the electric force. In fact, this force is what holds atoms together. ☑

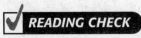

5. Identify What force holds atoms together?

_____

What Is an Atomic Number?

All atoms of an element have the same number of protons. This number is called the **atomic number** (Z) of the element. Neutral atoms have the same number of electrons as protons. Therefore, the atomic number of an element equals the number of electrons in an atom of the element.

SECTION 2 The Structure of Atoms *continued*

ATOMIC NUMBER AND PROTONS

Each element has a unique number of protons. Therefore, each element has its own unique atomic number. All atoms of a given element have the same atomic number. For example, hydrogen only has one proton, so its atomic number is 1. Uranium has 92 protons. Therefore, its atomic number is 92. The number of protons in an atom is equal to the atom's atomic number.

MASS NUMBER

The nuclei of most atoms contain both protons and neutrons. The **mass number** (A) of an element equals the number of protons plus the number of neutrons. All atoms of an element have the same number of protons. However, atoms of the same element can have different numbers of neutrons. Therefore, atoms of the same element always have the same atomic number, but can have different mass numbers. ☑

ISOTOPES

Atoms of a single element can have different numbers of neutrons. Atoms of an element with different numbers of neutrons are called **isotopes**. Isotopes contain the same number of protons as all atoms of an element. Therefore, they have the same atomic number. However, because isotopes have different numbers of neutrons, they have different mass numbers.

Look at the figure below. The figure shows three isotopes of hydrogen. Each hydrogen isotope has an atomic number of 1 because it contains one proton. However, each isotope has a different number of neutrons. Therefore, each isotope has a different mass number.

Isotopes of Hydrogen

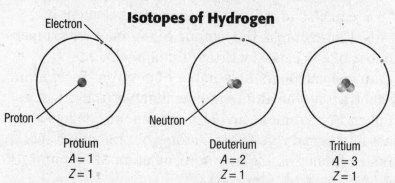

Protium	Deuterium	Tritium
$A = 1$	$A = 2$	$A = 3$
$Z = 1$	$Z = 1$	$Z = 1$

Each isotope of hydrogen has a different number of neutrons. However, all isotopes of hydrogen have the same number of protons.

Critical Thinking

6. Apply Concepts
Aluminum has an atomic number of 13. How many protons does an atom of aluminum have? How many electrons does it have?

_____

_____

✓ READING CHECK

7. Explain How can atoms of the same element have different mass numbers?

_____

_____

_____

LOOKING CLOSER

8. Identify How many electrons do all isotopes of hydrogen have?

_____

Some isotopes of an element are more common than others. For example, more than 99% of the oxygen atoms on Earth contain 8 protons and 8 neutrons. Only about 0.2% of the oxygen atoms on Earth contain 8 protons and 10 neutrons.

Some isotopes are unstable. These isotopes *decay*, or break down, over time. Sometimes, when an isotope decays, it forms a different isotope of the same element.

How Can You Show an Atom's Atomic and Mass Numbers?

You can use chemical symbols to represent atoms of different elements. For example, the symbol Cl represents an atom of the element chlorine. The chemical symbols for all the elements are in the periodic table at the back of this book.

Scientists use numbers placed before the symbol of an element to show an atom's mass number and atomic number. The mass number is always written above the atomic number, as shown below.

Critical Thinking

9. Apply Concepts What is the atomic number of most atoms of oxygen? What is the mass number of most atoms of oxygen?

_____

_____

Mass number
$\quad|$
$^{35}_{17}Cl$
$\quad|$
Atomic number

Mass number
$\quad|$
$^{37}_{17}Cl$
$\quad|$
Atomic number

This symbol represents an atom of an isotope of chlorine. This isotope of chlorine has a mass number of 35.

This symbol represents an isotope of chlorine with a mass number of 37.

LOOKING CLOSER

10. Identify How many protons are in the nucleus of an atom of chlorine?

_____

Critical Thinking

11. Calculate How many neutrons does an atom of chlorine-35 have? (Hint: Use the figure for reference.)

_____

You can also identify an isotope of an element in words. For example, the isotope of uranium with a mass number of 235 can be written "uranium-235."

You can calculate the number of neutrons in an atom by subtracting the atom's atomic number from its mass number. For example, an atom of uranium-235 has a mass number of 235. Like all atoms of uranium, it has an atomic number of 92. Therefore, an atom of uranium-235 has $235 - 92 = 143$ neutrons.

SECTION 2 The Structure of Atoms *continued*

ATOMIC MASS

The mass of a single atom is very small. For example, an atom of fluorine has a mass of less than one trillionth of one billionth of one gram. Therefore, scientists use a special unit to describe the masses of atoms. This unit is called a unified atomic mass unit. A **unified atomic mass unit** (u) is equal to one-twelfth the mass of a carbon-12 atom. This is about the same as the mass of a proton or a neutron. ☑

It can be easy to confuse atomic mass and mass number. *Atomic mass* is the mass of a single atom of an element. Atomic mass is measured in unified atomic mass units or in grams. *Mass number* is the sum of the number of protons and neutrons in an atom. Mass number does not have any units, and it is always a whole number.

> ✓ **READING CHECK**
>
> **12. Identify** What unit do scientists use to measure the masses of atoms?
>
> _____
> _____

AVERAGE ATOMIC MASS

The figure below shows the entry in the periodic table for chlorine. The number written above the chemical symbol is the atomic number of chlorine, 17. The number below the chemical symbol is the average atomic mass of chlorine. This number is related to the atomic masses of chlorine atoms.

| 17 |
| Cl |
| Chlorine |
| 35.453 |

About 76% of chlorine atoms are chlorine-35 atoms, with atomic masses of about 35 u. About 24% of chlorine atoms are chlorine-37 atoms, with atomic masses of about 37 u. The weighted average of these two numbers gives the average atomic mass of chlorine, 35.453 u.

There are two isotopes of chlorine: chlorine-35 and chlorine-37. However, both isotopes are not equally common in nature. If you could collect 100 atoms of chlorine, about 24 of them would be chlorine-37 atoms, and about 76 of them would be chlorine-35 atoms. In other words, about 24% of the chlorine atoms on Earth are chlorine-37 atoms. The other 76% are chlorine-35 atoms.

The average atomic mass of chlorine represents the average mass of all the chlorine atoms on Earth. It is a weighted average. That is, because most chlorine atoms are chlorine-35 atoms, the average atomic mass of chlorine is closer to 35 u than to 37 u.

> **LOOKING CLOSER**
>
> **13. Identify** What is the average atomic mass of chlorine?
>
> _____

How Can You Convert Atomic Masses to Grams?

Scientists use unified atomic mass units to describe the masses of single atoms. However, in most cases, chemists deal with huge numbers of atoms. For example, 1 g of table sugar contains about 1.8×10^{21} molecules of sugar. It is much easier to use grams to describe the masses of such large numbers of particles.

Chemists use a special unit called a mole to represent large numbers of particles. A **mole** (mol) is the basic unit used to measure the amount of a substance. One mole is equal to a very large number of particles: ☑

$$1 \text{ mol} = 602,213,670,000,000,000,000,000 \text{ particles}$$

This number, which is called *Avogadro's number*, is usually written as 6.022×10^{23}. The number is named after the Italian scientist Amedeo Avogadro.

Why is 6.022×10^{23} the number of particles in one mole? Chemists have defined a mole as the number of atoms in 12.00 g of carbon-12. From experiments, we know that there are 6.022×10^{23} atoms in 12.00 g of carbon-12.

MOLAR MASS

The mass of one mole of a substance is called its *molar mass*. For example, 1 mol of carbon-12 atoms has a mass of 12 grams. Therefore, the molar mass of carbon-12 is 12.00 g/mol. One mole of table sugar has a mass of 342.3 g. Therefore, the molar mass of table sugar is 342.3 g/mol.

You can use the mole to convert the average atomic masses on the periodic table into grams. The mass in grams of one mole of any element equals the element's average atomic mass in unified atomic mass units. An example is shown in the figure below.

READING CHECK

14. Define What is a mole?

_____

_____

_____

Critical Thinking

15. Apply Concepts The molar mass of sodium chloride is 58 g/mol. How many grams of sodium chloride are in 0.5 mol of sodium chloride?

_____

LOOKING CLOSER

16. Identify What is the molar mass of magnesium? Give your answer with three significant figures.

_____

The mass of one mole of magnesium atoms, in grams, equals the average atomic mass of magnesium in unified atomic mass units.

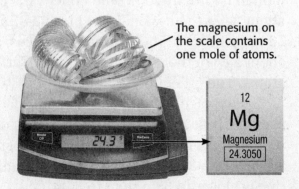

The magnesium on the scale contains one mole of atoms.

12
Mg
Magnesium
24.3050

SECTION 2 The Structure of Atoms *continued*

CONVERTING MOLES TO GRAMS

Let's look at an example of how to convert between moles and grams. What is the mass in grams of 5.50 mol of iron? Remember that the average atomic mass of each element is listed in the periodic table at the back of this book.

Step 1: List the given and unknown values.	Given: amount of iron = 5.50 mol molar mass of iron = 55.84 g/mol	Unknown: mass of iron
Step 2: Write the conversion factor. The numerator should have the units you are trying to find. The denominator should have the units you are trying to cancel.	conversion factor: $\dfrac{55.84 \text{ g Fe}}{1 \text{ mol Fe}}$	
Step 3: Multiply by the conversion factor to solve.	$5.50 \text{ mol Fe} \times \dfrac{55.84 \text{ g Fe}}{1 \text{ mol Fe}} = 307 \text{ g Fe}$	

Math *Skills*

17. Calculate What is the mass in grams of 3.20 mol of copper (Cu)? Show your work.

MOLAR MASSES OF COMPOUNDS

Remember that compounds are made of atoms joined together in specific ratios. Because compounds have fixed compositions, they also have molar masses. To find a compound's molar mass, add the masses of all the atoms in one molecule of the compound. For example, suppose you wanted to find the molar mass of water (H_2O). Follow these steps:

1. Look in the periodic table to find the molar masses of the elements in the compound.

   Water contains oxygen and hydrogen. Oxygen's molar mass is 16.00 g/mol. (For problems in this book, round all masses in the periodic table to the hundredths place.) Hydrogen's molar mass is 1.01 g/mol.

2. Use the chemical formula of water to determine how many atoms of each element are in the compound.

   The chemical formula H_2O tells you that each molecule of water contains two hydrogen atoms and one oxygen atom.

3. Add up the masses of all the atoms in the molecule.
   $(2) \times (1.01 \text{ g/mol}) + (1) \times (16.00 \text{ g/mol}) = 18.02 \text{ g/mol}$
   So, the molar mass of water is 18.02 g/mol.

Critical Thinking

18. Calculate What is the molar mass of methane, CH_4? Show your work.

Name _____ Class _____ Date _____

Section 2 Review

SECTION VOCABULARY

atomic number the smallest unit of an element that maintains the chemical properties of that element

isotope an atom that has the same number of protons (or the same atomic number) as other atoms of the same element do but that has a different number of neutrons (and thus a different atomic mass)

mass number the sum of the numbers of protons and neutrons in the nucleus of an atom

mole the SI base unit used to measure the amount of a substance whose number of particles is the same as the number of atoms of carbon in exactly 12 g of carbon-12

neutron a subatomic particle that has no charge and that is located in the nucleus of an atom

proton a subatomic particle that has a positive charge and that is located in the nucleus of an atom; the number of protons in the nucleus is the atomic number, which determines the identity of an element

unified atomic mass unit a unit of mass that describes the mass of an atom or molecule; it is exactly 1/12 of the mass of a carbon atom with mass number 12

1. **Compare** What is the difference between mass number and atomic mass?

_____

_____

2. **Apply Concepts** Fill in the blank spaces in the table below. Then, use the information in the table to answer questions 3 and 4.

Atom	Atomic number	Mass number	Number of neutrons
A	7	14	
B		15	8
C	13		14
D		87	50
E	38		49

3. **Identify** Which two atoms in the table are isotopes of the same element? Explain your answer.

_____

_____

4. **Describe** How many electrons does atom D contain? Explain your answer.

_____

_____

5. **Calculate** How many moles of glucose, $C_6H_{12}O_6$, are in 300 g of glucose? Show your work.

CHAPTER 4 | Atoms

SECTION 3 | # Modern Atomic Theory

KEY IDEAS

As you read this section, keep these questions in mind:

• How are electrons organized in an atom?

• Can the exact location of an electron be determined?

• How do electrons move between energy levels?

What Is the Modern Model of the Atom?

The modern model of the atom is very different from the model proposed by Rutherford. Remember that in Rutherford's atomic model, electrons could be found at any distance from the nucleus. Today, scientists know that electrons are found at only a few specific distances from the nucleus. In addition, we know today that it is impossible to determine exactly where an electron is at any specific time.

BOHR'S MODEL OF THE ATOM

In 1913, Danish physicist Niels Bohr showed that electrons can be found only in certain *energy levels*, or regions, around the nucleus. Electrons must gain energy to move to a higher energy level. They must lose energy to move to a lower level. ☑

You can use a house, such as the one in the figure below, to help you understand Bohr's model. Imagine that the nucleus of an atom is in a deep basement. Electrons can be on any floor, but they cannot be between floors. Electrons gain energy by riding up the elevator, and lose energy by riding down.

READING TOOLBOX

Summarize As you read this section, underline the main ideas in each paragraph. When you finish reading, write a summary of the section using the underlined ideas.

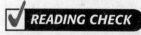

READING CHECK

1. Describe What must happen to an electron in order for it to move to a higher energy level?

_____

_____

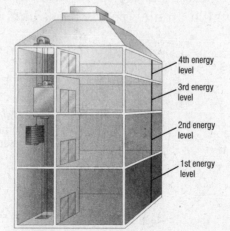

4th energy level

3rd energy level

2nd energy level

1st energy level

In the Bohr model, electrons can be found only in certain energy levels around the nucleus.

LOOKING CLOSER

2. Infer If an electron moves from the third energy level to the second energy level, has it gained or lost energy?

_____

_____

SECTION 3 **Modern Atomic Theory** *continued*

THE MODERN ATOMIC MODEL

In Bohr's model, electrons orbited the nucleus like planets orbit a star. However, Bohr's atomic model worked only for hydrogen. Other scientists realized that other elements were better described by combining Bohr's ideas about energy levels with ideas about probability. ☑

Imagine a spinning propeller on a plane, such as the one shown below. If someone asked you where a certain propeller blade was at a certain time, it would be difficult to answer. However, you could tell the person that the blade was probably somewhere within the blurred region at the front of the plane.

In a similar way, we cannot know the exact position, speed, and direction of an electron at the same time. This is because electrons exist as "clouds" around the nucleus. Therefore, scientists can determine only how likely it is that an electron is in a certain place. This region is called an orbital. An **orbital** is a region in which an electron is most likely to be. ☑

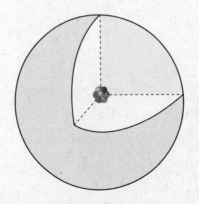

The shaded region is an orbital. The orbital is the region in which an electron is most likely to be.

✔ **READING CHECK**

3. Explain Why didn't scientists use Bohr's atomic model to describe all the elements?

_____

_____

✔ **READING CHECK**

4. Define What is an orbital?

_____

_____

_____

LOOKING CLOSER

5. Identify Label the orbital in the figure.

SECTION 3 Modern Atomic Theory *continued*

How Do Electrons Fill Energy Levels?

Within an atom, electrons have different amounts of energy and exist in different energy levels. Recall that there are many possible energy levels in an atom. Each energy level can hold a specific number of electrons. For example, the first energy level can hold up to two electrons. The more electrons an atom has, the more energy levels are "filled." The figure below shows how many electrons different energy levels can hold.

Electrons fill energy levels in order from lowest energy to highest energy. For example, lithium atoms have three electrons. Two of the electrons fill the first energy level. The third electron is located in the second energy level.

Electron Energy Levels

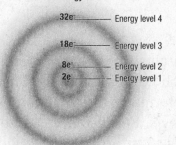

32e⁻ —— Energy level 4
18e⁻ —— Energy level 3
8e⁻ —— Energy level 2
2e⁻ —— Energy level 1

Each energy level can hold a different number of electrons.

The electrons in the outer energy level of an atom are called **valence electrons**. Valence electrons determine the chemical properties of an atom. For example, all atoms with one valence electron behave in a similar way. ☑

Each energy level contains one or more *subshells*. There are four different kinds of subshells. Each kind of subshell is represented by a different letter: s, p, d, or f. Each subshell has a different shape.

The lower the energy level, the fewer subshells are in the energy level. For example, the first energy level contains only an s subshell. The third energy level contains s, p, and d subshells.

Each subshell contains one or more orbitals. Each orbital can hold up to two electrons. An s subshell contains only one orbital, so it can hold up to two electrons. ☑

A p subshell contains three orbitals, as shown in the figures on the next page. The different orbitals have different *orientations*, or directions, in space. Each orbital can hold up to two electrons. Therefore, the three orbitals in the p subshell together can hold up to six electrons.

Critical Thinking

6. Infer How is the modern atomic model similar to Bohr's model of the atom?

_____

_____

_____

LOOKING CLOSER

7. Describe An atom contains nine electrons. In which energy levels are the electrons located?

_____

 **READING CHECK**

8. Define What are valence electrons?

_____

_____

 **READING CHECK**

9. Describe How many electrons can an s subshell hold?

_____

_____

LOOKING CLOSER

10. Compare How are the three p orbitals different from one another?

_____

_____

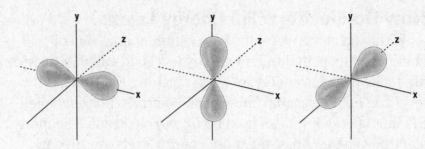

There are three kinds of p orbitals.

The shapes of the d and f orbitals are very complex. It is very difficult to show them in a drawing. There are five different kinds of d orbitals. Therefore, all the d orbitals together can hold up to ten electrons. There are seven different kinds of f orbitals, so all the f orbitals together can hold up to 14 electrons.

Talk About It

Discuss It can be difficult to understand energy levels and orbitals. After you read about energy levels and orbitals, discuss any questions you have with a small group.

ELECTRONS AND ORBITALS

Every energy level contains a certain number of orbitals. Each orbital can hold two electrons. Therefore, the number of orbitals determines the total number of electrons in that energy level. For instance, the second energy level of an atom has four orbitals: one s orbital and three p orbitals. Therefore, the second energy level can hold up to eight electrons. The figure below shows the maximum number of electrons in each energy level.

LOOKING CLOSER

11. Describe An atom has electrons in the first and second energy levels. What is the greatest number of electrons it could have?

_____

Energy level	Number of orbitals by type				Total number of orbitals	Maximum number of electrons
	s	p	d	f		
1	1				1	2
2	1	3			1 + 3 = 4	8
3	1	3	5		1 + 3 + 5 = 9	18
4	1	3	5	7	1 + 3 + 5 + 7 = 16	32

How Can Electrons Move in an Atom?

An electron is never found between energy levels. Instead, it "jumps" from one level to the next. What makes an atom move from one energy level to another? Electrons move between energy levels when an atom gains or loses energy.

GROUND STATE AND EXCITED STATE

The lowest state of energy of an electron is called its *ground state*. When an electron gains energy, it moves to an *excited state* in a higher energy level. Electrons gain energy by absorbing photons. A **photon** is the smallest unit of light energy. It is a little bit like an atom of light. When an electron falls to a lower energy level, it releases one photon. ☑

Photons have different energies. The energy of the photon affects which energy level an electron can move to. The higher the energy of the photon, the higher the energy level the electron can jump to.

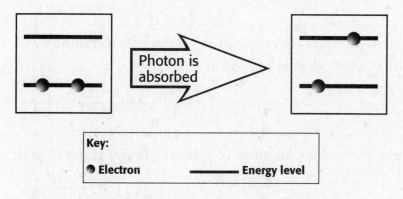

When an electron absorbs a photon, the electron can jump to a higher energy level.

✓ READING CHECK

12. Define What is the ground state of an electron?

_____

_____

LOOKING CLOSER

13. Identify On the figure, label the correct illustrations with "ground state" or "excited state."

ATOMS AND LIGHT

The energy of a photon is related to the wavelength of the light. Atoms of a given element can only gain or lose energy in specific amounts. These amounts of energy correspond to light of certain wavelengths, or colors. Therefore, the colors of light that are emitted or absorbed by an element can be used to identify the element.

For example, neon signs use energy from electricity to excite atoms of neon gas. The atoms of neon first gain the energy and then release it in the form of light. The wavelength of visible light determines the color of light. Fireworks are another example. The colors of fireworks are produced by burning compounds of magnesium, aluminum, and sodium salts.

Section 3 Review

SECTION VOCABULARY

orbital a region in an atom where there is a high probability of finding electrons **photon** a unit or quantum of light; a particle of electromagnetic radiation that has zero rest mass and carries a quantum of energy	**valence electron** an electron that is found in the outermost shell of an atom and that determines the atom's chemical properties

1. Apply Concepts An atom's valence electrons are in the second energy level. Which two orbitals could the valence electrons be in?

_____

2. Describe Relationships How are energy levels and orbitals related?

_____

_____

3. Describe An atom of nitrogen contains seven electrons. Describe the number of electrons in each energy level in an atom of nitrogen.

_____

_____

4. Infer How many valence electrons does an atom of nitrogen have? Explain your answer.

_____

_____

5. Explain According to the modern atomic theory, what can scientists not know about an electron?

_____

_____

6. Apply Concepts Aluminum has an atomic number of 13. In which energy levels are the electrons in an aluminum atom? (Hint: Remember that atoms have the same number of electrons as protons.)

_____

_____

7. Identify How many valence electrons does an atom of aluminum have? Explain your answer.

_____

_____

CHAPTER 5 The Periodic Table

SECTION 1 Organizing the Elements

As you read this section, keep these questions in mind:

- How did Dmitri Mendeleev organize his periodic table?
- How are the elements arranged in a modern periodic table?

How Are the Elements Organized?

People organize things so that a particular item is easier to find. For example, a person may organize her CDs by the names of the bands. Another person may organize his books by subject.

In the 1860s, scientists knew of about 60 elements. A Russian schoolteacher named Dmitri Mendeleev was trying to organize these elements. Mendeleev listed the properties of each element on a separate piece of paper. He then tried to arrange the pieces of paper into rows and columns so that they formed a pattern.

MENDELEEV'S PERIODIC TABLE

In 1869, Mendeleev published the first periodic table of the elements. In his periodic table, Mendeleev arranged elements in rows by increasing atomic mass. Within a row, elements with lower atomic masses were on the left. Mendeleev started a new row every time the chemical properties of the elements repeated. Thus, all the elements in a column had similar properties. ☑

READING TOOLBOX

Organize Create a Spider Map that has two legs and several lines on each leg. Use the map to compare Mendeleev's periodic table with the modern periodic table.

✓ READING CHECK

1. Identify What property did Mendeleev use to organize his periodic table?

_____

_____

		Ti=50	Zr=90	?=180.
		V=51	Nb=94	Ta=182.
		Cr=52	Mo=96	W=186.
		Mn=55	Rh=104,4	Pt=197,4
		Fe=56	Ru=104,4	Ir=198.
	Ni=Co=59		Pl=106,6	Os=199.
H=1		Cu=63,4	Ag=108	Hg=200.
Be=9,4	Mg=24	Zn=65,2	Cd=112	
B=11	Al=27,4	?=68	Ur=116	Au=197?
C=12	Si=28	?=70	Sn=118	
N=14	P=31	As=75	Sb=122	Bi=210
O=16	S=32	Se=79,4	Te=128?	
F=19	Cl=35,5	Br=80	I=127	
Li=7 Na=23	K=39	Rb=85,4	Cs=133	Tl=204
	Ca=40	Sr=87,6	Ba=137	Pb=207.
	?=45	Ce=92		
	?Er=56	La=94		
	?Yt=60	Di=95		
	?In=75,6	Th=118?		

Each row of Mendeleev's periodic table represented a repeating pattern. Because the pattern of chemical properties repeated by rows, all elements lined up in a column had similar properties.

PREDICTING ELEMENTS

When Mendeleev arranged the elements in a table, he left gaps, or spaces, in the table. Look again at Mendeleev's table on the last page. Notice that Mendeleev included question marks in his table. The question marks represented elements with certain properties that scientists had not discovered yet. Because he saw patterns of chemical properties, Mendeleev predicted that scientists would eventually find the elements that filled those gaps. ☑

Mendeleev was not the only person to develop a periodic table. However, he was the first to use the table to make predictions. For example, Mendeleev left a space in his table for an element after silicon. He predicted that this element would be a gray metal that had a high melting point. In 1886, the element germanium was discovered.

Properties of Germanium		
	Mendeleev's prediction	**Actual Property**
Atomic mass	70	72.6
Density	5.5 g/cm³	5.3 g/cm³
Appearance	Dark gray metal	Gray metalloid
Melting point	High	937 °C

Germanium has the properties similar to those that Mendeleev predicted.

PROBLEMS WITH MENDELEEV'S TABLE

Mendeleev found that some elements did not fit the pattern in his table. For example, Mendeleev had to place tellurium (Te) before iodine (I) in his table so that they fit the pattern of chemical properties. However, when he switched Te and I, they were no longer in order of increasing atomic mass. ☑

Mendeleev thought that the values for the atomic masses of Te and I might be incorrect. He thought that careful measurements would show that the atomic mass of Te was actually less than that of I. However, measurements by other scientists showed that the atomic masses of the two elements were correct. This problem was finally solved about 40 years later by an English chemist named Henry Moseley.

READING CHECK

2. Explain Why did Mendeleev leave gaps in the periodic table?

_____

_____

_____

_____

_____

READING CHECK

3. Explain Why did Mendeleev have problems arranging the elements Te and I?

_____

_____

_____

_____

SECTION 1 Organizing the Elements *continued*

How Is the Periodic Table Organized Today?

Unlike Mendeleev, Mosely did not organize elements by increasing atomic masses. Instead, he organized the elements into a periodic table by atomic number. Recall that an element's atomic number is the number of protons in an atom of the element. ☑

The new way of organizing did not change the locations of most elements in the periodic table. However, a few elements, including Te and I, did move. Although Te has a higher atomic mass than I, it has a lower atomic number. Thus, Mosely could place Te before I in the periodic table without disturbing the pattern of chemical properties.

The modern periodic table has more than 100 elements, and organizes the elements by atomic number. Because elements are arranged by atomic number, elements with similar properties are located in the same column. Therefore, the properties of the elements on the periodic table repeat at regular intervals. This principle is known as the **periodic law**.

PERIODS AND GROUPS

A horizontal row on the periodic table is called a **period**. There are seven periods on the periodic table. The properties of the elements in a period are different. A vertical column on the periodic table is called a **group**. All the elements in a group have similar chemical properties.

> ☑ **READING CHECK**
>
> **4. Identify** What property did Mosely use to organize the periodic table?
>
> _____
>
> _____

> **Critical Thinking**
>
> **5. Compare** Which information helps you predict the properties of an element—the period it is in, or the group it is in? Explain your answer.
>
> _____
>
> _____
>
> _____
>
> _____
>
> _____

	Group 1	Group 2	Group 13	Group 14	Group 15	Group 16	Group 17	Group 18
Period 1	1 H Hydrogen 1.0							2 He Helium 4.0
Period 2	3 Li Lithium 6.9	4 Be Beryllium 9.0	5 B Boron 10.8	6 C Carbon 12.0	7 N Nitrogen 14.0	8 O Oxygen 16.0	9 F Fluorine 19.0	10 Ne Neon 20.2
Period 3	11 Na Sodium 23.0	12 Mg Magnesium 24.3	13 Al Aluminum 27.0	14 Si Silicon 28.1	15 P Phosphorus 31.0	16 S Sulfur 32.1	17 Cl Chlorine 35.5	18 Ar Argon 39.9
Period 4	19 K Potassium 39.1	20 Ca Calcium 40.1	31 Ga Gallium 69.7	32 Ge Germanium 72.6	33 As Arsenic 74.9	34 Se Selenium 79.0	35 Br Bromine 79.9	36 Kr Krypton 83.8
Period 5	37 Rb Rubidium 85.5	38 Sr Strontium 87.6	49 In Indium 114.8	50 Sn Tin 118.7	51 Sb Antimony 121.8	52 Te Tellurium 127.6	53 I Iodine 126.9	54 Xe Xenon 131.3
Period 6	55 Cs Cesium 132.9	56 Ba Barium 137.3	81 Tl Thallium 204.4	82 Pb Lead 207.2	83 Bi Bismuth 209.0	84 Po Polonium (209)	85 At Astatine (210)	86 Rn Radon (222)
Period 7	87 Fr Francium (223)	88 Ra Radium (226)	113 Uut Ununtrium (284)	114 Unq Ununquadium (289)	115 Uup Ununpentium (288)			

63 Eu Europium 152.0	64 Gd Gadolinium 157.2	65 Tb Terbium 158.9	66 Dy Dysprosium 162.5	67 Ho Holmium 164.9	68 Er Erbium 167.3	69 Tm Thulium 168.9	70 Yb Ytterbium 173.0	71 Lu Lutetium 175.0
95 Am Americium (243)	96 Cm Curium (247)	97 Bk Berkelium (247)	98 Cf Californium (251)	99 Es Einsteinium (252)	100 Fm Fermium (257)	101 Md Mendelevium (298)	102 No Nobelium (259)	103 Lr Lawrencium (262)

Section 1 Review

SECTION VOCABULARY

group a vertical column of elements in the periodic table; elements in a group share chemical properties **period** in chemistry, a horizontal row of elements in the periodic table	**periodic law** the law that states that the repeating chemical and physical properties of elements change periodically with the atomic numbers of the elements

1. Compare Find oxygen, sulfur, and fluorine in the periodic table in the back of the book. Are the chemical properties of oxygen more similar to those of sulfur or to those of fluorine? Explain your answer.

_____

_____

_____

2. Identify Complete the table below to describe several elements. Use the periodic table in the back of the book to help you. Round off atomic masses to the nearest whole number. For example, change 15.9994 to 16.

Element	Symbol	Atomic number	Atomic mass	Period	Group
Gold					
		47			
				4	2
	Fe				

3. Predict If scientists found element 117, into which period and group would they place it? Identify one element that would have properties similar to those of element 117.

_____

_____

4. Infer Before 1937, scientists had not found element 43. Chemists predicted the properties of element 43. How was it possible for chemists to predict these properties?

_____

_____

_____

| CHAPTER 5 | The Periodic Table |

SECTION 2

Exploring the Periodic Table

As you read this section, keep these questions in mind:

• What are the three main categories of elements?

• Why do the elements in the same group have similar chemical properties?

• What happens to an atom that loses or gains an electron?

What Do Elements in a Group Have in Common?

All of the elements in a group on the periodic table have similar properties. Recall that an atom's electrons move in orbitals at various energy levels. The electrons in the outermost energy level are called *valence electrons*. The number of valence electrons in an atom determines many of the chemical properties of an element.

In general, the atoms of elements in the same group have the same number of valence electrons. For example, lithium (Li) and sodium (Na) are both members of Group 1. All atoms of these elements have one valence electron. Because of this, lithium and sodium have similar chemical properties.

READING TOOLBOX

Summarize On the periodic table in the back of the book, write notes to remind you of the periodic trends described in this section. Label the metals, nonmetals, and semiconductors.

Lithium

Valence electron

Sodium

Valence electron

| 3 |
| **Li** |
| Lithium |

| 11 |
| **Na** |
| Sodium |

Lithium and sodium atoms have different numbers of electrons. However, they have the same number of valence electrons.

LOOKING CLOSER

1. Compare How are the valence electrons in lithium and sodium atoms different?

_____

_____

_____

The repeating patterns of chemical properties shown in the periodic table are called *periodic trends*. Periodic trends are a result of the arrangement of electrons in atoms of each element.

SECTION 2 Exploring the Periodic Table *continued*

PREDICTING ELECTRON ARRANGEMENTS

If you know where an element is located on the periodic table, you can predict its arrangement of electrons. As you move to the right across a period, the number of valence electrons increases. As you move down a group, the number of energy levels increases. ☑

For example, boron and carbon are in the same period. Carbon has one more valence electron than boron has. Thus, carbon is located to the right of boron on the periodic table. Hydrogen and lithium are in the same group. Lithium has electrons in one more energy level than hydrogen does. Thus, lithium is located below hydrogen on the periodic table.

☑ **READING CHECK**

2. Describe How does the number of valence electrons change as you move to the right across the periodic table?

_____

_____

LOOKING CLOSER

3. Identify Which element has more valence electrons—neon or oxygen? Explain your answer.

_____

_____

_____

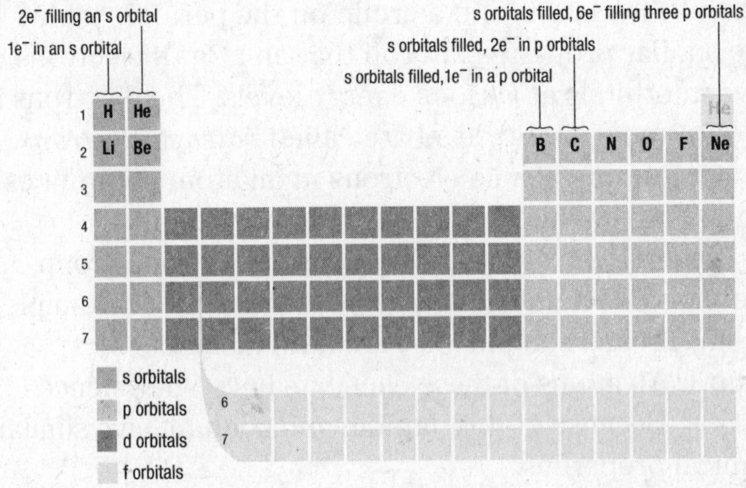

LOOKING CLOSER

4. Complete Use the periodic table in the back of the book to help you complete this table.

5. Identify What is the relationship between period and number of energy levels?

_____

_____

_____

Element and symbol	Period	Group	Number of valence electrons	Number of energy levels
	1	1	1	1
Nitrogen, N				
	3	2		
			1	4
	5		7	
Barium, Ba				
	7	2		

What Are Ions?

Some atoms do not have filled outermost energy levels. These atoms may undergo a process called ionization. During *ionization*, an atom may gain or lose valence electrons so that its outermost energy level is full. ☑

If an atom gains or loses electrons, it will no longer have an equal number of electrons and protons. When the numbers of electrons and protons are not equal, the charges do not cancel one another out. This gives the atom an electric charge. A charged atom is called an **ion**. Many atoms can form ions. However, atoms of elements in Groups 1 and 17 form ions most easily.

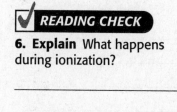

READING CHECK

6. Explain What happens during ionization?

_____

_____

_____

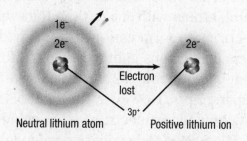

Neutral lithium atom   Positive lithium ion

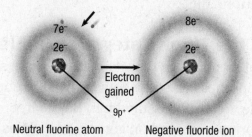

Neutral fluorine atom   Negative fluoride ion

Lithium is a group 1 element. When a lithium atom loses an electron, it becomes positively charged. Fluorine is a group 17 element. When a fluorine atom gains an electron, it becomes negatively charged.

LOOKING CLOSER

7. Describe How are the outermost energy levels of the atoms and ions in the figure different?

_____

_____

_____

_____

_____

GROUP 1

Atoms of elements in Group 1 are very reactive. That is, they react easily with atoms of other elements. Group 1 elements are very reactive because each of their atoms has one valence electron. A single valence electron can be removed easily from an atom. When an atom loses an electron, it becomes a positive ion. Positive ions are called *cations*. A positive ion has a superscript "+" next to the element symbol. For example, a lithium ion with a charge of +1 is written Li^+.

Critical Thinking

8. Infer Which atom would be more reactive—F or F⁻? Explain your answer.

_____

_____

_____

_____

_____

GROUP 17

Atoms of elements in Group 17 are also very reactive. Group 17 elements are very reactive because each of their atoms has seven valence electrons. Each of these atoms needs only one more electron to fill its outermost energy level. Atoms of Group 17 elements easily gain electrons. When an atom gains an electron, it becomes a negative ion. Negative ions are called *anions*. An anion has a superscript "−" next to the element symbol: F^-.

OTHER GROUPS

Atoms of elements in Groups 2 through 16 can also form ions. These atoms have to lose or gain more than one electron in order to have a filled outermost energy level. In general, atoms with fewer than four valence electrons lose electrons to form cations. Atoms with more than four valence electrons gain electrons to form anions.

Ions of elements in Groups 2 through 16 are also indicated with superscripts. However, the symbols for these ions also show how many electrons were gained or lost. For example, magnesium loses its two valence electrons to form a cation: Mg^{2+}.

What Are the Three Categories of Elements?

Recall that elements in the same group share similar chemical properties. The elements in the 18 groups of the periodic table are also classified into three larger categories. These categories are based on general properties that the elements share.

LOOKING CLOSER

9. Identify Which category contains the most elements?

_____

_____

10. Identify Which category contains the fewest elements?

_____

_____

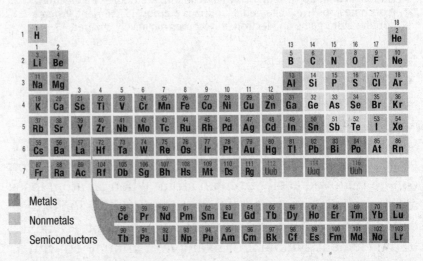

Name _____ Class _____ Date _____

SECTION 2 Exploring the Periodic Table *continued*

Three Categories of Elements

Category	Properties	Examples
Metals	• good conductors of electricity • good conductors of thermal energy • ductile (easily formed into wires) and malleable (easily shaped or formed) • generally shiny solids	**Lead**
Nonmetals	• poor conductors of electricity • poor conductors of thermal energy • not ductile or malleable • generally not shiny • may be solids, liquids, or gases	**Carbon**
Semiconductors	• share properties with metals and nonmetals • can conduct electricity under certain conditions	**Tellurium**

A **metal** is an element that is a good conductor of electricity and heat. An element that is not a good conductor of electricity and heat is called a **nonmetal**. Some elements conduct electricity only under certain conditions. Such elements are called **semiconductors**. Semiconductors are also called *metalloids*.

LOOKING CLOSER

11. Apply Concepts Into which category would you place a shiny substance that is used to make flexible bed springs?

_____

12. Apply Concepts Into which category would you place a brittle substance that does not conduct heat?

_____

Talk About It

Find Examples Find examples of objects you use every day that you think are made up of metals or nonmetals. With a partner, talk about why you think these objects contain metals or nonmetals.

Section 2 Review

SECTION VOCABULARY

ion an atom, radical, or molecule that has gained or lost one or more electrons and has a negative or positive charge **metal** an element that is shiny and that conducts heat and electricity well	**nonmetal** an element that conducts heat and electricity poorly and that does not form positive ions in an electrolytic solution **semiconductor** an element or compound that conducts electric current better than an insulator does but not as well as a conductor does

1. Compare Compare the number of valence electrons in an atom of oxygen and an atom of selenium. Are these two elements in the same period or the same group?

_____

_____

_____

2. Explain How does a cation differ from an anion?

_____

_____

_____

3. Predict Atoms of cesium can lose electrons to become cations. How many electrons does a single cesium atom lose? Explain your answer.

_____

_____

_____

4. Explain Why do elements in groups share more chemical properties than elements in a period?

_____

_____

_____

_____

5. Explain Why do some atoms gain electrons to form ions and some lose electrons?

_____

_____

_____

_____

CHAPTER 5 | The Periodic Table

SECTION 3 **Families of Elements**

KEY IDEAS

As you read this section, keep these questions in mind:

• What makes up a family of elements?

• What properties do the elements in a group share?

• Why does carbon form so many compounds?

What Are Element Families?

Recall that all elements can be classified into three categories: metals, nonmetals, and semiconductors. Scientists classify the elements further into five families. The atoms of all elements in most families have the same number of valence electrons. Thus, members of a family in the periodic table share some properties. ☑

Group number	Number of valence electrons	Name of family
Group 1	1	Alkali metals
Group 2	2	Alkaline-earth metals
Groups 3–12	varied	Transition metals
Group 17	7	Halogens
Group 18	8 (except helium, which has 2)	Noble gases

What Are the Families of Metals?

Many elements are classified as metals. Recall that metals can conduct heat and electricity. Most metals can be stretched and shaped into flat sheets or pulled into wires. Families of metals include the alkali metals, the alkaline-earth metals, and the transition metals.

THE ALKALI METALS

The elements in Group 1 form a family called the **alkali metals**. Because their atoms have only one valence electron, the alkali metals are very reactive. The valence electron can be easily removed to form a cation such as Na^+ or K^+. Alkali metals also have similar physical properties, such as melting point, boiling point, and density. ☑

READING TOOLBOX

Organize As you read this section, create a chart comparing the different families of elements. Include examples of each family and describe the common properties of elements in the family.

✓ READING CHECK

1. Identify In general, what do all elements in the same family have in common?

_____

_____

_____

✓ READING CHECK

2. Explain Why are alkali metals so reactive?

_____

_____

_____

SECTION 3 Families of Elements *continued*

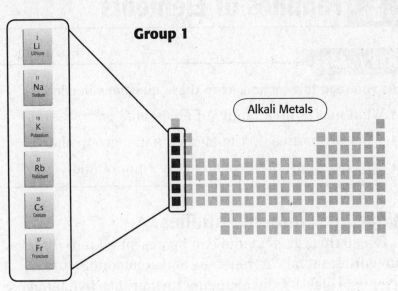

Group 1

Alkali Metals

The alkali metals are found on the left edge of the periodic table.

Because alkali metals are so reactive, they are rarely found in nature as pure elements. Rather, they are found combined with other elements as compounds. For example, the alkali metal sodium is found in the salt sodium chloride, NaCl. Sodium chloride is more commonly known as table salt. ☑

READING CHECK

3. Explain Why are alkali metals rarely found as pure elements?

_____

_____

_____

Alkali metals, such as sodium, are so soft that they can be cut with a knife.

THE ALKALINE-EARTH METALS

The elements in Group 2 form a family called the **alkaline-earth metals**. The atoms of alkaline-earth metals have two valence electrons. These elements are reactive, but not as reactive as alkali metals. ☑

READING CHECK

4. Describe Describe the reactivity of alkaline-earth metals.

_____

_____

_____

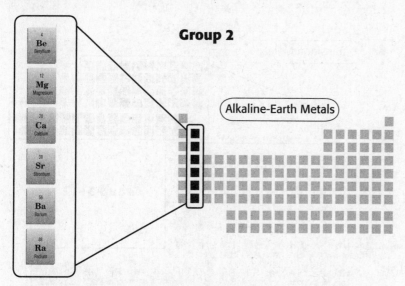

Group 2

Alkaline-Earth Metals

The alkaline-earth metals are found in Group 2 in the periodic table.

Alkaline-earth metals form cations with 2^+ charges, such as Mg^{2+} and Ca^{2+}. The alkaline-earth metals combine with other elements to form compounds. For example, two magnesium compounds—milk of magnesia and Epsom salts—are commonly used to treat minor medical problems. In addition, many calcium compounds are important to living things. Some make up the hard shells of many sea animals. Calcium compounds also make your bones and teeth strong.

The stalagmites and stalactites in limestone caves contain calcium carbonate deposits.

THE TRANSITION METALS

An element located in Groups 3-12 is known as a **transition metal**. Transition metals are not as reactive as the alkali metals or the alkaline-earth metals. In fact, some transition metals are quite unreactive. ☑

Critical Thinking

5. Apply Concepts Do alkaline-earth elements gain electrons or lose electrons to form ions?

_____

_____

✓ **READING CHECK**

6. Describe Describe the reactivity of transition metals.

_____

_____

_____

SECTION 3 Families of Elements *continued*

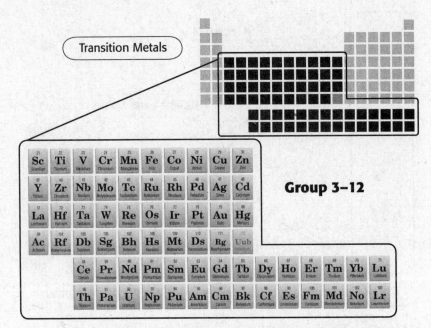

Transition Metals

Group 3–12

The transition metals are located in the middle of the periodic table.

LOOKING CLOSER

7. Identify Where are the transition metals located on the periodic table?

_____

_____

Although they are generally unreactive, transition metals can form ions. For example, an atom of gold, Au, can lose one electron to form Au^+ or three electrons to form Au^{3+}. Some transition metals can form as many as four different ions. Why? Transition metals have complex arrangements of electrons that make them behave differently than other elements. ☑

READING CHECK

8. Explain Why can transition metals form different kinds of ions?

_____

_____

_____

Both gold and platinum are shaped to make jewelry.

Like other metals, the transition metals are good conductors of electricity and heat. Most transition metals are harder, denser, and have higher melting points than alkali and alkaline-earth metals. Mercury is an exception. Mercury is the only metal that is a liquid at room temperature. For this reason, mercury is used in some thermometers.

SECTION 3 Families of Elements *continued*

SYNTHETIC ELEMENTS

All elements with atomic numbers greater than 92 are *synthetic*, or made in a laboratory. Technetium and promethium have atomic numbers lower than 92, but they are also synthetic elements. Synthetic elements are radioactive. Radioactive elements decay, or break down. They may become different elements. ☑

Examine the periodic table in the back of the book. Note that parts of Periods 6 and 7 are placed in two rows at the bottom of the periodic table. Many of these elements are synthetic. These two rows are placed separately so that the rest of the periodic table stays narrow. This placement also allows the other elements to line up according to periodic trends.

Synthetic elements have various uses. Plutonium is used to make nuclear weapons. Americium is used in smoke detectors.

> **READING CHECK**
>
> **9. Define** What are synthetic elements?
>
> _____
> _____
> _____

What Are the Families of Nonmetals?

Except for hydrogen, nonmetals are located on the right side of the periodic table. Nonmetals include some elements in Groups 13–16 and all the elements in Groups 17 and 18. Families of nonmetals include the noble gases and the halogens.

THE NOBLE GASES

The elements in Group 18 form a family called the **noble gases**.

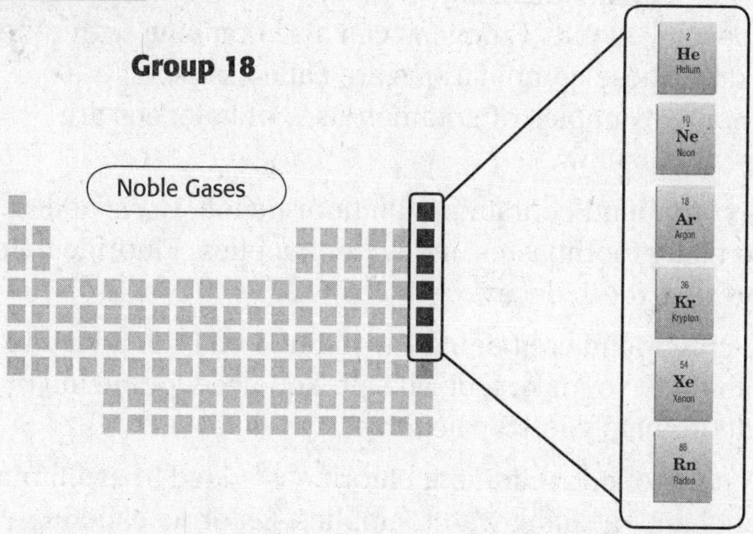

Group 18

Noble Gases

| 2 He Helium |
| 10 Ne Neon |
| 18 Ar Argon |
| 36 Kr Krypton |
| 54 Xe Xenon |
| 86 Rn Radon |

The noble gases are located along the right edge of the periodic table.

> **LOOKING CLOSER**
>
> **10. Infer** How many valence electrons do noble gases have? Explain your answer.
>
> _____
> _____
> _____

SECTION 3 Families of Elements *continued*

Neon produces the bright reddish orange light in neon signs. Other gases are added to make different colors.

Unlike most elements, the noble gases exist as single atoms, rather than as molecules or ions. Why? The outermost energy level of a noble gas atom is filled. Thus, noble gases are *inert*, or unreactive, and they do not typically react with other elements to form compounds. In other words, noble gases are very stable. ☑

Because noble gases are inert, they can be useful in many situations. For example, light bulbs are filled with argon gas because argon will not react with the bulb's metal filament.

THE HALOGENS

The elements in Group 17 form a family called the **halogens**. The halogens are the most reactive non-metals. They are very reactive because each atom has seven valence electrons. If it gains one electron, a halogen atom becomes stable.

Halogens combine easily with alkali metals because atoms of alkali metals need to lose one valence electron to become stable. Halogens can also combine with other metals. These combinations are called salts.

Some examples of common uses of halogens are described below.

- A compound containing the fluoride ion, F^-, is added to many toothpastes and water supplies. Fluoride helps prevent tooth decay.

- A compound containing the iodide ion, I^-, is added to table salt to make iodized salt. You need iodine in your diet to help you stay healthy.

- A compound containing chlorine is added to swimming pool and drinking-water supplies. Chlorine can kill bacteria.

READING CHECK

11. Explain Why do noble gases exist as single atoms rather than as compounds?

_____

_____

_____

_____

_____

Critical Thinking

12. Infer Why do Na and Cl readily combine to form a compound?

_____

_____

_____

_____

_____

SECTION 3 Families of Elements *continued*

Group 17

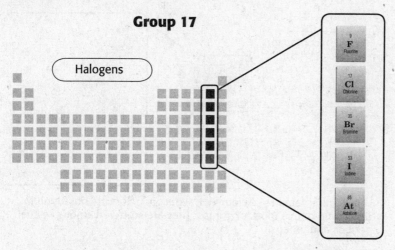

Halogens are located in the second column from the right on the periodic table.

HYDROGEN—A UNIQUE ELEMENT

Although hydrogen has one valence electron, it is not a member of the alkali metal family. Hydrogen has only one proton and one electron and has different properties from other Group 1 elements. ☑

Hydrogen is the most abundant element in the universe. About three out of every four atoms in the universe are hydrogen atoms. Most of these are located in clouds of gas and stars.

With only one electron, hydrogen can react with many other elements. For example, hydrogen reacts with oxygen to form water, H_2O, which is essential to life.

What Are the Semiconductors?

Recall that semiconductors can conduct electricity under certain conditions. The family of semiconductors contains six elements. These elements are not found in one particular group. Instead, they are found in different periods and groups. ☑

✓ READING CHECK

13. Explain Why is hydrogen not considered an alkali metal?

_____

_____

_____

✓ READING CHECK

14. Describe What are semiconductors?

_____

_____

_____

SECTION 3 Families of Elements *continued*

LOOKING CLOSER

15. Describe How does the location of semiconductors on the periodic table differ from the locations of other element families?

_____

_____

_____

_____

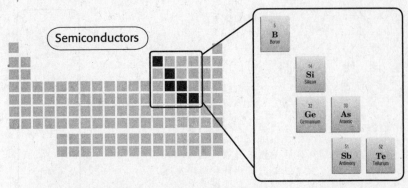

Semiconductors

Unlike other families of elements, semiconductors are not found in one group or in a block of groups. They are scattered among several periods and groups.

OTHER NONMETALS

In addition to the noble gases and halogens, there are six other nonmetals. Oxygen, nitrogen, and sulfur are very common nonmetals. They may gain electrons to form ions. For example, oxygen can form oxide, O^{2-}, nitrogen can form nitride, N^{3-}, and sulfur can form sulfide, S^{2-}.

Nitrogen and oxygen are the most plentiful gases in air. Sulfur is an odorless solid. However, many sulfur compounds, such as those in rotten eggs and skunk spray, have a terrible smell.

Critical Thinking

16. Apply Concepts How many electrons does an oxygen atom gain to form an oxide ion?

_____

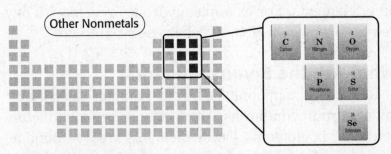

Other Nonmetals

The remaining nonmetals are carbon, nitrogen, oxygen, phosphorus, sulfur, and selenium.

SECTION 3 Families of Elements *continued*

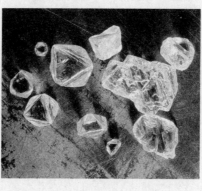

Graphite and diamond are both forms of carbon.

Carbon atoms can combine with one another in different ways to produce very different compounds. One way carbon atoms combine with one another produces graphite, which is used in pencil "lead." Carbon atoms can combine in another way to form diamonds.

Carbon atoms can also combine to form substances called *fullerenes*. The most famous has 60 carbon atoms and is known as *buckminsterfullerene*. The structure of this substance looks like a geodesic dome that was designed by American inventor R. Buckminster Fuller. A geodesic dome is a structure that looks like a large soccer ball.

Carbon can also combine with other elements to form millions of different compounds. These carbon-containing compounds are found in both living and nonliving things. Carbon compounds found in living things include sugars that you eat and chlorophyll in the cells of plants. Carbon compounds in nonliving things include rubber and isooctane in gasoline.

Critical Thinking

17. Explain Why is it not correct to refer to the material in pencils as "lead"?

_____

_____

_____

_____

_____

Section 3 Review

SECTION VOCABULARY

alkali metal one of the elements of Group 1 of the periodic table (lithium, sodium, potassium, rubidium, cesium, and francium)

alkaline-earth metal one of the elements of Group 2 of the periodic table (beryllium, magnesium, calcium, strontium, barium, and radium)

halogen one of the elements of Group 17 of the periodic table (fluorine, chlorine, bromine, iodine, and astatine); halogens combine with most metals to form salts

noble gas one of the elements of Group 18 of the periodic table (helium, neon, argon, krypton, xenon, and radon); noble gases are unreactive

transition metal one of the metals that can use the inner shell before using the outer shell to bond

1. Identify Which element is more reactive—lithium, Li, or beryllium, Be? Explain your answer.

_____

_____

2. Infer Scientists store some reactive chemicals in containers filled with argon. Why?

_____

_____

3. Classify Complete the following table to describe several elements. Use the periodic table in the back of the book to help you.

Symbol	Group number	Period number	Family name
Co			
		Period 2	semiconductor
		Period 6	halogen
Mg	Group 2		
		Period 5	noble gas

4. Infer A particular substance is typically found in nature as a pure element. What can you conclude about the reactivity of this element? (Hint: Which family contains elements that are generally found as pure elements?)

_____

_____

SECTION 1
Compounds and Molecules

KEY IDEAS

As you read this section, keep these questions in mind:

• What holds compounds and substances together?

• What determines the properties of a substance?

What Are Chemical Bonds?

Table salt and sugar look similar, but they have very different tastes. Their similarities and differences are partly due to the way their atoms or ions are joined.

Recall that compounds are substances that are made of two or more elements. **Chemical bonds** are forces that hold atoms or ions together in a compound. The chemical bonds can break and re-form during chemical changes. ☑

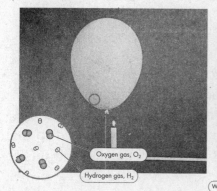 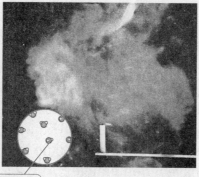

Oxygen gas, O_2

Hydrogen gas, H_2

Water vapor, H_2O

When a mixture of hydrogen gas and oxygen gas is heated, chemical bonds break and atoms rearrange. New bonds form and water is produced. The properties of water are very different from the properties of the original gases.

What Is a Chemical Structure?

A chemical formula tells you which atoms are in a compound, but not how they are connected. The structure of a building is the way its parts fit together. Similarly, a **chemical structure** is the way the atoms in a compound are bonded. Just as a blueprint represents the structure of a building, a chemical structure represents the structure of a compound.

READING TOOLBOX

Define As you read this section, write down any science terms you do not understand. Find the definitions of these terms in earlier chapters and write them in the sidebar.

✓ **READING CHECK**

1. Define What is a chemical bond?

_____

_____

_____

Talk About It

Discuss In a small group, talk about different ways you can represent structures such as buildings, roads, the solar system, etc. What are some advantages of using models like these? What are some disadvantages?

How Are Chemical Structures Represented?

Scientists use different chemical models to show different characteristics of compounds. Some models show the position of atoms in the molecule. Other models show the relative sizes of each atom in the compound. Ball-and-stick and space-filling models are two of the most commonly used chemical models.

LOOKING CLOSER
2. Compare What does the space-filling model of a water molecule tell you about the relative size of the atoms?

_____

_____

_____

Ball-and-stick model

95.8 pm

O

H   104.45°   H

Space-filling model

— Oxygen atom

Hydrogen atoms

The ball-and-stick model shows angles between bonds more clearly than the space-filling model does. However, the space-filling model shows the relative sizes of atoms more clearly than the ball-and-stick model does.

BALL-AND-STICK MODELS

Scientists use two terms to describe the relative positions of atoms in a compound. **Bond length** is the distance between the nuclei of two bonded atoms. **Bond angle** is the angle formed by two bonds connected to the same atom. A molecule must have three or more atoms to have a bond angle.

A ball-and-stick model uses balls to represent atoms and sticks to represent chemical bonds. This type of model is useful because it shows clearly the bonds and angles between atoms.

A ball-and-stick model shows you how the atoms or ions are arranged in a compound. Look again at the ball-and-stick model for water above. Hydrogen and oxygen atoms bond to form a molecule that appears bent. The molecule looks more like a boomerang than a straight line.

You can also use structural formulas to show the structure of a compound. Structural formulas are similar to ball-and-stick models. However, in a *structural formula*, chemical symbols represent the atoms. ☑

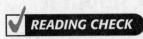

READING CHECK

3. Explain How do structural formulas differ from ball-and-stick models?

_____

_____

_____

_____

SECTION 1 Compounds and Molecules *continued*

Structural formula

SPACE-FILLING MODELS

A space-filling model shows the relative amount of space each atom takes up. In other words, a space-filling model can show relative sizes of atoms. However, unlike ball-and-stick or structural models, space-filling models do not show bond lengths clearly. ☑

REPRESENTING BONDS

Bonds are not really like sticks in a ball-and-stick model. Although bonds hold atoms tightly together, most bonds can bend, stretch, and rotate without breaking. Thus, you can think of bonds as flexible springs rather than rigid sticks.

Scientists generally use a straight, solid line to show a bond between two atoms. However, bonds are actually flexible like springs.

READING CHECK

4. Identify What is one disadvantage of space-filling models?

_____

_____

_____

LOOKING CLOSER

5. Explain Why are bonds more like springs than like sticks?

_____

_____

_____

How Does Chemical Structure Affect Chemical Properties?

The chemical structure of a compound determines the compound's properties. Some substances, such as quartz, are made up of large networks of bonded atoms. Other substances, such as table salt, are made up of networks of positive and negative ions. Some substances, such as water or sugar, are made of separate molecules.

The compounds that make up different substances join together in different ways when the substances are solids. The atoms in some substances, such as quartz, are connected strongly. These compounds tend to form strong or hard solids.

SECTION 1 Compounds and Molecules *continued*

The bonds that hold oxygen and silicon atoms together are very strong. The strength of the bonds between atoms makes quartz hard and rigid.

LOOKING CLOSER

6. Identify How does the chemical structure of quartz make the substance rigid?

_____

_____

_____

The molecules of substances such as sugar are bonded together more weakly. For example, atoms within each molecule of sugar are strongly attracted to each other, but individual molecules are not. Thus, sugar and similar substances tend to be softer and melt more easily.

Critical Thinking

7. Explain Why do substances such as sugar dissolve more easily than substances such as quartz?

_____

_____

_____

_____

_____

_____

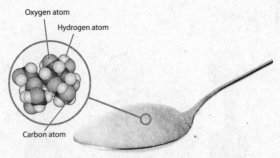

Oxygen atom

Hydrogen atom

Carbon atom

Each grain of sugar is made up of many sugar molecules, $C_{12}H_{22}O_{11}$.

Substances made of ions, such as sodium chloride, NaCl, are joined together by attractions between ions. The ions form a regular repeating network held together by strong bonds between ions with opposite charges. The strong attractions between ions give ionic compounds high melting and boiling points. ☑

READING CHECK

8. Explain Why do ionic compounds tend to have high melting and boiling points?

_____

_____

_____

Chloride ion, Cl⁻

Sodium ion, Na⁺

Each grain of table salt, or NaCl, is made of a tightly packed network of ions.

How Are Attractions Between Particles Related to State?

At room temperature, attractions between particles in a solid are stronger than those between particles of a liquid. Therefore, sugar molecules attract one another more strongly than water molecules do. Similarly, particles in a liquid attract one another more strongly than particles in a gas do. ☑

What Are Hydrogen Bonds?

The chemical structures of water and dihydrogen sulfide are similar. Why, then, does water have much higher melting and boiling points than dihydrogen sulfide does?

Water molecules are pulled together by attractions called hydrogen bonds. In a *hydrogen bond*, oxygen atoms and hydrogen atoms of different water molecules are attracted to one another. Although hydrogen bonds can pull water molecules together, hydrogen bonds are not as strong as chemical bonds. ☑

✔ READING CHECK

9. Compare How does the strength of attraction among particles differ in solids and liquids?

_____

_____

_____

_____

✔ READING CHECK

10. Compare Which is stronger—a hydrogen bond or a chemical bond?

_____

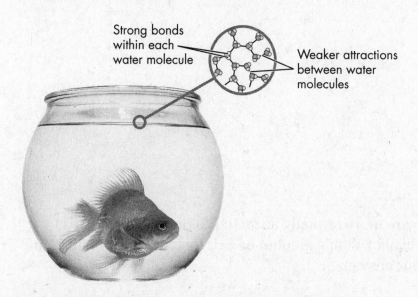

Strong bonds within each water molecule

Weaker attractions between water molecules

Water is a liquid at room temperature instead of a gas because hydrogen bonds hold water molecules together.

Section 1 Review

SECTION VOCABULARY

bond angle the angle formed by two bonds to the same atom	**chemical bond** the attractive force that holds atoms or ions together
bond length the distance between two bonded atoms at their minimum potential energy; the average distance between the nuclei of two bonded atoms	**chemical structure** the arrangement of the atoms in a molecule

1. Explain Why do scientists use different types of models to represent compounds?

_____

_____

2. Identify Which type of chemical model shows the bond angle and bond length between atoms in the compound? How does this type of model represent a compound?

_____

_____

3. Interpret Draw a ball-and-stick model of a boron trifluoride molecule. In this molecule, three fluorine atoms are attached to a boron atom. Each F-B-F bond angle is 120°, and all B-F bonds are the same length.

4. Predict Which molecules are more strongly attracted to one another—C_3H_8O molecules that make up liquid rubbing alcohol or CH_4 molecules that make up methane gas? Explain your answer.

_____

_____

_____

5. Apply Concepts What can you infer about the attraction between particles in a substance with a low melting point?

_____

CHAPTER 6 The Structure of Matter

SECTION 2 Ionic and Covalent Bonding

KEY IDEAS

As you read this section, keep these questions in mind:

• Why do atoms form bonds?

• How do ionic bonds and covalent bonds differ?

• What gives metals their distinctive properties?

• What makes a polyatomic ion different from other ions?

Why Do Chemical Bonds Form?

Atoms form bonds when their valence electrons interact. Recall that atoms with filled outermost energy levels are more stable than atoms with partially filled energy levels. In general, atoms join to form bonds so that each atom has a stable electron configuration. In other words, each atom binds in order to fill its outermost energy levels. ☑

There are two basic kinds of chemical bonding: ionic bonding and covalent bonding. The type of bonding in a compound determines many of the properties of the compound.

A Comparison of Ionic and Covalent Compounds		
	Ionic compounds	**Covalent compounds**
Structure	network of bonded ions	molecules
Valence electrons	transferred	shared
Electrical conductivity	good (when melted or dissolved)	poor
State at room temperature	solid	solid, liquid, or gas
Melting and boiling points	generally high	generally low

What Are the Properties of Ionic Bonds?

Ionic bonds form between oppositely charged ions. In general, atoms of metals, such as sodium and calcium, form positively charged ions. Atoms of nonmetals, such as chlorine and oxygen, form negatively charged ions. The attraction between ions with opposite charges holds ionic compounds together. ☑

READING TOOLBOX

Compare As you read, make a chart that describes and compares the different types of bonds.

☑ READING CHECK

1. Explain Why do atoms join to form bonds?

_____

_____

_____

LOOKING CLOSER

2. Compare How do the structures of ionic and covalent compounds differ?

_____

_____

_____

☑ READING CHECK

3. Identify What holds ionic compounds together?

_____

_____

_____

SECTION 2 Ionic and Covalent Bonding *continued*

TRANSFER OF ELECTRONS

Ionic bonds form when one atom transfers electrons to another atom. The atom that lost the electron has a positive charge. The atom that gained the electron has a negative charge. The figure below shows the transfer of an electron from a sodium atom to a chlorine atom. Chlorine attracts electrons more strongly than sodium does. Two atoms tend to form an ionic bond when one atom attracts electrons more strongly than the other atom.

LOOKING CLOSER

4. Identify In sodium chloride, which ion is negatively charged and which is positively charged?

_____

_____

_____

5. Compare Describe the outermost orbitals of Na$^+$ and Cl$^-$.

_____

_____

_____

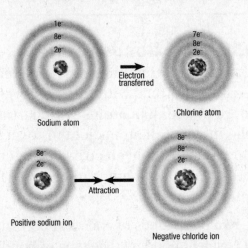

Ionic bonds form when one atom transfers electrons to another. The result is two ions with opposite charges. The oppositely charged ions attract each other.

NETWORKS OF IONIC COMPOUNDS

There is no such thing as "a molecule of NaCl." Sodium chloride is made up of a network of ions. In the network, each sodium ion is surrounded by six chloride ions. Why, then, is the chemical formula for sodium chloride not NaCl$_6$? In sodium chloride, each chloride ion is also surrounded by six sodium ions. Thus, in a sample of sodium chloride, there is one sodium ion for every chloride ion. ☑

Different ionic compounds have different ratios of ions. For example, in calcium fluoride, the ratio of calcium ions to fluoride ions is 1:2. That is, there are twice as many fluoride ions in a sample as calcium ions. Why?

Recall that calcium forms ions with +2 charges and fluorine forms ions with –1 charges. The total charge of an ionic compound is zero. For the total charge to be zero, the positive and negative charges must cancel each other.

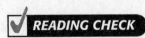 **READING CHECK**

6. Explain Why is the chemical formula for sodium chloride NaCl, and not NaCl$_6$ or Na$_6$Cl?

_____

_____

_____

SECTION 2 | Ionic and Covalent Bonding *continued*

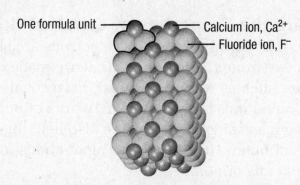

One formula unit — Calcium ion, Ca^{2+}
— Fluoride ion, F^-

The ionic compound calcium fluoride has twice as many fluoride ions
as calcium ions. Thus, the chemical formula for the compound is CaF_2.

CONDUCTING ELECTRICITY

Electrical current is moving charges. The ions in a
solid ionic compound are locked into place. Thus, the
charges are not free to move, and the compound cannot
conduct electricity. However, when an ionic compound
dissolves or melts, the ions are no longer locked in place.
The ions are free to move. Thus, dissolved or melted
ionic compounds can conduct electricity. ☑

✓ **READING CHECK**

7. Explain Why can a melted
ionic compound conduct
electricity, but a solid ionic
compound cannot?

_____

_____

_____

_____

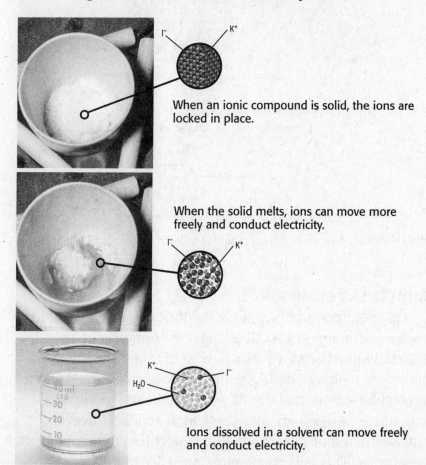

When an ionic compound is solid, the ions are
locked in place.

When the solid melts, ions can move more
freely and conduct electricity.

Ions dissolved in a solvent can move freely
and conduct electricity.

SECTION 2 Ionic and Covalent Bonding *continued*

What Are the Properties of Covalent Bonds?

A **covalent bond** forms when electrons are shared between two atoms. Compounds that are made of molecules, such as water and sugar, have covalent bonds. Compounds that exist as networks of bonded atoms, such as silicon dioxide, are also held together by covalent bonds. In general, covalent bonds form between atoms of nonmetals. ☑

The figure below shows electrons shared by two chlorine atoms. Before the chlorine atoms bond, each atom has seven electrons in its outermost energy level. By sharing a pair of electrons, both atoms can have full outermost energy levels.

A single line between two atoms in a structural formula represents a covalent bond. Each covalent bond indicates that two electrons are shared between the atoms.

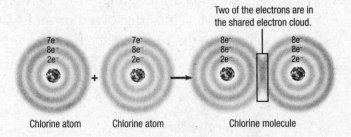

Chlorine atom   Chlorine atom   Chlorine molecule

Two of the electrons are in the shared electron cloud.

Each chlorine atom has six electrons that are not shared.

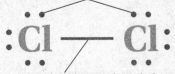

One covalent bond (two shared electrons)

Two chlorine atoms share electrons equally to form a nonpolar covalent bond.

MOLECULAR COMPOUNDS

Covalent compounds made up of molecules are called molecular compounds. Molecular compounds can be solids, liquids, or gases. Most molecular compounds have low melting points—generally below 300 °C. When a molecular compound dissolves or melts, the molecules can move more freely than they do in solids. However, unlike melted or dissolved ions, molecules cannot conduct electricity. This is because molecules are not charged.

READING CHECK

8. Define What is a covalent bond?

_____

_____

_____

LOOKING CLOSER

9. Identify How many electrons does each line between atoms represent?

_____

_____

10. Identify From where did the electrons that form the covalent bond between chlorine atoms come?

_____

_____

_____

SECTION 2 Ionic and Covalent Bonding *continued*

MULTIPLE BONDS

Some atoms need to share more than one pair of electrons to fill their outermost energy levels.

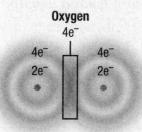

Oxygen
$4e^-$
$4e^-$ $4e^-$
$2e^-$ $2e^-$

Four electrons are in the shared electron cloud.

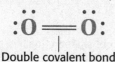

Double covalent bond

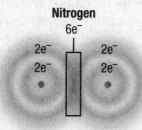

Nitrogen
$6e^-$
$2e^-$ $2e^-$
$2e^-$ $2e^-$

Six electrons are in the shared electron cloud.

Triple covalent bond

LOOKING CLOSER

11. Identify How many pairs of electrons are shared between oxygen atoms in O_2?

_____

12. Identify How many unshared valence electrons does each oxygen atom have?

_____

Notice that the covalent bond that joins the two oxygen atoms in the figure is shown as two lines. These two lines represent two pairs of electrons, or a total of four electrons. Two pairs of electrons shared between atoms are called a *double bond*.

The covalent bond that joins the two nitrogen atoms above is shown as three lines. These three lines represent three pairs of electrons. Three pairs of electrons shared between atoms are called a *triple bond*.

More energy is needed to break double and triple bonds than to break single bonds. A double bond is stronger than a single bond. A triple bond is stronger than both single and double bonds. Double and triple bonds are also shorter than single bonds. ☑

EQUAL SHARING

When two atoms of the same element share electrons, they share the electrons equally. That is, the electrons spend equal amounts of time near the nuclei of both atoms. For example, two chlorine atoms are exactly alike. When they bond, electrons are equally attracted to the positive nucleus of each atom. Bonds in which the electrons are shared equally are called *nonpolar covalent bonds*.

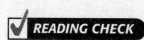
READING CHECK

13. Identify Which bond is strongest—a single, double, or triple bond?

_____

Critical Thinking

14. Explain In a molecule of ammonia, NH_3, three hydrogen atoms are attached to one nitrogen atom. Are the bonds in ammonia polar covalent or nonpolar covalent? Explain your answer.

_____

_____

_____

_____

UNEQUAL SHARING

When two atoms of different elements share electrons, they do not share them equally. The shared electrons are attracted to the nucleus of one atom more than to the other. Bonds in which electrons are not shared equally are called *polar covalent bonds*.

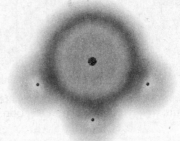

In a molecule of ammonia, NH_3, electrons are not shared equally.

In general, electrons are more attracted to elements located farther to the right and closer to the top of the periodic table. For example, within a molecule of ammonia, NH_3, the shared electrons are more attracted to the nitrogen atom than to the hydrogen atoms.

What Are the Properties of Metallic Bonds?

Critical Thinking

15. Infer Which element will attract electrons more strongly—fluorine or carbon? Explain your answer.

_____

_____

_____

_____

Metals, such as copper, can conduct electricity when they are solids. Metals are also flexible, so they can bend and stretch.

Atoms in metals pack tightly together. This happens because the nucleus of each atom strongly attracts the electrons from a neighboring atom. These strong attractions are called **metallic bonds**. Because the atoms are packed so tightly, the outermost energy levels of neighboring atoms overlap. Therefore, electrons are free to move from atom to atom.

What Are Polyatomic Ions?

The ions we have looked at so far are monatomic. That is, each is a single atom that has gained or lost an electron. However, some ions are made of groups of atoms that are covalently bonded. This kind of ion is a **polyatomic ion**. In a compound, a polyatomic ion acts as a single unit. A polyatomic ion can form ionic bonds with other polyatomic ions or with monatomic ions. ☑

✓ READING CHECK

16. Identify What kind of bond exists between atoms in a polyatomic ion?

_____

SECTION 2 Ionic and Covalent Bonding *continued*

Some Polyatomic Ions

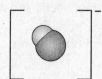 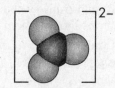 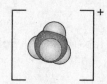

Hydroxide ion, OH⁻   Carbonate ion, CO_3^{2-} Ammonium ion, NH_4^+

Many compounds you may use contain polyatomic ions. For example, baking soda, $NaHCO_3$, contains the polyatomic ion hydrogen carbonate, HCO_3^-. Sodium carbonate, Na_2CO_3, which is used to make soaps and other cleaners, contains the carbonate ion, CO_3^{2-}.

Like other ions, polyatomic ions with opposite charges can bind to form compounds. For example, ammonium nitrate, NH_4NO_3, is made up of positively charged ammonium ions, NH_4^+, and negatively charged nitrate ions, NO_3^-.

PARENTHESES AND POLYATOMIC IONS

Why is the chemical formula for ammonium sulfate written as $(NH_4)_2SO_4$ instead of $N_2H_8SO_4$? Parentheses show you that the ammonium ion, NH_4^+, acts as a single ion. The subscript outside the parentheses tells you how many of that particular polyatomic ion are in the compound. ☑

Remember that the charge on a polyatomic ion applies to the whole ion, not just the last atom of the formula. The ammonium ion, NH_4^+, has a 1+ charge. This means that NH_4, not just the hydrogen atom, has a positive charge. This is why a polyatomic ion acts as a single unit.

OXYGEN-CONTAINING POLYATOMIC IONS

Many polyatomic ions contain oxygen. The names of many polyatomic ions that contain oxygen end with *-ite* or *-ate*. A polyatomic ion with a name that ends in *-ate* has one more oxygen atom than one with a name that ends in *-ite*. For example, the chlorite ion has one fewer oxygen atoms than the chlorate ion.

Notice that the hydroxide ion, OH⁻, and the cyanide ion, CN⁻, have unique names. These ions are not named according to any general rule.

✔ **READING CHECK**

17. Identify What do parentheses around a group of atoms in a chemical formula indicate?

_____

_____

_____

Critical Thinking

18. Apply Concepts The chemical formula for the chlorate ion is ClO_3^-. What is the chemical formula for the chlorite ion?

_____

Name _____ Class _____ Date _____

Section 2 Review

SECTION VOCABULARY

covalent bond a bond formed when atoms share one or more pairs of electrons **ionic bond** the attractive force between oppositely charged ions, which forms when electrons are transferred from one atom to another	**metallic bond** a bond formed by the attraction between positively charged metal ions and the electrons around them **polyatomic ion** an ion made of two or more atoms

1. Predict Would an atom of sodium and an atom of potassium join to form an ionic compound? Explain your answer.

_____

_____

2. Explain Why are electrons shared equally in oxygen, O_2, but not in carbon monoxide, CO?

_____

_____

3. Describe Examine the structural formula below. Complete the table to describe the bonds between atoms in the compound.

Bonded atoms	Number of shared electrons	Single, double, or triple bond?	Polar or nonpolar?
C–O			
C–Cl			

4. Identify Which of the bonds in calcium hydroxide, $Ca(OH)_2$, are ionic and which are covalent?

_____

_____

5. Identify Which of the following substances will conduct electric current: aluminum foil, sugar $(C_{12}H_{22}O_{11})$, or potassium hydroxide (KOH) dissolved in water? Explain your answer.

_____

_____

SECTION 3 Compound Names and Formulas

KEY IDEAS

As you read this section, keep these questions in mind:

• What are the rules for naming ionic compounds?

• What are the rules for naming covalent compounds?

• How can you determine an empirical formula?

Why Do We Name Compounds?

Compounds have names that distinguish them from other compounds. In general, the name of a compound comes from the elements that form it.

How Are Ionic Compounds Named?

Ionic compounds are formed by the strong attraction between two oppositely charged ions: cations (positive ions) and anions (negative ions). The name of an ionic compound identifies the cation first and the anion second.

CATION NAMES

In many cases, a cation name is the same as the element name. For example, when an atom of the element sodium loses an electron, the sodium ion, Na^+, forms. ☑

Recall that you can use the periodic table to help you determine which ions are formed by different elements. For example, Group 1 elements form cations with 1+ charges.

Some Common Cations	
Ion name and symbol	**Ion charge**
Lithium ion, Li^+	1+
Potassium ion, K^+	
Sodium ion, Na^+	
Calcium ion, Ca^{2+}	2+
Magnesium ion, Mg^{2+}	
Aluminum ion, Al^{3+}	3+

ANION NAMES

The name of an anion typically ends in -*ide*. Like most cations, anions of elements in the same group of the periodic table have the same charge. ☑

READING TOOLBOX

Summarize As you read this section, make a T-chart that lists the rules for naming ionic compounds and covalent compounds.

☑ READING CHECK

1. Explain In general, how is the name of a cation related to the name of the element?

_____

_____

_____

☑ READING CHECK

2. Describe How is the name of an anion different from the name of the element?

_____

_____

Some Common Anions		
Element	**Ion**	**Ion charge**
Fluorine, F	fluoride ion, F^-	$1-$
Chlorine, Cl	chloride ion, Cl^-	
Bromine, Br	bromide ion, Br^-	
Iodine, I	iodide ion, I^-	
Oxygen, O	oxide ion, O^{2-}	$2-$
Sulfur, S	sulfide ion, S^{2-}	
Nitrogen, N	nitride ion, N^{3-}	$3-$

LOOKING CLOSER

3. Identify What is the charge of a chloride ion?

_____

_____

TOTAL CHARGE OF IONIC COMPOUNDS

The sum of the charges of all of the ions in a compound must add up to zero. Therefore, if an ionic compound has two ions with different charges, the ratio of ions will not be 1:1. For example, calcium fluoride contains calcium ions, Ca^{2+}, and fluoride ions, F^-. For the compound to have a total charge of zero, there must be two fluoride ions for every calcium ion. Thus, the formula for calcium fluoride is CaF_2. ☑

✔ **READING CHECK**

4. Identify What is the total charge on an ionic compound?

_____

_____

CHARGES OF TRANSITION METALS

Many transition metals can form several cations—each with a different charge. The table below lists some common cations. For example, the compounds FeO and Fe_2O_3 both have iron cations, but the charges of the iron cations are different. If you used the naming rules described so far, you would name both of these iron oxide. However, they are different compounds, so they need different names.

To show the difference between FeO and Fe_2O_3, the charge of the iron cation is included in the name. Roman numerals in parentheses after the cation name show the charge on the cation. The cation in FeO is Fe^{2+}, so it is named iron (II) oxide. The cation in Fe_2O_3 is Fe^{3+}, so it is named iron (III) oxide. ☑

✔ **READING CHECK**

5. Explain What do the roman numerals after the cation name of a transition metal represent?

_____

_____

Some Transition Metal Cations			
Ion name	**Ion symbol**	**Ion name**	**Ion symbol**
Copper(I) ion	Cu^+	Chromium(II) ion	Cr^{2+}
Copper(II) ion	Cu^{2+}	Chromium(III) ion	Cr^{3+}
Iron(II) ion	Fe^{2+}	Cadmium(II) ion	Cd^{2+}
Iron(III) ion	Fe^{3+}	Titanium(II) ion	Ti^{2+}
Nickel(II) ion	Ni^{2+}	Titanium(III) ion	Ti^{3+}
Nickel(III) ion	Ni^{3+}	Titanium(IV) ion	Ti^{4+}

DETERMINING TRANSITION METAL CHARGES

How can you tell that the iron ion in Fe_2O_3 has a $3+$ charge? Examine the total charge on the oxide ion. An oxide ion has a $2-$ charge. Thus, three oxide ions have a total charge of $6-$. If the total anion charge is $6-$, the total cation charge must be $6+$. Because there are two Fe ions in Fe_2O_3, each Fe ion must have a $3+$ charge.

DETERMINING FORMULAS OF IONIC COMPOUNDS

You can find the charge of each ion in a compound if you know the compound's formula. You can find the formula for a compound if you know the compound's name.

What is the chemical formula for aluminum fluoride?

Step 1: List the known and unknown values.	**Known:** aluminum ion: Al^{3+} fluoride ion: F^-	**Unknown:** chemical formula
Step 2: Write the symbols for the ions with the cation first.	Al^{3+}, F^-	
Step 3: Find the least common multiple of the ions' charges. Write the chemical formula. Use subscripts to show the number of each ion needed to make a neutral compound.	The least common multiple of 3 and 1 is 3. Three positive charges and three negative charges are needed. $(1 \times 3+) = 3+$ Only one Al^{3+} ion is needed. $(3 \times 1-) = 3-$ Three F^- ions are needed.	

So, the chemical formula for aluminum fluoride is AlF_3.

How Are Covalent Compounds Named?

The rules for naming covalent compounds are different from those used to name ionic compounds. The names of covalent compounds have prefixes to indicate how many atoms of each element are in the molecule. The table below shows some prefixes used to name covalent compounds. ☑

Prefixes Used to Name Covalent Compounds			
Number of atoms	Prefix	Number of atoms	Prefix
1	mono-	6	hexa-
2	di-	7	hepta-
3	tri-	8	octa-
4	tetra-	9	nona-
5	penta-	10	deca-

Critical Thinking
6. Apply Concepts What is the charge on the titanium ion in the compound TiO_2?

_____

LOOKING CLOSER
7. Apply Concepts What is the chemical formula for beryllium chloride? Use the steps described in the table to help you.

_____

READING CHECK
8. Identify What do the prefixes in the names of covalent compounds tell you?

_____

_____

_____

Name _____ Class _____ Date _____

SECTION 3 Compound Names and Formulas *continued*

USING NUMERICAL PREFIXES TO NAME COMPOUNDS

The element farthest to the left in the periodic table is named first in a compound. If there is only one atom of the first element, its name does not get a prefix. The element farthest to the right in the periodic table is named second. Its name ends in –*ide*. ☑

For example, N_2O_4 has two nitrogen atoms and four oxygen atoms. Nitrogen is farther to the left in the periodic table than oxygen, so it is named first. The name of this compound is dinitrogen tetroxide. The *a* in tetra is dropped to make the name easier to say.

What Are Empirical Formulas?

An **empirical formula** gives the smallest whole-number ratio of atoms in a compound. For example, the empirical formula for water is H_2O. This tells you that the ratio of hydrogen atoms to oxygen atoms is 2:1. For most ionic compounds, the empirical formula is the same as the chemical formula. However, for many covalent compounds, the empirical and chemical formulas are different.

One mole of a compound contains 62 g of phosphorus and 80 g of oxygen. What is the empirical formula of this compound?

Step 1: List the given and unknown values.	Given: Mass, *m* of phosphorus: 62 g Mass, *m* of oxygen: 80 g	Unknown: empirical formula
Step 2: Write the atomic masses.	phosphorus: 30.97 g/mol oxygen: 16.00 g/mol	
Step 3: Write the molar ratio of the elements. The molar ratio of elements in the compound will be the compound's empirical formula.	$\dfrac{62 \text{ g P} \times 1 \text{ mol P}}{30.97 \text{ g P}} = 2.0 \text{ mol P}$ $\dfrac{80 \text{ g O} \times 1 \text{ mol O}}{16.00 \text{ g O}} = 5.0 \text{ mol O}$	

So, the empirical formula of the compound is P_2O_5.

READING CHECK

9. Identify Which element in a compound is named first?

_____

_____

Math *Skills*

10. Calculate A sample of a compound contains 160 g of oxygen and 20.2 g of hydrogen. What is the compound's empirical formula?

_____

SECTION 3 Compound Names and Formulas *continued*

THE SAME EMPIRICAL FORMULA

Empirical formulas only show the ratio of atoms in a compound. They do not show the actual number of atoms of each element that is in the compound. So, it is possible for two different compounds to have the same empirical formula. ☑

For example, formaldehyde, acetic acid, and glucose all have the empirical formula CH_2O. That is, the ratio of the atoms in each of the compounds is 1:2:1. However, these three compounds are very different from one another. Formaldehyde is used to preserve dead organisms. Acetic acid gives vinegar its sour taste. Glucose is a sugar that your body uses for energy.

MOLECULAR FORMULAS

A **molecular formula** tells you how many atoms are in one molecule of the compound. You can use the empirical formula of a compound and its molar mass to find its molecular formula.

Compound	Empirical formula	Molar mass (g/mol)	Molecular formula	Structure
Formaldehyde	CH_2O	30.03	CH_2O	Oxygen Carbon Hydrogen
Acetic acid	CH_2O	60.06	$2 \times CH_2O$ $= C_2H_4O_2$	
Glucose	CH_2O	180.2	$6 \times CH_2O$ $= C_6H_{12}O_6$	

☑ **READING CHECK**

11. Explain Why is it possible for different compounds to have the same empirical formulas?

_____

_____

_____

_____

_____

Critical Thinking

12. Predict A particular compound has the empirical formula CH_2O. Its molar mass is 240.0 g/mol. Predict the molecular formula for this compound.

_____

Section 3 Review

SECTION VOCABULARY

empirical formula a chemical formula that shows the composition of a compound in terms of the relative numbers and kinds of atoms in the simplest ratio	molecular formula a chemical formula that shows the number and kinds of atoms in a molecule, but not the arrangement of the atoms

1. Identify Complete the table below to identify and name several ionic compounds.

Chemical Formula	Chemical Name	Cation	Anion
$CaBr_2$			
	Nickel(II) oxide		
	Cadmium(II) nitride	Cd^{2+}	N^{3-}

2. Identify Complete the table below to identify and name several covalent compounds.

Chemical Formula	Chemical Name
SiI_4	
	Dinitrogen monoxide
P_4O_{10}	

3. Explain What is the charge of the cadmium ion in cadmium bromide, $CdBr_2$? Explain your answer.

_____

_____

4. Calculate One mole of an unknown sample contains 120 g of carbon and 30.3 g of hydrogen. What is the empirical formula of the compound? Show your work.

5. Compare How does a molecular formula differ from an empirical formula?

_____

_____

CHAPTER 6 | The Structure of Matter
SECTION
4 **Organic and Biochemical Compounds**

KEY IDEAS

As you read this section, keep these questions in mind:
• What is an organic compound?
• What is a polymer?
• What organic compounds are essential to life?

What Are Organic Compounds?

What do you think of when you hear the word *organic*? Many people think of living things or a way of growing food. Scientists use the word organic to describe a type of compound. An **organic compound** is a covalently bonded compound that contains carbon. Most organic compounds also contain hydrogen. Many organic compounds contain oxygen, nitrogen, phosphorus, and sulfur. ☑

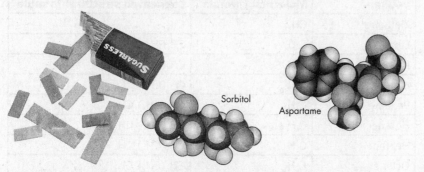

Many familiar substances contain organic compounds. For example, the sweeteners sorbitol, $C_6H_{14}O_6$, and aspartame, $C_{14}H_{18}N_2O_5$, are found in sugarless chewing gum.

A carbon atom can form four covalent bonds. It forms a single bond by sharing one valence electron with another atom. A carbon atom forms a double bond if it shares two of its electrons with another atom. A carbon atom forms a triple bond if it shares three of its electrons. A carbon atom cannot form more than four total bonds at one time.

What Is an Alkane?

When a compound is made of only carbon and hydrogen atoms, it is called a *hydrocarbon*. *Alkanes* are hydrocarbons that have only single covalent bonds. Methane, CH_4, is the simplest alkane. It forms when living matter, such as plants, decay. Methane is also a component of the gas used in stoves.

READING TOOLBOX

Summarize As you read this section, make a table that lists each type of organic compound and its main characteristics.

☑ READING CHECK

1. Identify What kind of bonds exists between atoms in an organic compound?

_____

_____

Critical Thinking
2. Apply Concepts If two carbon atoms are joined by a triple bond, how many other atoms can each carbon atom bond with?

_____

_____

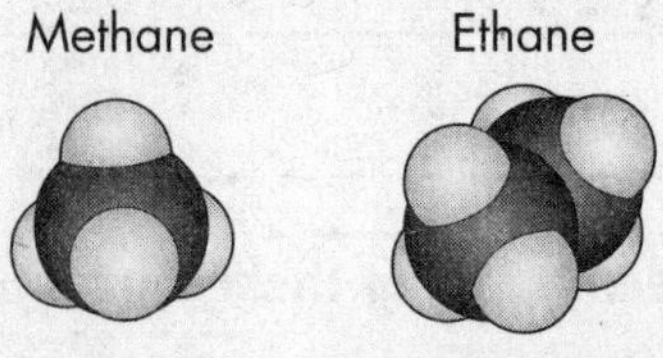

Methane   Ethane

Methane and ethane are the two simplest hydrocarbons.

Methane has only C—H single bonds. However, all other alkanes have one or more C—C single bonds. Molecular models of methane and ethane, C_2H_6, are shown above.

The carbon atoms in methane, ethane, and propane are all bonded in a single line. There are no other arrangements possible for these three hydrocarbons. When an alkane's carbon atoms are bonded in a straight line, it is called a *normal alkane* (*n*-alkane). Several normal alkanes are shown in the table below. ☑

☑ **READING CHECK**

3. Define What is a normal alkane?

_____

_____

_____

n-Alkane	Molecular formula	Condensed structural formula
Methane	CH_4	CH_4
Ethane	C_2H_6	CH_3CH_3
Propane	C_3H_8	$CH_3CH_2CH_3$
Butane	C_4H_{10}	$CH_3(CH_2)_2CH_3$
Pentane	C_5H_{12}	$CH_3(CH_2)_3CH_3$
Hexane	C_6H_{14}	$CH_3(CH_2)_4CH_3$
Heptane	C_7H_{16}	$CH_3(CH_2)_5CH_3$
Octane	C_8H_{18}	$CH_3(CH_2)_6CH_3$
Nonane	C_9H_{20}	$CH_3(CH_2)_7CH_3$
Decane	$C_{10}H_{22}$	$CH_3(CH_2)_8CH_3$

Carbon atoms in an alkane that has more than three carbon atoms can have more than one possible arrangement. Carbon atom chains may have branches or form rings. The figure on the next page shows several ways that six carbon atoms can be arranged.

Except for *cyclic alkanes*, or alkanes that form rings, the chemical formula for alkanes follows a special pattern:

Math *Skills*

4. Calculate If a normal alkane contains 15 carbon atoms, how many hydrogen atoms does it contain?

_____

$$C_nH_{2n + 2}$$

Some alkanes may share a chemical formula. For example, all of the six-carbon alkanes on the next page, except cyclohexane, have the chemical formula C_6H_{14}, or $(C_6H_{2(6) + 2})$.

SECTION 4 Organic and Biochemical Compounds *continued*

Some Six-Carbon Alkanes

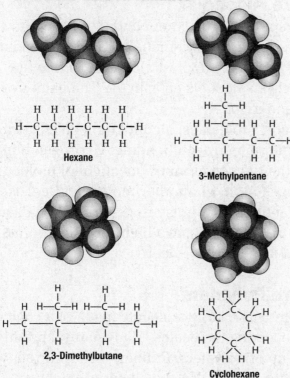

Hexane

3-Methylpentane

2,3-Dimethylbutane

Cyclohexane

LOOKING CLOSER

5. Compare All of these alkanes, except cyclohexane, have the same chemical formula. Why, then, are these three different compounds?

_____

_____

_____

6. Identify What is the chemical formula for cyclohexane?

_____

What Are Alkenes?

Alkenes are hydrocarbons with a double bond between at least two carbon atoms. A double bond is represented by two lines between the two carbon atoms, C=C. Alkenes are named by replacing the *-ane* ending used for alkanes with *-ene*.

The simplest alkene is ethene (also called ethylene), C_2H_4. Ethene forms when fruit ripens. Propene (propylene), C_3H_6, is used in some plastics.

Critical Thinking

7. Infer Can an alkene contain single bonds between carbon atoms? Explain your answer.

_____

_____

_____

_____

_____

Double bond

Ethene

Double bond

Propene

The peaches in the plastic bowl release ethene gas as they ripen. The plastic that forms the bowl was made by joining propene molecules.

What Are Alcohols?

Alcohols are organic compounds that contain a hydroxyl, –OH, group. Methanol, CH_3OH, and ethanol, CH_3CH_2OH, are the simplest alcohols. Notice that the names of these alcohols ends in *-ol*. The names of most alcohols end in *-ol*.

Like water molecules, alcohol molecules attract one another due to hydrogen bonding. Hydrogen bonds form between the oxygen atom of one alcohol molecule and the hydrogen atom of another molecule. Because of these attractions, alcohols are generally liquids at room temperature. Alcohols have higher boiling points than alkanes of a similar size do. ☑

What Are Polymers?

A **polymer** is a large molecule made of a chain of smaller, repeating molecules. Many natural products are made up of polymers. Rubber, wood, cotton, wool, starch, protein, and DNA are all natural polymers.

Human-made polymers are usually plastics, such as the milk jug shown in the figure below, or fibers, such as nylon. Most plastics are flexible and easily molded, and fibers form long, thin strands.

Polypropene (polypropylene) can be used to make both plastics and fibers. Polypropene is molded to make plastic containers, some car parts, and appliances. It is also used to make carpets and artificial turf for athletic fields.

Critical Thinking

8. Compare How does the structure of methanol differ from the structure of methane?

_____

_____

_____

_____

✓ **READING CHECK**

9. Explain Why do alcohols have higher boiling points than alkanes of similar sizes do?

_____

_____

_____

_____

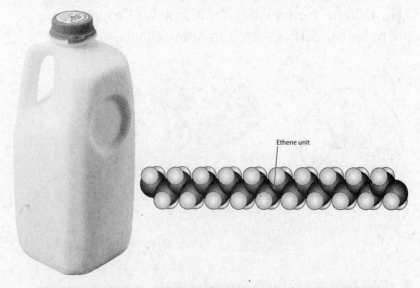

Ethene unit

This plastic milk jug is made of polyethene. Polyethene is a polymer made of repeating units of ethene.

MONOMERS

The name polyethene (also called polyethylene or polythene) tells you the basic structure of the polymer. Ethene is an alkene that has the chemical formula C_2H_4. Poly means "many." Thus, polyethene means "many ethenes."

Polyethene is a polymer made up of monomers of ethene. A *monomer* is a repeating unit that makes up a polymer.

POLYMER PROPERTIES

The way polymer chains join together to form substances determines the properties of the substance. The arrangement of polymer chains in some substances makes the substance flexible. For example, you can crush or dent a milk jug because the plastic is flexible. However, the plastic is not elastic, so it will not return to its original shape.

The arrangement of polymer chains in other substances makes the polymer elastic. For example, rubber bands are made up of elastic polymers. As long as you do not stretch a rubber band too far, it can return to its original shape.

What Are Biochemical Compounds?

Biochemical compounds are organic compounds that can be made by living things. Biochemicals are essential to life. They include carbohydrates, proteins, and DNA. Each of these biochemicals is a polymer. ☑

Critical Thinking

10. Infer What does the name *polystyrene* tell you about the structure of the compound?

_____

_____

✓ **READING CHECK**

11. List What are three biochemical polymers?

_____

_____

_____

Carbohydrates give athletes plenty of quick energy. The athletes also need plenty of protein in their diets to help build up their muscles.

SECTION 4 Organic and Biochemical Compounds *continued*

CARBOHYDRATES

Carbohydrates are biochemical compounds made up of carbon, hydrogen, and oxygen. Some carbohydrates, such as sugars, are small molecules. However, many carbohydrates are large molecules made of chains of sugars. For example, starch is made of glucose monomers. Potatoes and pasta are some foods that contain starch. ☑

When you eat starchy foods, enzymes in your body break down the carbohydrate polymers into their monomers. Your body uses enzymes to break down starches so that your cells can use the molecules of glucose.

Your cells use glucose for energy. However, your body can store extra glucose as glycogen. Glycogen is another polymer made up of glucose molecules. When you need energy later, your body breaks down glycogen into glucose monomers that your cells can use.

PROTEINS

Proteins are organic compounds made of chains of amino acids. **Amino acids** are smaller molecules made of carbon, hydrogen, oxygen, and nitrogen. Some amino acids contain sulfur. Each protein is made of a specific combination and number of amino acids. The sequence of amino acids in a protein determines the protein's structure and function. ☑

Foods that contain proteins include cheeses and meats. When you eat foods that contain protein, your body breaks down the protein into individual amino acids. Your cells use the amino acids to make other proteins that your body needs.

> **READING CHECK**
>
> **12. List** What three elements make up a carbohydrate?
>
> _____
>
> _____
>
> _____

> **READING CHECK**
>
> **13. Identify** What monomers make up proteins?
>
> _____

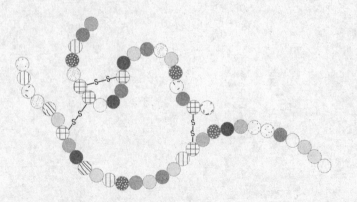

Proteins are made up of monomers called amino acids. Each ball in the chain represents an amino acid. Different chains may be linked together by sulfur ions. These links are called disulfide bridges.

SECTION 4 Organic and Biochemical Compounds *continued*

DNA

All of your genes are made of DNA molecules. *DNA* is a long molecule made of carbon, hydrogen, oxygen, nitrogen, and phosphorus. DNA is made up of monomers called *nucleotides*. Each nucleotide has one of four bases: adenine, thymine, guanine, and cytosine. ☑

The figure below shows the complex structure of DNA. The shape of a DNA molecule is a double helix. A double helix looks like a twisted ladder.

Two chains of nucleotides form the strands of DNA. The strands are held together by attractions between bases on opposite strands.

READING CHECK

14. Identify What monomers make up DNA?

_____

_____

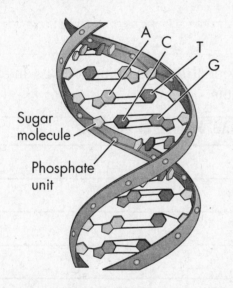

In DNA, cytosine, C, always pairs with guanine, G. Adenine, A, always pairs with thymine, T.

DNA carries the instructions for making proteins. Each group of three bases along a strand of DNA represents a specific amino acid. The sequence of bases in DNA determines the sequence of amino acids in proteins. ☑

Almost every cell in your body contains a copy of your DNA. When a cell divides, DNA strands separate and a copy is made from the old strands.

READING CHECK

15. Identify Relationships How is the sequence of bases in DNA related to the sequence of amino acids in proteins?

_____

_____

_____

_____

Section 4 Review

SECTION VOCABULARY

amino acid any one of 20 different organic molecules that contain a carboxyl and an amino group and that combine to form proteins	**organic compound** a covalently bonded compound that contains carbon, excluding carbonates and oxides
carbohydrate any organic compound that is made of carbon, hydrogen, and oxygen and that provides nutrients to the cells of living things	**polymer** a large molecule that is formed by more than five monomers, or small units
	protein an organic compound that is made of one or more chains of amino acids and that is a principal component of all cells

1. Apply Concepts A particular alkane and a particular alkene have the same number of carbon atoms joined in a chain. Which compound contains more hydrogen atoms? Explain your answer.

_____

_____

2. Identify Complete the table below to identify each compound as an alkane, an alkene, or an alcohol based on its name.

Compound	Alkane, alkene, or alcohol?
2-methylpentane	
3-methyloctane	
1-nonene	
2-butanol	
3-heptene	
cyclohexanol	

3. Identify Which of the following compounds is an alkane: CH_2O, C_6H_{14}, or C_3H_4? Explain your answer.

_____

_____

4. Analyze Patterns Alkynes are hydrocarbons that have triple bonds between at least two carbons. What is the name of the compound that has the chemical formula C_3H_4?

_____

5. Identify Relationships What is the relationship between monomers and polymers?

_____

CHAPTER 7 Chemical Reactions
SECTION 1
The Nature of Chemical Reactions

KEY IDEAS

As you read this section, keep these questions in mind:

- What happens in a chemical reaction?
- What is the role of energy in a chemical reaction?
- What is the difference between an exothermic and an endothermic reaction?

What Is a Chemical Reaction?

Scientists often carry out chemical reactions in laboratories. However, chemical reactions also happen outside science laboratories. In fact, chemical reactions happen around you and inside you all the time. A tree growing, an apple ripening, a leaf decaying, and a log burning are all chemical reactions. Digestion and respiration are also chemical reactions. In a *chemical reaction*, substances go through chemical changes to form new substances. ☑

Consider what happens when you combine sugar, water, flour, and yeast to make bread. The yeast breaks down the sugar to form new substances. One of these substances is carbon dioxide gas, which causes the bread to rise.

The formation of a gas is a clue that a chemical reaction has happened. Sometimes a gas from a chemical reaction forms bubbles that you can see. For example, if you mix baking soda and vinegar, gas bubbles will form. The gas bubbles indicate that a reaction has happened. Other clues that a chemical reaction has happened are shown below.

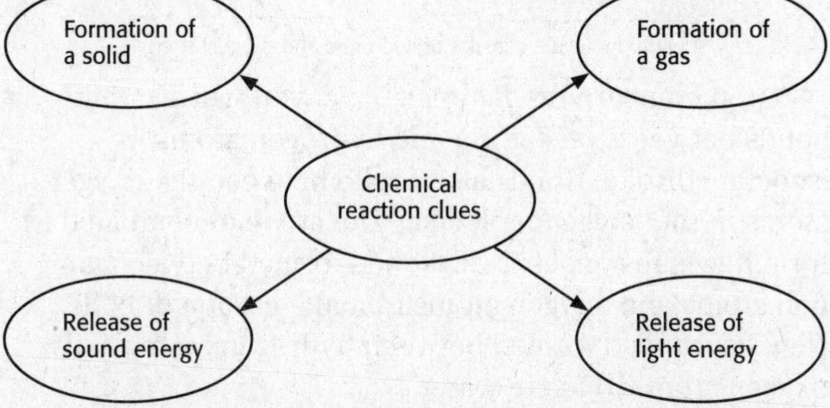

READING TOOLBOX

Organize After you read this section, make a Concept Map using the section vocabulary terms. Review your Concept Map with a partner. You and your partner may have organized the terms differently.

☑ READING CHECK

1. Describe What happens in a chemical reaction?

_____

_____

_____

SECTION 1 The Nature of Chemical Reactions *continued*

BREAKING BONDS AND REARRANGING ATOMS

Recall that matter is made of atoms. Compounds consist of atoms of two or more different elements bonded to one another. During a chemical reaction, the bonds between some atoms break. The atoms rearrange and new bonds form. In other words, the atoms recombine to form new substances. Atoms are never destroyed in a chemical reaction. ☑

Consider what happens when gasoline burns in an engine. Gasoline contains isooctane (C_8H_{18}). When gasoline burns, isooctane reacts with oxygen gas (O_2). These molecules are shown below.

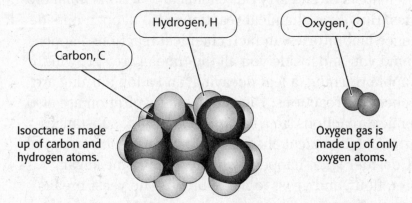

Carbon, C

Hydrogen, H

Oxygen, O

Isooctane is made up of carbon and hydrogen atoms.

Oxygen gas is made up of only oxygen atoms.

Isooctane and oxygen react to form carbon dioxide (CO_2) and water (H_2O).

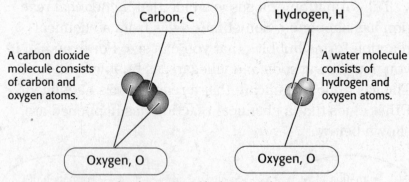

Carbon, C

Hydrogen, H

A carbon dioxide molecule consists of carbon and oxygen atoms.

A water molecule consists of hydrogen and oxygen atoms.

Oxygen, O

Oxygen, O

A water molecule consists of hydrogen and oxygen atoms.

If you compare the figures above, you will see that bonds between the carbon and hydrogen atoms in isooctane broke. Bonds also broke between the oxygen atoms in the oxygen molecule. The atoms recombined to form new substances. New bonds formed between carbon atoms and oxygen atoms to make carbon dioxide. New bonds also formed between hydrogen atoms and oxygen atoms to make water.

✓ READING CHECK

2. Explain How do new substances form in a chemical reaction?

_____

_____

_____

_____

LOOKING CLOSER

3. Compare Examine the molecules in this figure and those in the figure above. Where did the oxygen and hydrogen atoms in H_2O come from?

_____

_____

_____

SECTION 1 The Nature of Chemical Reactions *continued*

REACTANTS AND PRODUCTS

When gasoline burns in an engine, isooctane and oxygen are the reactants. A **reactant** is a substance that participates in a chemical reaction. Isooctane and oxygen react to produce carbon dioxide and water, which are the products. A **product** is a substance that forms during a chemical reaction. ☑

You can use a word equation to show what happens in a chemical reaction. For example, the following word equation shows what happens when gasoline burns.

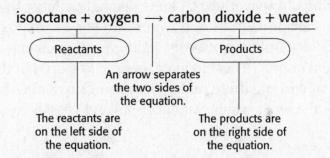

isooctane + oxygen $\longrightarrow$ carbon dioxide + water

Reactants

Products

An arrow separates the two sides of the equation.

The reactants are on the left side of the equation.

The products are on the right side of the equation.

READING CHECK

4. Identify What do scientists call a substance that forms during a chemical reaction?

_____

_____

What Is the Role of Energy in Chemical Reactions?

Chemical reactions always involve changes in energy. Most chemical reactions need added energy to start. Some chemical reactions produce, or release, energy. Other chemical reactions absorb energy.

Chemical compounds store energy in the bonds between their atoms. Energy that is stored in the form of chemical bonds is called **chemical energy**.

During a chemical reaction, chemical energy may change form. For example, it could become light or heat energy. However, the total amount of energy in the reactants must equal the total amount of energy in the products. In other words, energy in a chemical reaction can change form, but no energy is created or destroyed. ☑

FORMING BONDS

Recall that new bonds form in chemical reactions. When new bonds form, energy is released. For example, when gasoline burns, energy is released as heat and light.

LOOKING CLOSER

5. Identify On what side of the equation are reactants found?

_____

_____

READING CHECK

6. Identify Where is energy stored in chemical compounds?

_____

_____

BREAKING BONDS

Recall that some bonds between atoms break in a chemical reaction. Breaking bonds requires energy. For example, energy is needed to break bonds between the atoms in isooctane and oxygen. A spark from a spark plug provides the energy needed to break these bonds. An open flame can also start this reaction. For this reason, sparks and flames are not allowed near a gas pump.

LIGHT ENERGY AND PHOTOSYNTHESIS

During photosynthesis, plants use light energy to change carbon dioxide and water into sugars and oxygen. As a result of photosynthesis, light energy is changed into chemical energy. This chemical energy is stored in the bonds of carbohydrate molecules. You gain some of this chemical energy when you eat fruits and vegetables.

Critical Thinking

7. Infer The cells in your body get energy from the foods you eat. However, your cells must use energy to get this energy. Why?

_____

_____

_____

_____

_____

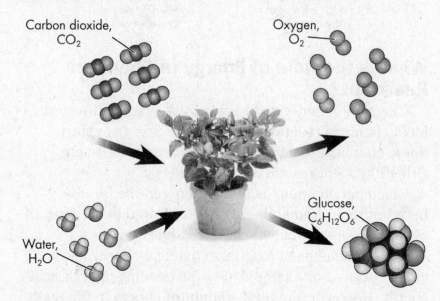

Carbon dioxide, CO_2

Oxygen, O_2

Water, H_2O

Glucose, $C_6H_{12}O_6$

8. Describe How does the energy of the reactants and products differ in an endothermic reaction?

_____

_____

_____

What Are Endothermic and Exothermic Reactions?

Recall that during a chemical reaction, energy is needed to break bonds in the reactants. Energy is released as new bonds form in the products. In an **endothermic reaction**, more energy is needed to break the bonds in the reactants than is released when new bonds form in the products. In other words, endothermic reactions absorb more energy than they release. In an endothermic reaction, the products have more chemical energy than the reactants do. ☑

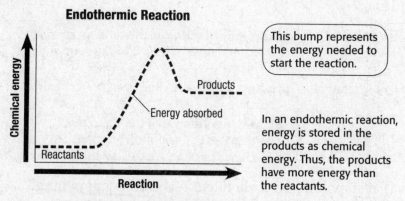

Endothermic Reaction

This bump represents the energy needed to start the reaction.

Products

Energy absorbed

Reactants

In an endothermic reaction, energy is stored in the products as chemical energy. Thus, the products have more energy than the reactants.

In an **exothermic reaction**, more energy is released when new bonds form than is needed to break bonds. In other words, exothermic reactions release more energy than they absorb. In an exothermic reaction, the products have less chemical energy than the reactants do. All combustion reactions are exothermic.

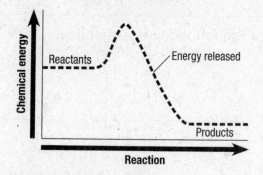

Exothermic Reaction

Reactants

Energy released

Products

In an exothermic reaction, chemical energy is released, often as heat.

Graphing *Skills*

9. Interpret How does the energy of the products differ from the energy of the reactants in an exothermic reaction?

_____

_____

_____

CONSERVATION OF ENERGY

All chemical reactions obey the law of conservation of energy. The *law of conservation of energy* states that energy cannot be created or destroyed. In both endothermic and exothermic reactions, energy changes from one form into another form. However, no energy is created or destroyed.

If no energy is created or destroyed, how can the products of an exothermic reaction have less energy than the reactants? How can the products of an endothermic reaction have more energy than the reactants?

LOOKING CLOSER

10. Explain How can products and reactants have different amounts of energy without violating the law of conservation of energy?

_____

_____

_____

_____

_____

_____

_____

Endothermic reaction:

Energy of reactants + energy absorbed = energy of products

Exothermic reaction:

Energy of reactants = energy of products + energy released

Section 1 Review

SECTION VOCABULARY

chemical energy the energy released when a chemical compound reacts to produce new compounds	**exothermic reaction** a chemical reaction in which energy is released to the surroundings as heat
endothermic reaction a chemical reaction that requires energy input	**product** a substance that forms in a chemical reaction
	reactant a substance or molecule that participates in a chemical reaction

1. List What are three clues that may tell you a chemical reaction is happening?

_____

_____

_____

2. Predict Caramel forms when table sugar, $C_{12}H_{22}O_{11}$, reacts with oxygen. What elements make up caramel?

_____

3. Apply Concepts Identify whether or not each of the following is a chemical reaction. Explain your answers.

a. melting ice

_____

b. burning a candle

_____

c. rusting iron

_____

4. Describe What is the role of energy in forming bonds? What is the role of energy in breaking bonds?

_____

_____

5. Apply Concepts Is a firecracker exploding an example of an endothermic reaction or an exothermic reaction? Explain your answer.

_____

_____

_____

CHAPTER 7 Chemical Reactions
SECTION 2 Chemical Equations

KEY IDEAS

As you read this section, keep these questions in mind:
• What is a chemical equation?
• What can a chemical equation tell you?

How Can Chemical Reactions Be Described?

Suppose you watched a beautiful sunset. How would you describe it to someone else? You could write a description, take a photograph, or even draw a picture. There is more than one way to describe what you saw.

You can also describe chemical reactions in more than one way. For example, a gas stove burns methane gas to cook food. Methane gas reacts with oxygen to produce carbon dioxide and water. The figure below shows three ways you can describe this chemical reaction.

READING TOOLBOX

Review As you read this section, be sure to connect what you read with material that you learned in previous chapters. Go back if you need to review a concept or definition. Write definitions or explanations in the sidebar as reminders.

Word equation

methane and oxygen yield carbon dioxide and water

Molecular model

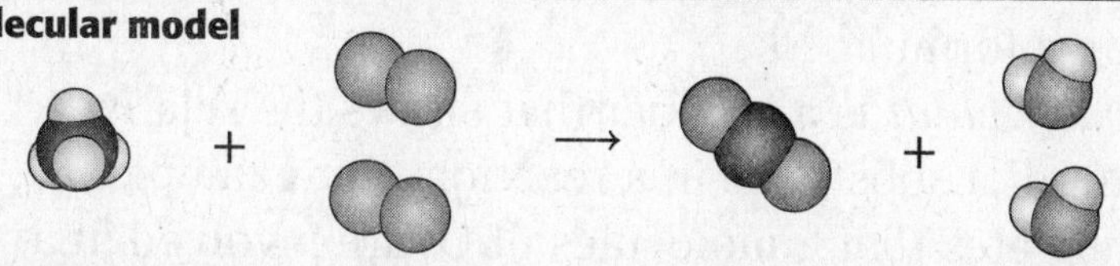

Chemical equation

$$CH_4 + 2O_2 \longrightarrow CO_2 + 2H_2O$$

Talk About It

Discuss Examine the three ways of describing a chemical reaction that are shown in the figure. In a small group, discuss possible advantages and disadvantages of each type of description. Think of possible reasons scientists use chemical equations more frequently than word equations.

Each way of describing a chemical reaction has advantages and disadvantages. For example, molecular models show how the atoms are rearranged in a chemical reaction. However, the models can be very confusing if the reactants and products are composed of many atoms.

Scientists generally use chemical equations to describe chemical reactions. A **chemical equation** uses symbols to show the relationship between the reactants and products of a reaction.

LOOKING CLOSER

1. Explain Why does this equation disobey the law of conservation of mass?

_____

_____

_____

_____

CONSERVATION OF MASS

Recall that during a chemical change, matter cannot be created or destroyed. In other words, the total mass of the products must equal the total mass of the reactants. Look again at the chemical equation for the reaction between methane and oxygen.

$$CH_4 + O_2 \longrightarrow CO_2 + H_2O$$

The equation shows what substances are involved in the reaction. The same elements appear on both sides of the equation. Notice that there are four H atoms on the left, but only two H atoms on the right. Also notice that there are two O atoms on the left and three O atoms on the right. The chemical equation cannot be correct because it does not obey the law of conservation of mass. How can you correct the equation?

BALANCED EQUATIONS

A chemical equation can correctly describe what happens in a reaction only when it is balanced. In a *balanced* chemical equation, the number of atoms of each element is the same on both sides of the arrow. You can balance a chemical equation by placing a coefficient in front of a chemical formula. ☑

A *coefficient* is a number that shows the relative amount of a substance in a reaction. For example, $2O_2$ indicates that 2 molecules of O_2 are involved in a reaction.

READING CHECK

2. Describe When is a chemical equation balanced?

_____

_____

_____

LOOKING CLOSER

3. Identify How many total oxygen atoms are represented by "$2O_2$"?

_____

_____

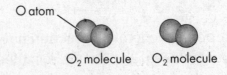

O atom

O_2 molecule O_2 molecule

BALANCING EQUATIONS

How would you write a balanced equation for the reaction between magnesium (Mg) and oxygen (O_2) that forms magnesium oxide (MgO)?

SECTION 2 Chemical Equations *continued*

Step 1: Write a word equation for the reaction.	magnesium + oxygen $\longrightarrow$ magnesium oxide
Step 2: Write the formula for each reactant and product.	$Mg + O_2 \longrightarrow MgO$

Step 3: Count the atoms of each element on both sides of the equation.	Reactants $Mg + O_2$ Mg: 1 O: 2	Products MgO Mg: 1 O: 1

Step 4: Add one or more coefficients to balance the number of atoms.	Place the coefficient 2 in front of MgO to balance the O atoms. $Mg + O_2 \longrightarrow 2\ MgO$	
	Reactants Mg: 1 O: 2	Products Mg: 2 ✘ O: 2 ✔
	Place the coefficient 2 in front of Mg to balance the Mg atoms $2Mg + O_2 \longrightarrow 2\ MgO$	
	Reactants Mg: 2 O: 2	Products Mg: 2 ✔ O: 2 ✔

The total number of Mg and O atoms is the same on both sides of the equation. Therefore, the equation is balanced.

$$2Mg + O_2 \longrightarrow 2MgO$$

HINTS FOR BALANCING EQUATIONS

Keep the following points in mind when you balance a chemical equation:

- Be sure that you write each formula correctly.

- You cannot change the subscripts within a chemical formula. You can only place a coefficient in front of a formula.

- The number 1 is never written as a coefficient in an equation or as a subscript in a formula.

- When you add a coefficient to balance one element, look to see if another element becomes unbalanced.

- Do a final check to see if the atoms for all elements are balanced.

Math Skills

4. Balance Equations
Sodium sulfide, Na_2S, reacts with silver nitrate, $AgNO_3$, to form sodium nitrate, $NaNO_3$, and silver sulfide, Ag_2S. Write the balanced equation for this reaction.

_____

Critical Thinking

5. Infer Why must you add coefficients to balance an equation instead of changing subscripts in a chemical formula?

_____
_____
_____
_____
_____

LOOKING CLOSER

6. Explain Does this equation obey the law of conservation of mass? Explain your answer.

_____

_____

_____

_____

✓ **READING CHECK**

7. Identify What do the coefficients in a balanced equation tell you?

_____

_____

What Are Mole Ratios?

Consider again the reaction between magnesium and oxygen to produce magnesium oxide.

$$2Mg + O_2 \longrightarrow 2MgO$$

The balanced equation tells you that two Mg atoms react with one O_2 molecule to produce two MgO molecules. The coefficients in a balanced equation also tell you the mole ratio. The **mole ratio** is the proportion of reactants and products in a chemical reaction.

Recall that chemists use a counting unit called the mole to indicate the number of particles in a sample of a substance. One mole is the amount of a substance that contains 6.022×10^{23} particles. The coefficients in a balanced equation tell you the relative number of moles of reactant and product in the reaction. ☑

In the reaction between Mg and O_2 atoms, 2 moles of Mg are needed for every 1 mole of O_2. The reaction produces 2 moles of MgO. No matter how much magnesium and oxygen combine or how much MgO is made, the balanced equation does not change. This follows the *law of definite proportion*.

Law of Definite Proportion
A compound always contains the same elements in the same proportion. This is true regardless of how the compound forms or how much of it forms.

USING MOLE RATIOS

You can use mole ratios to predict how much of a substance is involved in a chemical reaction. For example, consider what happens when electrical energy causes water to form hydrogen and oxygen. The balanced equation for the reaction is shown below. Notice that 2 moles of H_2O produce 2 moles of H_2 and 1 mole of O_2.

$$2\,H_2O \longrightarrow 2\,H_2 + O_2$$

 Chemical Reactions

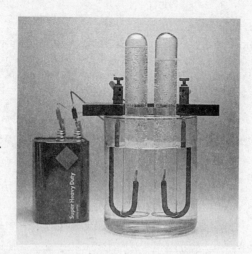

Electrical energy causes water molecules to break into oxygen and hydrogen.

The equation tells you the mole ratio between any two substances in this reaction. For example, the mole ratio of H_2O to O_2 is 2:1. You can use this mole ratio to predict what will happen under certain conditions.

Assume that 4 moles of O_2 are produced in this reaction. How many moles of H_2O reacted? The balanced equation gives you the mole ratio.

$$2 \text{ moles } H_2O : 1 \text{ mole } O_2$$

Therefore, twice as many moles of H_2O are needed as moles of O_2. If 4 moles of O_2 are produced, how many moles of reactant (H_2O) did you have?

$$2x = 4 \text{ moles}$$
$$x = 8 \text{ moles of } H_2O$$

If you know the mole ratios of substances in a reaction, you can determine the relative masses of the substances. Consider again the reaction of magnesium and oxygen to produce magnesium oxide. What mass of Mg would you need to react with 2 moles of oxygen?

Step 1: Write the balanced equation and identify the coefficients for the substances.	$2Mg + O_2 \longrightarrow 2MgO$ Mg: 2 O_2: 1 MgO: 2
Step 2: Calculate the molar masses of the substances.	Mg: 24.3 g/mol O_2: 32.0 g/mol MgO: 40.3 g/mol
Step 3: Mutiply the mole ratio for each substance by its molar mass.	Mg: 2 mol × 24.3 g/mol = 48.6 g O_2: 1 mol × 32.0 g/mol = 32.0 g MgO: 2 mol × 40.3 g/mol = 80.6 g

You would need to use 48.6 g of Mg to react completely with 2 moles of O.

Critical Thinking

8. Apply Concepts How many moles of Mg would you need to react with 2.5 moles of O_2?

_____

_____

Math Skills

9. Calculate Chlorine gas can be produced in the following reaction:

$2NaCl + 2H_2O \longrightarrow$

$Cl_2 + H_2 + 2NaOH$

What mass of NaCl do you need to make 71 g of Cl_2? (Hint: Use the periodic table in the back of the book to help you calculate the molar masses.)

_____

Section 2 Review

SECTION VOCABULARY

chemical equation a representation of a chemical reaction that uses symbols to show the relationship between the reactants and products	**mole ratio** the relative number of moles of the substances required to produce a given amount of product in a chemical reaction

1. Balance Equations Write balanced equations for the reactions below.

$N_2 + H_2 \longrightarrow NH_3$

_____

$KOH + HCl \longrightarrow KCl + H_2O$

_____

$Pb(NO_3)_2 + KI \longrightarrow KNO_3 + PbI_2$

_____

2. Explain Why must you balance an equation to describe correctly what happens in a chemical reaction?

_____

_____

_____

3. Interpret What does $4H_2O$ tell you about the number of molecules and the total number of atoms of each element?

_____

_____

_____

4. Calculate What is the mole ratio of C_5H_{12} to H_2 in the following reaction?

$C_5H_{12} \longrightarrow C_5H_8 + 2H_2$

_____

5. Identify Relationships Does adding coefficients to a chemical equation disobey the law of definite proportions? Explain your answer.

_____

_____

_____

_____

CHAPTER 7 Chemical Reactions
SECTION 3 Reaction Types

KEY IDEAS

As you read this section, keep these questions in mind:
• How can chemical reactions be classified?
• How are electrons involved in chemical reactions?

What Are the Various Types of Reactions?

There are millions of possible chemical reactions. However, all these reactions can be classified into several general types. Classifying reactions makes it easier to identify any similarities or differences. Knowing the type of reaction can also help you predict the products that will form. ☑

SYNTHESIS REACTIONS

Plastics are used to make many items, such as compact discs (CDs), eyeglasses, telephones, and toys. The plastics used to make these products are hard and durable. Plastics can also be soft and flexible. An example of such a plastic is shown below.

Plastics are made in synthesis reactions. In a **synthesis reaction**, two or more substances join to form a new compound. Synthesis reactions have the following general form: ☑

> **Synthesis Reaction**
> $$A + B \longrightarrow AB$$

Many kinds of plastics are made from a molecule called ethene. These plastics are made by combining many ethene molecules to form one large molecule, called polyethene.

READING TOOLBOX

Find Examples As you read, make a list of all the chemical reactions listed in the section. When you finish reading, classify each reaction in as many ways as possible.

☑ **READING CHECK**

1. Identify What does classifying reactions allow you to do?

_____

_____

☑ **READING CHECK**

2. Identify What happens in a synthesis reaction?

_____

_____

_____

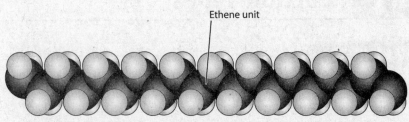

Ethene unit

A single molecule of polyethene is made up of as many as 3,500 ethene molecules.

The synthesis reaction used to make polyethene is called polymerization. In *polymerization*, many units of a substance combine to form a new compound. The products that form in this type of synthesis reaction are called *polymers*. Not all synthesis reactions form polymers. In fact, some synthesis reactions form simple molecules, such as water. ☑

$$2H_2 + O_2 \longrightarrow 2H_2O$$

DECOMPOSITION REACTIONS

Your body must digest the foods you eat before you can use them for energy. During digestion, your body breaks down complex molecules into simpler ones. Digestion is an example of a decomposition reaction. In a **decomposition reaction**, substances break apart. Decomposition reactions have the following general form:

Decomposition Reaction
AB $\longrightarrow$ A + B

Water molecules can break apart in a decomposition reaction called *electrolysis*. The prefix *electro-* means that electrical energy is supplied. The suffix *–lysis* means "break apart."

$$2H_2O \longrightarrow 2H_2 + O_2$$

SINGLE-DISPLACEMENT REACTIONS

Potassium metal is very reactive. If you add potassium to water, the H_2 gas that is produced may explode and burn instantly. The reaction between potassium and water is a single-displacement reaction. In a **single-displacement reaction**, one atom or ion replaces another atom or ion in a compound. Single-displacement reactions have the following general form:

READING CHECK

3. Describe What happens in a polymerization reaction?

_____

_____

_____

Critical Thinking

4. Identify Relationships How are decomposition reactions related to synthesis reactions?

_____

_____

_____

SECTION 3 Reaction Types *continued*

```
┌─────────────────────────────────────┐
│  Single-Displacement Reaction        │
│         AX + B ⟶ BX + A               │
└─────────────────────────────────────┘
```

Recall that some elements are more reactive than others. In general, an atom or ion of a more reactive element will replace a less reactive one in a single-displacement reaction.

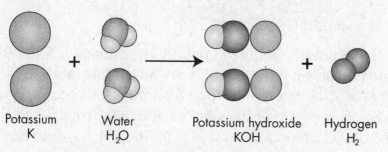

Potassium reacts with water in a single-displacement reaction.

LOOKING CLOSER

5. Identify When potassium reacts with water, which element does potassium replace?

_____

6. Infer Is potassium more reactive or less reactive then hydrogen?

_____

DOUBLE-DISPLACEMENT REACTIONS

The stomach sometimes produces excess acid (HCl) that can cause a stomach ache. Some antacid tablets contain magnesium hydroxide, $Mg(OH)_2$. This compound can neutralize excess acid.

$$Mg(OH)_2 + 2HCl \longrightarrow MgCl_2 + 2H_2O$$

Notice in the equation above that Mg and H appear to trade places. This equation shows a double-displacement reaction. In a **double-displacement reaction**, two atoms or ions appear to replace one another in compounds. Double-displacement reactions have the following general form:

```
┌─────────────────────────────────────┐
│  Double-Displacement Reaction        │
│        AX + BY ⟶ AY + BX              │
└─────────────────────────────────────┘
```

Lead chromate, $PbCrO_4$, is a compound found in the yellow paint that is used to make lines on roads. Lead chromate forms in a double-displacement reaction.

$$Pb(NO_3)_2 + K_2CrO_4 \longrightarrow PbCrO_4 + 2KNO_3$$

Critical Thinking

7. Compare How does a double-displacement reaction differ from a single-displacement reaction?

_____

_____

_____

_____

_____

_____

Lead nitrate is insoluble in water.

Lead nitrate, $Pb(NO_3)_2$, potassium chromate, K_2CrO_4, and potassium nitrate, KNO_3, are all soluble in water. That is, they dissolve to form ions. Recall that ions form when atoms gain or lose one or more electrons. Unlike the other compounds in this reaction, $PbCrO_4$ does not dissolve in water. Instead, lead chromate is a yellow solid that settles to the bottom of the solution.

COMBUSTION REACTIONS

A fire may be the small flame of a lighted match, or it may cover thousands of acres of land. No matter how small or large, fire is an example of a combustion reaction. In a **combustion reaction**, organic compounds react with oxygen. All combustion reactions produce carbon dioxide and water. ☑

READING CHECK

8. Identify What are the products of a combustion reaction?

_____

_____

Combustion reactions are used to generate much of the electrical energy used by homes, schools, businesses, and many forms of transportation.

INCOMPLETE COMBUSTION

When there is not enough oxygen during a combustion reaction, only some of the fuel is converted to CO_2. The combustion reaction is incomplete. In this case, the reaction produces soot, which is unburned carbon, and some carbon monoxide, CO. Carbon monoxide is a poisonous gas. ☑

READING CHECK

9. Identify What factor leads to incomplete combustion?

_____

_____

SECTION 3 Reaction Types *continued*

How Are Electrons Involved in Reactions?

Chemists started classifying reactions before they knew about the parts of the atom. After chemists learned about electrons, they could classify reactions in new ways. The new classification systems looked at changes in the number of electrons that atoms have.

Recall that a covalent bond forms when electrons are shared between two atoms. Sometimes when a covalent bond breaks, a single electron is left on each piece of the molecule. Each piece is called a free radical. A **free radical** is an atom or group of atoms that has one unpaired electron. Because they have unpaired electrons, free radicals are very reactive. Free radicals react with O_2 molecules high in the atmosphere to form the protective ozone layer. ☑

REDOX REACTIONS

In many reactions, one atom transfers electrons to another. Such reactions are called oxidation-reduction, or *redox*, reactions. In an **oxidation-reduction reaction**, one substance loses electrons and another substance gains electrons.

Before they knew about electrons, scientists used the terms *oxidation* and *reduction* to describe reactions that involve oxygen. Combustion is an example of such a reaction. Oxygen gas reacts with carbon compounds to form carbon dioxide. Carbon atoms in CO_2 are oxidized, and oxygen atoms in O_2 are reduced.

Scientists now know that not all oxidation reactions require oxygen. However, the terms oxidation and reduction remain. In any redox reaction, the substance that loses electrons is *oxidized*. The substance that gains electrons is *reduced*.

Recall that an ionic bond forms when an atom transfers one or more electrons to another atom. The formation of an ionic compound is a common type of redox reaction. For example, NaCl forms when Na transfers an electron to Cl.

Process	Gain or loss of electrons?	The substance is...
Oxidation	loss	oxidized
Reduction	gain	reduced

READING CHECK

10. Explain Why are free radicals so reactive?

_____

_____

Critical Thinking

11. Analyze In the reaction that forms NaCl, which atom is reduced? Which atom is oxidized?

_____

_____

Section 3 Review

SECTION VOCABULARY

combustion reaction the oxidation reaction of an organic compound, in which heat is released

decomposition reaction a reaction in which a single compound breaks down to form two or more simpler substances

double-displacement reaction a reaction in which a gas, a solid precipitate, or a molecular compound forms from the apparent exchange of atoms or ions between two compounds

free radical an atom or group of atoms that has one unpaired electron

oxidation-reduction reaction any chemical change in which one species is oxidized (loses electrons) and another species is reduced (gains electrons); also called redox reaction

single-displacement reaction a reaction in which one element or radical takes the place of another element or radical in a compound

synthesis reaction a reaction in which two or more substances combine to form a new compound

1. **Classify** Complete the table to identify the types of reaction each chemical equation represents. Some reactions may be classified in more than one way.

Chemical equation	Type of reaction
$S_8 + O_2 \longrightarrow 8SO_2$	
$6Li + N_2 \longrightarrow 2Li_3N$	
$AgNO_3 + KBr \longrightarrow AgBr + KNO_3$	
$CaCO_3 \longrightarrow CaO + CO_2$	
$Mg + Pb(NO_3)_2 \longrightarrow Pb + Mg(NO_3)_2$	

2. **Compare** How does oxidation differ from reduction?

_____

_____

3. **Apply Concepts** Substances in a fire extinguisher help prevent air from reaching a burning material. Why would this be a good way to fight a fire?

_____

_____

4. **Infer** Why must reduction take place whenever oxidation occurs?

_____

_____

CHAPTER 7 Chemical Reactions

SECTION 4 Reaction Rates and Equilibrium

As you read this section, keep these questions in mind:

• How can you increase the rate of a reaction?

• What does a catalyst do?

• What happens when a reaction goes backward and forward?

What Are Some Ways to Increase the Rate of a Reaction?

Chemical reactions can happen at different rates, or speeds. You can change the speed of a reaction by changing certain factors. You may already know some ways to change reaction rates. In fact, you may use the factors that affect reaction rates every day.

Think about the following observations and hypotheses:

• A potato slice cooks in 5 minutes at 200 °C. A potato slice cooks in 10 minutes at 100 °C. Thus, potatoes cook more quickly at higher temperatures.

• Potato slices cook in 10 minutes. A whole potato cooks in 30 minutes. Thus, many small pieces of potato cook more quickly than a whole potato.

These observations reveal changes in the speed of chemical reactions. In both situations, the contact between particles of potato and particles of boiling water was increased. When contact between particles increased, the reaction (cooking) happened more quickly. This relationship reflects a general principle: ☑

> Anything that increases contact between particles will increase the rate of a reaction.

Factors that affect the rate of a reaction include:

• temperature
• concentrations of the reactants
• surface area of the reactants
• particle mass, shape, and size
• pressure

READING TOOLBOX

Summarize As you read, make a chart that shows different ways to speed up a chemical reaction. In your chart, include columns for examples and for explanations of how each method increases reaction rate.

Talk About It

Discuss In a small group, talk about other chemical reactions you may see or use in your daily life. Do you use any methods to speed up the reactions?

READING CHECK

1. Identify In general, what will increase the rate of a chemical reaction?

_____

_____

_____

SECTION 4 Reaction Rates and Equilibrium *continued*

TEMPERATURE AND REACTION RATE

When you heat food, you add energy to the particles. Cooking at higher temperatures cooks food more quickly. Why? Chemical reactions are faster at higher temperatures.

2. Describe What is the relationship between temperature and reaction rate?

_____

_____

_____

Bread stored at room temperature | Bread stored in the freezer

Cooling food slows down the chemical reactions that cause food to spoil.

Recall that as particles move more quickly, temperature increases. An increase in temperature can speed up a reaction in two main ways:

1. Faster-moving molecules collide more frequently.

2. Faster-moving molecules transfer more energy when they collide.

Fast-moving particles in a substance at a high temperature collide more frequently. They are more likely to react because they collide with more energy to break bonds.

CONCENTRATION AND REACTION RATE

In most cases, the rate of a chemical reaction increases when you increase the concentrations of the reactants. Consider what would happen if you doubled the concentration of reactants. There would be twice as many collisions between reactant particles. ✓

3. Explain Why does increasing concentration increase reaction rate?

_____

_____

Recall that if you add baking soda to vinegar, gas bubbles form. If you mix some water with the vinegar first, you make a less concentrated solution. When you add the baking soda, the same amount of bubbles will not be produced as quickly. Thus, a lesser concentration of reactants decreased the reaction rate.

SECTION 4 Reaction Rates and Equilibrium *continued*

SURFACE AREA AND REACTION RATE

If you place a whole potato in boiling water, only the surface of the potato touches the water. The energy from the water molecules has to go through the whole potato in order for the potato to cook. However, if you cut up the potato and put the pieces into boiling water, you expose more of the potato. This causes the potato to cook more quickly.

Many small pieces of potato have more surface area than one whole potato. Increasing the surface area of a reactant speeds up a reaction.

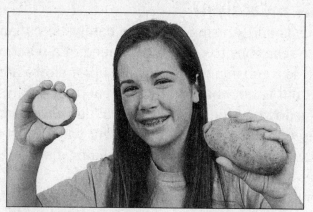

When you divide a solid into pieces, the total surface area becomes larger.

LOOKING CLOSER
4. Explain How does dividing a solid into smaller pieces affect surface area?
_____
_____

MASS AND REACTION RATE

Recall that according to the kinetic theory of matter, more massive particles move more slowly than less massive ones at the same temperature. Because they move more slowly, the more massive particles collide less frequently with other particles. Thus, reactants with massive particles will not react as readily as those with less massive particles. ☑

✔ **READING CHECK**
5. Explain Why do more massive particles collide less frequently than smaller particles do?
_____
_____
_____

SIZE, SHAPE, AND REACTION RATE

Particles of reactants must be in a certain position relative to other particles in order to react. Large reactant particles generally have more branches or bulky parts than smaller particles. Therefore, larger particles cannot get into the correct position as quickly as smaller particles. Thus, reactants with larger particles generally do not react as readily as those with smaller, simpler particles.

PRESSURE AND REACTION RATE

The concentration of a gas is the number of particles in a certain volume. A gas at higher pressure has a higher concentration than the same amount of gas at lower pressure. Gases react more quickly at higher pressures. Why? ☑

Gas at high pressure is squeezed into a smaller space. When gas particles have less space to move, they collide more frequently with one another. More frequent collisions cause more reactions.

What Is a Catalyst?

Chemists add substances called catalysts to many chemical reactions to change the speed of a reaction. A **catalyst** is a substance that speeds up or slows down a reaction but is not changed by the reaction. Catalysts that slow down reactions are also called *inhibitors*. ☑

Different catalysts work in different ways. Most solid catalysts speed up reactions by providing a surface where the reactant particles can meet and react.

Various industries use catalysts. For example, catalysts are used to help make ammonia, to process crude oil, and to make plastics. Catalysts can be very expensive. However, because they are not used up by a reaction, they can be cleaned or renewed and reused.

To help reduce air pollution, cars have special devices called catalytic converters. A *catalytic converter* reduces pollution by speeding up reactions that break down harmful substances into harmless ones. In general, platinum is the catalyst in catalytic converters.

A car's catalytic converter reduces air pollution by helping pollutant molecules react to form less harmful substances.

What Is an Enzyme?

Catalysts are very important in living things. A catalyst produced by a living thing is called an **enzyme**. A reactant that is acted on, or *catalyzed*, by an enzyme is called a **substrate**.

✓ **READING CHECK**

6. Identify What is the relationship between gas pressure and reaction rate?

_____

_____

_____

✓ **READING CHECK**

7. Explain Why may a chemist add a catalyst to a chemical reaction?

_____

_____

_____

LOOKING CLOSER

8. Identify What reactions do catalytic converters catalyze?

_____

_____

_____

SECTION 4 Reaction Rates and Equilibrium *continued*

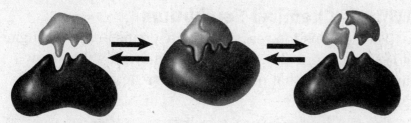

An enzyme has an active site that fits a particular substrate.

The substrate undergoes a reaction.

The substrate then leaves the active site and another substrate enters the active site.

An enzyme is a large molecule that has one region on its surfaces called the *active site*. Only a particular substrate can fit into the active site of a particular enzyme. Only a substance that can fit into this active site can participate in a reaction catalyzed by the enzyme. Therefore, each enzyme is very specific and catalyzes only one reaction or one set of similar reactions. ☑

Enzymes are very efficient. The cells of most organisms contain an enzyme called catalase. *Catalase* breaks down hydrogen peroxide, which is poisonous to cells. In 1 min., one molecule of catalase can catalyze the decomposition of 6 million molecules of hydrogen peroxide.

$$2H_2O_2 \longrightarrow 2H_2O + O_2$$

Recall that an enzyme is not affected by the reaction it catalyzes. Therefore, the same catalase molecule can catalyze the decomposition of H_2O_2 molecules over and over again.

✓ **READING CHECK**

9. Explain Why does an enzyme catalyze only one reaction or a set of similar reactions?

_____

_____

_____

_____

Critical Thinking

10. Apply Concepts In the decomposition of hydrogen peroxide catalyzed by catalase, which substance is the substrate?

_____

_____

Common Enzymes and Their Uses		
Enzyme	**Substrate**	**Role of the enzyme**
Amylase	starch	to break down starch into smaller molecules
Cellulase	cellulose	to break down long cellulose molecules into sugars
DNA polymerase	nucleic acid	to build up DNA chains in cell nuclei
Lipase	fat	to break down fat into smaller molecules
Protease	protein	to break down proteins into amino acids

What Is Chemical Equilibrium?

The combustion reaction that happens in a car's engine goes in only one direction. This is shown by the arrow in the equation that points from the reactants to the products.

$$2C_8H_{18} + 25O_2 \longrightarrow 18H_2O + 16CO_2$$

Because the reaction goes in only one direction, the reactants must always be present for the reaction to continue. For this reason, a car will stop running if there is no gasoline in the fuel tank.

Not all reactions go in only one direction. Some reactions occur in both directions. These reactions are reversible. A reversible reaction is shown in a chemical equation by arrows that point in both directions.

$$\text{reactants} \leftrightarrows \text{products}$$

Equilibrium can be described as a balance that is reached by two opposing forces. A reaction that proceeds equally in both directions is in a state of **chemical equilibrium**. The rates of the forward reaction and the reverse reaction are equal. ☑

To help you understand equilibrium, think of a football game. Eleven players from each team are on the field at one time. If one player enters the game, then another player from the team must leave the game. Even though changes are made, each team always has 11 players on the field. Therefore, the teams are in equilibrium.

✓ READING CHECK

11. Compare For a reaction in chemical equilibrium, how do the rates of the forward and reverse reactions compare?

_____

_____

LOOKING CLOSER

12. Explain Why is the carbonated water no longer at equilibrium when you remove the bottle cap?

_____

_____

_____

Carbonated water in a closed bottle is at equilibrium. Gas particles dissolve in the liquid at the same rate that they leave it.

If you remove the top of the bottle, gas particles leave the liquid faster than they dissolve in it. The carbonated water is no longer at equilibrium.

SECTION 4 | Reaction Rates and Equilibrium *continued*

A DYNAMIC PROCESS

Chemical equilibrium is a dynamic process. That is, changes happen all the time. However, when a change is made, the chemical reaction adjusts to maintain equilibrium.

Consider the Haber process, which is used to make ammonia, NH_3. Ammonia is a chemical used in fertilizers, dyes, plastics, cosmetics, cleaning products, and fire retardants. The Haber process is shown in the following equation.

$$N_2(gas) + 3H_2(gas) \leftrightarrows 2NH_3(gas) + energy$$

Notice that the process is reversible. However, manufacturers want more NH_3 than N_2 or H_2. In other words, they want to change the equilibrium so that the right side of the equation is *favored*. Some conditions that affect equilibrium are shown below.

The Effects of Change on Equilibrium	
Condition	**Effect**
Temperature	Increasing temperature favors the reaction that absorbs energy.
Pressure	Increasing pressure favors the reaction that produces fewer molecules of gas.
Concentration	Increasing the concentration of one substance favors the reaction that produces less of that substance.

LOOKING CLOSER

13. Apply Concepts What could you do if you wanted to favor an endothermic reaction?

_____

_____

LE CHÂTELIER'S PRINCIPLE

Le Châtelier's principle is a general rule that describes how equilibrium systems respond to changes.

> **Le Châtelier's principle**
>
> If a change is made to a system at chemical equilibrium, the equilibrium shifts until the system reaches a new equilibrium.

Look again at the equation for the Haber process above. Recall that increasing pressure favors the reaction that produces the fewer gas molecules. Thus, if you increase pressure, the equilibrium shifts and the right side of the equation is favored. As a result, more NH_3 forms. For this reason, the Haber process is carried out under extremely high pressure.

Critical Thinking

14. Apply Concepts What factor would you change in the Haber process if you wanted to favor the left side of the equation? Explain your answer.
(Hint: Use the table in the text above.)

_____

_____

_____

_____

_____

Section 4 Review

SECTION VOCABULARY

catalyst a substance that changes the rate of a chemical reaction without being consumed or changed significantly	**enzyme** a type of protein that speeds up metabolic reactions in plants and animals without being permanently changed or destroyed
chemical equilibrium a state of balance in which the rate of the forward reaction equals the rate of the reverse reaction and the concentrations of products and reactants remain unchanged	**substrate** the reactant in reactions catalyzed by enzymes

1. List Identify five factors that may affect the rate of a chemical reaction.

_____

_____

2. Explain If you add a piece of potato to hydrogen peroxide, tiny gas bubbles will form. However, if you crush the piece of potato first, more gas bubbles will form. Explain these observations.

_____

_____

_____

3. Compare What is the relationship between a catalyst and an inhibitor?

_____

_____

_____

4. Predict How will an increase in pressure affect the following chemical equilibrium: $2NOCl$ (gas) $\leftrightarrows$ $2NO$ (gas) $+ Cl_2$(gas)? Explain your answer.

_____

_____

_____

5. Evaluate Assumptions A person tells you that a reaction must have stopped because the amounts of products and reactants have not changed. What is wrong with the person's reasoning?

_____

_____

_____

_____

CHAPTER 8 Solutions

SECTION 1 Solutions and Other Mixtures

KEY IDEAS

As you read this section, keep these questions in mind:

• What is a heterogeneous mixture?

• What is a homogeneous mixture?

What Is a Mixture?

Recall that matter can be classified into two main groups: 1) pure substances, such as elements and compounds, and 2) mixtures. Unlike the components of a compound, the components of a mixture can be separated by physical changes. In addition, the amount of each component in a mixture is not fixed. ☑

What Is a Heterogeneous Mixture?

Examine the two spoonfuls of fruit salad in the figure below. Notice that one spoonful has more strawberries than the other. Both samples came from the same mixture, but the samples are not exactly the same. Fruit salad is an example of a heterogeneous mixture. In a *heterogeneous mixture*, the components are not spread out, or *distributed*, evenly throughout the mixture. ☑

The components of a heterogeneous mixture are not spread out evenly throughout the mixture. Different samples of the mixture have different amounts of each component.

The amount of each component in different samples of the same heterogeneous mixture may vary. You can even add more of one component, or take out some of another component. You would still have a mixture. If you take out some of the strawberries or add more grapes, you will still have a fruit salad.

READING TOOLBOX

Organize As you read, make a chart that describes the different kinds of heterogeneous and homogeneous mixtures.

☑ READING CHECK

1. Identify What are the two main groups of matter?

_____

_____

☑ READING CHECK

2. Describe How are the components of a heterogeneous mixture distributed?

_____

_____

_____

_____

SUSPENSIONS

Have you ever forgotten to shake the orange juice carton? When you poured yourself a glass of orange juice, it was probably watery. Orange juice is a heterogeneous mixture. Shaking the mixture mixes the components of the orange juice. However, eventually the mixture will settle again into layers.

Orange juice is an example of a suspension. In a **suspension**, the components that make up the mixture may seem to be distributed almost evenly. However, when the mixture is allowed to sit, one component settles to the bottom. When orange juice sits for a while, the pulp settles to the bottom of the container.

Right after you shake the juice, the pulp is spread throughout the mixture.

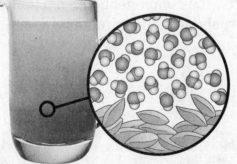

Over time, the pulp settles out of the mixture, and two layers form.

LOOKING CLOSER

3. Explain What happens to the particles in a suspension over time?

_____

_____

_____

Particles in a suspension are large enough to be filtered out of the mixture. For example, to remove the pulp from orange juice, you can pour the juice through a filter of porous paper. This filter will catch the pulp but will let the juice pass through. ☑

✓ **READING CHECK**

4. Explain Why is it generally easy to filter out particles in suspension?

_____

_____

_____

Suspensions
☑ Particles are relatively large.
☑ Particles settle out or can be filtered.

SECTION 1 Solutions and Other Mixtures *continued*

LIQUIDS IN SUSPENSION

Many suspensions, such as orange juice, are a mixture of a liquid and a solid. However, some mixtures are made up of two liquids. For example, you can combine oil, vinegar, and spices to make salad dressing. If you shake the ingredients, they will mix. However, if the dressing sits for a while, the liquids will separate into layers. Why? Oil and vinegar are immiscible. Liquids that are *immiscible* do not mix or do not stay mixed. ☑

5. Define What are immiscible liquids?

_____

_____

_____

Many salad dressings are made of oil and vinegar, which form a suspension when shaken. Oil is less dense than vinegar. When the salad dressing sits for a while, the oil rises and floats on top of the vinegar.

LOOKING CLOSER

6. Explain Why does the oil rise above the vinegar?

_____

_____

_____

COLLOIDS

Colloids are another type of heterogeneous mixture. Like a suspension, a **colloid** has particles dispersed throughout the mixture. However, the particles of a colloid are smaller than the particles of a suspension. The particles of colloids are so small that they can pass through most filters and remain spread throughout the mixture.

Latex paint is an example of a colloid. The color in latex paint comes from particles of colored pigments in water. Gelatin, egg whites, and blood plasma are all examples of colloids. Whipped cream is a colloid made by dispersing gas in a liquid. Fog is a colloid of water droplets in air. Smoke is a colloid of small solid particles in air.

Critical Thinking

7. Compare What is the main difference between a suspension and a colloid?

_____

_____

_____

_____

Colloids

☑ Particles are relatively small.

☑ Particles cannot be filtered easily.

LOOKING CLOSER

8. Describe What is the Tyndall effect?

_____

_____

_____

_____

The liquid in the jar on the right is a colloid. A colloid may look clear, but the particles may be large enough to scatter light. This scattering of light is called the *Tyndall effect*.

EMULSIONS

An **emulsion** is a colloid made of liquids that are generally immiscible. Mayonnaise is made of tiny droplets of oil suspended in vinegar. Unlike the oil and vinegar of salad dressing, the oil and vinegar in mayonnaise stay mixed because of egg yolks. Egg yolks act as an emulsifier. An *emulsifier* coats one type of particles in the mixture so that they cannot join to form a separate layer. ☑

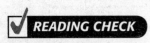
READING CHECK

9. Explain How is an emulsion different from other colloids?

_____

_____

_____

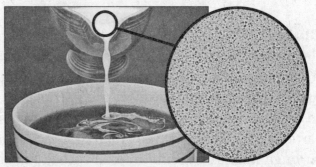

Like other colloids, an emulsion, such as cream, has particles so small that the mixture looks like a pure substance. However, cream is a mixture of fats, proteins, and carbohydrates dispersed in water. Proteins act as emulsifiers to coat the droplets of fats and keep them dispersed.

Emulsions

☑ An emulsion is a colloid made of immiscible liquids.

☑ Emulsifiers keep layers from separating.

Name _____ Class _____ Date _____

What Is a Homogeneous Mixture?

In a *homogeneous mixture*, the particles are dispersed evenly throughout. In other words, a homogeneous mixture is *uniform*. A sample from one part of a homogeneous mixture is the same as any other sample of the mixture. A homogeneous mixture looks uniform even under a microscope. ☑

If you stir a small amount of salt into water, the mixture will look like pure water. Every part of the mixture has the same relative amounts of salt and water particles. Like any mixture, a mixture of salt and water can be separated physically into its components. The components of a mixture also keep their separate identities. Thus, you can separate the salt from the mixture by evaporating the water.

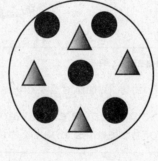

_____   _____
_____   _____

SOLUTIONS

Solutions are homogeneous mixtures. A **solution** is a homogenous mixture in which one or more components dissolves in another. For examples, if you stir salt into water, the salt dissolves in the water and seems to disappear. What happens to the salt when it dissolves?

When a substance *dissolves*, it separates into the smallest particles that make up the substance. These particles may be atoms, ions, or molecules. For example, in water, salt separates into Na^+ and Cl^- ions. In this solution, salt is called the solute. A **solute** is the substance that dissolves. In a saltwater solution, water is the solvent. A **solvent** is the substance in which the solute dissolves. Together, a solute and solvent make up a solution. ☑

✓ READING CHECK

10. Describe How are the components of a homogeneous mixture distributed?

_____
_____
_____

LOOKING CLOSER

11. Label Use *homogeneous mixture* and *heterogeneous mixture* to label the diagrams.

✓ READING CHECK

12. Describe What happens to a substance when it dissolves?

_____
_____
_____

SECTION 1 Solutions and Other Mixtures *continued*

Water is a pure substance.

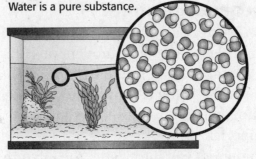

LOOKING CLOSER

13. Identify Into what small particles does salt separate when it dissolves?

_____

_____

14. Apply Concepts What kind of mixture is the gravel at the bottom of the fish tank?

_____

_____

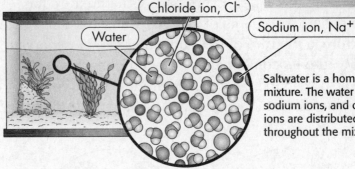

Chloride ion, Cl⁻

Water

Sodium ion, Na⁺

Saltwater is a homogeneous mixture. The water molecules, sodium ions, and chloride ions are distributed evenly throughout the mixture.

Solutions

☑ One substance dissolves in another.

☑ Solute separates into atoms, ions, or molecules when it dissolves.

SOLUTIONS OF LIQUIDS

A solution may be made up of liquids. Two or more liquids that mix easily and stay mixed are *miscible*. For example, water mixes with isopropanol to form a solution called rubbing alcohol. Water and isopropanol are miscible, so they stay mixed. You can use rubbing alcohol to disinfect cuts and scrapes. ☑

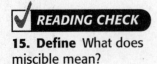

READING CHECK

15. Define What does miscible mean?

_____

_____

_____

Window cleaner, rubbing alcohol, and gasoline are all mixtures of liquids

SECTION 1 Solutions and Other Mixtures *continued*

OTHER KINDS OF SOLUTIONS

Water is not the only liquid that can be a solvent. For example, gasoline is a homogeneous mixture of liquids that contains no water. Nail polish remover is another solution that contains no water.

Other states of matter can also form solutions. Gases can dissolve in liquids, and solids can dissolve in solids. For example, many carbonated drinks are solutions of a gas (carbon dioxide), a liquid (water), and a solid (sugar).

ALLOYS

An **alloy** is a homogeneous mixture that is made up of two or more metals. Liquid metals are mixed together, and a solid solution of metals forms when the mixture cools.

Alloys are important because they have properties that the individual metals do not have. For example, copper is very soft and bends easily. Copper could not be used to make a sturdy musical instrument. However, when zinc is dissolved in copper, the brass that forms is harder than copper, but bends more easily than zinc. ☑

Some solutions are made of two or more metals. For example, brass is a solution of zinc metal dissolved in copper.

> **Alloys**
> ☑ An alloy is one or more metals dissolved in another.
> ☑ Properties differ from those of the individual metals.

Critical Thinking

16. Apply Concepts What states of matter are present in a seawater solution? Give examples of each state.

_____

_____

_____

✓ READING CHECK

17. Explain Why are alloys sometimes more useful than pure metals?

_____

_____

_____

Section 1 Review

SECTION VOCABULARY

alloy a solid or liquid mixture of two or more metals	**solution** a homogenous mixture throughout which two or more substances are uniformly dispersed
colloid a mixture consisting of tiny particles that are intermediate in size between those in solutions and those in suspensions and that are suspended in a liquid, solid, or gas	**solvent** in a solution, the substance in which the solute dissolves
emulsion any mixture of two or more immiscible liquids in which one liquid is dispersed in the other	**suspension** a mixture in which particles of a material are more or less evenly dispersed throughout a liquid or gas
solute in a solution, the substance that dissolves in the solvent	

1. **Compare** What is the main difference between a heterogeneous and a homogeneous mixture?

_____

_____

2. **Organize** Complete the concept map to show the relationships between alloys, colloids, emulsions, heterogeneous mixtures, homogeneous mixtures, matter, mixtures, pure substances, solutions, and suspensions.

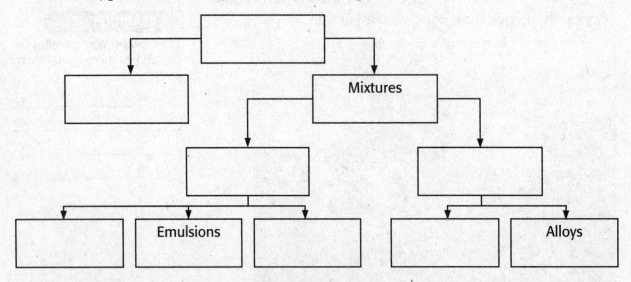

3. **Apply Concepts** You suspect that a clear liquid is actually a colloid. How could you find out?

_____

_____

4. **Apply Concepts** Imagine you have dissolved a small amount of baking soda in a glass of water. Identify the solute and solvent.

_____

CHAPTER 8 Solutions

SECTION 2 How Substances Dissolve

As you read this section, keep these questions in mind:
• Why is water called the universal solvent?
• How do substances dissolve?

Why Do Substances Dissolve in Certain Solvents?

Water is often called a universal solvent because many substances dissolve in it. However, no one substance can dissolve every solute. A general rule in chemistry is that "like dissolves like." This rule means that a solvent will dissolve substances that have similar molecular structures. ☑

A solvent must be able to attract solute particles and pull them away from one another. Thus, solvent particles must attract solute particles more strongly than the solute particles attract one another.

POLAR MOLECULES

Recall that atoms bonded together do not all share electrons equally. For example, a water molecule is made up of two hydrogen atoms bonded to one oxygen atom. The oxygen atom attracts electrons more strongly than the hydrogen atoms do. Thus, the electrons spend more time near the oxygen atom. This gives each hydrogen atom a partial positive charge (δ^+) and the oxygen atom a partial negative charge (δ^-). ☑

Molecules that have partially charged positive and negative areas are **polar**. Because water molecules are polar, water can dissolve many other polar substances. Water can also dissolve ionic compounds such as table salt.

READING TOOLBOX

Summarize Read each page of the section silently to yourself. With a partner, take turns summarizing each page.

☑ **READING CHECK**

1. Identify Why is water called a universal solvent?

_____

_____

☑ **READING CHECK**

2. Explain Why does a water molecule have partial charges?

_____

_____

_____

Water is a polar molecule because the oxygen atom strongly attracts electrons. Because the electrons spend more time near the oxygen atom, the oxygen atom has a partial negative charge.

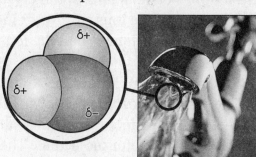

SECTION 2 How Substances Dissolve *continued*

WATER AND IONIC COMPOUNDS

Recall that charged particles attract particles with an opposite charge. Because a water molecule has areas of partial positive charge and partial negative charge, it can attract charged particles. The two partially positive hydrogen atoms attract negative particles. The one partially negative oxygen atom attracts positive particles.

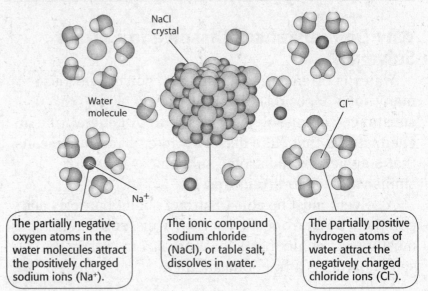

NaCl crystal

Water molecule

Na^+

Cl^-

The partially negative oxygen atoms in the water molecules attract the positively charged sodium ions (Na^+).

The ionic compound sodium chloride (NaCl), or table salt, dissolves in water.

The partially positive hydrogen atoms of water attract the negatively charged chloride ions (Cl^-).

LOOKING CLOSER

3. Describe On the diagram, circle the solute particles that have already dissolved. Describe the arrangement of the particles.

_____

_____

_____

The attractions between ions in crystals of table salt are strong. However, the attraction between a water molecule and Na^+ ions and Cl^- ions is even stronger. NaCl dissolves in water because attractions between its ions and water molecules are stronger than attractions between the ions. The water molecules pull the ions away from the crystal and surround them.

Water dissolves many other ionic compounds in the same way that it dissolves NaCl. However, some ionic compounds, including silver chloride (AgCl), do not dissolve in water. Why do some ionic compounds dissolve in water and some do not? In compounds such as AgCl, attractions between ions in the crystal are stronger than those between the ions and water molecules. Thus, the water molecules cannot pull the ions apart. ☑

READING CHECK

4. Explain Why can water dissolve NaCl but not AgCl?

_____

_____

_____

_____

WATER AND POLAR MOLECULAR COMPOUNDS

The partially positive hydrogen atoms in a water molecule are attracted to the partially negative oxygen atoms of other water molecules. These attractions are known as **hydrogen bonds**.

SECTION 2 How Substances Dissolve *continued*

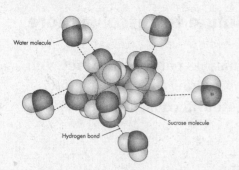

Water molecule

Sucrose molecule

Hydrogen bond

Hydrogen bonds between water molecules and sucrose molecules help pull sucrose molecules toward water molecules and away from one another. However, individual sucrose molecules do not break apart.

LOOKING CLOSER
5. Explain When a molecular compound dissolves, do the molecules break apart? Explain your answer.

_____

_____

_____

_____

Many molecular compounds, including ethanol, vitamin C, and table sugar, are polar. Like water, these compounds contain hydrogen atoms bonded to oxygen atoms. Thus, hydrogen bonds can form between the partially charged atoms of water molecules and other polar molecules.

NONPOLAR COMPOUNDS

The electrons of a **nonpolar** molecule are distributed evenly over the whole molecule. Thus, a nonpolar molecule has no partial charges. Most nonpolar compounds do not dissolve in polar compounds. In other words, they are *insoluble* in polar compounds. For example, olive oil is a mixture of nonpolar compounds. Olive oil does not dissolve in water. Most nonpolar substances dissolve only in nonpolar solvents.

What Is the Role of Energy in Dissolving a Solute?

Attractions between particles of a solute and solvent help keep solute particles apart. However, for a solute to dissolve, energy is needed to break the attractions between particles of solute. Where does this energy come from?

Recall that particles of matter, such as atoms and molecules, move constantly. When you add sugar to a glass of water, water molecules collide with sugar molecules. When they collide, the water molecules transfer energy to the sugar molecules. This energy helps break the hydrogen bonds between sugar molecules. Thus, a solute such as sugar, dissolves due to the following: ☑

• attractions between particles in the solute and solvent; and

• a transfer of energy that breaks attractions between solute particles.

Critical Thinking
6. Infer Could NaCl dissolve in olive oil? Explain your answer.

_____

_____

_____

_____

_____

☑ **READING CHECK**

7. Explain Why is energy needed to dissolve a solute?

_____

_____

_____

What Can Cause a Solute to Dissolve More Quickly?

A solute dissolves because its particles interact with the particles of a solvent. Anything that allows more solvent to touch more solute will cause a solute to dissolve more quickly.

INCREASE IN SURFACE AREA

Small pieces of a substance dissolve faster than large pieces. For a given amount of a substance, many smaller pieces will have more *surface area* than a single larger piece. Greater surface area allows more solute to touch the solvent. As a result, there are more collisions between solute particles and solvent particles.

1 cm

0.1 cm

If you break a solute into smaller pieces, you will increase the total amount of surface area. Because more of the solute touches the solvent at one time, more collisions happen between solute and solvent particles.

TEMPERATURE INCREASE

If you heat a sample of matter, its particles move more quickly. This causes the solute to dissolve more quickly in two ways. First, faster moving particles collide more frequently. Second, at higher temperatures, collisions among particles transfer more energy.

Larger amounts of energy help break bonds between solute particles more easily.

LOOKING CLOSER

8. Explain How does an increase in surface area help a solute dissolve more quickly?

_____

_____

_____

_____

LOOKING CLOSER

9. Explain How does an increase in temperature help a solute dissolve?

_____

_____

_____

STIR OR SHAKE

If you pour some sugar into a glass of water and let it sit, the sugar will dissolve slowly. However, if you stir or shake the water, the sugar will dissolve more quickly.

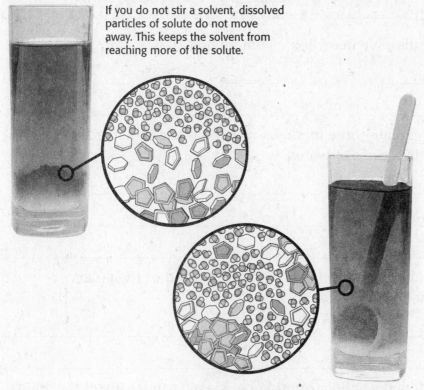

If you do not stir a solvent, dissolved particles of solute do not move away. This keeps the solvent from reaching more of the solute.

Stirring or shaking moves the dissolved solute particles away from the rest of the solute. Then, more solvent can reach the solute that has not dissolved.

LOOKING CLOSER

10. Explain How does stirring a solution allow more contact between solvent and solute particles?

_____

_____

_____

_____

_____

_____

How Can a Solute Affect a Solution's Physical Properties?

A solute can change the physical properties of the pure solvent. For example, the boiling point of pure water is 100 °C and the freezing point is 0 °C. If you dissolve 12 g of sodium chloride in 100 mL of water, the boiling point of the solution increases from 100 °C to 102 °C. The freezing point decreases from 0 °C to –8 °C.

The effect of a solute on freezing and melting point of a solvent can be useful. For example, a car's radiator contains a solution of water and ethylene glycol. This solution acts as antifreeze because the freezing point is –30 °C. It also helps prevent boiling in hot weather because the boiling point is 109 °C.

Talk About It

Research Copy the ingredients from the labels of several household products that are solutions. For each, try to identify the solvent from the list of ingredients. What does the solvent tell you about how the product is used? Make a poster that describes your findings and present it to the class.

Name _____ Class _____ Date _____

Section 2 Review

SECTION VOCABULARY

hydrogen bond the intermolecular force occurring when a hydrogen atom that is bonded to a highly electronegative atom of one molecule is attracted to two unshared electrons of another molecule	**nonpolar** describes a molecule in which centers of positive and negative charge are not separated **polar** describes a molecule in which the positive and negative charges are separated

1. **Explain** Why can water dissolve many ionic compounds?

_____

_____

2. **Describe** Describe and explain three methods you could use to make a spoonful of salt dissolve quickly in a glass of water.

_____

_____

_____

3. **Predict** Use the rule of "like dissolves like" to predict whether the polar compound glycerol is soluble in water.

_____

_____

4. **Identify Relationships** How does the attraction between particles affect the ability of a solvent to dissolve a substance?

_____

_____

_____

5. **Apply Concepts** You combine water, sugar, and drink mix to make a fruit-flavored drink. You decide to freeze the mixture to make ice cubes. Into the freezer you place one ice cube tray filled with the drink and one ice cube tray filled with plain water. Two hours later you find that the water has frozen but the drink has not. Explain this result.

_____

_____

_____

_____

CHAPTER 8 | Solutions

SECTION
3 **Solubility and Concentration**

What Is Solubility?

Have you ever mixed a large amount of sugar in a glass of tea? You may have found that only some of the sugar dissolved. Some of the sugar may not have dissolved, no matter how much you stirred the water. Sugar is *soluble* in water, which means that it can dissolve. However, once a certain amount of sugar has been added to water, no more sugar will dissolve.

The **solubility** of a substance is the maximum amount that can dissolve in 100 g of solvent at a certain temperature. For example, 36 g of salt is the maximum amount that can dissolve in 100 g of water at 20 °C. Some substances, such as acetic acid and ethanol, are completely soluble in water in any amount. Other substances, such as AgCl, are almost completely insoluble in water.

No matter how much you heat, shake, or stir a mixture of oil and water, the oil will not dissolve.

LOOKING CLOSER
1. Describe Describe the solubility of oil in water.

_____

_____

DIFFERENT SUBSTANCES, DIFFERENT SOLUBILITIES

You may think that compounds with some of the same elements have similar solubilities. However, the solubilities of related compounds can vary greatly. Use the table on the next page to compare the solubilities of compounds that contain sodium. Why are their solubilities so different?

SECTION 3 Solubility and Concentration *continued*

Solubilities of Some Ionic Compounds in Water		
Compound	Formula	Solubility in grams per 100 g of H_2O at 20 °C
Calcium chloride	$CaCl_2$	75
Calcium fluoride	CaF_2	0.0015
Calcium sulfate	$CaSO_4$	0.32
Iron (II) sulfide	FeS	0.0006
Silver chloride	AgCl	0.00019
Silver nitrate	$AgNO_3$	216
Sodium chloride	NaCl	35.9
Sodium fluoride	NaF	4.06
Sodium iodide	NaI	178
Sodium sulfide	Na_2S	26.3

LOOKING CLOSER

2. Compare Which compound is more soluble in water—sodium fluoride or sodium iodide?

_____

_____

Critical Thinking

3. Infer How does the strength of attraction between Na^+ and F^- compare to the attraction between Na^+ and I^-? Explain your answer.

_____

_____

_____

_____

_____

_____

The solubility of a substance depends on the strength of attractions between particles of the solvent and solute. In a highly soluble substance, attractions between solute particles are weak compared to attractions between solvent and solute particles.

What Is Concentration?

How could you compare a solution with one teaspoon of salt to a solution with one tablespoon of salt? You would need to indicate that the solutions have different amounts of solute. The amount of a solute dissolved in a particular amount of solution is known as **concentration**. A *concentrated* solution has a large amount of solute. A *dilute* solution has a small amount of solute.

How Is Concentration of a Solution Expressed?

The terms *concentrated* and *dilute* can help you compare two solutions. However, they do not tell you how much solute is in the solution. Scientists express the amount of solute in a solution, or concentration, in several ways. One common expression of concentration is molarity. **Molarity** is the number of moles of solute per liter of solution. ☑

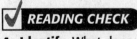

READING CHECK

4. Identify What does molarity express?

_____

_____

$$\text{Molarity (M)} = \frac{\text{moles of solute}}{\text{liters of solution}} = \frac{\text{mol}}{\text{L}}$$

A 1.0 M solution is read as "one molar solution."

SECTION 3 Solubility and Concentration *continued*

CALCULATING MOLARITY

What is the molarity of a 0.500 L sucrose ($C_{12}H_{22}O_{11}$) solution that contains 124 g of solute?

Step 1: List the given and unknown values.	**Given:** mass of sucrose, $m = 124$ g volume of solution, $V = 0.500$ L	**Unknown:** molarity, M
Step 2: Write the equations.	moles $C_{12}H_{22}O_{11} = \dfrac{\text{mass of } C_{12}H_{22}O_{11}}{\text{molar mass of } C_{12}H_{22}O_{11}}$ molarity $= \dfrac{\text{moles of } C_{12}H_{22}O_{11}}{\text{liters of solution}}$	
Step 3: Insert the known values and solve for the unknown value.	molar mass $C_{12}H_{22}O_{11} = 342$ g/mol moles $C_{12}H_{22}O_{11} = \dfrac{124 \text{ g}}{324 \text{ g/mol}} = 0.362$ mol molarity $= \dfrac{0.362 \text{ mol } C_{12}H_{22}O_{11}}{0.500 \text{ L solution}} = 0.724$ M	

Math Skills

5. Calculate What is the molarity of 525 g of lead(II) nitrate, $Pb(NO_3)_2$, dissolved in 1,250 mL of solution? Tip: When volume is given in mL, you must change milliliters to liters. To do this, multiply by 1 L/1,000 mL.

What Is an Unsaturated Solution?

If you add a small amount of sugar to water and stir, the sugar will probably dissolve. If you add another small amount, it will probably dissolve as well. The solution is unsaturated. An **unsaturated solution** contains less solute than the maximum amount that could dissolve in the solvent.

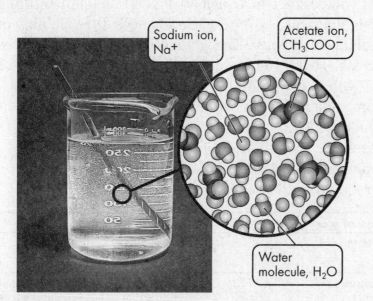

Sodium ion, Na^+

Acetate ion, CH_3COO^-

Water molecule, H_2O

This sodium acetate solution is unsaturated. A solution is unsaturated as long as more solute can dissolve in it.

LOOKING CLOSER

6. Infer How will the concentration of Na^+ change if you add more sodium acetate?

What Is a Saturated Solution?

When you add the maximum amount of solute that will dissolve in a solvent, you have a **saturated solution**. In a saturated solution, the dissolved solute is in *equilibrium* with undissolved solute. If you add more solute, some of it will dissolve, but other solute particles will settle out of the solution. Thus, the total amount of dissolved solute stays the same. ☑

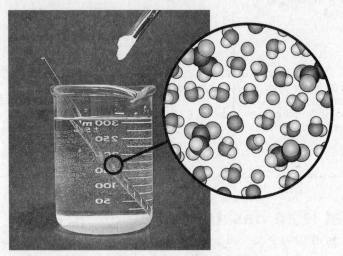

This sodium acetate solution is saturated. No more sodium acetate will dissolve in the solution.

✓ **READING CHECK**

7. Describe If you add more solute to a saturated solution, what will happen to the total amount of dissolved solute?

_____

_____

What Is a Supersaturated Solution?

Recall that solubility of a substance refers to how much of it will dissolve in a solvent at a certain temperature. If the temperature of the solvent changes, the solubility of a solute can change. The solubility of most solid solutes increases as the temperature of the solution increases. ☑

If you heat a saturated solution of sodium acetate, more sodium acetate will dissolve. If you let the solution cool, the extra solute you added may stay dissolved. Then the solution is supersaturated. A **supersaturated solution** holds more solute than it normally would at a lower temperature.

✓ **READING CHECK**

8. Describe How does the solubility of solid solutes change as temperature of the solution increases?

_____

_____

Type of solution	Description
Unsaturated	
Saturated	Contains the maximum amount of solute that will dissolve in the solvent
Supersaturated	

LOOKING CLOSER

9. Describe Complete the table to describe three types of solutions.

SECTION 3 Solubility and Concentration *continued*

How Do Temperature and Pressure Affect Solubility of Gases?

The solubility of a solid generally increases as the temperature of the solvent increases. However, the solubility of gases generally decreases as the temperature of the solvent increases. Carbonated beverages contain carbon dioxide, CO_2, gas dissolved in water. Because gases are less soluble in warmer solvents, less CO_2 stays dissolved in warm soda than in cold soda. You may have noticed this if you've ever sipped a warm, flat soda. ☑

Solubility of gases also depends on pressure. Carbon dioxide is dissolved in soda under high pressure. When you open the bottle, gas pressure decreases. Soda fizzes as the carbon dioxide comes out of solution.

READING CHECK

10. Describe How does an increase in the temperature of a solution affect the solubility of a gas?

_____

_____

_____

The pressure inside the bottle is higher than the pressure outside the bottle. At this high pressure, carbon dioxide gas is dissolved in water.

CO$_2$ under high pressure above solvent

Dissolved CO$_2$ molecules

LOOKING CLOSER

11. Explain How does pressure affect the solubility of a gas?

_____

_____

_____

When you open the bottle, the pressure inside the bottle decreases. Bubbles form as carbon dioxide comes out of solution.

Air at atmospheric pressure

Dissolved CO$_2$ molecules

CO$_2$ gas bubble

12. Infer Will more bubbles come out of a warm soda or a cold one? Explain your answer.

_____

_____

_____

_____

The solubility of gases is important to scuba divers. Increased pressure underwater causes more nitrogen gas to dissolve in their blood. If divers returns to the surface too quickly, nitrogen comes out of solution and forms bubbles in their blood vessels. This condition is known as the bends. It is very painful and can be dangerous.

Name _____ Class _____ Date _____

Section 3 Review

SECTION VOCABULARY

concentration the amount of a particular substance in a given quantity of a mixture, solution, or ore	**solubility** the ability of one substance to dissolve in another at a given temperature and pressure; expressed in terms of the amount of solute that will dissolve in a given amount of solvent to produce a saturated solution
molarity a concentration unit of a solution expressed as moles of solute dissolved per liter of solution	**supersaturated solution** a solution that holds more dissolved solute than is required to reach equilibrium at a given temperature
saturated solution a solution that cannot dissolve any more solute under the given conditions	**unsaturated solution** a solution that contains less solute than a saturated solution does and that is able to dissolve additional solute

1. Explain If you add salt continuously to a glass of water, eventually some salt will remain at the bottom. Why?

_____

_____

2. Compare Use the chart below to compare the solubilities of silver nitrate and silver chloride in water. Explain why their solubilities are different.

Compound	Formula	Solubility in grams per 100 g of H_2O at 20 °C
Silver nitrate	$AgNO_3$	216
Silver chloride	$AgCl$	0.00019

_____

_____

3. Calculate What is the molarity of 2 mol of calcium carbonate, $CaCl_2$, dissolved in 1 L of solution?

4. Explain Why do scientists typically use molarity to express the concentration of a solution rather than the words *dilute* and *concentrated*?

_____

_____

CHAPTER 9 | Acids, Bases, and Salts
SECTION
1 | **Acids, Bases, and pH**

What Are the Properties of Acids?

Does the thought of eating a lemon cause your mouth to pucker? You expect a lemon to taste sour. All the foods in the figure below taste sour because they contain acids.

READING TOOLBOX

Outline Make an outline of the material in this section. Use the headers in the section to help you organize your outline.

Citrus fruits, such as lemons, grapefruits, limes, and oranges, contain citric acid. Apples contain malic acid. Grapes contain tartaric acid.

When acids dissolve in water, they ionize, or form ions. When acids ionize, they form hydrogen ions, H^+. The hydrogen ions bond to water molecules, H_2O, to form hydronium ions, H_3O^+. An **acid** is a compound that increases the number of hydronium ions when it dissolves in water. Hydronium ions give acids their properties. Some properties of acids are listed below. ☑

- sour taste
- conduct electricity
- turn blue litmus paper red
- corrosive (able to destroy or eat away certain materials)

READING CHECK

1. **Define** What is an acid?

_____

_____

_____

_____

What Is the Difference Between Strong and Weak Acids?

All acids ionize when they are dissolved in water. However, some acids ionize completely, while others do not. The relative numbers of acid molecules that ionize in water determine if the acid is strong or weak. ☑

STRONG ACIDS

The figure below shows what happens to nitric acid when it is dissolved in water. The arrow pointing to the right shows that all of the nitric acid ionizes.

Nitric acid is a strong acid. When strong acids are dissolved in water, they ionize completely. This means that all the dissolved acid molecules break apart into ions.

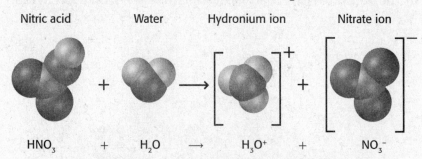

| Nitric acid | Water | Hydronium ion | Nitrate ion |

$$HNO_3 \;+\; H_2O \;\longrightarrow\; H_3O^+ \;+\; NO_3^-$$

When nitric acid ionizes, it forms hydronium ions and nitrate ions. The ions move around freely in the water and can conduct electricity. A substance that conducts electricity when it is dissolved in water is called an **electrolyte**. Strong acids are strong electrolytes. This is because solutions of these acids contain as many hydronium ions as the acid can possibly form. ☑

WEAK ACIDS

Weak acids, such as acetic acid, do not completely ionize. Only some of the molecules of acid ionize in water. Examine the figure at the top of the next page. The arrow pointing to the right shows that dissolved acetic acid molecules break apart into ions. The arrow pointing to the left shows that ions are also recombining to form molecules. Therefore, a solution of a weak acid contains fewer hydronium ions than a solution of a strong acid with the same concentration.

READING CHECK

2. Identify What determines whether an acid is strong or weak?

_____

_____

_____

LOOKING CLOSER

3. Identify What happens to the total charge of the solution when HNO_3 dissolves?

_____

_____

READING CHECK

4. Define What is an electrolyte?

_____

_____

_____

_____

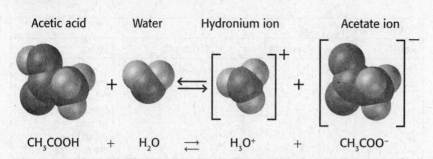

Acetic acid   Water   Hydronium ion   Acetate ion

$$CH_3COOH + H_2O \rightleftharpoons H_3O^+ + CH_3COO^-$$

Because there are few ions in a solution of a weak acid, the solution does not conduct electricity very well. Thus, weak acids are weak electrolytes.

Both of these beakers contain acids. One contains a weak acid and one contains a strong acid.

ACID DANGERS

Although many products you use every day contain acids, strong and concentrated acids can be very dangerous. For example, your stomach makes a very strong acid called hydrochloric acid. You need this acid to help you digest food. Normally, your stomach has a thick lining that protects it from the strong acid. However, if your body makes too much acid, the acid can destroy your stomach.

Even weak acids are not always safe to handle. Acids can damage your skin. The vapors are also harmful to your eyes, lungs, and mouth. This is why you should always wear goggles, gloves, and a laboratory apron when you work with acids. Never taste a chemical to determine if it is an acid. ☑

LOOKING CLOSER

5. Infer Which of the two beakers contains more ions? How do you know?

_____

_____

_____

_____

6. Identify Which beaker contains a strong acid? Explain your answer.

_____

_____

_____

✓ READING CHECK

7. List Identify three pieces of safety equipment you should use when you work with an acid.

_____

_____

_____

SECTION 1 Acids, Bases, and pH *continued*

Some Common Acids			
Acid	**Formula**	**Strength**	**Uses**
Hydrochloric acid	HCl	strong	Cleaning masonry; treating metals before plating or painting; adjusting pH of swimming pools
Sulfuric acid	H_2SO_4	strong	making fertilizers; the acid in car batteries
Nitric acid	HNO_3	strong	making fertilizers and explosives
Acetic acid	CH_3COOH	weak	making chemicals, plastics, and medicines; the acid in vinegar
Formic acid	HCOOH	weak	dying cloth; the acid used by stinging ants
Citric acid	$H_3C_6H_5O_7$	weak	making flavorings and soft drinks; the acid in citrus fruits

LOOKING CLOSER

8. Identify Which common acid is found in car batteries?

_____

9. Identify Is the acid in vinegar strong or weak?

_____

All these products contain acids.

What Are the Properties of Bases?

Baking soda is an example of a common base. It is used to make cakes and cookies and may be found in toothpastes and cleaning supplies. A **base** is a compound that forms hydroxide ions, OH^-, when it is dissolved in water. Hydroxide ions give bases their properties. Some of these properties are listed below. ☑

- bitter taste
- feel slippery
- conduct electricity
- turn red litmus paper blue
- corrosive

✔ READING CHECK

10. Identify What kind of ions do bases form when they are dissolved in water?

_____

SECTION 1 Acids, Bases, and pH *continued*

STRONG BASES

When strong bases are dissolved in water, they ionize completely. Most strong bases are made up of metal ions and hydroxide ions. These kinds of bases are called metal hydroxides.

Sodium hydroxide is an example of a metal hydroxide. Some drain cleaners contain sodium hydroxide. Sodium hydroxide completely ionizes when it is put into water. Sodium hydroxide and other strong bases are strong electrolytes. That is, they conduct electricity well when they are dissolved in water.

WEAK BASES

Ammonia is an example of a weak base. Ammonia, NH_3, does not contain hydroxide ions. Where do the oxygen and hydrogen that make up the hydroxide ion come from? Ammonia reacts with water to form OH^-. This reaction is shown in the figure below. ☑

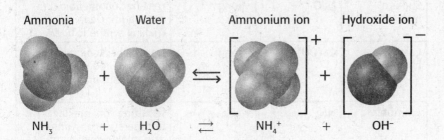

Ammonia		Water		Ammonium ion		Hydroxide ion

NH_3 + H_2O ⇌ NH_4^+ + OH^-

The double arrow tells you that ammonia does not ionize completely when it is dissolved in water. Therefore, ammonia is a weak base and a weak electrolyte.

DANGERS OF BASES

The table on the next page gives examples of common bases. Many bases are used in soaps, dyes, and fertilizer. However, concentrated bases can be very dangerous. They may dissolve many materials, including skin. When you work with bases, you should wear safety goggles, gloves, and a laboratory apron to protect yourself.

Critical Thinking

11. Compare In terms of ionization, how are strong acids and strong bases similar?

_____

_____

_____

_____

☑ READING CHECK

12. Explain How do bases that do not contain hydroxide ions form hydroxide ions?

_____

_____

SECTION 1 Acids, Bases, and pH *continued*

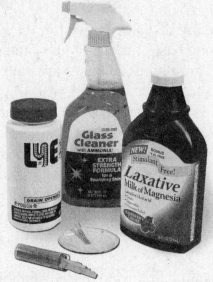

All these products contain bases.

Some Common Bases			
Base	**Formula**	**Strength**	**Uses**
Potassium hydroxide	KOH	strong	making soap; dyeing products
Sodium hydroxide	NaOH	strong	making soap; refining petroleum; cleaning drains; making synthetic fibers
Calcium hydroxide	$Ca(OH)_2$	strong	treating acid soil; treating lakes polluted by acid rain; making mortar, plaster, and cement
Ammonia	NH_3	weak	fertilizing soil; making fertilizers; making nitric acid; making cleaning solutions
Methylamine	CH_3NH_2	weak	making dyes and medicines; tanning leather
Aniline	$C_6H_5NH_2$	weak	making dyes and varnishes; used as a solvent

LOOKING CLOSER

13. Identify Identify two common bases used in making soap.

_____

_____

What Is the Difference Between Strong and Concentrated?

Many people think the words concentrated and strong mean the same thing. Similarly, many people think that weak and dilute mean the same thing. In chemistry, however, these words have different meanings.

Recall that the *concentration* of a solution refers to the number of solute particles in a particular amount of solution. A solution with a large number of solute particles is concentrated. A solution with a small number of solute particles is dilute.

STRONG AND DILUTE

Suppose a scientist added a very small amount of hydrochloric acid to a liter of water. Because the solution contains only a small amount of solute, you could describe it as dilute. However, when any amount of hydrochloric acid is dissolved in water, it ionizes completely. At any concentration, hydrochloric acid is a strong acid. Thus, a strong acid may form a dilute solution.

What Is pH?

How can you tell if a solution is acidic or basic? One way is to use an indicator. An **indicator** is a substance that changes color if a solution is acidic or basic. Litmus paper and pH paper are examples of indicators.

An indicator can tell you something is an acid or a base. However, in many cases, you need to know how acidic or basic a solution is. The **pH** of a solution is a value that expresses how acidic or basic a solution is. The pH scale ranges from 0 to 14. Solutions with a pH less than 7 are acids. Solutions with a pH greater than 7 are bases. Solutions with a pH of 7 are neutral. A *neutral* solution is not acidic or basic. ☑

> Acidic: pH < 7
>
> Basic: pH > 7
>
> Neutral: pH = 7

Critical Thinking
14. Infer Can a weak base form a concentrated solution? Explain your answer.

_____

_____

_____

_____

_____

✓ READING CHECK

15. Identify Is a solution with a pH greater than 7 basic or acidic?

_____

LOOKING CLOSER

16. Identify Is a soft drink more acidic or less acidic than milk?

_____

17. Analyze Relationships What happens to acidity as pH increases? What happens to basicity as pH increases?

_____

_____

_____

_____

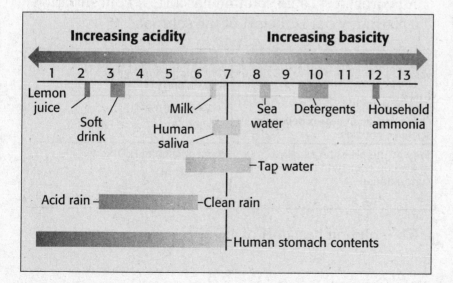

Increasing acidity   Increasing basicity

1   2   3   4   5   6   7   8   9   10   11   12   13

Lemon juice

Soft drink

Milk

Human saliva

Sea water   Detergents   Household ammonia

Tap water

Acid rain — Clean rain

Human stomach contents

SECTION 1 Acids, Bases, and pH *continued*

RELATIVE CONCENTRATIONS OF IONS

The pH of a solution indicates the concentration of hydronium ions. An acidic solution has a greater concentration of hydronium ions than hydroxide ions. A basic solution has a greater concentration of hydroxide ions than hydronium ions. A neutral solution has equal concentrations of hydronium ions and hydroxide ions. ☑

CONCENTRATION AND pH

Recall that you can use molarity (M) to describe the concentration of a substance in a solution. You can use the concentration of hydronium ions in a solution to determine the solution's pH.

In a solution, strong acids like HCl and HNO_3 produce one hydronium ion for each dissolved acid particle. The concentration of a strong acid indicates how many particles are in the solution. Because every particle of a strong acid that dissolves will ionize, the hydronium ion concentration equals the acid concentration.

Writing the H_3O^+ concentration in scientific notation can help you determine pH. When the concentration of hydronium ions is one times ten to a power, the pH is the negative of the power of 10. For example, pure water has a hydronium ion concentration of 0.0000001 mol/L, or 1×10^{-7} M. Thus, pure water has a pH of 7.

CALCULATING pH

A hydrochloric acid solution has a H_3O^+ concentration of 0.0001 M. What is the pH of the solution?

Math *Skills*

19. Calculate HNO_3 is a strong acid. What is the pH of a 0.01 M solution of HNO_3?

_____

Step 1: List the given and unknown values.	Given: concentration of HCl = 0.0001 M	Unknown: pH
Step 2: Write the molar concentration of hydroxide ions in scientific notation.	concentration of H_3O^+ = 0.0001 M = 1×10^{-4} M	
Step 3: The pH is the negative of the power of 10 in the H_3O^+ concentration.	concentration of H_3O^+ ions = 1×10^{-4} M pH = -(-4) = 4	

The solution has a pH of 4.

INTERPRETING pH DIFFERENCES

As you have seen, pH is based on powers of 10. Because of this, small differences in pH reflect big differences in hydronium concentrations. For example, the pH of apple juice is about 3. The pH of coffee is about 5. The difference in pH of the two liquids seems small. However, the difference of two pH units is actually quite large.

Because each pH unit represents a power of 10, a pH difference of two represents a difference in acidity of 10^2, or 100. Thus, apple juice is 100 times more acidic than coffee. Antacid tablets are basic. When antacid tablets are dissolved in water, the solution they form has a pH of about 8. Thus, coffee is 10^3, or 1,000 times, as acidic as an antacid tablet solution.

MEASURING pH

Indicators such as litmus paper do not measure pH very precisely. To measure pH precisely, you can use a pH meter. Because ions in a solution have electric charge, they can conduct electric current. A pH meter measures pH by determining the electric current created by the movement of ions.

Math *Skills*

20. Calculate Solution A has a pH of 9. Solution B has a pH of 3. How much more acidic is solution B than solution A?

_____

_____

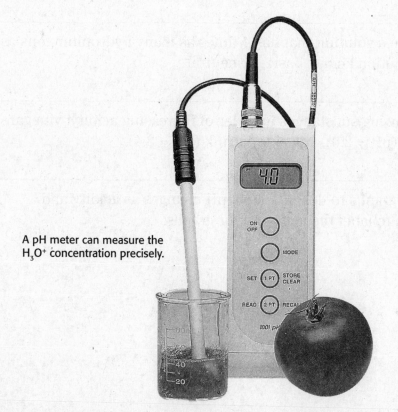

A pH meter can measure the H_3O^+ concentration precisely.

LOOKING CLOSER

21. Apply Concepts Is the tomato acidic or basic? Explain your answer.

_____

_____

22. Infer How is the pH value shown on the pH meter more precise than pH values you have seen so far?

_____

_____

Name _____ Class _____ Date _____

Section 1 Review

SECTION VOCABULARY

acid any compound that increases the number of hydronium ions when dissolved in water **base** any compound that increases the number of hydroxide ions when dissolved in water **electrolyte** a substance that dissolves in water to give a solution that conducts an electric current	**indicator** a compound that can reversibly change color depending on conditions such as pH **pH** a value that is used to express the acidity or basicity of a system; each whole number on the scale

1. Write Equations Write an equation showing the ionization of hydrochloric acid in water.

_____

2. Explain How do a strong acid and a weak acid behave differently when each is dissolved in water?

_____

_____

_____

3. Identify Relationships What is the relationship between the strength of an acid or base and the strength of the electrolyte that it forms?

_____

_____

4. Classify Suppose you have a solution that has 4 times as many hydronium ions as hydroxide ions. Is this solution acidic, basic, or neutral?

_____

5. Arrange Arrange the following substances in order of increasing acidity: vinegar (pH = 2.8), stomach acid (pH = 2.0), and a soft drink (pH = 3.4).

_____

6. Graph Trends Create two graphs to describe how pH changes as acidity and basicity increase. Be sure to label the axes of your graphs.

CHAPTER 9 | Acids, Bases, and Salts

SECTION
2 Reactions of Acids with Bases

KEY IDEAS

As you read this section, keep these questions in mind:

• What happens when you combine an acid with a base?

• In what ways can you use salts?

What Is an Acid-Base Reaction?

Have you ever used an antacid to feel better when you had an upset stomach? You can get an upset stomach if the acid in your stomach irritates your esophagus. An antacid contains a base. Taking an antacid reduces the amount of acid in your stomach.

The reaction between an acid and a base is called a **neutralization reaction**. Neutralization reactions have many uses.

REACTIONS BETWEEN IONS

Recall that a strong acid, such as hydrochloric acid, ionizes completely when it is dissolved in water, as shown below:

$$HCl + H_2O \longrightarrow H_3O^+ + Cl^-$$

A strong base, such as sodium hydroxide, also ionizes completely in water, as shown here:

$$NaOH \longrightarrow Na^+ + OH^-$$

If the acid and base are mixed together, a neutralization reaction occurs, as shown below:

$$H_3O^+ + Cl^- + Na^+ + OH^- \longrightarrow Na^+ + Cl^- + 2H_2O$$

A chemical reaction occurs between the hydronium ions and hydroxide ions to form water molecules. In this case, the Na^+ and Cl^- are spectator ions. *Spectator ions* do not change during the reaction between H_3O^+ and OH^- ions. If you combine equal amounts and concentrations of a strong acid and a strong base, the H_3O^+ and OH^- ions react to form H_2O. Thus, the solution that results is neutral.

READING TOOLBOX

Summarize Before you read, copy the three equations on this page onto a large sheet of paper. As you read, label the hydronium ions, the hydroxide ions, and spectator ions. Indicate which parts of the third equation are from a base and which are from an acid.

LOOKING CLOSER
1. Identify What uncharged product results from a neutralization reaction?

_____

SECTION 2 Reactions of Acids with Bases *continued*

FORMATION OF SALTS

If you remove the spectator ions from the equation for a neutralization reaction, you will have the following:

$$H_3O^+ + OH^- \longrightarrow 2\ H_2O$$

The spectator ions do not chemically react or change their identity. However, they do combine to form a salt. A **salt** is an ionic compound made of a positive ion from the base (Na^+) and the negative ion from the acid (Cl^-), as shown below: ☑

$$Na^+ + Cl^- \longrightarrow NaCl$$

Examine the figure below. The middle beaker looks like the others, even though the neutralization reaction has produced new compounds. This is because the salt stays dissolved in the water. However, when the water evaporates, the salt will remain in the beaker as a solid.

2. Explain What happens to the spectator ions in a neutralization reaction?

_____

_____

_____

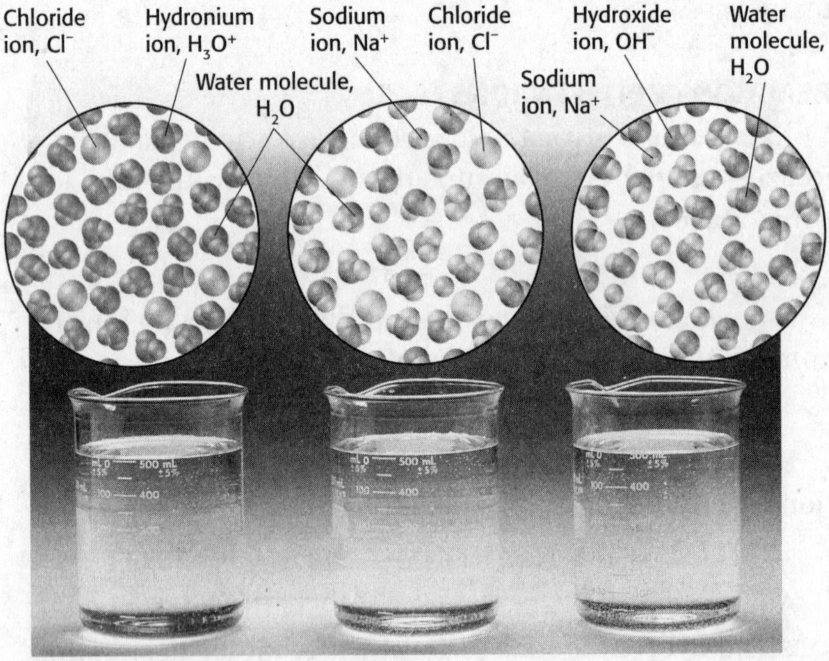

LOOKING CLOSER

3. Explain The center beaker contains the products of a neutralization reaction. Why do you not see the salt that has formed?

_____

_____

_____

Chloride ion, Cl^- Hydronium ion, H_3O^+ Sodium ion, Na^+ Chloride ion, Cl^- Hydroxide ion, OH^- Water molecule, H_2O

Water molecule, H_2O Sodium ion, Na^+

What Are Some Common Salts?

When you hear the word *salt*, you probably think of the salt you sprinkle on food. However, to a scientist, a salt can be almost any combination of a cation and an anion. The table on the next page gives some examples of salts.

                                                                             Acids, Bases, and Salts

SECTION 2 Reactions of Acids with Bases *continued*

Some Common Salts		
Salt	**Formula**	**Uses**
Aluminum sulfate	$Al_2(SO4)_3$	purifying water; used in antiperspirants
Ammonium sulfate	$(NH_4)_2SO_4$	flameproofing fabrics; used as fertilizer
Barium sulfate	$BaSO_4$	used to diagnose some medical conditions
Calcium chloride	$CaCl_2$	used to de-ice streets and highways; used in some kinds of concrete
Potassium chloride	KCl	treating potassium deficiency; used as substitute for table salt
Sodium carbonate	Na_2CO_3	making glass; added to wash to soften water
Sodium chloride	$NaCl$	flavoring food
Sodium hydrogen carbonate	$NaHCO_3$	treating upset stomach; ingredient in baking powder; used in fire extinguishers
Sodium stearate	$NaOOCC_{17}H_{34}$	used as soap; used in deodorants
Sodium lauryl sulfonate	$NaSO_3C_{12}H_{25}$	used as detergent

All of these products contain salts.

Like all animals, we need elements such as potassium, sodium, calcium, magnesium, iron, phosphorus, and iodine to stay healthy. However, many of these nutrients are harmful in their elemental forms. You get the ions of these elements from minerals. Minerals contain the salts that you need. ☑

Salts that contain calcium are important for your teeth and bones. Your nerves and muscles need calcium, potassium, and sodium ions in order to work properly. Sodium and potassium salts help balance the amount of water that goes in and out of your cells.

READING CHECK
5. Explain Why do we get the many of the nutrients we need from salts rather than from elemental forms?

_____

_____

_____

Why Don't Some Neutralization Reactions Produce Neutral Solutions?

Reactions between acids and bases do not always produce neutral solutions. The pH of the final solution depends on how much acid and base you combine. The pH also depends on the strength of the acid and base you use. ☑

Recall that weak acids and bases do not ionize completely and that strong acids and bases do ionize completely. If a strong acid reacts with an equal amount of a weak base, the solution will be acidic. If a weak acid reacts with an equal amount of a strong base, the solution will be basic.

How Can You Use Acid-Base Reactions?

Suppose you were given a solution of sodium hydroxide, but you didn't know its concentration. How could you find out? One way would be to carry out a titration. A *titration* is a process in which you add carefully measured amounts of one solution to another solution. In an acid-base titration, the concentration of one solution is generally known. The concentration of the other solution is unknown. ☑

Think about how pH changes as an acid and a base mix. For example, the graph below shows how the pH of a solution of HCl changed as potassium hydroxide (KOH) was added to it. Hydrochloric acid, HCl, was titrated with potassium hydroxide, KOH.

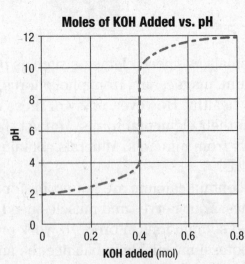

Moles of KOH Added vs. pH

✔ **READING CHECK**

6. Identify What two factors determine the pH of solution formed in an acid-base reaction?

_____

_____

_____

_____

✔ **READING CHECK**

7. Define What is a titration?

_____

_____

_____

_____

Graphing Skills

8. Identify What is the initial pH of the solution before KOH is added?

_____

9. Analyze Does the solution's acidity increase or decrease as KOH is added?

_____

SECTION 2 Reactions of Acids with Bases *continued*

INTERPRETING A TITRATION GRAPH

As KOH was added to the acid solution, the pH increased slowly. Then, when 0.4 mol of KOH had been added, the pH increased very quickly. The pH at that point is equal to the pH at the center of the vertical line: about 7. When more KOH was added, the pH rose above 7.

Recall that a pH below 7 indicates an acidic solution. Therefore, when fewer than 0.4 mol of KOH had been added to the solution, the solution was acidic. This shows that not all of the HCl reacted with the KOH. When more than 0.4 mol of KOH was added, the pH was above 7. This shows that the solution was basic. In other words, there was no HCl left in the solution to react with the KOH.

Remember that when a strong acid reacts with an equal amount of a strong base the resulting solution has a pH of 7. It took 0.4 mol of KOH to produce a solution with a neutral pH. Therefore, there must have been 0.4 mol of HCl in the original acid solution.

The point at which there is no extra acid or base in the mixture is called the *equivalence point* of the titration. In the example on the previous page, the equivalence point occurred when 0.4 mol of KOH were added to the HCl. At that point, all of the HCl had reacted with the KOH, but there was no extra KOH in the solution. How many moles of KOH were added to reach the equivalence point? Use the steps below to figure it out: ☑

| **Step 1:** Locate the equivalence point on the graph. | A strong acid was titrated with a strong base. The y-axis indicated pH, so the equivalence point in the titration curve has a y-value of 7. |
| **Step 2:** Read the moles of KOH from the graph. | The x-axis indicates how many moles of KOH were added. At pH = 7, 0.4 mol of KOH was added. |

The pH of the mixture at the equivalence point depends on which acids and bases are reacting. If a strong acid reacts with a strong base, the pH at the equivalence point will be 7. If a strong acid reacts with a weak base, the pH at the equivalence point will be less than 7. If a weak acid reacts with a strong base, the pH at the equivalence point will be greater than 7.

Critical Thinking

10. Apply Concepts When enough KOH had been added to the HCl solution to create a neutral solution, what were the components of the solution?

_____

_____

✓ READING CHECK

11. Define What is the equivalence point of a titration?

_____

_____

Section 2 Review

SECTION VOCABULARY

neutralization reaction the reaction of the ions that characterize acids and the ions that characterize bases to form water molecules and a salt	**salt** an ionic compound that forms when a metal atom or a positive radical replaces the hydrogen of an acid

1. **Compare** How does the everyday definition of salt differ from the one used by scientists?

_____

_____

2. **Identify** What two types of compounds are produced by a neutralization reaction?

_____

3. **Identify** In the reaction described by the equation below, what are the spectator ions?

$$H_3O^+ + Br^- + Li^+ + OH^- \longrightarrow Li^+ + Br^- + 2H_2O$$

_____

4. **Predict** Suppose you combine a weak acid with an equal amount of a strong base. Will the final solution be acidic or basic?

_____

5. **Write Equations** Write two equations for the neutralization of nitric acid, HNO_3, with magnesium hydroxide, $Mg(OH)_2$. In the first equation, include the spectator ions. In the second, do not include the spectator ions.

_____

_____

6. **Predict** If you react equal amounts of sulfuric acid, H_2SO_4, and ammonia, NH_3, will the solution that results be acidic, basic, or neutral? Explain your answer.

_____

_____

_____

7. **Identify** What are two ways calcium salts are important for your health?

_____

_____

CHAPTER 9 Acids, Bases, and Salts

SECTION 3

Acids, Bases, and Salts in the Home

KEY IDEAS

As you read this section, keep these questions in mind:

• Why do you add cleaning products to water?

• What are some of the products in your home that contain acids, bases, or salts?

Why Do You Add Cleaning Products to Water?

Acids, bases, and salts are not just found in a science laboratory. Many items in your home or school contain acids, bases, and salts. These items include soaps, detergents, shampoos, antacids, vitamins, sodas, and juices.

Cleaning products that contain salts are very useful. For example, if your hands are greasy after you eat french fries, you cannot clean them with just water. This is because water does not mix with oil. Instead, you need to wash your hands with soap. Soaps and other cleaning products help water mix with oily substances.

SOAPS

Soap is made of sodium or potassium ions and fatty acids. *Fatty acids* are molecules made of long chains of hydrogen and carbon atoms. The fatty acids mix well with oil. The sodium or potassium ions mix well with water. Because of its two different parts, soap can dissolve in both oil and water. ☑

Soap forms a mixture of oil and water called an emulsion. Recall that in an emulsion, liquids that normally do not mix are spread throughout each other. Soap acts as an emulsifier by surrounding drops of oil. When you rinse the soap away, the water also washes away the oil, leaving your skin clean.

READING TOOLBOX

Underline As you read this section, use colored pens or pencils to underline examples of acids, bases, and salt. Use red for acids, blue for bases, and purple for salts.

✓ READING CHECK

1. Describe What is the basic structure of soap? How does this structure help soap clean?

_____

_____

_____

_____

How Does Soap Work?

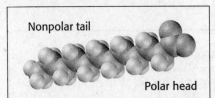

Nonpolar tail

Polar head

❶ Soap is an ionic compound. Its negative ion is made of long fatty acid chains. Its positive ion is a sodium or potassium ion.

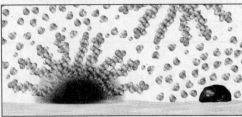

❷ Soap acts as an emulsifier. It surrounds droplets of oily dirt. The fatty acids mix with the oil. The positive ion mixes with the water.

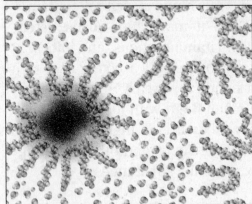

❸ The droplets of oil and dirt surrounded by soap stay suspended in water. Because the oily dirt is suspended in water, you can rinse it away.

LOOKING CLOSER

2. Identify What are the positive and negative ions in soap?

_____

_____

_____

3. Explain Why can soap mix with both oil and water?

_____

_____

_____

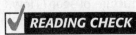

READING CHECK

4. Explain How does soap scum form?

_____

_____

_____

DETERGENT

Have you ever noticed a greasy ring around the bathtub after a bath? Soap is good for cleaning many things. However, soap does not work well in hard water. *Hard water* contains dissolved ions, such as Mg^{2+}, Ca^{2+}, and Fe^{3+}. The fatty acids in soap can combine with these ions to form *soap scum*. Soap scum is a salt that is insoluble in water. ☑

Like soaps, **detergents** are salts made of ions and fatty acids. They also emulsify oils and dissolve in water. However, the ends of the fatty chains in detergents are different from those in soaps. Because of these differences, detergents do not form insoluble salts in hard water. Therefore, detergents do not form soap scum. For this reason, detergents are used in most shampoos, liquid hand cleansers, and body washes.

The source of detergents is also different from soaps. Soaps are made from animal fats or plant oils. Detergents are made from petroleum products.

SECTION 3 Acids, Bases, and Salts in the Home *continued*

BLEACH

A **disinfectant** is a substance that kills viruses and bacteria. **Bleach** is an example of a disinfectant made of a base, sodium hypochlorite, NaOCl. Bleach can also remove colors and stains from fabrics.

Although bleach can be very useful, it can also be dangerous. If you mix bleach with an acid, poisonous gases form. You should never mix bleach with an acid such as vinegar. In addition, you should not mix bleach with ammonia because a toxic gas will form. ☑

AMMONIA

Ammonia solutions are also good cleansers. Recall that ammonia is a weak base. When it is dissolved in water, it does not ionize completely. The concentration of hydroxide ions in an ammonia solution is low. However, an ammonia solution contains enough hydroxide ions to remove fingerprints and oily smears from windows. Many ammonia cleaners sold in stores are a combination of alcohols, detergents, and other cleaning agents.

What Are Some Examples of Acids, Bases, and Salts in Your Home?

In addition to household cleaners, many other items in your home contain acids, bases, or salts. These items include many of the health, beauty, and food products you may use every day.

HEALTH AND BEAUTY PRODUCTS

Have you ever used an antacid when you had a stomach ache? An **antacid** is a weak base that neutralizes excess stomach acid that can make you feel sick. Some other health and beauty products that contain acids, bases, or salts are listed below. ☑

- Toothpastes and contact lens solution contain salts.
- Shaving cream and face lotion contain weak acids.
- Makeup and hair products may contain acids or bases.

✔ **READING CHECK**

5. Explain Why should you not mix bleach with acids or ammonia?

_____

_____

_____

✔ **READING CHECK**

6. Explain How can an antacid make you feel better when you have a stomach ache?

_____

_____

_____

SHAMPOOS

Most shampoos are made of detergents. People use shampoos to remove dirt and oil from their hair. However, shampoos are not meant to remove all the oil from hair. Some oil is needed to make your hair shiny and to keep it from becoming dry and brittle. Shampoos are typically pH balanced. That is, they are made to be in a specific pH range. Hair looks its best when it is at a slightly acidic pH.

ANTIOXIDANTS

Have you ever noticed that a piece of apple will turn brown after a short time? Many cut fruits turn brown when they are exposed to air. They turn brown as molecules in the fruit react with oxygen.

If you rub a piece of apple with lemon juice, it will look fresher longer. Why? The citric acid in lemon juice acts as an antioxidant. An *antioxidant* prevents oxygen from reacting with other molecules. Lemon juice prevents oxygen from reacting with molecules in the piece of apple. ☑

Vitamin C, or ascorbic acid, is another antioxidant. Citric acid and vitamin C prevent the enzyme in the oxidation reaction from working. Vitamin C also reacts with oxygen molecules before the oxygen can react with the molecules in the fruit.

FOOD PRODUCTS

Some acids are useful in cooking because they can change proteins in foods. For example, acids such as vinegar or citric acid can unravel the proteins in meats. This makes meat more tender. Healthy bacteria produce lactic acid as they use the sugar lactose in milk for energy. Lactic acid changes the milk protein casein into a thick gel. This gel is an important ingredient in yogurt.

Critical Thinking

7. Infer Why do you think most shampoos are made of detergents rather than soaps?

_____

_____

_____

_____

☑ **READING CHECK**

8. Define What is an antioxidant?

_____

_____

SECTION 3 Acids, Bases, and Salts in the Home *continued*

Baking powder releases CO_2 during baking. The CO_2 in the batter causes biscuits to rise.

LOOKING CLOSER
9. Identify What is the role of baking powder in making biscuits rise?

_____
_____
_____

In addition to table salt, people use other salts for baking. For example, baking soda, or sodium hydrogen carbonate, forms carbon dioxide gas at high temperatures. Baking soda is added to cookies to make them rise as they bake.

Like baking soda, baking powder is a salt that can be added to some foods to make them rise. Baking powder contains baking soda and an acidic substance. When mixed with water, these compounds react to produce CO_2. Carbon dioxide makes cake batter light and fluffy and helps biscuits rise.

Talk About It
Investigate Choose a health or beauty item you use every day. Read the back label of the item and write down all the ingredients. Research the ingredients to find out if they are acids, bases, or salts. Make a poster that describes your findings and present it to the class.

CLEANING PRODUCTS

Bases are also found in many cleaning products in the kitchen. For example, many drain cleaners are made from bases. Strong bases such as sodium hydroxide break down grease and other food material that cause clogs in drains.

Name _____ Class _____ Date _____

Section 3 Review

SECTION VOCABULARY

antacid a weak base that neutralizes stomach acid	**disinfectant** a chemical substance that kills harmful bacteria or viruses
bleach a chemical compound used to whiten or make lighter, such as hydrogen peroxide or sodium hypochlorite	**soap** a substance that is used as a cleaner and that dissolves in water
detergent a water-soluble cleaner that can emulsify dirt and oil	

1. Explain Why do soaps and other cleaning products clean better than water alone?

_____

2. Compare Identify one similarity between soaps and detergents. Identify two differences.

_____

_____

_____

_____

3. Summarize Complete the Spider Map below to describe four common types of cleaners. On the lines, indicate whether each is an acid, base, or salt, and give examples of products that contain each.

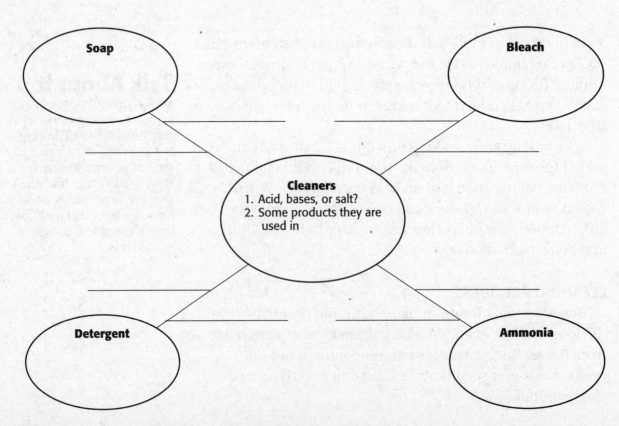

CHAPTER 10 Nuclear Changes

SECTION
1 # What Is Radioactivity?

KEY IDEAS

As you read this section, keep these questions in mind:

• What is radioactivity?

• What are the different types of nuclear radiation?

• How does nuclear decay change an atom?

What Is Radioactivity?

Our lives are affected by radioactivity, or nuclear radiation, in many ways. Technology that uses radioactivity has helped people detect disease, kill cancer cells, and generate electricity. However, too much nuclear radiation can be harmful. We need to know where radiation exists and how to protect ourselves from it. First, we need to know what radioactivity is.

What Happens During Nuclear Decay?

Recall that an element may be found in different forms called isotopes. Isotopes of an element have the same number of protons in their nuclei but different numbers of neutrons. In contrast, different elements have different numbers of protons in their nuclei.

Certain isotopes of some elements go through a process called radioactive decay. During **radioactive decay**, an unstable atom releases energy or particles from its nucleus. Sometimes, decay must happen many times before a nucleus is stable. ☑

After radioactive decay, the element may change into a different isotope of the same element or into a completely different element. The energy and matter released by the nuclei of unstable isotopes is called **nuclear radiation**.

READING TOOLBOX

Compare As you read, make a table that compares the main types of nuclear radiation. In the table, describe their similarities and differences.

✓ READING CHECK

1. Describe What happens during radioactive decay?

_____

_____

_____

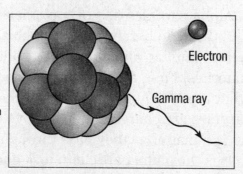

This diagram shows what happens when a particular unstable isotope emits, or gives off, nuclear radiation. This nucleus is emitting both energy and a particle.

Electron

Gamma ray

What Are Different Types of Nuclear Radiation?

There are four main types of nuclear radiation: alpha particles, beta particles, gamma rays, and neutrons. Nuclear radiation can interact with nearby matter. The charge, mass, and energy of nuclear radiation determine how it will interact with matter.

Types of Nuclear Radiation				
Radiation type	Symbol	Mass (kg)	Charge	Graphic
Alpha particle	$_2^4\text{He}$	6.646×10^{-27}	+2	
Beta particle	$_{-1}^0\text{e}$, $_{+1}^0\text{e}$	9.109×10^{-31}	−1, (+1)	
Gamma ray	γ	none	0	
Neutron	$_1^0\text{n}$	1.675×10^{-27}	0	

LOOKING CLOSER

2. Identify Which type of radiation has the most massive particles?

_____

3. Identify Which two types of radiation have no charge?

_____

ALPHA PARTICLES

Ernest Rutherford discovered the alpha particle while studying the decay of uranium-238, a radioactive isotope. Rutherford named the radiation *alpha* (α) *rays* after the first letter of the Greek alphabet. Later, he discovered that alpha rays were actually particles. **Alpha particles** are positively charged particles made of two protons and two neutrons—the same makeup as a helium nucleus. ☑

Alpha particles do not travel far through materials. In fact, they can barely pass through a sheet of paper. Two factors limit an alpha particle's ability to pass through materials. First, alpha particles are more massive than other types of nuclear radiation. Second, because alpha particles are charged, they remove electrons from, or *ionize*, matter as they pass through it. This process causes the alpha particle to lose energy and slow down.

✓ **READING CHECK**

4. Identify Which element has the same number of protons and neutrons as an alpha particle?

_____

BETA PARTICLES

Some decaying nuclei emit a type of nuclear radiation that travels farther through matter than alpha particles do. This nuclear radiation is made up of beta particles, which are named after the second Greek letter, beta (β). **Beta particles** are typically fast moving electrons. However, beta particles can also be positively charged particles called *positrons*. Positrons have the same mass as electrons.

Scientists wondered how negatively charged beta particles could come from a positively charged nucleus. A theory introduced in the 1930s helped explain this. Recall that a neutron has no charge. Scientists found that a neutron decays to form a proton and an electron. The nucleus then ejects, or shoots out, an electron at a high speed as a beta particle. ☑

GAMMA RAYS

Unlike alpha or beta particles, gamma rays are not made of matter and do not have an electric charge. Instead, **gamma rays** are a form of electromagnetic energy, or light. Gamma rays are named for the third Greek letter, gamma (γ). Like visible light and X rays, gamma rays consist of energy packets called *photons*. Gamma rays, however, have much more energy than light or X rays do.

Although gamma rays have no electric charge, they can ionize matter easily and cause damage. Clothing or most building materials cannot stop gamma rays. Thus, gamma rays are more dangerous to the health of living things than alpha or beta particles are.

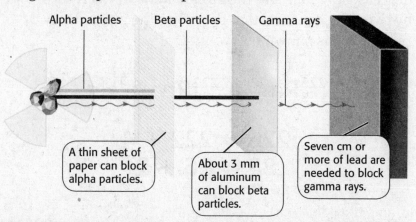

A thin sheet of paper can block alpha particles.

About 3 mm of aluminum can block beta particles.

Seven cm or more of lead are needed to block gamma rays.

Different kinds of nuclear radiation can pass through, or penetrate, different materials.

READING CHECK

5. Explain How is it possible for a positively charged nucleus to release a negatively charged beta particle?

_____

_____

_____

_____

LOOKING CLOSER

6. Identify Which of the three materials shown in the figure can block alpha particles, beta particles, and gamma rays?

_____

SECTION 1 What Is Radioactivity? *continued*

What Is Neutron Emission?

During *neutron emission*, a nucleus releases neutrons. Several processes may cause neutron emission. For example, sometimes, neutrons are released when atoms are hit by large particles such as alpha particles or other neutrons. ☑

Recall that charged particles can ionize matter. Because neutrons have no charge, they do not ionize matter. Neutrons don't lose energy ionizing matter as alpha and beta particles do. Thus, neutrons travel farther through matter than either alpha or beta particles do.

How Does Nuclear Decay Change an Atom?

Nuclear decay causes changes in the nucleus of an atom. When an unstable nucleus releases an alpha or beta particle, the number of protons and neutrons changes. For instance, when radium-226 emits an alpha particle, it changes to radon-222. Nuclear decay changed the number of protons, so the atom becomes a different element. ☑

Nuclear-decay equations are written in a way similar to chemical reaction equations. The original nucleus is like a reactant, so it is placed on the left side of the equation. The products of the reaction are placed on the right side of the equation.

What Happens During Alpha Decay?

During alpha decay, a large unstable nucleus becomes smaller by emitting an alpha particle. Recall that an alpha particle is the same as the nucleus of a helium atom. The equation for alpha decay shows that the atomic mass decreases by four and the atomic number decreases by two. The equation that describes the alpha decay of radium-226 is shown below.

$$^{226}_{88}\text{Ra} \longrightarrow {}^{222}_{86}\text{Rn} + {}^{4}_{2}\text{He}$$

$$226 = 222 + 4$$
$$88 = 86 + 2$$

READING CHECK

7. Identify What is one cause of neutron emission?

_____

_____

_____

READING CHECK

8. Explain Why does alpha or beta decay cause an atom to become a different element?

_____

_____

_____

_____

LOOKING CLOSER

9. Identify What is the atomic number of radon, Rn? How many protons does an atom of radon have?

_____

10. Identify How many neutrons are in an atom of $^{222}_{86}\text{Rn}$?

_____

SECTION 1 What Is Radioactivity? *continued*

MASS NUMBER AND ATOMIC NUMBER

The mass number of the radium atom before decay is 226. This number is the same as the sum of the mass numbers of the decay products. Similarly, the radium atom has 88 protons before alpha decay. This number is the same as the sum of the protons produced by the decay.

What Happens During Beta Decay?

During beta decay, the mass number of an atom before and after the decay will not change. However, the atomic number after the decay increases or decreases by one. Remember that the atomic number is equal to the number of protons. Recall that the number of protons an atom has determines what element that atom belongs to. Therefore, the atom after beta decay will change to a different element.

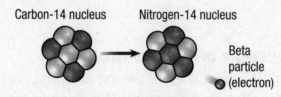

Carbon-14 nucleus → Nitrogen-14 nucleus

Beta
particle
(electron)

During beta decay, a neutron in the nucleus decays to form a proton and an electron. The electron is emitted from the nucleus, but the proton stays. Thus, the nucleus has one more proton after beta decay.

LOOKING CLOSER
11. Explain After beta decay, why is the atom a different element?

_____

_____

_____

An electron does not have an atomic number because it is not an atom. Most beta particles have only a single negative charge. However, scientists typically represent an electron using an atomic number of –1 in a nuclear-decay equation. A beta particle's mass is very small compared to the mass of a proton or neutron. Thus, the particle can be considered to have a mass of zero. The symbol for a negatively charged beta particle symbol is $_{-1}^{0}e$.

"Atomic mass"
of an electron

$_{-1}^{0}e$ ———— An electron

"Atomic number"
of an electron

LOOKING CLOSER
12. Identify What does the zero represent in the symbol for a beta particle?

_____

_____

SECTION 1 What Is Radioactivity? *continued*

$$^{14}_{6}\text{C} \longrightarrow \,^{14}_{7}\text{N} + \,^{0}_{-1}\text{e} \qquad \begin{array}{c} 14 = 14 + 0 \\ 6 = 7 + (-1) \end{array}$$

Critical Thinking

13. Apply Concepts Why does the mass number of an atom stay the same before and after beta decay?

_____

_____

_____

_____

_____

Through the process of beta decay, a carbon-14 nucleus becomes a nitrogen-14 nucleus. The equation that describes this process is shown above. During beta decay of carbon-14, a neutron decays to form a proton and an electron. Because the nucleus gains a proton, the new isotope has a new atomic number. Thus, the new isotope is a different element.

What Happens During Gamma Decay?

Recall that gamma rays are not made of particles. Thus, when an isotope emits gamma rays, the number of protons and neutrons does not change. However, the energy content of the nucleus will be lower after gamma decay.

WRITING NUCLEAR DECAY EQUATIONS

Actinium-217 decays by releasing an alpha particle. Write the equation that describes this decay process, and determine which element formed.

Step 1: Write the equation with the original element on the left side and the products on the right side.	**Given:** $^{217}_{89}\text{Ac} \longrightarrow \,^{A}_{Z}X + \,^{4}_{2}\text{He}$
	Unknown: X = unknown decay product A = unknown mass Z = unknown atomic number

Math *Skills*

14. Write Equations Complete the following radioactive decay equation. Indicate whether alpha or beta decay takes place.

$$^{12}_{5}\text{B} \longrightarrow \,^{12}_{6}\text{C} + \,^{A}_{Z}X$$

_____

_____

Step 2: Write math equations for atomic and mass numbers. Rearrange the equations.	$217 = A + 4$ $A = 217 - 4$	$89 = Z + 2$ $Z = 89 - 2$
Step 3: Solve for the unknown values, and rewrite the equation with all nuclei represented.	$A = 213$ $Z = 87$ According to the periodic table, 87 is the atomic number of francium. The unknown element is $^{213}_{87}\text{Fr}$. $^{217}_{89}\text{Ac} \longrightarrow \,^{213}_{87}\text{Fr} + \,^{4}_{2}\text{He}$	

SECTION 1 What Is Radioactivity? *continued*

How Do Scientists Use Radioactive Decay?

Scientists can use radioactive decay to determine the age of rocks and materials that were once alive. Radioactive decay can help scientists learn the ages of materials found at ancient graves and villages, and even Earth itself.

It is impossible to predict the precise moment a nucleus of a single atom will decay. However, it is possible to know how long it will take for half a sample of radioactive material to decay. This is because the decay rate is the same for any sample of an isotope. The time needed for half the nuclei in a sample to decay is called the isotope's **half-life**. ☑

Half-Lives of Selected Isotopes		
Isotope	**Half-life**	**Nuclear radiation emitted**
Thorium- 219	1.05×10^{-6} s	α
Hafnium-156	2.5×10^{-2} s	α
Radon-222	3.82 days	α, γ
Iodine-131	8.1 days	β, γ
Radium-226	1,599 years	α, γ
Carbon-14	5,715 years	β
Plutonium-239	2.412×10^4 years	α, γ
Uranium-235	7.04×10^8 years	α, γ
Potassium-40	1.28×10^9 years	β, γ
Uranium-238	4.47×10^9 years	α, γ

READING CHECK

15. Define What is a half-life?

_____

_____

_____

LOOKING CLOSER

16. Identify Which of these radioactive isotopes has the shortest half-life? Which has the longest half-life?

_____

_____

Different radioactive isotopes have different half-lives. Half-lives can last from nanoseconds to billions of years. The length of a half-life depends on the stability of the nuclei of a particular isotope.

An isotope's half-life can make the isotope useful in particular situations. For example, doctors use isotopes with short half-lives, such as iodine-131, to help diagnose medical problems. Geologists calculate the ages of rocks by using the half-lives of long-lasting isotopes, such as potassium-40.

USING HALF-LIFE

Radium-226 has a half-life of 1,599 years. How much time is needed for seven-eighths (7/8) of a sample of radium-226 to decay?

Step 1: List the given and unknown values.	**Given:** half-life = 1,599 years fraction of sample decayed = $\frac{7}{8}$
	Unknown: • fraction of sample remaining • total time of decay
Step 2: Subtract the fraction decayed from 1 to find how much of the sample remains. Determine how much of the sample remains after each half-life.	fraction of sample remaining = 1 − fraction decayed = $1 - \frac{7}{8} = \frac{1}{8}$ amount of sample remaining after one half-life = $\frac{1}{2}$ amount of sample remaining after two half-lives = $\frac{1}{2} \times \frac{1}{2} = \frac{1}{4}$ amount of sample remaining after three half-lives = $\frac{1}{2} \times \frac{1}{2} \times \frac{1}{2} = \frac{1}{8}$
Step 3: Multiply the number of half-lives by the time needed for each half-life. This is the total time needed for $\frac{7}{8}$ of the sample to decay.	Each half-life lasts 1,599 years. total time of decay = 3 half-lives × $\frac{1{,}599 \text{ y}}{\text{half-life}}$ = 4,797 y

Math *Skills*

17. Calculate The half-life of iodine-131 is 8.1 days. How much time is needed for three-fourths of the sample of iodine-131 to decay?

Critical Thinking

18. Infer As the number of carbon-14 atoms decreases over time, why does the number of nitrogen-14 atoms increase?

EXPONENTIAL RATE OF RADIOACTIVE DECAY

After the first half-life of a radioactive sample has passed, half of the sample remains unchanged. After the next half-life, half of the remaining sample decays. That is, only a quarter of the original element remains. After the next half life, only one-eighth will remain unchanged. This relationship is called an *exponential decay*.

The original radioactive nuclei are called parent nuclei. A *decay curve* is a graph that shows the change in number of parent nuclei in a given sample over time. Examine the graph on the next page. The total number of nuclei remains the same, but the number of carbon nuclei decreases over time. As the number of carbon-14 atoms decrease, the number of nitrogen-14 atoms increases.

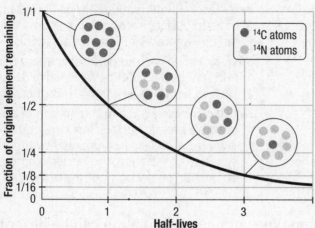

Radioactive Decay of ¹⁴C

During each half-life, half of the remaining sample decays to form another element.

LOOKING CLOSER
19. Predict What fraction of the original element will remain after four half-lives?

_____

_____

CARBON-14 DATING

Carbon is found in all living things. Living things may use any of the carbon isotopes in their bodies. The most common carbon isotope is carbon-12. Plants take in carbon dioxide during photosynthesis. A small fraction of the CO_2 molecules they take in contain the carbon-14 isotope instead of carbon-12. While a plant or an animal that eats the plant is alive, the ratio of the carbon isotopes in its body stays about the same.

When an organism dies, however, it does not take in any more carbon. The nuclei of the carbon-14 atoms decay, but those of carbon-12 do not. Scientists can compare the ratio of carbon-14 to carbon-12 to estimate how long ago an organism died. This is sometimes called carbon-14 dating. Scientists use carbon-14 dating to estimate the ages of objects made of materials that were once alive.

Critical Thinking
20. Infer Can scientists use carbon-dating to estimate the age of a gold ring? Explain your answer.

_____

_____

_____

_____

_____

Scientists may use carbon-14 dating to estimate the age of a piece of ancient clothing or the age of a mummy.

Section 1 Review

SECTION VOCABULARY

alpha particle a positively charged particle that consists of two protons and two neutrons and that is emitted from a nucleus during radioactive decay; it is identical to the nucleus of a helium atom and has a charge of +2

beta particle an electron or positron that is emitted from a nucleus during radioactive decay

gamma ray the high-energy photon emitted by a nucleus during fission and radioactive decay

half-life the time required for half of a sample of a radioactive isotope to break down by radioactive decay to form a daughter isotope

nuclear radiation the particles that are released from the nucleus during radioactive decay, such as neutrons, electrons, and photons

radioactive decay the disintegration of an unstable atomic nucleus into one or more different nuclides, accompanied by the emission of radiation, the nuclear capture or ejection of electrons, or fission

1. Identify Which of the four common types of nuclear radiation can be described as an uncharged particle?

_____

2. Explain Why are gamma rays more dangerous than alpha particles or beta particles?

_____

_____

3. Describe What happens to the mass number and the atomic number of an atom during beta decay?

_____

_____

_____

4. Analyze An archaeologist finds an old piece of wood. The carbon-12 to carbon-14 ratio is 1/16 the ratio measured in a newly fallen tree. Estimate the age of the piece of wood. (Hint: Use the table "Half-Lives of Selected Isotopes" to help you.)

_____

5. Calculate What product is formed in the following alpha decay? Use the periodic table in the back of the book to help you identify the element.

$$^{212}_{86}\text{Rn} \longrightarrow \, ^{A}_{Z}X + \, ^{4}_{2}\text{He}$$

_____

CHAPTER 10 | Nuclear Changes
SECTION
2 **Nuclear Fission and Fusion**

KEY IDEAS

As you read this section, keep these questions in mind:

• What holds the nucleus of an atom together?

• What happens when the nucleus of a heavy atom splits apart?

• What happens when the nucleus of a small atom joins with the nucleus of another small atom?

Who Discovered Nuclear Fission?

In 1939, German scientists Otto Hahn and Fritz Strassman were trying make uranium atoms with heavier nuclei. To do this, they used a device that shot neutrons at a sample of uranium. They hoped that at least a few uranium nuclei would gain one or more neutrons. To their surprise, new elements formed. Instead of uranium isotopes, they detected barium and krypton. They thought they had made a mistake.

Soon after, a scientist named Lise Meitner and her nephew Otto Frisch read the results of the experiments. Meitner realized that Hahn and Strassman had not made a mistake. They had actually split the uranium nuclei into smaller elements. ☑

This nuclear reactor was used in the late 1940s and early 1950s to study controlled nuclear fission.

In the early 1940s, Enrico Fermi and other scientists at the University of Chicago built a stack of graphite and uranium blocks. These materials formed the nuclear reactor that was used to create the first controlled nuclear fission chain reaction. This work launched the Manhattan Project, which led to the creation of nuclear weapons.

READING TOOLBOX

Define As you read, write down any terms in the section that you do not understand. Use the section vocabulary boxes or a dictionary to find the definitions of these terms. Write the definitions in your own words in the text margin.

☑ **READING CHECK**

1. Explain What did Lise Meitner conclude about the work of Hahn and Strassman?

_____

_____

_____

SECTION 2 Nuclear Fission and Fusion *continued*

What Holds a Nucleus Together?

Protons and neutrons are packed tightly in the tiny nucleus of an atom. Recall that some atomic nuclei are unstable and emit nuclear radiation as they decay. The stability of a nucleus depends on the nuclear forces that hold the nucleus together. If like charges repel one another, how can positively charged protons fit together into an atomic nucleus without flying apart?

THE STRONG NUCLEAR FORCE

The *strong nuclear force* holds the neutrons and protons together in a nucleus. This attraction is much stronger than the electric force that causes protons to repel other protons. However, the attraction only happens over a very short distance (3×10^{-15} meters). This is less than the width of three protons. ☑

✔ READING CHECK

2. Compare Compare the relative strengths of the nuclear force and the electric force.

_____

_____

_____

_____

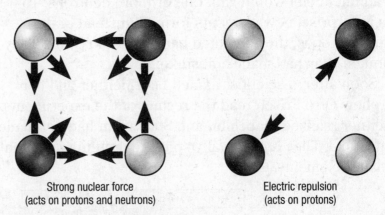

Strong nuclear force
(acts on protons and neutrons)

Electric repulsion
(acts on protons)

The strong nuclear force that holds protons and neutrons together is stronger than the electrical force that pushes protons apart.

THE STRONG NUCLEAR FORCE AND STABILITY

Because neutrons have no charge, they do not attract or repel protons or one another. However, protons repel one another due to the electric force and attract one another due to the nuclear force. In stable nuclei, the attractive forces are stronger than the repulsive forces. Under these conditions, the element does not undergo decay. ☑

✔ READING CHECK

3. Describe What are the relative strengths of attractive and repulsive forces in a stable nucleus?

_____

_____

_____

SECTION 2 Nuclear Fission and Fusion *continued*

What Causes a Nucleus to Decay?

An element decays when the repulsive forces in the nucleus are stronger than the attractive forces. A large number of neutrons in an atom can help hold a nucleus together. However, there is a limit to how many neutrons a nucleus can have. Nuclei with too many or too few neutrons are unstable and undergo decay. ☑

UNSTABLE NUCLEI

Nuclei with more than 83 protons are always unstable, no matter how many neutrons they have. These nuclei always decay and release large amounts of energy and nuclear radiation. Some of the energy is passed to the particles that leave the nucleus. The rest of the energy leaves the nucleus in the form of gamma rays. This radioactive decay helps produce a more stable nucleus. ☑

What Is Nuclear Fission?

The process of splitting atoms with heavy nuclei into atoms with lighter nuclei is called **fission**. When the nucleus splits, both neutrons and energy are released.

In their experiments, Hahn and Strassman used a device that shot at, or *bombarded*, a uranium-235 nucleus with neutrons. One set of products from this type of fission includes two lighter nuclei, barium-140 and krypton-93, and neutrons and energy.

$$^{235}_{92}U + ^{1}_{0}n \longrightarrow ^{140}_{56}Ba + ^{93}_{36}Kr + 3^{1}_{0}n + \text{energy}$$

Notice that the products include three neutrons plus energy. Uranium-235 can also undergo fission to produce different pairs of lighter nuclei. For example, uranium-235 can undergo fission to produce strontium-90, xenon-143, and three neutrons.

How Does Nuclear Fission Produce Energy?

During fission, the nucleus breaks into smaller nuclei. The process releases large amounts of energy. Each dividing nucleus releases about 3.2×10^{-11} joules of energy. In comparison, the chemical reaction of one molecule of the explosive trinitrotoluene (TNT) releases 4.8×10^{-18} joules.

✓ **READING CHECK**

4. Identify Under what conditions does a nucleus decay?

_____

_____

_____

✓ **READING CHECK**

5. Identify What is the maximum number of protons that can be found in a stable nucleus?

_____

LOOKING CLOSER

6. Analyze How many total neutrons are on the left side of the equation? How many total neutrons are found on the right?

_____

Math *Skills*

7. Compare How much more energy is released by a dividing nucleus than by a molecule of TNT?

_____

SECTION 2 Nuclear Fission and Fusion *continued*

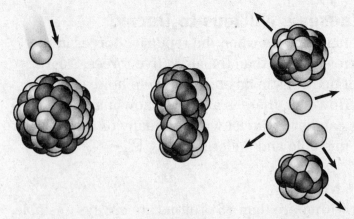

When a uranium-235 nucleus is bombarded by a neutron, the nucleus breaks apart into smaller nuclei. The process releases energy through fast moving neutrons.

In their experiment, Hahn and Strassman recorded the masses of all of the nuclei and particles before and after the reaction. They found the overall mass had decreased after the reaction. Hahn and Strassman also found that the process had released energy. They concluded that the missing mass must have changed into energy. ☑

What Is Mass-Energy Equivalence?

Recall that, according to Newton's laws, no mass or energy can be created or destroyed during physical or chemical changes. The laws of conservation of mass and energy do not apply to nuclear reactions such as fission. During fission, some matter changes to energy.

Albert Einstein explained the equivalence of mass and energy by the special theory of relativity. This *equivalence* means that matter can be converted into energy, and energy can be converted into matter. Equivalence is described by the equation below. ☑

> **Mass-Energy Equation**
> *Energy = mass × (speed of light)²*
> $E = mc^2$

The speed of light, c, equals 3.0×10^8 m/s. If you multiply c^2 by even a very small mass, the energy value is very large. For example, the mass-equivalent energy of 1 kg of matter is 9×10^{16} joules. That is more than the energy of 22 million tons of the explosive TNT.

✔ READING CHECK

8. Explain Why is some mass missing after fission?

_____

_____

_____

✔ READING CHECK

9. Explain What does mass-energy equivalence mean?

_____

_____

_____

_____

SECTION 2 Nuclear Fission and Fusion *continued*

STABILITY OF MATTER

Obviously, the objects around us do not change suddenly into their equivalent energies. The results of that would be disastrous. Under ordinary conditions, matter is very stable.

What Is the Mass Defect?

Suppose you measured the mass of a carbon-14 nucleus, which has six protons and eight neutrons. Suppose you then measured the mass of six individual protons and eight individual neutrons. You would expect the mass of the nucleus to be the same as the total mass of the individual particles. However, you find that the mass of the nucleus is less than the sum of the individual masses. What happened to the missing mass?

Mass of 1 proton = 1.673×10^{-27} kg	Mass of 6 protons =
Mass of 1 neutron = 1.675×10^{-27} kg	Mass of 8 neutrons =
Actual mass of a carbon-14 nucleus = 2.325×10^{-26} kg	Expected mass of a carbon-14 nucleus =

Math Skills

10. Calculate Complete the table to compare the expected and actual values for the mass of a carbon-14 nucleus.

The missing mass is called the *mass defect*. Einstein's theory of special relativity explains: the missing mass changes into energy. When nuclei form, energy is released. Note, however, that the mass defect of a nucleus is very small. ☑

What Is a Nuclear Chain Reaction?

Have you ever watched balls moving on a pool table? When one ball hits another, the collision can cause the second ball to hit another. Some nuclear reactions work the same way. One reaction triggers another reaction.

A nucleus that splits when it is hit by a neutron forms smaller nuclei. The smaller nuclei need fewer neutrons to be held together. Therefore, they release extra neutrons. If one of those neutrons collides with another large nucleus, that nucleus undergoes fission, or splits. A **nuclear chain reaction** is a continuous series of nuclear fission reactions.

READING CHECK

11. Define What is the mass defect?

_____

_____

_____

_____

SECTION 2 Nuclear Fission and Fusion *continued*

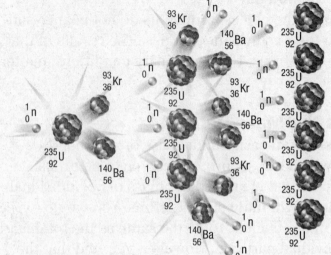

A nuclear chain reaction may be triggered, or started, by a single neutron.

LOOKING CLOSER

12. Predict How many total neutrons will probably be released in the next stage of this chain reaction?

_____

_____

Scientists found that on average, each uranium nucleus that divides produces two or three extra neutrons. Each one of these neutrons could trigger, or start, another fission reaction. The ability to start a nuclear chain reaction depends partly on the number of neutrons released during each fission reaction.

What Is a Controlled Chain Reaction?

Energy produced in a nuclear chain reaction can be used to generate electricity. The diagram describes this process.

Using Nuclear Chain Reactions to Generate Electricity

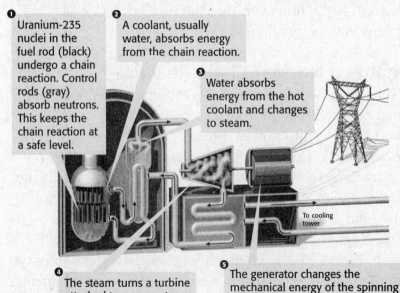

❶ Uranium-235 nuclei in the fuel rod (black) undergo a chain reaction. Control rods (gray) absorb neutrons. This keeps the chain reaction at a safe level.

❷ A coolant, usually water, absorbs energy from the chain reaction.

❸ Water absorbs energy from the hot coolant and changes to steam.

To cooling tower

❹ The steam turns a turbine attached to a generator.

❺ The generator changes the mechanical energy of the spinning turbine into electrical energy.

LOOKING CLOSER

13. Identify What is the function of the control rods?

_____

_____

_____

NUCLEAR WEAPONS

The chain-reaction principle is also used to make a nuclear bomb. In a nuclear bomb, two or more quantities of uranium-235 are packed into a container. The uranium is surrounded by a powerful chemical explosive. When the explosives are detonated, or set off, the uranium is pushed together to exceed the critical mass. The **critical mass** is the smallest amount of a substance that provides enough neutrons to start a nuclear chain reaction. ☑

If the amount of a substance is less than the critical mass, a chain reaction will not continue. Fortunately, the concentration of uranium-235 in nature is too low to start a chain reaction naturally. In nuclear power plants, control rods are used to slow the chain reaction. In a nuclear bomb, reactions are not controlled.

✓ **READING CHECK**

14. Define What is a critical mass?

_____

_____

_____

_____

_____

What Is Nuclear Fusion?

Nuclear fission is not the only nuclear process that can produce energy. Energy can also be produced when light atomic nuclei join, or *fuse*, to form heavier nuclei. This process is called **fusion**. ☑

In the sun and other stars, huge amounts of energy are produced when hydrogen nuclei fuse. However, a large amount of energy is needed to start a fusion reaction. Energy is needed to push nuclei close enough so that the strong nuclear force can overcome the repulsive electrical force. In stars, extremely high temperatures provide the energy to bring hydrogen nuclei together.

✓ **READING CHECK**

15. Describe What happens during nuclear fusion?

_____

_____

_____

$$^1_1H + ^1_1H \rightarrow ^2_1H + \text{other particles}$$

$$^2_1H + ^1_1H \rightarrow ^3_2He + ^0_0\gamma$$

$$^3_2He + ^3_2He \rightarrow ^4_2He + ^1_1H + ^1_1H$$

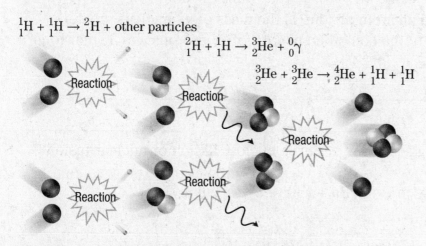

The process of nuclear fusion releases large amounts of energy.

Section 2 Review

SECTION VOCABULARY

critical mass the minimum mass of a fissionable isotope that provides the number of neutrons needed to sustain a chain reaction	**fusion** the process in which light nuclei combine at extremely high temperatures, forming heavier nuclei and releasing energy
fission the process by which a nucleus splits into two or more fragments and releases neutrons and energy	**nuclear chain reaction** a continuous series of nuclear fission reactions

1. Summarize Complete the process chart to describe how nuclear fission is used to produce electricity.

```
┌────────────────────────────────────────────────────────────────┐
│                                                                  │
│                                                                  │
└────────────────────────────────────────────────────────────────┘
                                │
                                ▼
┌────────────────────────────────────────────────────────────────┐
│         A coolant absorbs energy from the chain reaction.        │
│                                                                  │
└────────────────────────────────────────────────────────────────┘
                                │
                                ▼
┌────────────────────────────────────────────────────────────────┐
│                                                                  │
│                                                                  │
└────────────────────────────────────────────────────────────────┘
                                │
                                ▼
┌────────────────────────────────────────────────────────────────┐
│                                                                  │
│                                                                  │
└────────────────────────────────────────────────────────────────┘
                                │
                                ▼
┌────────────────────────────────────────────────────────────────┐
│ A generator changes the mechanical energy of the spinning turbine into electrical energy. │
└────────────────────────────────────────────────────────────────┘
```

2. Predict Suppose you had an atom of $^{56}_{26}\text{Fe}$. Is the mass of its nucleus greater than, less than, or equal to the combined masses of 26 protons and 30 neutrons? Explain your answer.

_____

_____

3. Identify Do the following equations describe nuclear fission or nuclear fusion? Explain your answers.

$$^{235}_{92}\text{U} + {}^{1}_{0}\text{n} \longrightarrow {}^{140}_{56}\text{Ba} + {}^{93}_{36}\text{Kr} + 3{}^{1}_{0}\text{n} + \text{energy}$$

_____

$$^{208}_{82}\text{Pb} + {}^{58}_{26}\text{Fe} \longrightarrow {}^{265}_{108}\text{Hs} + {}^{1}_{0}\text{n}$$

_____

CHAPTER 10 | Nuclear Changes

SECTION 3 · Nuclear Radiation Today

KEY IDEAS

As you read this section, keep these questions in mind:

• Where are some common sources of radiation?

• What are some beneficial uses of nuclear radiation?

• What factors determine the risks of nuclear radiation?

• How is the energy produced by nuclear fission used?

Is All Radiation Harmful?

You may be surprised to learn that you are exposed to some form of nuclear radiation every day. Some forms of nuclear radiation are beneficial. Others may be harmful. As you read this section, you will learn about some benefits and risks of nuclear radiation.

Where Is Radiation?

Nuclear radiation is all around you. Every day, we are exposed to radiation from natural sources, such as the sun, soil, and rocks. Nuclear radiation that comes from natural sources is known as **background radiation**. About 80% of all radiation we are exposed to comes from natural sources. The living tissues of most organisms are adapted to survive the low levels of natural nuclear radiation. ☑

About 20% of our exposure to nuclear radiation comes from human-made sources. These sources include smoke detectors and X rays.

READING TOOLBOX

Outline As you read this section, make an outline to summarize the main points. Use the headers throughout the section to help you organize your outline.

☑ **READING CHECK**

1. Define What is background radiation?

_____

_____

_____

LOOKING CLOSER

2. Identify Give two sources of background radiation that you can see in this picture.

_____

_____

MEASURING RADIATION

Levels of radiation absorbed by the human body are measured in **rems** or millirems (1 rem = 1,000 millirems). An X ray at the dentist's office exposes a patient to about 1 millirem of radiation. ☑

In the United States, many people work in jobs that involve nuclear radiation. These include nuclear engineers, medical technicians, and some scientists. A safe limit for such workers has been set at 5,000 millirems per year. This level does not include exposure to natural background radiation.

EXPOSURE BY LOCATION

People in the United States receive different amounts of natural radiation. People who live at higher elevations are exposed to more nuclear radiation than those who live at lower elevations. Those who live in areas with many rocks are exposed to more nuclear radiation than those in areas with few rocks.

Talk About It

Research In a small group, choose one of the cities listed in the table. Compare the level of radiation exposure for that city with others in the table. Is the level higher or lower? Research the geography and climate of this city. What factors may cause this city to have a higher or lower level of radiation exposure than other cities? Present your findings and ideas to the class.

Radiation Exposure per Location

Location	Radiation exposure (millirems/year)	Location	Radiation exposure (millirems/year)
Tampa, FL	63.7	Portland, OR	86.7
Richmond, VA	64.1	Rochester, NY	88.1
Las Vegas, NV	69.5	Wheeling, WV	111.9
Los Angeles, CA	73.6	Denver, CO	164.6

Some activities increase a person's exposure to nuclear radiation. Some of these activities are shown in the table below.

Radiation Exposure per Activity

Activity	Radiation exposure (millirems/year)
Smoking 1 1/2 packs of cigarettes per day	8,000
Flying for 720 hours (airline crew)	267
Inhaling radon from the environment	360
Giving or receiving medical X rays	100

What Are Some Beneficial Uses of Nuclear Radiation?

Radioactive substances are used in many different ways. Some uses of nuclear radiation include medical diagnosis and treatment, smoke detectors, manufacturing, and agriculture.

Small radioactive sources in smoke detectors release alpha particles. The charged alpha particles produce an electric current. When there is a fire, smoke particles reduce the flow of electric current. This drop in current sets off the alarm.

LOOKING CLOSER
4. Identify What type of radiation is used in a smoke detector?

_____

_____

TREATING CANCER

Doctors can treat some cancers with controlled doses of nuclear radiation. This is known as *radiotherapy*. For example, some brain tumors can be treated with small beams of gamma rays. Thyroid cancer can be treated with an iodine isotope. Leukemia treatments also use radiotherapy. Large doses of nuclear radiation are used to kill defective bone marrow in leukemia patients. Then the patient can receive healthy bone marrow from a donor.

DETECTING DISEASE

Nuclear radiation is used in much of the medical equipment that doctors use to detect disease. For example, CT scans show bones and dense tissue. PET scans use radioactive tracers to show how organs function. **Radioactive tracers** are radioactive isotopes with short half-lives that are added to a substance. Doctors can use tracers in the human body to locate tumors.

Critical Thinking
5. Infer Why do you think the beams of gamma rays used to treat brain tumors must be focused carefully?

_____

_____

_____

_____

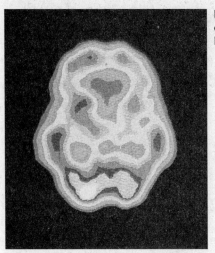

Doctors can use PET scans to detect disease. However, scientists can also use PET scans to study how the brain works.

LOOKING CLOSER

6. Identify What are two uses for PET scans?

_____

_____

AGRICULTURAL RESEARCH

Scientists also use radioactive tracers in agricultural research. For example, scientists can add radioactive tracers to flowing water and study where and when the tracers reappear. This can tell them how fast water moves through soil or through the stems and leaves of crops.

What Are Some Risks of Nuclear Radiation?

Nuclear radiation has many benefits, but there are also risks. For example, nuclear radiation can be harmful to living tissue. Nuclear radiation can change the number of electrons in the molecules of living materials. This process is known as *ionization*. Ionized molecules may form substances that are harmful to life. ☑

The risk of damage from nuclear radiation depends on two main factors: the type of radiation and the amount of radiation exposure.

✓ **READING CHECK**

7. Identify How is nuclear radiation harmful to living things?

_____

_____

_____

_____

EFFECT OF RADIATION TYPE

Recall that different types of nuclear radiation can pass through different materials. For example, a layer of clothing or one inch of air is enough to stop alpha particles. However, beta particles are lighter and faster than alpha particles. Beta particles can pass through several feet of air or thin samples of solids and liquids. Several feet of material may be needed to protect people from high-energy gamma rays.

Name _____ Class _____ Date _____

SECTION 3 Nuclear Radiation Today *continued*

EFFECT OF EXPOSURE AMOUNT

Low levels of nuclear radiation may not have a large effect on living cells. However, studies have shown that a link between cancer and exposure to high levels of nuclear radiation.

RADIATION SICKNESS

Exposure to high levels of nuclear radiation can cause *radiation sickness*. This sickness may be caused by a single large exposure, such as a nuclear explosion. Radiation sickness may also be caused by many exposures to high levels of nuclear radiation over time. People who work with nuclear radiation wear dosimeters. A *dosimeter* is a device that measures the amount of nuclear radiation exposure. ☑

A dosimeter contains a piece of film that detects radiation in the environment.

✔ **READING CHECK**

8. Identify What is the function of a dosimeter?

_____

RADON GAS

Radon is produced by the decay of uranium-238, an isotope found in soil and rock. Radon gas emits alpha particles and gamma rays. Studies have shown that people who have been exposed to radon gas have a greater risk of developing lung cancer. The risk is even higher for people who smoke. ☑

Some areas have higher radon levels than others do. Tests for radon gas in homes and office buildings are widely available. Installing vents that draw air out of a building can help reduce high levels of radon. Sealing cracks in building foundations can also help reduce radon levels.

✔ **READING CHECK**

9. Describe How does smoking change the risk of cancer for a person exposed to radon gas?

_____

How Can We Use Nuclear Power?

Dozens of countries use nuclear reactors, such as the one in the figure below, to generate electricity. Energy produced from nuclear fission is used to provide electrical energy to millions of homes and businesses.

Nuclear reactors are used in many parts of the world to generate electricity.

ADVANTAGES OF NUCLEAR FISSION

There are many advantages to using nuclear fission as a source of energy.

- Nuclear fission does not produce gases that pollute the air.
- There is more energy in known uranium reserves than in known gas and oil reserves. ☑

DISADVANTAGES OF NUCLEAR FISSION

There are also disadvantages to using nuclear fission as a source of energy.

- Radioactive products of fissions may escape into the environment and spread nuclear radiation.
- Nuclear reactors need many safety features. Thus, nuclear power plants are expensive to build. ☑

READING CHECK

10. Describe How does the energy in uranium reserves compare to those of coal and oil?

_____

_____

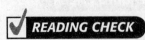

READING CHECK

11. Identify What is one reason nuclear power plants are expensive to build?

_____

_____

SECTION 3 Nuclear Radiation Today *continued*

STORING NUCLEAR WASTES

Nuclear wastes, such as the fuel rods that were used in the reactor, cannot simply be thrown away. Radioactive wastes must be stored safely for thousands of years until they have decayed to less harmful elements. Storage facilities must be well shielded so that nuclear radiation does not leak out and harm living things. ☑

An ideal place for storing nuclear wastes would have few people. It would also have little surface water, such as ponds, rivers, or groundwater. The area must also be free from earthquakes.

READING CHECK

12. Explain Why must radioactive wastes be stored safely for thousands of years?

_____

_____

_____

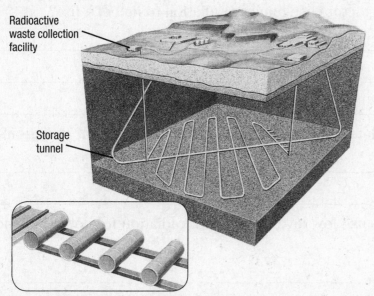

Radioactive waste collection facility

Storage tunnel

Storage facilities for nuclear wastes must be able to contain radioactive materials safely for thousands of years.

Critical Thinking

13. Analyze Why do you think an ideal place to store nuclear waste would be an area without earthquakes?

_____

_____

_____

_____

NUCLEAR FUSION

Recall that energy in stars, such as our sun, is produced by fusion. Scientists are looking for ways to use fusion as an energy source here on Earth.

Nuclear fusion releases very large amounts of energy, and the reaction releases very little waste or pollution. However, a large amount of energy is needed to start a fusion reaction. Thus, nuclear fusion reactions are difficult to produce in a laboratory. With current technology, the use of fusion as an energy source is not practical. ☑

READING CHECK

14. Explain Why are nuclear fusion reactions difficult to produce in a laboratory?

_____

_____

_____

Section 3 Review

SECTION VOCABULARY

background radiation the nuclear radiation that arises naturally from cosmic rays and from radioactive isotopes in the soil and air **radioactive tracers** a radioactive material that is added to a substance so that its distribution can be detected later	**rems** the quantity of ionizing radiation that does as much damage to human tissue as 1 roentgen of high-voltage X rays does

1. Identify List three activities that add to an individual's exposure to radiation.

_____

_____

2. Describe How do smoke detectors use nuclear radiation to detect a fire?

_____

_____

3. Identify What two factors determine the risk of damage from nuclear radiation?

_____

_____

4. Infer Why is it important to use low levels of nuclear radiation for detection and treatment of diseases?

_____

_____

5. Describe What are two ways to reduce the levels of radon gas in a building?

_____

_____

6. Identify What are two advantages and two disadvantages of using nuclear fission to generate electricity?

_____

_____

_____

_____

CHAPTER 11 | Motion
SECTION 1 | Measuring Motion

As you read this section, keep these questions in mind:
• What is motion?
• What is the difference between velocity and speed?
• How can you use graphs to show the motion of an object?

What Is Motion?

Objects move in many ways. Cars travel in straight lines along busy roads. Satellites travel in circles around Earth. Motion is so common that it probably seems very simple. However, in science, we must be careful to define motion precisely.

Imagine sitting in a moving car with your eyes closed. If you could not see the road moving by the car, it would be hard to tell the car was moving. Motion must be defined relative to other objects. The objects used to define motion are called a **frame of reference**. In physics, any object can be a frame of reference. The objects that make up the frame of reference are treated as if they are not moving. ☑

In science, **motion** is the change in position of an object relative to a frame of reference. In the image shown below, trees provide a frame of reference for the motion of the snowboarder.

In this multiple-exposure photograph, the trees and ski jump provide a frame of reference for the motion of the snowboarder. You can tell the snowboarder is moving because his position relative to the trees is changing.

When we describe motion, we are often interested in how far an object has moved. Scientists describe how far an object has moved using two terms: distance and displacement.

READING TOOLBOX

Summarize As you read, underline the main ideas in each paragraph. When you finish reading, write a summary of the section using the underlined ideas.

✓ READING CHECK

1. Define What is a frame of reference?

_____

_____

LOOKING CLOSER

2. Infer Give another example of a frame of reference for the motion of the snowboarder.

_____

_____

DISTANCE AND DISPLACEMENT

You are probably familiar with what distance means. *Distance* is how far an object moves. If you run one lap around a soccer field, you have run a distance of about 350 m. In contrast, **displacement** is a measure of how far the starting point is from the ending point. If you run seven laps around a soccer field and end up exactly where you started, your displacement is 0 m. In many cases, displacement is shorter than distance.

LOOKING CLOSER
3. Identify Which is longer, the runner's distance traveled or displacement?

_____

_____

When you describe distance and displacement, you need to give both a length and a direction. You can describe the direction of displacement using cardinal directions, such as north, south, east, or west. You can also describe direction relative to a reference point. For example, in the figure above, the direction of the student's displacement could be described as "away from the goal."

How Are Speed and Velocity Different?

Critical Thinking
4. Apply Concepts A scientist records the motion of an object in a notebook. She writes down that the object moved 10 m in 3 s. Did the scientist record a speed or a velocity? Explain your answer.

_____

_____

_____

_____

_____

In everyday language, we often use the words *speed* and *velocity* as if they mean the same thing. However, in science, speed is different from velocity.

You know from experience that some objects travel faster than others. A running horse travels faster than a jogger. A race car travels faster than a running horse. **Speed** describes how far an object travels in a certain amount of time. In other words, it describes how fast an object moves.

In contrast, **velocity** describes both how fast an object is moving and in what direction it is moving. As when you describe displacement, you can describe the direction of motion using words such as *up, down, left,* and *right.*

SECTION 1 Measuring Motion *continued*

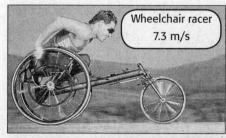

Wheelchair racer
7.3 m/s

Galloping horse
19 m/s

Speeding race car
96 m/s

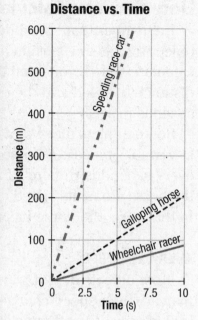

Distance vs. Time

Objects can move at many different speeds. The faster the object is moving, the steeper the slope of its line on a graph of distance versus time.

LOOKING CLOSER

5. Apply Concepts Could you determine the velocities of these objects from the information in the graph? Explain your answer.

_____

_____

_____

_____

ADDING VELOCITIES

Imagine a person sitting on a bus. The bus is traveling east at 15 m/s relative to the street. The person gets up and walks toward the back of the bus at 1 m/s. How can you determine the person's velocity relative to the street? Before the person starts walking, her velocity is the same as the bus—15 m/s east relative to the street. However, when she is walking toward the back of the bus, her velocity decreases.

You can use positive and negative numbers to figure out the person's velocity when she is walking on the bus. First, you have to define which direction is "positive" motion. In this case, you can define "positive" motion as motion eastward. Therefore, the bus and everyone on it has a velocity of +15 m/s.

The person walking toward the back of the bus is moving in the opposite direction from the bus. Therefore, she has a "negative" velocity. Her velocity is −1 m/s. To determine her total velocity, add the two velocities together. Her total velocity is (+15 m/s) + (−1 m/s) = +14 m/s. Since we have defined "positive" motion as motion eastward, the person is moving 14 m/s east.

Critical Thinking

6. Predict Consequences Suppose you defined "positive" motion as motion westward. What would be the person's total velocity?

_____

SECTION 1 Measuring Motion *continued*

How Can You Calculate Speed?

Remember that speed describes the distance an object travels in a certain amount of time. Therefore, to calculate speed, you need to measure two quantities: the distance traveled and the time it took. The SI unit for speed is m/s. ☑

Some objects move at a constant speed. Others move at variable speeds. A horse that runs a distance of 19 m every second is running at a constant speed of 19 m/s. If the horse stops, its speed changes from 19 m/s to 0 m/s. In that case, the horse has a variable speed.

AVERAGE SPEED

Most objects do not travel at one constant speed. Instead, their speed changes from one instant to another. In this case, it is often useful to describe the average speed of the object. *Average speed* is the total distance traveled divided by the total time it took to travel that distance. The equation below describes this relationship:

$$speed = \frac{distance}{time}$$

$$v = \frac{d}{t}$$

Let's look at an example. A sledder moves 132 m down a hill in 18 s. What is the average speed of the sledder?

Step 1: List the given and unknown values.	**Given:** distance, $d = 132$ m time, $t = 18$ s	**Unknown:** average speed, v
Step 2: Write the equation.	$v = \dfrac{d}{t}$	
Step 3: Insert the known values and solve for the unknown value.	$v = \dfrac{132 \text{ m}}{18 \text{ s}}$ $v = 7.3$ m/s	

So, the sledder has an average speed of 7.3 m/s. The sledder's speed may have changed many times as he moved down the hill. At some points, he may have been traveling faster than 7.3 m/s. At other points, he may have been moving more slowly.

✓ READING CHECK

7. Identify What two quantities do you need to know to calculate speed?

_____

_____

Critical Thinking

8. Infer It is often easier to calculate the average speed of an object than to calculate its speed at each point along its path. What do you think is the reason for this?

_____

_____

_____

_____

_____

_____

_____

SECTION 1 Measuring Motion *continued*

INSTANTANEOUS SPEED

The *instantaneous speed* of an object is its speed at a given *instant*, or point in time. Because we cannot divide by zero, we cannot use the equation for speed to calculate instantaneous speed. However, tools like the speedometers in cars can measure instantaneous speed. If an object is moving at a constant speed, its instantaneous speed is equal to its constant speed. ☑

How Can You Calculate Velocity?

Remember that velocity is the speed of an object in a particular direction. To calculate the velocity of an object, you must first find the speed of the object. Then, you must indicate the direction of the object. Let's look at an example.

For several days in 1936, Alaska's Black Rapids glacier moved at 89 m per day down the valley. What is the velocity of the glacier in meters per second?

Step 1: List the given and unknown values.	Given: $d = 89$ m $t = 1$ day direction = down the valley	Unknown: velocity, v
Step 2: Perform conversions, and write the equation.	$1 \text{ day} \times \dfrac{24 \text{ h}}{1 \text{ day}} \times \dfrac{60 \text{ min}}{1 \text{ h}} \times \dfrac{60 \text{ s}}{1 \text{ min}} = 86{,}400 \text{ s}$ $v = \dfrac{d}{t}$	
Step 3: Insert the known values and solve for the unknown value.	$v = \dfrac{89 \text{ m}}{86{,}400 \text{ s}}$ $v = 0.0010$ m/s down the valley	

So, the glacier moved at a velocity of 0.0010 m/s down the valley. Notice that the symbol for velocity, v, is the same as the symbol for speed. You can use the speed equation to calculate velocity. Just remember to include a direction when you describe an object's velocity.

How Can You Show Motion on a Graph?

You can show motion on a graph by recording distance on the vertical axis and time on the horizontal axis. Then, you can use the shape of the line on the graph to learn about the motion of an object.

READING CHECK

9. Explain Why can't you use the speed equation to calculate instantaneous speed?

_____

_____

Math *Skills*

10. Calculate A swimmer swims 110 m toward the shore in 72 s. What is the swimmer's velocity in meters per second? Show your work.

SECTION 1 Measuring Motion *continued*

CALCULATING SPEED FROM A GRAPH

On a graph of distance versus time, the motion of an object moving at a constant speed is a straight line. The slope of the line is equal to the speed of the object. You can calculate the *slope* of the line by dividing the vertical change of the line by its horizontal change. The equation below describes this relationship: ☑

$$slope = \frac{vertical\ change}{horizontal\ change}$$

If you show distance on the vertical axis and time on the horizontal axis, the slope of the line is:

$$slope = \frac{change\ in\ distance}{change\ in\ time}$$

Remember that speed equals distance divided by time. Therefore, the slope of a line on a graph of distance versus time is the speed of the object. For example, you can determine the speed of the object in the plot below.

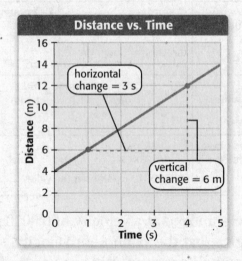

Distance vs. Time

✓ READING CHECK

11. Describe On a graph of distance versus time, what does the motion of an object moving at a constant speed look like?

_____

Graphing Skills

12. Identify What is the independent variable in the graph in the figure?

_____

Critical Thinking

13. Apply Concepts
Suppose you chose two different points on the line to calculate slope. Would you get the same result for slope? Explain your answer.

_____
_____
_____
_____
_____
_____

Step 1: Choose two points to use to calculate the slope.	**Point 1:** time, $t = 1$ s distance, $d = 6$ m	**Point 2:** time, $t = 4$ s distance, $d = 12$ m
Step 2: Calculate the vertical change and the horizontal change.	*vertical change* = 12 m − 6 m = 6 m *horizontal change* = 4 s − 1 s = 3 s	
Step 3: Divide the vertical change by the horizontal change.	$slope = \frac{vertical\ change}{horizontal\ change} = \frac{6\ m}{3\ s} = 2$ m/s	

So, the slope of the line—and the speed of the object—is 2 m/s.

SECTION 1 Measuring Motion *continued*

INTERPRETING SLOPE

Remember that the speed of an object is equal to the slope of the line describing its motion. The steeper the slope of the line, the faster the object is moving. For example, the graphs below show the motion of two cars traveling at different constant speeds.

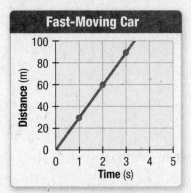

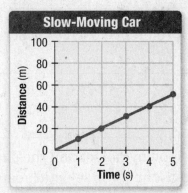

The slopes of the lines on these graphs indicate the speeds of the cars. The graph of the motion of a fast-moving car has a steeper slope than that of a slow-moving car. The fact that these graphs are straight lines indicates that the cars are moving at constant speeds.

On a graph of distance versus time, the motion of an object moving at a variable speed is a curved line. For example, the graph below shows distance versus time for a car that is speeding up.

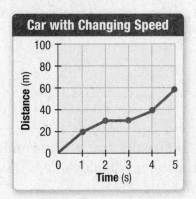

The graph of this car's motion is not a straight line. Therefore, the car is not moving at a constant speed.

Even if an object's speed is changing, you can use a graph of its motion to find its average speed. Remember that average speed equals total distance traveled divided by total time. You can find both total distance and total time from the graph. Then, divide distance by time to calculate average speed.

LOOKING CLOSER

14. Identify How can you tell that the cars are moving at constant speeds based on the information in the graphs?

_____

_____

Graphing *Skills*

15. Apply Concepts What is the car's average speed between 0 s and 5 s? Show your work.

Section 1 Review

SECTION VOCABULARY

displacement the change in position of an object	**speed** the distance traveled divided by the time interval during which the motion occurred
frame of reference a system for specifying the precise location of objects in space and time	**velocity** the speed of an object in a particular direction
motion an object's change in position relative to a reference point	

1. Describe How is a frame of reference used to describe motion?

_____

_____

_____

2. Interpret Label the fastest moving object and the slowest moving object in the plot below. Explain your reasoning for selecting each line.

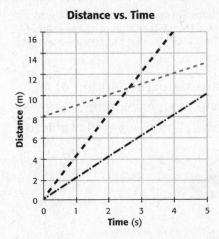

Distance vs. Time

_____

_____

3. Apply Concepts A runner runs a 1,500 m race on a circular track. The runner stops 100 m from the starting point. What are the distance and displacement traveled by the runner?

_____

_____

4. Calculate Scientists tracking a flock of ducks found that, on average, the ducks flew 740 km south in 12 h. What were the speed and velocity of the flock of ducks in meters per second? Show your work.

SECTION 2 Acceleration

KEY IDEAS

As you read this section, keep these questions in mind:

• What two things may change when an object accelerates?

• How can you calculate constant acceleration?

• How can graphs show acceleration?

How Is Acceleration Related to Velocity?

Acceleration occurs when an object changes velocity. Remember that velocity has both a speed and a direction. Therefore, acceleration also has two components: a magnitude and a direction. When the speed or the direction of an object changes, the object is accelerating.

ACCELERATION AND SPEED

An object that changes speed is accelerating. An accelerating object may speed up or slow down. An object that is speeding up has a positive acceleration. An object that is slowing down has a negative acceleration. ☑

Suppose a cyclist starts peddling south and speeds up down the road. Every second, the velocity of the cyclist increases by 1 m/s. After 1 s, the cyclist's velocity is 1 m/s south. After 2 s, the cyclist's velocity is 2 m/s south. After 5 s, the cyclist's velocity is 5 m/s south.

You can describe the cyclist's acceleration by saying that his velocity is increasing by one meter per second per second (1 m/s/s or 1 m/s^2). In this case, the cyclist is speeding up. Therefore, his acceleration is +1 m/s^2 south.

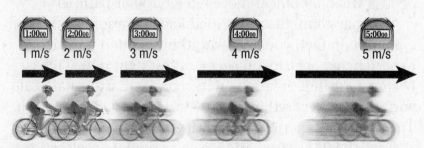

This cyclist's speed increases by 1 m/s every second. Therefore, his acceleration is 1 m/s/s, or 1 m/s^2.

READING TOOLBOX

Define As you read this section, underline any words you don't know. When you learn what they mean, write the words and their definitions in your notebook.

☑ READING CHECK

1. Describe A car slows down as it comes up to a stop sign. Is its acceleration positive or negative?

_____

_____

LOOKING CLOSER

2. Identify Relationships What happens to the cyclist's speed as time increases?

_____

_____

SECTION 2 Acceleration *continued*

Talk About It
Brainstorm Make a list of 10 examples of acceleration. With a partner or in a small group, identify how velocity is changing in each example.

ACCELERATION AND DIRECTION
An object that changes direction is accelerating, even if its speed is constant. For example, the skaters in the figure below are moving at a nearly constant speed. However, they must change direction to stay on the track. As they go around the curves in the track, they accelerate.

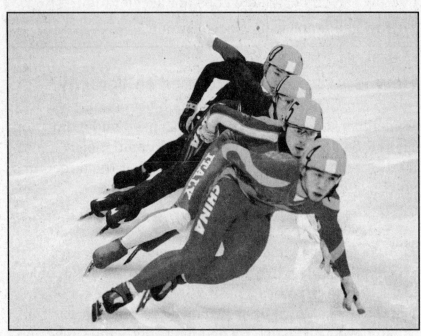

As these skaters change direction, they accelerate, even if their speed doesn't change.

LOOKING CLOSER
3. Identify Give two ways the skaters may be accelerating.

_____

_____

CENTRIPETAL ACCELERATION
Imagine moving at a constant speed in a circle. At each point in the circle, your direction is changing. Therefore, you are constantly accelerating, even though your speed does not change. You are experiencing centripetal acceleration. *Centripetal acceleration* is the acceleration that occurs when an object moves in a circular path. ☑

You may think that centripetal acceleration is not very common. In fact, you and everything around you are experiencing centripetal acceleration right now. This is because Earth is rotating on its axis. As Earth rotates, its surface—and everything on it—travels in a circular path. Therefore, it experiences centripetal acceleration.

Earth itself also experiences centripetal acceleration as it orbits the sun. Our moon is constantly accelerating as it orbits Earth. In fact, every object that orbits another object is experiencing centripetal acceleration.

✓ **READING CHECK**

4. Explain How can an object moving in a circular path be accelerating if its speed does not change?

_____

_____

_____

SECTION 2 Acceleration *continued*

How Can You Calculate Acceleration?

For an object moving in a straight line, acceleration occurs only because of changes in speed. Therefore, you can calculate the object's acceleration if you know its speed at two different times. You can use the equation below to calculate acceleration:

$$acceleration = \frac{final\ speed - initial\ speed}{time}$$

$$a = \frac{\Delta v}{t}$$

In this equation, the symbol "delta" (Δ) means "change in." You calculate acceleration by dividing the change in speed by the time in which the change occurred.

If the acceleration is small, the velocity is changing slowly. For example, a person can accelerate at about 2 m/s². If the acceleration is large, the velocity is changing more quickly. A sports car can accelerate at about 7.2 m/s².

CALCULATING ACCELERATION FROM VELOCITY

Let's look at an example. A cyclist slows along a straight line from 5.5 m/s to 1.0 m/s in 3.0 s. What is the average acceleration of the cyclist?

Step 1: List the given and unknown values.	**Given:** initial speed, $v_i = 5.5$ m/s final speed, $v_f = 1.0$ m/s time, $t = 3.0$ s	**Unknown:** acceleration, a
Step 2: Write the equation.	$a = \frac{\Delta v}{t} = \frac{v_f - v_i}{t}$	
Step 3: Insert the known values and solve for the unknown value.	$a = \frac{1.0\ m/s - 5.5\ m/s}{3.0\ s}$ $a = \frac{-4.5\ m/s}{3.0\ s}$ $a = -1.5$ m/s²	

So, the cyclist accelerated at –1.5 m/s². The acceleration was negative because the cyclist was slowing down. Her initial, or starting, speed was higher than her final speed.

Critical Thinking

5. Infer Can you use the equation to the left to calculate centripetal acceleration? Explain your answer.

_____
_____
_____
_____
_____
_____
_____
_____

Math *Skills*

6. Calculate A turtle swimming in a straight line toward shore has a speed of 0.50 m/s. After 4.0 s, its speed is 0.80 m/s. What is its average acceleration? Show your work.

How Can You Graph Accelerated Motion?

Remember that you can determine the speed of an object by examining a graph of distance versus time. Similarly, you can determine an object's acceleration by examining a graph of speed versus time.

A straight line on a graph of speed versus time indicates a constant acceleration. *Constant acceleration* is acceleration that does not change with time. The slope of a straight line on a graph of speed versus time is equal to an object's acceleration. A line with a positive slope indicates that the object is speeding up. A line with a negative slope indicates that the object is slowing down. Let's look at an example of how to graph accelerated motion. ☑

Imagine a bus traveling on a straight road at 20 m/s. For the first 20 s, the bus slows to a stop at a constant rate. The bus stays stopped for 20 s. For the next 10 s, the bus accelerates at 1.5 m/s². For the last 10 s, the bus continues at a constant speed. Graph the speed of the bus versus time from 0 s to 60 s. What is the bus's acceleration from 0 s to 20 s? What is its final speed?

Step 1: Determine the x-axis and y-axis of the graph. Here, the x-axis is time (t) in seconds and the y-axis is speed (v) in meters per second.

Step 2: Starting from the origin, graph each part of the motion. (The graph is shown at the top of the next page.)

A. The bus began at $t = 0$ s and $v = 20$ m/s. It slowed with a constant acceleration to $t = 20$ s and $v = 0$ m/s. Draw a straight line connecting these two points.

B. From 20 s to 40 s, the bus's speed was 0 m/s. Draw a horizontal line at $v = 0$ m/s from $t = 20$ s to $t = 40$ s.

C. From 40 s to 50 s, the bus accelerated at 1.5 m/s². Draw a line from $t = 40$ s and $v = 0$ m/s with a slope of 1.5 m/s². End the line at $t = 50$ s.

D. From 50 s to 60 s, the bus's speed was constant. Draw a horizontal line from $t = 50$ s to $t = 60$ s at $v = 15$ m/s.

Step 3: Read the graph to determine the bus's acceleration and final speed. The acceleration between 0 s and 20 s is equal to the slope of the line between these two points. Therefore, the acceleration was −1 m/s². From the graph, you know that the bus was traveling 15 m/s at $t = 50$ s. Therefore, the bus's final speed was 15 m/s.

READING CHECK

7. Define What is constant acceleration?

_____

_____

Graphing *Skills*

8. Explain Why should you use a horizontal line to indicate where the bus is not accelerating?

_____

_____

_____

_____

_____

SECTION 2 Acceleration *continued*

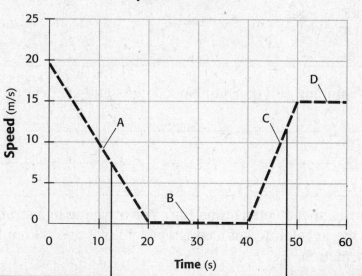

Speed vs. Time

The slope of this part of the graph is -1 m/s². Therefore, the bus's acceleration during this time period was -1 m/s². Because the bus's acceleration was constant, this part of the graph is a straight line.

From 40 s to 50 s, the bus accelerated at 1.5 m/s². Therefore, its speed increased by $(1.5 \text{ m/s}^2) \times (10 \text{ s}) = 15$ m/s. Since its starting speed was 0 m/s, its final speed was 15 m/s.

Graphing *Skills*

9. Apply Concepts
Suppose the bus accelerated at 1.0 m/s² from 40 s to 50 s. Draw a line showing this acceleration.

10. Calculate What would be the bus's speed at 50 s if the bus accelerated at 1.0 m/s² from 40 s to 50 s?

DETERMINING ACCELERATION FROM DISTANCE VERSUS TIME GRAPHS

You've just seen that you can determine whether an object is accelerating by examining a graph of speed versus time. You can also identify acceleration by examining a graph of distance versus time. On a graph of distance versus time, a curved line indicates acceleration. For example, compare the two graphs in the figure below. They show the motion of a bicyclist in a race.

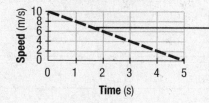

Speed vs. Time

On a speed versus time graph, the bicyclist's motion is a straight line with a negative slope. Therefore, the bicyclist was slowing down with a constant acceleration.

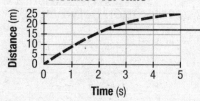

Distance vs. Time

On a distance versus time graph, the bicyclist's motion is a curved line. The curve of the line indicates that the bicyclist was accelerating.

LOOKING CLOSER

11. Explain Is the bicyclist speeding up or slowing down? Explain your answer.

_____

_____

_____

Section 2 Review

SECTION VOCABULARY

acceleration the rate at which velocity changes over time; an object accelerates if its speed, direction, or both change	

1. Explain Why is a fan blade spinning at a constant speed constantly accelerating?

_____

_____

_____

2. Graph The graph below shows speed versus time for a car traveling in a straight line. From 40 s to 50 s, the car accelerated at a constant rate of 1 m/s². Complete the graph to show this information.

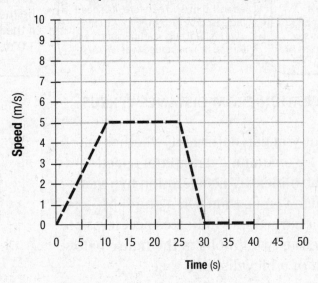

Speed vs. Time for a Moving Car

3. Interpret Based on the graph above, what is the car's acceleration between 25 s and 30 s? Explain your answer.

_____

_____

_____

4. Calculate Based on the graph above, what is the car's acceleration between 10 s and 25 s? Explain your answer.

_____

_____

_____

Name _____ Class _____ Date _____

Motion and Force

KEY IDEAS

As you read this section, keep these questions in mind:
- What are the four fundamental forces in nature?
- How can forces affect the motion of an object?
- Why is friction sometime necessary?

What Are the Fundamental Forces?

You often hear the word force used in everyday conversation. For example, "Our basketball team is an awesome force!" What exactly is force? In science, **force** means any action that can affect the motion of an object. Like velocity and acceleration, force has both *magnitude*, or size, and direction.

There are four *fundamental forces* in nature. The four fundamental forces are gravity, the electromagnetic force, the strong nuclear force, and the weak nuclear force.

What Are the Properties of the Fundamental Forces?

Each of the four fundamental forces is similar in that they act to change the motions of objects. However, they each have different properties, and each works in a different way. ☑

The strong and weak nuclear forces act over only short distances. These are the forces that hold atoms together. The strong and weak nuclear forces are important, but you do not experience them directly in your everyday life.

The force of gravity and electromagnetic forces are forces you feel every day. Gravity acts over long distances and pulls objects toward each other. Electromagnetic forces produce friction, magnetism, and static electricity.

READING TOOLBOX

Compare As you read this section, make a chart comparing the four fundamental forces. Include in your chart the relative strength of each and the effects of each.

✓ READING CHECK

1. Compare How are the four fundamental forces similar?

_____

_____

_____

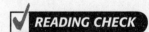
Earth

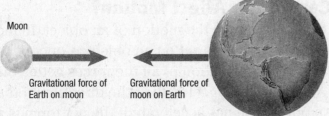

Moon

Gravitational force of Earth on moon | Gravitational force of moon on Earth

LOOKING CLOSER

2. Identify Which fundamental force acts between Earth and the moon?

_____

SECTION 3 Motion and Force *continued*

FORCES OF DIFFERENT STRENGTHS

The strong nuclear force is the strongest of all the forces. The *strong nuclear force* holds together the protons and neutrons in the nuclei of atoms. However, it only acts over short distances. The maximum range of the strong nuclear force is about the size of an atomic nucleus.

The *weak nuclear force* is about ten trillion times weaker than the strong nuclear force. The weak nuclear force affects some kinds of radioactive decay.

Electromagnetic forces can act over longer distances and are about 1% of the strength of the strong nuclear force. *Electromagnetic forces* hold electrons near the nucleus of an atom and hold molecules together.

Gravity is the weakest of the fundamental forces. It is about 10^{40} times weaker than the strong nuclear force. It also works over longer distances than any of the other fundamental forces. Gravity is an important force in shaping the structure of our galaxy and the universe.

Critical Thinking
3. Explain Electromagnetic forces cause protons to repel each other. Why don't the nuclei of atoms fly apart due to the electromagnetic forces between the protons?

_____

_____

_____

_____

CONTACT FORCES AND FIELD FORCES

Scientists put forces into two main groups: contact forces and field forces. *Contact forces* require two objects to physically be in contact with each other. When you push or pull on an object, you are applying a contact force. Friction is another example of a contact force.

Field forces act over distances and do not require two objects to be in direct contact. Gravity and magnetism are examples of field forces. Field forces can attract two objects together, or push two objects apart.

LOOKING CLOSER
4. Describe Fill in the blank spaces in the table.

Type of Force	Description	Examples
Contact force		
	act over distances on objects that may not be touching	gravity, magnetism

How Can Forces Affect Motion?

Forces act to change the motion of an object. In most situations, several forces act on an object at once. The *net force* is the combination of all the forces acting on an object. An object will accelerate in the direction of the net force. An object will not accelerate if the net force is zero.

SECTION 3 Motion and Force *continued*

BALANCED FORCES

Balanced forces produce a net force of zero. Therefore, an object experiencing balanced forces will not change its motion. This means that an object at rest will remain at rest if the forces are balanced. An object in motion will remain in motion if the forces are balanced. ☑

There are many examples of balanced forces in daily life. A light hanging from the ceiling does not move up or down. The force of tension in the cord pulls the light up. This balances the force of gravity, which pulls the light down. A car moving at a constant velocity is another example of an object affected by balanced forces.

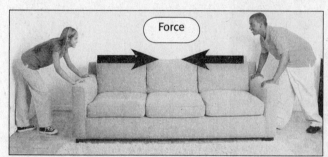

In this picture, both people are pushing with the same force. They are pushing in opposite directions. Therefore, the forces are balanced. The couch does not move.

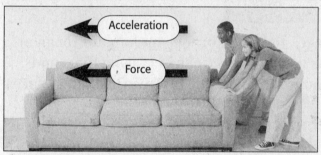

Here, the two people are pushing in the same direction. Therefore, the force is unbalanced and the couch moves. The couch moves in the direction of the net force.

UNBALANCED FORCES

When the net force acting on an object is greater than zero, the object will accelerate in the direction of the net force. Look at the image of the two students pushing a couch above. When the two students are pushing on opposite sides of the couch, the forces oppose each other. If one student pushes harder, the couch will move in the direction that student is pushing.

When the two students are pushing on the same side of the couch, the forces combine. The couch accelerates in the direction both students are pushing. What happens if one student pushes the couch west, and the other student pushes the couch north? The net force is a combination of the two forces. The couch will move in a north-west direction.

✔ **READING CHECK**

5. Describe How do balanced forces affect an object's motion?

_____

_____

_____

LOOKING CLOSER

6. Explain Why does the couch move in the bottom picture, but not in the top?

_____

_____

_____

Critical Thinking

7. Infer An object moves at a constant speed along a circular path. Is the object experiencing balanced or unbalanced forces? Explain your answer.

_____

_____

_____

_____

SECTION 3 Motion and Force *continued*

What Is the Force of Friction?

Friction is a force that opposes the relative motion between two objects in contact. Friction results from electromagnetic forces. It occurs as a result of the interactions between atoms on the surfaces of two objects. The rougher the surfaces, the greater the friction between them. ☑

Friction can produce heat when surfaces rub together. For example, you can warm your hands on a cool morning by rubbing them together. The heat from friction can cause a match to light, as shown in the figure below.

There is friction between the match head and the surface it moves against. The friction produces heat. The heat causes the match to catch on fire.

Even surfaces that look or feel smooth are rough at the molecular level. Interactions between atoms and molecules produce friction even between smooth surfaces.

TYPES OF FRICTION

There are two main types of friction: kinetic friction and static friction. **Kinetic friction** is the friction between two moving surfaces. There are two main types of kinetic friction: sliding friction and rolling friction. *Sliding friction* occurs when two objects slide past each other. *Rolling friction* occurs when a round object rolls over a flat surface. ☑

In most cases, rolling friction is less than sliding friction. This is why it is easier to push a chair on wheels across a floor than a chair without wheels.

Static friction is the friction between two surfaces that are not sliding past each other. Forces act between molecules on the surface of two objects, holding them together. Static friction is usually greater than kinetic friction. Therefore, in most cases, it takes a greater force to start an object moving than to keep it moving.

READING CHECK

8. Identify Which of the four fundamental forces causes friction?

_____

_____

LOOKING CLOSER

9. Infer If there was no friction between the match and the surface, would the match light? Explain your answer.

_____

_____

_____

_____

READING CHECK

10. List What are the two main types of kinetic friction?

_____

_____

How Does Friction Impact Everyday Life?

Friction allows you to hold a pencil and use it to write on a piece of paper. Friction even keeps you from slipping when you walk.

Friction between the tires of a car and the road allows a car to move. As the wheels of a car turn, they push against the road. As a result, the road pushes forward on the car. The force pushing the car forward must be greater than the friction that opposes the motion of the car. Due to friction, a constant force must be applied to keep the car moving. Friction also keeps cars from moving when parked.

Balanced forces (constant speed)

The car's engine produces a forward force. Friction resists this force. When the forward force balances the force of friction, the car's motion does not change. The car moves at a constant speed.

Unbalanced forces (acceleration)

If the forward force is greater than the force of friction, the car's motion changes. The car accelerates forward.

Balanced forces (no motion)

The force of gravity pulls the truck down the hill. Friction between the truck's wheels and the road resists the force of gravity. When the force of friction is equal to the force of gravity, the truck's motion does not change. The truck does not move.

INCREASING AND DECREASING FRICTION

Sometimes, people need to decrease the friction between surfaces. For example, car engines have many moving parts. If there is too much friction between these parts, the engine can become too hot. Therefore, people add oil to their engines. Oil is a *lubricant*. It reduces the friction between surfaces. ☑

Sometimes, people need to increase the friction between surfaces. For example, people in cold climates may put sand on icy roads and sidewalks. The sand increases friction between the ground and people or cars moving on it.

Talk About It

Discuss With a partner or in a small group, identify 10 different examples of how friction affects your everyday life. For each example, talk about whether friction makes things easier or more difficult.

LOOKING CLOSER

11. Apply Concepts What would happen to the truck in the bottom picture if the force of gravity were larger than the force of friction?

_____

_____

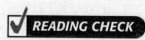
READING CHECK

12. Define What is a lubricant?

_____

_____

Name _____ Class _____ Date _____

Section 3 Review

SECTION VOCABULARY

force an action exerted on a body in order to change the body's state of rest or motion; force has magnitude and direction	**kinetic friction** the force that opposes the movement of two surfaces that are in contact and are sliding over each other
friction a force that opposes motion between two surfaces that are in contact	**static friction** the force that resists the initiation of sliding motion between two surfaces that are in contact and at rest

1. Compare What is the difference between kinetic friction and static friction?

_____

_____

2. Describe Fill in the table below for the relative strengths of the three remaining fundamental forces. List the forces from strongest to weakest. Indicate the relative strength of each force.

Fundamental Force	Approximate Relative Strength
Strong nuclear force	1
	1 : ten trillion

3. Describe What happens to an object when an unbalanced force acts on it?

_____

4. Apply Concepts A cyclist peddling at a constant rate sees the finish line and speeds up to finish the race sooner. Explain when the forces between the cyclist and the ground are balanced and when they are unbalanced.

_____

_____

_____

5. Explain Why is it easier to move a chair with wheels across a floor than a chair without wheels?

_____

_____

CHAPTER 12 Forces

SECTION
1 # Newton's First and Second Laws

KEY IDEAS

As you read this section, keep these questions in mind:
- What makes an object's motion change?
- What is inertia?
- What affects how much an object speeds up or slows down?

What Are Newton's Laws of Motion?

Imagine rolling a basketball across a smooth wooden floor. How far will the ball roll before it stops? Now imagine rolling the ball across a floor covered with carpet. The ball will not roll as far on the carpet as it did on the smooth floor. What causes this?

Hundreds of years ago, an English scientist named Sir Isaac Newton noticed similar effects. He also wondered what caused them. He discovered the relationship between motion and forces. He described the relationships in three laws. Today, we call these laws *Newton's laws of motion.*

What Is Newton's First Law of Motion?

A ball that stops after rolling along the floor is an example of Newton's first law of motion. This law states that an object's motion will not change until an unbalanced force acts on the object. The law also states that an object will not start to move until an unbalanced force acts on it. A rolling ball stops moving because the force of friction acts on it and slows it down. If there were no friction, the ball would keep rolling. ☑

This bowling ball slows down as it rolls because of the force of friction. If no forces acted on the ball, it would not stop rolling.

READING TOOLBOX

Find Examples As you read, make a table listing examples of Newton's first and second laws.

☑ **READING CHECK**

1. Describe State Newton's first law of motion in your own words.

_____

_____

_____

_____

SECTION 1 Newton's First and Second Laws *continued*

What Is Inertia?

Another way of stating Newton's first law is that matter resists any change in motion. All objects resist changes in motion. However, not all objects resist changes in motion by the same amount. For example, it does not take very much force to change the motion of a baseball. It takes much more force to change the motion of a bowling ball. The bowling ball resists changes in motion more than the baseball does.

The tendency of an object to resist changes in motion is called **inertia**. All objects have inertia. The amount of inertia an object has depends on the object's mass. The greater the mass of an object, the greater its inertia. ☑

READING CHECK

2. Explain How is mass related to inertia?

_____

_____

SEAT BELTS AND CAR SEATS

Think about the last time you rode in a car. What happened when the car stopped suddenly? You probably felt like you were being pushed toward the front of the car. Objects in the seats near you may have fallen over. Newton's first law of motion explains why this happens.

When a car stops, the inertia of the objects inside the car prevents them from stopping right away. Therefore, they may slide or fall over as the car stops suddenly.

Seat belts help to protect people inside a car from being hurt when the car stops. When the car stops, you start to slide toward the front of the car. The seat belt catches you and stops you from sliding.

Car seats help keep babies from being hurt when a car stops. These seats face toward the back of the car, as you can see in the figure below. This kind of car seat keeps the baby from sliding forward.

LOOKING CLOSER

3. Describe How does the car seat protect the baby?

_____

_____

_____

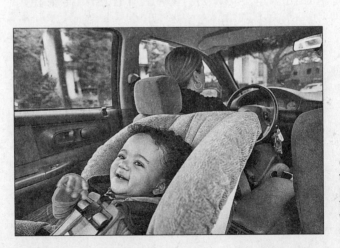

Car seats like this one help prevent babies from being hurt when a car stops.

What Is Newton's Second Law of Motion?

Newton's first law describes what happens when no unbalanced forces act on an object: the object's motion does not change. What happens when an unbalanced force does act on an object?

Newton's second law states that the larger the unbalanced force on an object, the more the object's motion will change. It also states that the larger the object's mass, the smaller its acceleration will be. *Acceleration* is the change in motion of an object.

Think about a baseball. If you throw the baseball gently, it will not move very fast. If you throw it more forcefully, it will move much more quickly. Now, imagine using the same force to throw a bowling ball. What will happen? The bowling ball will move much more slowly than the baseball.

We can write Newton's second law of motion as a mathematical equation:

$$net\ force = mass \times acceleration$$

or

$$F = ma$$

You can use this equation to calculate how much force is needed to make an object accelerate. You can also use it to calculate how much an object will accelerate when a force acts on it. Before you can use the equation, though, you need to know how scientists measure force.

What Are the Units of Force?

The SI unit scientists use to measure force is the newton (N). One newton is the amount of force needed to make a one-kilogram mass accelerate at one meter per second squared:

$$1\ N = 1\ kg \times 1\ m/s^2$$

Although scientists use newtons to measure force, sometimes people use pounds instead. One pound (lb) is equal to 4.45 N. One newton is equal to 0.225 lb.

Units of force	
newtons (N)	$1\ N = 1\ kg \times m/s^2$ $1\ N = 0.225\ lb$
pounds (lb)	$1\ lb = 4.45\ N$ $1\ lb = 4.45\ kg \times m/s^2$

Critical Thinking
4. Apply Concepts In many cases, large trucks move more slowly up hills than small cars. What do you think is the reason for this?

_____
_____
_____
_____
_____

LOOKING CLOSER
5. Calculate How many newtons are equal to 10 lb?

_____

SECTION 1 Newton's First and Second Laws *continued*

How Does Mass Affect Acceleration?

Look at the two pictures below. The football players are pushing with the same amount of force in both pictures. However, the mass of the sled is smaller in the picture on the left than the one in the picture on the right. Therefore, the sled on the left accelerates more than the one on the right.

LOOKING CLOSER
6. Infer What could the football players pushing the sled do to make it move more quickly?

_____

_____

The sled on the left accelerates more because its mass is smaller.

Talk About It

Give Examples In a small group, talk about times you have seen examples of Newton's second law of motion.

How Does Force Affect Acceleration?

Look at the other two pictures below. In the picture on the left, one person is pushing the car. The car has a large mass, and it does not accelerate very much. In the picture on the right, several people are pushing the same car. The mass of the car is the same as in the left-hand picture. However, the force is greater. Therefore, the car on the right accelerates more.

LOOKING CLOSER
7. Infer What would happen if the mass of the car on the right was greater?

_____

_____

The car in the right-hand picture accelerates more because the force acting on it is greater.

SECTION 1 Newton's First and Second Laws *continued*

CALCULATING FORCE FROM ACCELERATION

Zoo keepers lift a lion on a stretcher. The total mass of the lion and the stretcher is 175 kg. The acceleration of the lion and the stretcher is 0.657 m/s² upward. What force do the zoo keepers use to produce this acceleration?

Step 1: List the given and unknown values.	Given: mass, $m = 175$ kg acceleration, $a = 0.657$ m/s²	Unknown: force, F
Step 2: Write the equation.	$F = ma$	
Step 3: Insert the known values and solve for the unknown value.	$F = (175$ kg$) \times (0.657$ m/s²$)$ $F = 115$ kg $\times$ m/s² $= 115$ N	

So, the zoo keepers apply 115 N of force to lift the lion and the stretcher.

Math Skills

8. Calculate An object with a mass of 10.0 kg accelerates upward at 5.0 m/s². What force acts on the object? Show your work.

CALCULATING ACCELERATION FROM FORCE

A sailboat has a mass of 655 kg. A force of 895 N pushes the sailboat forward. What is the sailboat's acceleration?

Step 1: List the given and unknown values.	Given: mass, $m = 655$ kg force, $F = 895$ N	Unknown: acceleration, a
Step 2: Write the equations.	$F = ma$ $a = \dfrac{F}{m}$	
Step 3: Insert the known values and solve for the unknown value.	$a = \dfrac{895 \text{ N}}{655 \text{ kg}} = \dfrac{895 \text{ kg} \times \text{m/s}^2}{655 \text{ kg}}$ $a = 1.37$ m/s²	

So, the sailboat accelerates at 1.37 m/s².

Math Skills

9. Manipulate Equations Show how to rearrange the equation for Newton's second law of motion in order to solve for mass.

Section 1 Review

SECTION VOCABULARY

inertia the tendency of an object to resist a change in motion unless an outside force acts on the object	

1. Apply Concepts Which has more inertia, a car with a mass of 900 kg or a car with a mass of 1,500 kg? Explain your answer.

_____

_____

2. Infer Newton's first law of motion is sometimes called the "law of inertia." Why?

_____

_____

3. List Give two examples of Newton's second law of motion.

_____

_____

4. Calculate A baseball accelerates downward at 9.8 m/s². The force pulling the ball downward is 1.4 N. What is the mass of the baseball? Show your work.

5. Calculate A model airplane has a mass of 3.2 kg. Its propeller pulls it forward with a force of 7.0 N. What is the airplane's acceleration? Show your work.

6. Make Predictions Two cars are driving at the same speed. The cars have the same mass. One car is driving on an icy road. The other is driving on a dry road. Which car will be able to stop more quickly? Explain your answer.

_____

_____

_____

CHAPTER 12 | Forces
SECTION 2 | Gravity

As you read this section keep these questions in mind:

• What is free fall?

• How are weight and mass related?

• How does gravity affect the motion of objects?

What Is Gravity?

Have you ever seen movie footage of the Apollo astronauts walking on the moon? If so, you may have seen them bouncing up and down in their large spacesuits. Why could the astronauts jump so high on the moon? The answer is that gravity is weaker on the moon than it is on Earth.

Gravity is a force that pulls objects together. Sir Isaac Newton described the *law of universal gravitation*, which has three main parts:

1. Every object in the universe pulls with a gravitational force on every other object.

2. The strength of the gravitational force between two objects depends on the masses of the objects.

3. The strength of the gravitational force between two objects depends on the distance between the objects. ☑

Newton developed an equation that shows these relationships between gravitational force, mass, and distance.

READING TOOLBOX

Summarize As you read this section, underline the main ideas in each paragraph. When you finish reading, make an outline of the section using the ideas you underlined.

READING CHECK

1. Identify On what two factors does the strength of the gravitational force between two objects depend?

_____

_____

_____

Universal Gravitation Equation

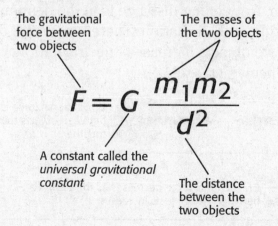

The gravitational force between two objects

The masses of the two objects

$$F = G \frac{m_1 m_2}{d^2}$$

A constant called the *universal gravitational constant*

The distance between the two objects

SECTION 2 Gravity *continued*

2. Summarize How do the masses of objects affect the gravitational force between them?

_____

_____

_____

How Does Mass Affect Gravitational Force?

Look back at the equation describing the law of universal gravitation. Notice that the two masses, m_1 and m_2, are multiplied together on the right side of the equation. Therefore, the gravitational force between two objects increases as the masses of the objects increase.

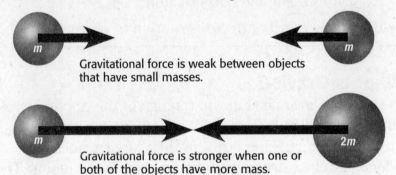

Gravitational force is weak between objects that have small masses.

Gravitational force is stronger when one or both of the objects have more mass.

Imagine an elephant and a cat standing on Earth. Earth's gravity pulls on the elephant and the cat. The elephant has a larger mass than the cat does. Therefore, the gravitational force between Earth and the elephant is greater than between Earth and the cat. This is one reason it is easier to pick up a cat than an elephant.

There is also a gravitational force between the elephant and the cat. However, Earth has a much larger mass than either the elephant or the cat. Therefore, the gravitational force between the elephant and the cat is very small compared to Earth's gravitational force on them.

Critical Thinking
3. Infer The gravitational force between the sun and Earth is larger than the force between the sun and the moon. What do you think is the reason for this?

_____

_____

_____

How Does Distance Affect Gravitational Force?

Look again at the equation for the law of universal gravitation. Notice that distance is in the denominator on the right side of the equation. Therefore, as the distance between two objects increases, the gravitational force between them decreases.

LOOKING CLOSER
4. Explain Why is the gravitational force between the bottom two balls smaller than that between the top two balls?

_____

_____

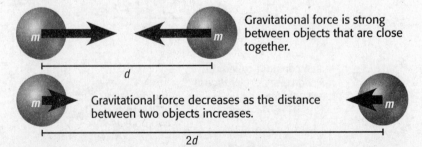

Gravitational force is strong between objects that are close together.

Gravitational force decreases as the distance between two objects increases.

SECTION 2 Gravity *continued*

THE STRENGTH OF EARTH'S GRAVITATIONAL FORCE

Earth's gravitational force pulls every object toward Earth's center. All other objects in the universe also pull on the objects on Earth. However, other objects are very far away, have very small masses, or both. Therefore, Earth's gravitational force affects objects on Earth most significantly. Gravitational forces from other objects are usually small enough to ignore.

What Is Free Fall?

Imagine dropping a ball. It will fall toward the ground because Earth's gravitational force acts on it. Remember Newton's second law of motion: an unbalanced force that acts on an object causes the object to accelerate. Therefore, Earth's gravity causes the ball to accelerate toward the ground.

When Earth's gravity is the only force acting on an object, the object is in **free fall**. During free fall, objects accelerate toward Earth's center. The acceleration caused by Earth's gravity is called *free-fall acceleration*. ☑

All objects have the same free-fall acceleration. Recall that acceleration depends on both force and mass. A heavy object experiences a greater gravitational force than a lighter object. However, it is harder to accelerate a heavy object than a lighter one because the heavy object has more mass.

Mass: 20 kg

Force: 196 N

Mass: 10 kg

Force: 98 N

Acceleration: 9.8 m/s²

The gravitational force on the larger ball is twice as great as the force on the smaller ball. However, the larger ball has a larger mass, so it is harder to accelerate. Therefore, both balls have the same free-fall acceleration.

Critical Thinking

5. Explain Why don't you feel a gravitational force between you and your desk?

_____

_____

_____

_____

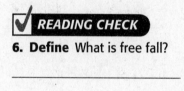

READING CHECK

6. Define What is free fall?

_____

_____

_____

LOOKING CLOSER

7. Identify Why do the two balls have the same free-fall acceleration, even though they have different masses?

_____

_____

_____

_____

SECTION 2 Gravity *continued*

AIR RESISTANCE AND TERMINAL VELOCITY

You may have seen objects falling through the air at different rates. For example, a piece of paper falls more slowly than a ball. This may seem to contradict the statement that all objects have the same free-fall acceleration. However, free fall happens when gravity is the only force that acts on an object.

On Earth, objects fall through the atmosphere. The gases in the atmosphere produce friction on the object. This friction is called *air resistance*. It acts in a direction opposite that of the gravitational force. ☑

As an object falls through the air, air resistance increases. If the object falls far enough, the air resistance on the object will equal the gravitational force on the object. Then, there will be no unbalanced forces acting on the object.

Recall Newton's first law of motion: if no unbalanced forces act on an object, the object's motion will not change. Therefore, when the force of air resistance balances the gravitational force, the object will no longer accelerate. Instead, it falls at a constant velocity called its **terminal velocity**.

✓ READING CHECK

8. Define What is air resistance?

_____

_____

_____

LOOKING CLOSER

9. Infer What would happen to the skydiver's velocity if she opened her parachute? Explain your answer. (Hint: Air resistance increases as the area of an object increases.)

_____

_____

_____

_____

_____

_____

_____

When the skydiver first jumps out of the plane, gravitational force is much larger than the force of air resistance. Therefore, she accelerates downward.

When the force of air resistance equals the gravitational force, the skydiver stops accelerating. She falls at a constant velocity.

The gravitational force and the force of air resistance are different on different objects. Therefore, different objects can have different terminal velocities.

What Is Weight?

Think back to the astronauts on the moon. The moon's mass is much smaller than Earth's mass. Therefore, objects near the moon experience a smaller gravitational force than objects near Earth. The astronauts could jump very high on the moon because the gravitational force on them was small. Another way to say this is the astronauts weighed less on the moon.

Weight is the gravitational force on an object. Remember that Earth's gravity is the main gravitational force we feel at Earth's surface. Therefore, on Earth, the weight of an object is the same as Earth's gravitational force on the object. ☑

The moon is very far from Earth. When astronauts walk on the moon, Earth's gravitational force on them is very weak. The moon's gravitational force is the main force acting on the astronauts. On the moon, the weights of the astronauts were smaller than on Earth.

To jump into the air, you must push yourself up with a force greater than your weight. If your weight is smaller, you need less force to jump into the air. On the moon, the astronauts only weighed one-sixth of what they weighed on Earth. Therefore, they needed less force to jump into the air.

You may have heard that astronauts are "weightless" in space. However, this is not true. Because gravity exists everywhere in space, an object has weight everywhere in space. Astronauts in the space shuttle seem to be weightless because they are in free fall. The astronauts and the space shuttle are falling toward Earth with the same acceleration. This is why the astronauts appear to float. ☑

Astronauts in orbit on the space shuttle seem to float in midair. This is because the astronauts and the space shuttle are both in free fall.

> ☑ **READING CHECK**
>
> **10. Define** What is weight?
>
> _____
>
> _____

> ☑ **READING CHECK**
>
> **11 Explain** Why can an object never be truly "weightless"?
>
> _____
>
> _____
>
> _____
>
> _____
>
> _____

SECTION 2 Gravity *continued*

THE DIFFERENCE BETWEEN MASS AND WEIGHT

Many people confuse mass and weight. Remember that mass is the amount of matter in an object. Mass is measured in kilograms (kg). In contrast, weight is a force. Like all forces, weight is measured in newtons (N). ☑

The weight of an object will change if the gravitational force on it changes. For example, an astronaut with a mass of 66 kg weighs about 650 N (about 150 lb) on Earth. On the moon, the astronaut has the same mass, 66 kg, because he contains the same amount of matter. However, his weight is smaller: only about 110 N (about 25 lb). The table below shows how the weights of some objects would be different on the moon.

12. Compare How is weight different from mass?

_____

_____

_____

LOOKING CLOSER

13. Apply Concepts A small can of soup has a mass of about 400 g. What would its mass be on the moon?

_____

Object	Mass	Weight on Earth	Weight on the moon
Apple	100 g	1 N (0.225 lb)	0.16 N (0.04 lb)
Elephant	5,000 kg	49,000 N (11,025 lb)	8,000 N (1,800 lb)
Train locomotive	25,000 kg	245,000 N (55,125 lb)	40,000 N (9,000 lb)

CALCULATING WEIGHT

You can use the equation for Newton's second law of motion to calculate the weight of an object. Recall the equation for Newton's second law of motion:

$$F = ma$$

Remember that free-fall acceleration is the acceleration of an object because of gravity. Also, remember that weight is the force on an object because of gravity. Therefore, you can rewrite the equation like this:

$$weight = mass \times free\text{-}fall\ acceleration$$

$$w = mg$$

On Earth, the free-fall acceleration, or g, is about 9.8 m/s². Therefore, the weight of an object is equal to its mass in kilograms multiplied by 9.8 m/s². On the moon, free-fall acceleration is about 1.6 m/s².

Math *Skills*

14. Calculate An object has a mass of 2,000 kg. What is its weight on Earth? Show your work.

How Does Gravity Affect Moving Objects?

Imagine throwing a baseball in a straight, horizontal line. What happens to the baseball? It does not travel in a straight line for very long. Instead, it follows a curved path through the air until it hits the ground. This is because gravity pulls the baseball toward the ground.

SECTION 2 Gravity *continued*

PROJECTILE MOTION

A thrown baseball shows projectile motion. **Projectile motion** is the curved path followed by any object that is thrown or launched near Earth's surface. Gravity causes these objects to move along curved paths. ☑

All objects in projectile motion are moving in two directions: horizontally and vertically. These two motions combine to give the object its curved path. However, the horizontal and vertical motions do not affect each other. You can see this in the figure below.

☑ **READING CHECK**

15. Identify What causes a thrown baseball to follow a curved path?

_____

_____

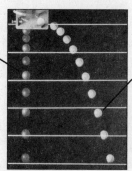

This ball has no horizontal motion. It does not fall along a curved path.

This ball was pushed off the ledge. It is moving both horizontally and vertically. The motions combine to form a curved path.

The downward acceleration on both balls is the same. The horizontal motion of the light-colored ball does not affect its vertical motion.

ORBITS

You have probably heard people talk about the space shuttle or the moon orbiting Earth. An *orbit* is a circular or oval-shaped path that one object follows as it moves around another object in space. For example, the moon orbits Earth, and Earth orbits the sun. Gravity controls the orbits of all of the objects in the universe.

A space shuttle orbiting Earth may seem very different from a baseball falling to the ground after you throw it. However, both are examples of projectile motion. The space shuttle in the figure below is moving forward, or horizontally. Earth's gravity is pulling the shuttle down, or vertically, toward Earth. These two motions combine to produce the curved orbit of the shuttle.

LOOKING CLOSER

16. Compare If the dark colored ball reached the ground after 5 seconds, how long did it take the light colored ball to reach the ground?

_____

_____

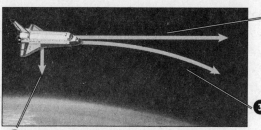

1 The shuttle moves forward at a constant speed. If Earth's gravity did not pull on it, the shuttle would move away from the planet.

3 The horizontal and vertical forces on the shuttle combine to produce a curved path. This path is called an *orbit*.

2 Earth's gravity pulls the shuttle downward. If it were not moving horizontally, the shuttle would fall straight down to Earth's surface.

LOOKING CLOSER

17. Identify How would the shuttle's motion change if there were no gravitational force between it and Earth?

_____

_____

Section 2 Review

SECTION VOCABULARY

free fall the motion of a body when only the force of gravity is acting on the body **projectile motion** the curved path that an object follows when thrown, launched, or otherwise projected near the surface of Earth; the motion of objects that are moving in two dimensions under the influence of gravity	**terminal velocity** the constant velocity of a falling object when the force of air resistance is equal in magnitude and opposite in direction to the force of gravity **weight** a measure of the gravitational force exerted on an object; its value can change with the location of the object in the universe

1. **Apply Concepts** If Earth had no atmosphere, would a falling object ever reach terminal velocity? Explain your answer.

_____

_____

_____

2. **Calculate** Fill in the blank spaces in the table below. Free-fall acceleration on Earth is 9.8 m/s². On the moon, free-fall acceleration is 1.6 m/s².

Object	Mass (kg)	Weight on Earth (N)	Weight on the moon (N)
Bowling ball	5		8
Textbook		19.6	
Large dog	50		

3. **Identify** In the space below, write the equation for the law of universal gravitation. Explain what each variable in the equation represents.

_____

_____

_____

4. **Explain** Why do astronauts in orbit in the space shuttle seem to float?

_____

_____

5. **Identify** What two kinds of motion combine to produce projectile motion?

_____

CHAPTER 12 Forces
SECTION 3 Newton's Third Law

KEY IDEAS

As you read this section keep these questions in mind:

- What happens when one object exerts a force on another object?
- How can you calculate the momentum of an object?
- How does momentum change after a collision?

What Is Newton's Third Law of Motion?

Imagine kicking a soccer ball. The ball would move in a different direction. From Newton's first law, you know that the ball's motion could not have changed unless a force acted on it. Therefore, there must be a force acting on the ball. This force came from your foot. However, if you kicked a soccer ball, you would probably also feel a force on your foot. Where did this force come from?

When you kick a soccer ball, your foot exerts a force on the ball. This force is called an *action force*. At the same time, the ball exerts a force on your foot. That force is called a *reaction force*. Sir Isaac Newton described the relationship between action forces and reaction forces in his third law of motion.

Newton's third law of motion states that action forces always produce reaction forces. It also states that action forces and reaction forces are always equal in size, but act in opposite directions. The figure below shows the sizes and directions of action and reaction forces when a person kicks a soccer ball.

According to Newton's third law, the foot and the soccer ball exert equal and opposite forces on each other.

READING TOOLBOX

Organize After you read this section, create a Concept Map for momentum. Include the words *momentum*, *mass*, *velocity*, and *direction* in your map.

LOOKING CLOSER

1. Identify On the figure, label the action force and the reaction force.

Critical Thinking

2. Apply Concepts A student has a weight of 534 N. The student sits in a chair. When the student sits in a chair, how much force does the chair apply to the student?

_____

_____

LOOKING CLOSER

3. Explain Why don't the action and reaction forces in the figure cancel each other out?

_____

_____

_____

FORCE PAIRS

An action force and the reaction force that results are called a *force pair*. Newton's third law states that the forces in a force pair are equal in size, but opposite in direction. You may wonder why these forces do not cancel each other out, since they happen at the same time. The answer is that the forces act on different objects. For example, in the figure below, the action force acts on the water. The reaction force acts on the swimmer.

The action force is the swimmer pushing the water backward.

The reaction force is the water pushing the swimmer forward.

EQUAL FORCES, UNEQUAL EFFECTS

Imagine dropping a soccer ball. Earth's gravitational force pulls the soccer ball toward the ground. This is the action force. At the same time, the soccer ball exerts an equal gravitational force on Earth. This is the reaction force. The action force and the reaction force are the same size, but opposite in direction.

It is easy to see the effect of the action force—the ball falls to the ground. Why don't you notice the effect of the reaction force—Earth being pulled upward? The answer is that these two equal forces act on objects with very different masses.

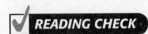
READING CHECK

4. Explain Why don't we notice Earth moving upward when an object falls toward the ground?

_____

_____

Recall Newton's second law of motion: A large mass will accelerate less than a small mass when you apply the same amount of force. For example, the same amount of force acts on the soccer ball and Earth, but Earth's mass is much greater than the soccer ball's. Therefore, Earth's acceleration is much smaller than that of the soccer ball. Earth does move upward, but this acceleration is so small it is almost impossible to measure. ☑

SECTION 3 Newton's Third Law *continued*

SUMMARY OF NEWTON'S THIRD LAW OF MOTION

To summarize, there are four main ideas in Newton's third law of motion:

• Forces occur in pairs made up of an action force and a reaction force.

• Action and reaction forces are equal in size, but opposite in direction.

• Action and reaction forces act on different objects.

• Equal forces acting on different objects may have different effects.

DETERMINING THE EFFECTS OF FORCES

You can use Newton's third law of motion to determine how an object will move. For example, think again about the falling soccer ball. You can measure its weight, which is equal to the gravitational force on it—the action force. Once you know the weight of the soccer ball, you know the size of the reaction force acting on Earth. If you know Earth's mass, you can calculate Earth's acceleration using Newton's second law of motion.

What if you do not know the size of the force acting on an object? You may still be able to predict the object's motion using a quantity called momentum.

What Is Momentum?

Momentum is a property of all moving objects. The momentum of an object moving in a straight line is equal to its mass multiplied by its velocity. Momentum is represented by the variable p.

Momentum Equation

$$momentum = mass \times velocity$$

$$p = mv$$

The SI unit of momentum is kilograms times meters per second (kg • m/s). Like velocity, momentum has both size and direction. An object's velocity and momentum are in the same direction. ☑

Talk About It

Brainstorm Think of 10 examples of force pairs. Describe each action force with a partner. Ask your partner to try to think of the reaction force. Then, have your partner share his or her list of action forces with you. Try to think of the reaction force for each of your partner's action forces.

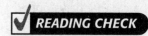
READING CHECK

5. Apply Concepts An object has a velocity of 10 m/s south. In what direction is its momentum?

_____

_____

SECTION 3 Newton's Third Law *continued*

EFFECTS OF VELOCITY AND MASS ON MOMENTUM

Look back at the equation for momentum. How does the velocity of an object affect its momentum? Mass and velocity are multiplied together to calculate momentum. Therefore, as an object's velocity increases, its momentum also increases. For example, a fast-moving car has more momentum than a slow-moving car of the same mass.

How does mass affect momentum? If velocity stays the same, increasing mass also increases momentum. For example, a tractor-trailer truck has more momentum than a sports car moving at the same velocity. ☑

CALCULATING MOMENTUM

Imagine a bowling ball rolling toward bowling pins. The ball has a mass of 6.00 kg. Its velocity is 10.0 m/s down the alley. What is the ball's momentum?

Step 1: List the given and unknown values.	Given: mass, $m = 6.00$ kg velocity, $v = 10.0$ m/s down the alley	Unknown: momentum, p
Step 2: Write the equation for momentum.	$p = mv$	
Step 3: Insert the known values and solve for the unknown value.	$p = (6.00$ kg$) \times (10.0$ m/s down the alley$)$ $p = 60.0$ kg · m/s down the alley	

FORCE AND MOMENTUM CHANGES

Recall Newton's first law: an object's motion will not change until an unbalanced force acts on it. When you apply a force to a moving object, its motion changes. If its velocity changes, its momentum also changes. For example, a moving car has a certain velocity and momentum. When the driver applies the brakes, the car slows down. In other words, its velocity changes. Therefore, its momentum also changes.

If you give an object more time to change its momentum, you will need to use less force to make that change. For example, if you move your arm back when you catch a baseball, the ball's momentum has more time to change. Your hand has to use less force to change the ball's momentum. This also means your hand feels less of a sting!

READING CHECK

6. Identify How does mass affect momentum?

_____

_____

_____

Math *Skills*

7. Calculate An ostrich has a mass of 135 kg. It is running with a velocity of 16.2 m/s north. What is its momentum? Show your work.

Critical Thinking

8. Infer What is the momentum of a car that has stopped moving?

_____

SECTION 3 Newton's Third Law *continued*

What Happens to Momentum When Objects Collide?

You can use the law of conservation of momentum to predict how objects will move after they collide, or hit. The *law of conservation of momentum* states that the total amount of momentum in an isolated system is conserved. Let's look at each part of this law to understand what it means.

An *isolated system* is a group of objects that does not gain or lose mass or energy to its environment. Imagine a cue ball rolling across a table toward other billiard balls. The cue ball and the other balls are almost an isolated system. The balls do not gain or lose mass to the environment. They may lose a small amount of energy to friction, but the amount is generally small enough to ignore.

Conserved means *kept the same*. The amount of momentum in an isolated system stays the same, no matter what happens within the system.

Think again about the cue ball rolling across a table. When the cue ball hits the other balls, they move. Before the collision, the other balls are not moving; they have no momentum. Therefore, the total momentum in the system is equal to the momentum of the cue ball.

When the cue ball hits another ball, it passes some of its momentum to the other ball. After the collision, all the balls have a different momentum. However, their total momentum is the same as it was before the collision.

Critical Thinking
9. Rephrase Write the law of conservation of momentum in your own words.

_____

_____

_____

_____

_____

_____

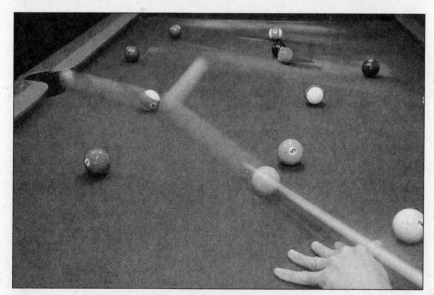

When a cue ball hits another ball on the table, the cue ball slows down. The other ball begins to move. The total momentum of the system stays the same.

LOOKING CLOSER
10. Explain Why does the cue ball slow down after it hits another ball?

_____

_____

_____

Section 3 Review

SECTION VOCABULARY

momentum a quantity defined as the product of the mass and velocity of an object	

1. Explain How is velocity related to momentum?

_____

_____

2. Identify What is Newton's third law of motion?

_____

_____

3. Apply Concepts A skier pushes her ski poles against the ground. She begins to move across the snow. Earth does not seem to move. Identify the action and reaction forces in this example, and explain why the skier moves but Earth does not seem to.

_____

_____

_____

_____

4. Calculate A baby has a mass of 5.0 kg. The baby is on a train that is traveling east at 72 m/s. What is the baby's momentum? Show your work.

5. Calculate A kitten has a mass of 0.8 kg. It is moving forward with a momentum of 0.5 kg • m/s. What is the kitten's velocity? Show your work.

6. Compare Describe the total momentum of billiard balls before and after the cue ball collides with another ball.

_____

_____

CHAPTER 13 Work and Energy
SECTION 1

Work, Power, and Machines

As you read this section, keep these questions in mind:

• What is work, and how is it measured?

• How are work and power related?

• How do machines make work easier?

What Is Work?

Imagine trying to lift the front end of a car without a jack. You might exert a lot of force and not move the car at all. Exerting all that force may seem like hard work, but in scientific terms, you did no work at all.

In science, there are many different kinds of work. Here, we will deal only with work against gravity. This kind of **work** occurs when a force causes an object to move away from Earth's surface. You can use the equation below to calculate the work done on an object:

$$work = force \times distance$$
$$W = Fd$$

In this equation, *distance* is the distance the object moves above Earth's surface. Work only occurs when the object is moving. If the object is not moving, no work is occurring.

This weightlifter did work on the barbell to lift it over her head.

Work is measured in newton-meters (N • m). You can also use *joules* (J) to measure work. One newton-meter equals one joule. Remember that one newton is equal to one kilogram-meter per second squared (kg • m/s²). Therefore, one joule is also equal to one kilogram-meter squared per second squared (kg • m²/s²):

$$1 \text{ N} \bullet \text{m} = 1 \text{ J} = 1 \text{ kg} \bullet \text{m}^2/\text{s}^2$$

You can use different units for work to make solving problems easier.

READING TOOLBOX

Compare As you read this section, create a table comparing work, power, and mechanical advantage. Include the equations used to calculate each, the units used to measure each, and the definition of each.

LOOKING CLOSER

1. Apply Concepts Is the weightlifter doing any work when she holds the barbell motionless above her head? Explain your answer.

_____

_____

_____

_____

SECTION 1 Work, Power, and Machines *continued*

CALCULATING WORK FROM FORCE AND DISTANCE

To calculate the amount of work done on an object, you must know the force applied and the distance the object moved. Let's look at an example of how to calculate the work done on an object. A crane uses an average force of 5,200 N to lift a metal beam 25 m into the air. How much work does the crane do on the beam?

Math *Skills*

2. Calculate A student lifts an apple to a height of 1 m. The apple weighs 1 N. How much work does the student do on the apple? Show your work.

Step 1: List the given and unknown values.	Given: force, $F = 5,200$ N distance, $d = 25$ m	Unknown: work, W
Step 2: Write the equation.	$W = Fd$	
Step 3: Insert the known values and solve for the unknown value.	$W = (5,200$ N$) \times (25$ m$)$ $W = 130,000$ N $\cdot$ m $W = 130$ kJ	

So, the crane does about 130 kJ of work on the beam.

CALCULATING WORK FROM MASS AND DISTANCE

If you know the mass of an object, you can calculate how much work it takes to lift the object. For example, suppose a car has a mass of 1,200 kg. A mechanic uses an electric lift to raise the car 0.50 m off the ground. How much work does the lift do on the car?

In order to use the work equation, you must know the force exerted on the car. Because the car is being lifted straight up, the force on the car is equal to the car's weight. Therefore, you can use the equation for weight, $w = mg$, to find the force on the car. In this equation, g is free-fall acceleration (9.8 m/s^2). Here's how to solve this problem:

Critical Thinking

3. Explain If the car were being moved sideways, could you determine the force on the car by using the weight equation? Explain your answer.

_____
_____
_____
_____
_____
_____
_____
_____

Step 1: List the given and unknown values.	Given: mass, $m = 1,200$ kg distance, $d = 25$ m	Unknown: force, F (equal to weight, w) work, W
Step 2: Write the equations.	$w = mg$ $W = Fd$	
Step 3: Insert the known values and solve for the unknown values.	$w = (1,200$ kg$) \times (9.8$ m/s$^2)$ $w = 12,000$ kg $\cdot$ m/s$^2 = 12,000$ N $W = (12,000$ N$) \times (0.50$ m$)$ $W = 6,000$ N $\cdot$ m $= 6.0$ kJ	

So, the lift does about 6.0 kJ of work on the car.

How Are Work and Power Related?

Like work, power has a very specific meaning in science. **Power** is the rate at which work is done or energy is used. In other words, power is how much work is done in a given amount of time. The equation for power is: ☑

$$power = \frac{work}{time}$$

$$P = \frac{W}{t}$$

READING CHECK

4. Define What is power?

_____

_____

The SI unit for power is the *watt* (W). One watt is the amount of power needed to do one joule of work in one second (1 J/s). Be careful not to confuse the symbol for work, *W*, which is in italics, with the symbol for watt, W, which is not in italics.

Power increases when more work is done in a given amount of time. Power also increases when you do work in less time. For example, imagine climbing a flight of stairs slowly. Now, imagine running up the stairs. In both cases, you do the same amount of work, because you move your weight through the same distance. However, it takes less time to climb the stairs running. Therefore, your power output is higher if you run up the stairs. ☑

Let's look at an example of how to calculate power. Lifting an elevator 18 m takes 100 kJ of work. If the elevator moves 18 m in 20 s, what is the power output of the elevator?

READING CHECK

5. Identify Name two things that can cause power output to decrease.

_____

_____

_____

_____

Step 1: List the given and unknown values.	Given: work, $W = 100$ kJ time, $t = 20$ s	Unknown: power, P
Step 2: Write the equation.	$P = \frac{W}{t}$	
Step 3: Insert the known values and solve for the unknown value.	$P = \frac{100 \text{ kJ}}{20 \text{ s}}$ $P = 5 \text{ kJ/s} = 5{,}000 \text{ J/s}$ $P = 5{,}000 \text{ W} = 5 \text{ kW}$	

So, it takes about 5 kW of power to lift the elevator.

SECTION 1 Work, Power, and Machines *continued*

How Do Machines Make Work Easier?

Many people think that machines reduce the amount of work we have to do to move an object. However, machines do not change the amount of work done on an object. Instead, they make work easier by changing the way the force is applied. For example, in the picture below, the ramp increases the distance over which the force is applied. ☑

☑ **READING CHECK**

6. Describe How do machines make work easier?

_____

_____

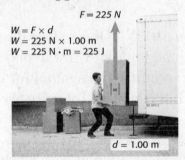

$W = F \times d$
$W = 225 \text{ N} \times 1.00 \text{ m}$
$W = 225 \text{ N} \cdot \text{m} = 225 \text{ J}$

$F = 225 \text{ N}$

$d = 1.00 \text{ m}$

To lift a box straight up, the mover applies a large force over a small distance.

LOOKING CLOSER

7. Compare How does the amount of work done in the top picture compare with the work done in the bottom picture?

_____

_____

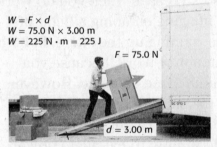

$W = F \times d$
$W = 75.0 \text{ N} \times 3.00 \text{ m}$
$W = 225 \text{ N} \cdot \text{m} = 225 \text{ J}$

$F = 75.0 \text{ N}$

$d = 3.00 \text{ m}$

To move the box up the ramp, the mover applies a smaller force over a longer distance.

Many machines make work easier by changing the size or direction of the force we apply. The force we apply is called the *input force*. For example, people use jacks to lift cars off the ground. A person applies a light, downward input force to the handle of the jack. The jack changes the input force into a stronger, upward force, the *output force*. The output force lifts the car. In this way, a person can lift a very heavy car.

It may seem that changing a small force into a large force breaks the law of conservation of energy. However, the jack doesn't only increase the force applied. It also decreases the distance over which the force is applied. Therefore, the total amount of work stays the same. ☑

READING CHECK

8. Explain Why doesn't a machine that increases force break the law of conservation of energy?

_____

_____

_____

Many machines increase force by decreasing the distance over which the force is applied. This process is called *multiplying the force*. The car jack is an example of a machine that multiplies force. Other machines, such as ramps, multiply distance. They make work easier by allowing you to exert a smaller force over a longer distance.

What Is Mechanical Advantage?

Scientists and engineers use a quantity called **mechanical advantage** to describe how much a machine multiplies force or distance. Mechanical advantage is the ratio between output force and input force. It is also the ratio between input distance and output distance. The mechanical advantage equation is: ☑

$$mechanical\ advantage = \frac{output\ force}{input\ force} = \frac{input\ distance}{output\ distance}$$

A machine with a mechanical advantage greater than one multiplies force. Such machines can help you move or lift large objects, such as cars and heavy boxes, more easily. Jacks and many pulleys multiply force.

A machine with a mechanical advantage of one does not multiply force. Such machines only change the direction of the force. Some pulleys work this way.

A machine with a mechanical advantage less than one multiplies distance. It also produces an output force that is smaller than the input force. Ramps work this way. Some of the joints in your body, such as your elbow, also work this way.

CALCULATING MECHANICAL ADVANTAGE

You can calculate mechanical advantage if you know input and output forces or distances. For example, imagine a jack that lifts a 9,900 N car with an input force of 150 N. What is the mechanical advantage of the jack? Follow these steps to solve this problem:

Step 1: List the given and unknown values.	**Given:** input force = 150 N output force = 9,900 N	**Unknown:** mechanical advantage
Step 2: Write the equation.	$mechanical\ advantage = \frac{output\ force}{input\ force}$	
Step 3: Insert the known values and solve for the unknown value.	$mechanical\ advantage = \frac{9,900\ N}{150\ N}$ $mechanical\ advantage = 66$	

The jack has a mechanical advantage of 66. Therefore, the output force from the jack is 66 times greater than the input force.

READING CHECK

9. Identify What does mechanical advantage measure?

_____

_____

_____

Talk About It

Apply Concepts How can you tell without doing any calculations whether a machine has a mechanical advantage greater or less than one? In a small group, brainstorm some ideas about how you could figure this out.

Math *Skills*

10. Calculate A ramp is 5.0 m long and 1.5 m high. What is the mechanical advantage of the ramp? Show your work. (Hint: The height of the ramp is the output distance.)

Section 1 Review

SECTION VOCABULARY

mechanical advantage a number that tells how many times a machine multiplies force; it can be calculated by dividing the output force by the input force **power** a quantity that measures the rate at which work is done or energy is transformed	**work** the transfer of energy to a body by the application of a force that causes the body to move in the direction of the force; it is equal to the product of the magnitude of the component of a force along the direction of displacement and the magnitude of the displacement

1. Apply Concepts A short ramp and a long ramp each reach a height of 1 m. Which ramp has a greater mechanical advantage? Explain your answer.

_____

_____

_____

2. Calculate A student weighs 565 N. She climbs 3.25 m vertically up a flight of stairs. It takes her 12.6 s. What is her power output? Show your work.

3. Describe The student from the question above carries a stack of books up the same flight of stairs. If she still takes 12.6 s, how will her power output change? Explain your answer.

_____

_____

_____

4. Compare What is the difference between work and power?

_____

_____

5. Apply Concepts A certain machine changes a large input force into a smaller output force. How does the machine affect the distance over which the force is applied? Explain your answer.

_____

_____

CHAPTER 13 Work and Energy
SECTION 2 Simple Machines

KEY IDEAS

As you read this section, keep these questions in mind:

- What are simple machines?
- What simple machines are in the lever family?
- What simple machines are in the inclined plane family?
- What are compound machines?

What Are Simple Machines?

We are surrounded by many different electronics and machines. In physics, a *machine* is a mechanical device that changes the motion of an object. Remember that machines make work easier by changing the way a force is applied. Many machines, such as cars and bicycles, are complicated. However, even the most complicated machine is made from a combination of just six simple machines. **Simple machines** are the most basic machines.

Scientists divide the six simple machines into two families: the lever family and the inclined plane family. The lever family includes the simple lever, the pulley, and the wheel and axle. The inclined plane family includes the simple inclined plane, the wedge, and the screw.

READING TOOLBOX

Compare As you read this section, make a chart showing the similarities and differences between the six simple machines. Describe how each machine affects input and output forces and distances. Include the mechanical advantage each machine provides.

| The lever family | Simple lever | Pulley | Wheel and axle |
| The inclined plane family | Simple inclined plane | Wedge | Screw |

LOOKING CLOSER
1. Infer What do you think is the reason that the wedge and the simple inclined plane are in the same family of simple machines?

_____

_____

How Do Levers Work?

If you have ever used a claw hammer to remove a nail from a piece of wood, you have used a simple lever. All *levers* have a rigid arm that *pivots*, or turns, around a point. This point is called the *fulcrum*.

SECTION 2 Simple Machines *continued*

CLASSES OF LEVERS

Scientists divide levers into three main classes based on where the fulcrum, input force, and output force are. In a *first-class lever*, the fulcrum is between the input and output forces. The mechanical advantage of a first-class lever depends on the position of the fulcrum.

First-class lever

Output force

Input force

Fulcrum

In a first-class lever, the fulcrum is between the input force and the output force.

LOOKING CLOSER
2. Identify What part of the hammer acts as the fulcrum when the hammer is used to remove a nail?

_____

_____

In a *second-class lever*, the output force is located between the fulcrum and the input force. Wheelbarrows are examples of second-class levers. The mechanical advantage of a second-class lever is always greater than one. Therefore, second-class levers multiply force.

Second-class lever

Output force

Fulcrum

Input force

In a second-class lever, the output force is between the fulcrum and the input force.

LOOKING CLOSER
3. Compare How do the directions of the input and output forces in a second-class lever compare?

_____

_____

In a *third-class lever*, the input force is located between the fulcrum and the output force. The output force of a third-class lever is less than the input force. Therefore, the mechanical advantage of a third-class lever is less than one.

Third-class levers multiply distance. A person's forearm is a third-class lever. The elbow is the fulcrum. The biceps muscle attaches to the bone near the elbow. The muscle contracts a short distance to move the hand a long distance.

Critical Thinking
4. Apply Concepts How does the input distance of a third-class lever compare to the output distance?

_____

_____

_____

Third-class lever

Output force

Fulcrum

Input force

In a third-class lever, the input force is between the fulcrum and the output force.

SECTION 2 Simple Machines *continued*

PULLEYS

A *pulley* is another kind of simple machine in the lever family. You may have used a pulley to lift things, such as a flag on a flagpole.

As shown below, the point in the middle of a fixed pulley is like the fulcrum of a lever. The rest of the pulley acts like the fixed arm of a first-class lever, because it pivots around a point. The distance from the fulcrum is the same on both sides of a fixed pulley. A fixed pulley has a mechanical advantage of one. Therefore, a fixed pulley does not increase force. It simply changes the direction of the force. ☑

A moveable pulley or a combination of pulleys can produce a mechanical advantage greater than one. Moveable pulleys are attached to the object being moved. Fixed and moveable pulleys can be combined into a single unit to produce a greater mechanical advantage.

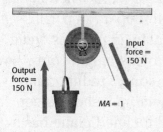

A fixed pulley has a mechanical advantage of one. It changes only the direction of a force.

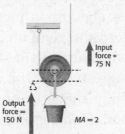

A single moveable pulley has a mechanical advantage of two.

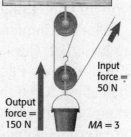

Combining several pulleys produces an even higher mechanical advantage.

✓ **READING CHECK**

5. Describe How does a fixed pulley change the input force?

_____

_____

_____

LOOKING CLOSER

6. Infer Of the three pulleys in the figure, which one requires the largest input distance? Explain your answer.

_____

_____

_____

_____

WHEEL AND AXLE

A wheel and axle is made of a lever or pulley (wheel) connected to a shaft (axle). Bicycle gears, doorknobs, wrenches, and screwdrivers are wheel-and-axle machines. When a small input force turns a wheel, the output force is multiplied. The output force increases because the axle is smaller than the wheel. Therefore, the axle rotates through a smaller distance. The figure at the top of the next page shows a wheel and axle.

SECTION 2 Simple Machines *continued*

LOOKING CLOSER
7. Identify What are the input and output forces on a steering wheel?

_____

_____

_____

_____

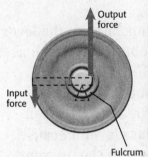

A wheel and axle changes a small input force into a larger output force.

What Are Inclined Planes?

Remember that a ramp makes work easier by reducing the force needed to move an object. Ramps are examples of simple inclined planes. *Simple inclined planes* are simple machines with a straight, slanted surface.

Inclined planes, like all machines, do not reduce the amount of work needed to move an object. They reduce the force you apply by increasing the distance over which you apply it. You do the same amount of work whether you lift something straight up or push it up a ramp. ☑

The mechanical advantage of an inclined plane is equal to its length (input distance) divided by its height (output distance). Pushing an object up a long, gradual ramp takes less force than pushing the object up a short, steep ramp. In other words, a long, gradual inclined plane has a greater mechanical advantage than a short, steep plane.

✔ **READING CHECK**

8. Explain How do ramps reduce the force needed to move an object?

_____

_____

_____

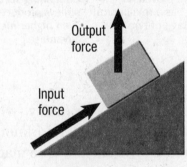

A short, steep inclined plane has a small mechanical advantage.

LOOKING CLOSER
9. Apply Concepts A student wants to use one of the two ramps in the figure to move a box of books. If the student wants to use the smallest possible force to move the books, which ramp should he use? Explain your answer.

_____

_____

_____

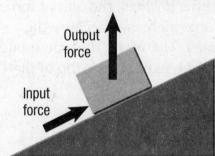

A long, gently sloping inclined plane has a greater mechanical advantage.

SECTION 2 Simple Machines *continued*

WEDGES AND SCREWS

A wedge is formed from two inclined planes placed back to back. Ax blades, splitting wedges, and door-stops are examples of wedges. As shown in the figure below, using a wedge is like pushing down on a ramp. In other words, a wedge is a moving inclined plane. A wedge turns a single downward force into two forces directed out to the sides. It both multiplies force and changes the direction of the force.

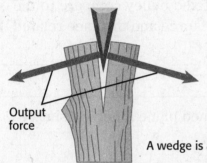

Input force

Output force

A wedge is a moving inclined plane.

LOOKING CLOSER
10. Describe How does the wedge affect the input force?

_____

_____

_____

A screw is an inclined plane wrapped around a cylinder. When you tighten a screw with gently sloping threads, you apply a small input force over a large distance. The screw then exerts a large output force over a small distance. A screw with steeper threads requires more force to tighten, because the input force is applied over a shorter distance.

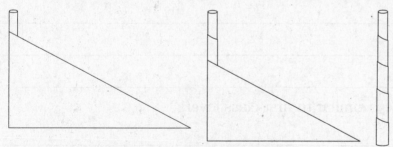

A screw is an inclined plane wrapped around a cylinder.

LOOKING CLOSER
11. Identify Relationships How is a screw related to a simple inclined plane?

_____

_____

_____

What Are Compound Machines?

Many of the things you use every day are compound machines. A **compound machine** is a machine that combines two or more simple machines. For example, a pair of scissors is made of two first-class levers joined at a common fulcrum. Each lever arm is a wedge. Together, the wedges can cut paper. Bicycles and cars are made of many simple machines, so they are also compound machines.

Name _____ Class _____ Date _____

Section 2 Review

SECTION VOCABULARY

compound machine a machine made of more than one simple machine	**simple machine** one of the six basic types of machines, which are the basis for all other forms of machines

1. List What are the six simple machines?

_____

_____

2. Compare How does the input distance of a single fixed pulley compare to the output distance? Explain your answer. (Hint: How are force and distance related?)

_____

_____

3. Infer Why are wedges and screws part of the inclined plane family of simple machines?

_____

_____

4. Compare How are second-class levers and third-class levers similar? How are they different?

_____

_____

_____

5. Explain How are fixed pulleys similar to first-class levers?

_____

_____

6. Infer Can a simple inclined plane have a mechanical advantage less than one? Explain your answer. (Hint: Can the height of a ramp ever be greater than its length?)

_____

_____

_____

CHAPTER 13 | Work and Energy
SECTION
3 **What Is Energy?**

KEY IDEAS

As you read this section, keep these questions in mind:
- How are energy and work related?
- Why is potential energy called energy of position?
- What is kinetic energy?
- What is mechanical energy?

What Is Energy?

The world around you is full of energy. A lightning bolt has electrical energy. Your body contains chemical energy from the food you eat. Obviously, energy exists in many forms, but what is energy? **Energy** is the ability to do work.

Whenever work is done, energy is transformed or transferred from one object to another object. For example, suppose you use a hammer to pound a nail into a piece of wood. You do work on the hammer. The hammer does work on the nail. The nail does work on the board. Each time one object does work on another, energy flows between the objects.

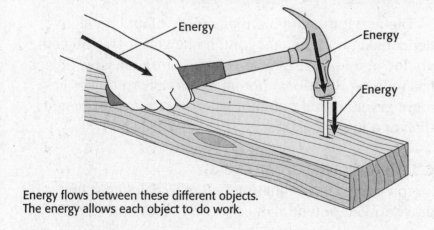

Energy flows between these different objects.
The energy allows each object to do work.

What Is Potential Energy?

An object at rest is not doing work, but it can have energy. How can that be? Such an object has potential energy. **Potential energy** is the energy an object has because of its position or shape. Potential energy is sometimes called *energy of position*, because it results from the relative positions of objects. ☑

READING TOOLBOX

Organize As you read this section, make a table listing the different forms of energy. Include definitions for each form of energy, an example of each form, and any equations used to calculate each form.

LOOKING CLOSER

1. Infer If your hand supplies the energy for the hammer to do work, where does the energy to move your hand come from?

_____

_____

READING CHECK

2. Identify Where does potential energy come from?

_____

_____

SECTION 3 What Is Energy? *continued*

TYPES OF POTENTIAL ENERGY

When you stretch a rubber band, you do work on it to change its shape. The energy you use to stretch the rubber is stored as potential energy until you release the rubber band. Any object that can be stretched or compressed has potential energy called *elastic potential energy*. Bungee cords, balls, and springs also have elastic potential energy.

An object that is above Earth's surface can fall to the ground and do work. Therefore, it has stored energy. This kind of stored energy is called *gravitational potential energy*. It is a result of the gravitational attraction between objects. Earth's gravitational force pulls on all objects near its surface. Therefore, all objects above Earth's surface have gravitational potential energy. ☑

The car at the top of a hill on a roller coaster has gravitational potential energy. The car can do work when it moves down the hill.

✔ **READING CHECK**

3. Explain Why do all objects above Earth's surface have gravitational potential energy?

_____

_____

_____

Critical Thinking

4. Explain Why does gravitational potential energy depend on both mass and height?
(Hint: What two factors affect the strength of gravitational force?)

_____

_____

_____

_____

_____

_____

_____

_____

The gravitational potential energy of an object depends on both its mass and its height. If two objects are located at the same height, the more massive object has more gravitational potential energy. An object has more gravitational potential energy at a greater height than at a lower height.

CALCULATING POTENTIAL ENERGY

You can use the equation below to calculate the gravitational potential energy (*PE*) of an object:

gravitational PE = mass × free-fall acceleration × height

$$PE = mgh$$

Remember that an object's weight is equal to its mass (*m*) times gravitational free-fall acceleration (*g*). Therefore, gravitational potential energy is simply an object's weight multiplied by its height. The units of gravitational potential energy are the same as those of all types of energy: joules (J).

RELATIVE HEIGHT AND POTENTIAL ENERGY

In the potential energy equation, height usually means the distance of the object from the ground. However, in some cases a different height may be more useful.

For example, imagine an apple attached to the branch of a tree. Below the branch, there is a bird's nest. If the apple falls onto the nest, the apple will do work on the nest. The farther the apple falls before it hits the nest, the more work it will be able to do on the nest. To calculate the apple's gravitational potential energy relative to the nest, use the height of the apple above the nest.

Let's try an example. A 65 kg rock climber climbs 35 m up a cliff. What is the climber's gravitational potential energy? Remember that free-fall acceleration is equal to 9.8 m/s².

Step 1: List the given and unknown values.	**Given:** mass, $m = 65$ kg height, $h = 35$ m free-fall acceleration, $g = 9.8$ m/s²	**Unknown:** gravitational potential energy, *PE*
Step 2: Write the equation.	$PE = mgh$	
Step 3: Insert the known values and solve for the unknown value.	$PE = (65$ kg$) \times (9.8$ m/s²$) \times (35$ m$)$ $PE = 22{,}000$ kg $\cdot$ m²/s² $PE = 2.2 \times 10^4$ J	

So, the climber's potential energy is 2.2×10^4 J.

What Is Kinetic Energy?

Think back to the apple hanging from a tree branch. When the apple is hanging, it has gravitational potential energy. What kind of energy does it have when it falls toward the ground? The energy an object has because it is moving is called **kinetic energy**.

The kinetic energy of an object depends on both the object's mass and its speed. A bowling ball can do more work than a tennis ball if both balls are moving at the same speed. This is because the bowling ball has more mass. On the other hand, two bowling balls rolling at different speeds have different kinetic energies. The ball rolling faster has more kinetic energy. ☑

Talk About It

Brainstorm In a small group, think of some examples of situations in which you shouldn't use the height of an object above the ground to calculate its gravitational potential energy.

Math Skills

5. Calculate A chef holds a 55 g egg above the floor. The egg has 0.65 J of gravitational potential energy. How far above the ground is the egg? Show your work. (Hint: Rearrange the equation for gravitational potential energy to solve for height.)

✓ READING CHECK

6. Identify What two factors affect an object's kinetic energy?

_____

_____

SECTION 3 What Is Energy? *continued*

KINETIC ENERGY AND SPEED

In fact, kinetic energy depends more on speed than on mass. To understand why this is, examine the equation for kinetic energy below:

$$kinetic\ energy = \frac{1}{2} \times mass \times speed\ squared$$

$$KE = \frac{1}{2}mv^2$$

In the kinetic energy equation, speed is squared. Therefore, even a small change in speed causes a large change in kinetic energy. This is why car crashes at high speeds are much more dangerous than crashes at low speeds. A car has much more kinetic energy at high speeds, so it can do more work—damage—in a collision. The graph below shows the effect of speed on kinetic energy for a snowboarder.

Critical Thinking

7. Apply Concepts What will happen to the kinetic energy of an object if its speed doubles?

_____

_____

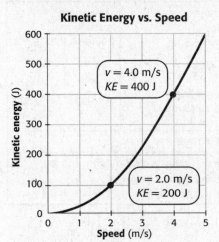

Kinetic Energy vs. Speed

A small increase in speed produces a larger increase in kinetic energy. This is because kinetic energy is proportional to speed squared.

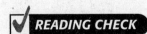

8. Read a Graph What is the snowboarder's kinetic energy when her speed is 5 m/s?

_____

_____

KINETIC ENERGY OF ATOMS AND MOLECULES

Atoms and molecules are always moving, so they have kinetic energy. The faster the particles in a substance are moving, the higher its temperature. This is because temperature is a measure of the average kinetic energy of the particles in a substance. For example, the molecules in a glass of water have more kinetic energy than molecules in an ice cube. ☑

Another quantity that describes the kinetic energy of particles is thermal energy. Thermal energy is the total kinetic energy of all the particles in an object. Unlike temperature, thermal energy depends on the mass of an object, as well as how fast its particles are moving.

✓ READING CHECK

9. Describe What happens to an object's temperature if the kinetic energy of its particles decreases?

_____

_____

SECTION 3 What Is Energy? *continued*

CALCULATING KINETIC ENERGY

You can use the kinetic energy equation to calculate the energy of a moving object. For example, if a 44 kg cheetah is running at a speed of 31 m/s, what is its kinetic energy?

Step 1: List the given and unknown values.	Given: mass, $m = 44$ kg speed, $v = 31$ m/s	Unknown: kinetic energy, *KE*
Step 2: Write the equation.	$KE = \frac{1}{2}mv^2$	
Step 3: Insert the known values and solve for the unknown value.	$KE = \frac{1}{2}$ (44 kg) $\times$ (31 m/s^2) $KE = 21{,}000$ kg $\cdot$ m^2/s^2 $KE = 2.1 \times 10^4$ J	

So, the cheetah has 2.1×10^4 J of kinetic energy.

What Is Mechanical Energy?

How would you describe the energy of an apple falling from a tree? Because the apple is moving, it has kinetic energy. Until the apple hits the ground, the apple also has potential energy. As the apple falls, its potential energy changes into kinetic energy.

Both gravitational potential energy and kinetic energy are forms of mechanical energy. **Mechanical energy** is the amount of work something can do because of its kinetic and potential energies. The mechanical energy of an object is equal to the sum of its gravitational potential energy and its kinetic energy: ☑

mechanical energy = kinetic energy + potential energy

An object's mechanical energy can be all potential energy, all kinetic energy, or some of both. An object's mechanical energy remains the same as long as no energy is added it. If an object's potential energy increases because its position has changed, its kinetic energy must decrease. If its potential energy decreases, its kinetic energy must increase.

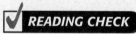Math **Skills**

10. Calculate A bowling ball travels at 2.0 m/s. It has 16 J of kinetic energy. What is the mass of the bowling ball in kilograms? Show your work. (Hint: Rearrange the kinetic energy equation to solve for mass.)

✓ **READING CHECK**

11. Define What is mechanical energy?

_____

_____

What Is Nonmechanical Energy?

There are forms of energy other than mechanical energy. For example, your body uses energy from the food you eat. The energy in food comes from the sun. The appliances in your home run on electrical energy. Many of these forms of *nonmechanical energy* come from the interactions between atoms and molecules. ☑

CHEMICAL ENERGY

Chemical energy is a kind of potential energy. In a chemical reaction, bonds between the atoms of a substance break apart. When the atoms form new bonds, different substances are formed. The breaking and making of bonds involves energy. *Chemical energy* is energy stored in the bonds of substances. The amount of chemical energy in a substance depends on the arrangement of atoms in the substance.

READING CHECK

12. Identify Where do many forms of nonmechanical energy come from?

_____

_____

_____

LOOKING CLOSER

13. Describe Where does the energy in an unburned match come from?

_____

_____

Matches contain chemical energy in the form of chemical compounds. When the matches burn, the chemical energy is converted to heat and light energy.

CHEMICAL ENERGY IN LIVING THINGS

All living things require energy. They use energy to grow, reproduce, move, and defend themselves. The energy they use comes from food.

Plants, algae, and certain bacteria can make their own food. These organisms use energy from the sun to change carbon dioxide and water into sugar and oxygen. This process is called *photosynthesis*.

Sugars and other foods, like all chemical compounds, contain chemical energy. Living things obtain the energy they need from food. They break the bonds in the chemicals they eat and store the energy in other compounds. ☑

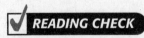
READING CHECK

14. Identify What kind of energy do plants convert sunlight into during photosynthesis?

_____

_____

SECTION 3 What Is Energy? *continued*

NUCLEAR ENERGY

Remember that the strong nuclear force holds protons and neutrons together in the nuclei of atoms. As a result of this force, atomic nuclei contain potential energy called *nuclear energy.* Some kinds of reactions can release this energy. For example, within the sun and most other stars, atomic nuclei *fuse*, or combine. This *nuclear fusion* releases energy. People use *nuclear fission*, or the breaking apart of nuclei, to produce electricity. ☑

15. Identify Name two kinds of nuclear energy.

_____

_____

ELECTRICAL ENERGY

Most of the appliances that we use every day are powered by electricity. Electricity is a form of *electrical energy,* which comes from the movements of charged particles.

Electrical energy is similar to gravitational potential energy. Charged particles move from areas of high electric potential to areas of low electric potential. This is similar to what happens when an object falls to the ground. When the charged particles move, they transmit energy.

LIGHT ENERGY

Think about a hot, sunny day at the beach such as the one in the figure below. Is the sand hotter under the shade of the umbrella or where sunlight is shining directly on the sand? You might guess, correctly, that the sand in the direct sunlight is hotter. The reason is that sunlight carries energy. The energy from the sun heats the Earth.

Electromagnetic waves carry energy from the sun to Earth. Most objects absorb some of these waves. The energy in the waves is then converted to heat energy.

LOOKING CLOSER

16. Explain Why is the sand cooler under the umbrella than outside the umbrella?

_____

_____

_____

_____

Light energy travels from the sun to the Earth across empty space in the form of *electromagnetic waves.* Electromagnetic waves can travel through empty space.

Section 3 Review

SECTION VOCABULARY

energy the capacity to do work	**mechanical energy** the amount of work an object can do because of the object's kinetic and potential energies
kinetic energy the energy of an object that is due to the object's motion	**potential energy** the energy that an object has because of the position, shape, or condition of the object

1. Explain A boy on a bicycle is resting at the top of a hill. Then, he rides his bicycle down the hill. Describe how the boy's potential and kinetic energy differ at the top, middle, and bottom of the hill.

_____

_____

_____

2. Describe Fill in the table. Decide what form or forms of energy apply to each situation and whether each form is mechanical or nonmechanical energy.

Situation	Form(s) of Energy	Mechanical or nonmechanical?
Frisbee moving through the air	kinetic and potential energy	
Cup of hot soup		nonmechanical
Sunlight	light energy	
Boulder sitting at the top of a hill		
A lit lightbulb	electrical energy and light energy	

3. Apply Concepts Why are water storage tanks usually built on towers or hilltops?

_____

_____

_____

4. Calculate What is the potential energy of a 35 kg child sitting at the top of a slide that is 3.5 m above the ground? What is her kinetic energy if she moves down the slide at a speed of 5.0 m/s? Show your work.

CHAPTER 13 | Work and Energy

SECTION

4 Conservation of Energy

KEY IDEAS

As you read this section, keep these questions in mind:

• How can energy change from one form to another?

• What is the law of conservation of energy?

• How much of the work done by a machine is useful work?

• What is efficiency?

How Can Energy Change from One Form to Another?

Imagine you are sitting in a roller coaster car. A conveyer belt pulls the car slowly up the first hill. When you reach the top of the hill, you are barely moving. Then the car goes over the top, and you race down the hill. You speed faster and faster down the hill to the bottom. You continue moving up and down through smaller hills, twists, and turns until you coast to the end.

This roller coaster, like many others, relies on the fact that energy is conserved to move riders up and down hills.

During your roller coaster ride, energy changes from one form to another many times. All of the energy required for the whole ride comes from the conveyer belt on the first hill. It does work as it lifts the car and passengers up the hill. The energy from that work is stored as gravitational potential energy at the top of the hill.

Before the ride is over, the energy changes from potential energy into kinetic energy and back again several times. In addition, a small amount of the stored energy is transferred to the wheels as heat. Some energy also makes the air vibrate and creates the roaring sound. The energy changes easily from one form to another, but the total amount of energy always remains the same.

READING TOOLBOX

List As you read this section, make a list of real-life examples that demonstrate the law of conservation of energy.

LOOKING CLOSER

1. Identify Where does the roller coaster car have the most gravitational potential energy?

_____

_____

_____

SECTION 4 Conservation of Energy *continued*

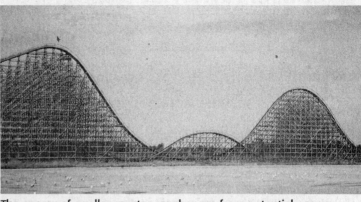

The energy of a roller coaster car changes from potential energy to kinetic energy and back again many times during a ride.

LOOKING CLOSER

2. Identify On the figure, circle the location at which the roller coaster car has the least gravitational potential energy.

POTENTIAL ENERGY TO KINETIC ENERGY AND BACK

At the top of a hill, all the energy of a roller coaster car is potential energy. The potential energy slowly changes to kinetic energy as the car accelerates down the hill. At the bottom of the hill, almost all of the potential energy has changed to kinetic energy. However, the system has the same total energy whether the car is at the top or bottom.

This kinetic energy of the car at the bottom of the hill can carry the car up another smaller hill. As the car climbs the hill, the car slows down and its kinetic energy decreases. Where does that energy go? Most of it turns back into potential energy.

At the top of the smaller hill, the car still has some kinetic energy, along with some potential energy. The kinetic energy carries the car forward over the top of the hill. This process continues to the end of the ride—potential energy to kinetic energy and back again.

Remember that the initial energy for the ride came from the work the conveyer belt did to lift the car. The roller coaster cannot climb a hill as tall or taller than the first hill without more work being done. The car does not have enough energy.

The car also cannot glide on forever. If the changes from potential energy to kinetic energy were complete, the roller coaster ride would never have to end. Where does the energy go? It is transformed into other forms of energy. ☑

Talk About It

Discuss In a small group, identify several situations in everyday life in which an object's energy changes from one form to another. For each situation, identify the different types of energy the object has at different times.

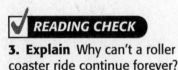

READING CHECK

3. Explain Why can't a roller coaster ride continue forever?

_____

_____

_____

MECHANICAL ENERGY TO OTHER FORMS OF ENERGY

Imagine dropping a tennis ball on the ground. With each bounce, the ball loses height. Eventually, it stops bouncing. If no energy were lost, the ball would bounce to its starting height forever.

The ball stops bouncing because not all of its kinetic energy changes to elastic potential energy when it bounces. With each bounce, the ball loses some of its mechanical energy.

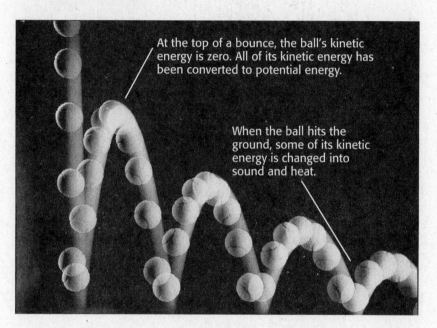

At the top of a bounce, the ball's kinetic energy is zero. All of its kinetic energy has been converted to potential energy.

When the ball hits the ground, some of its kinetic energy is changed into sound and heat.

Critical Thinking
4. Apply Concepts Identify two forms of potential energy that the tennis ball has.

_____

_____

LOOKING CLOSER
5. Identify On the figure, circle a place where the ball has both kinetic and gravitational potential energy.

Is the energy really "lost"? When the ball bounces, some of its kinetic energy compresses the air around the ball, which makes a sound. Some of the kinetic energy also heats the ball, air, and ground. Sound and heat are forms of nonmechanical energy. In most cases, when it seems that an object has "lost" mechanical energy, the energy has just changed form.

Similarly, a moving roller coaster car loses mechanical energy as it rolls, because of friction and air resistance. This energy is not "lost." Some of it increases the temperature of the track, the car's wheels, and the air. Some of the energy compresses the air around the wheels and causes a roaring sound. The car's mechanical energy has not disappeared. Some mechanical energy has just changed to nonmechanical forms.

Name _____ Class _____ Date _____

GRAPHING MECHANICAL ENERGY

Graphs are a useful way to show relationships between variables. The bar graph below presents data about the mechanical energy of a roller coaster car.

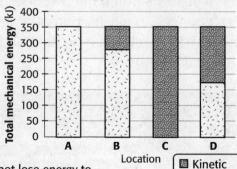

Mechanical Energy of a Roller Coaster Car

> **Graphing** *Skills*

6. Read a Graph At which location does the roller coaster car have the most kinetic energy?

_____

If the roller coaster car did not lose energy to friction, its total energy would stay the same throughout the ride. It would change from kinetic to potential energy and back again.

Legend:
- ▦ Kinetic energy
- ☐ Potential energy

Use the steps below to learn about the relationship between potential and kinetic energy that is illustrated in the graph:

Step 1: Study the axes to determine the variables being plotted.

x-axis variable: location
y-axis variable: mechanical energy

Critical Thinking

7. Identify Name two things about the roller coaster car that you cannot learn by examining the graph.

_____

_____

_____

_____

Step 2: Identify the dependent and independent variables.

Location is the independent variable, because location does not depend on the energy of the car.

Kinetic and potential energy are the dependent variables, because the car's energy depends on its location.

Step 3: Examine the legend and decide what it tells you about how it relates to the graph.

The legend indicates that mechanical energy consists of both kinetic and potential energy.

Step 4: Examine the graph to decide what the data tell you about the relationship between kinetic and potential energy.

The graph shows that total mechanical energy stays the same. An increase in kinetic energy produces an equal decrease in potential energy. A decrease in kinetic energy produces an equal increase in potential energy.

SECTION 4 Conservation of Energy *continued*

What Is the Law of Conservation of Energy?

The energy present in a roller coaster car at the beginning of the ride is present throughout the ride. The same amount of energy is present at the end of the ride, even though the energy has changed form. The energy of a bouncing ball changes form, but none is "lost." The work done on a machine is equal to the work it can do.

These simple observations are based on one of the most important principles in science—the law of conservation of energy. Simply put, the law of conservation of energy states that *energy cannot be created or destroyed*. In other words, the total amount of energy in the universe never changes. Energy may change from one form to another, but energy never disappears. ☑

Mechanical energy can change to nonmechanical forms of energy, such as heat, light, and sound. Energy in a system may move into the surrounding environment, but the total amount of energy does not change. Energy does not disappear.

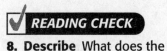

When fireworks explode, chemical potential energy is converted into other kinds of energy. However, the total energy of the system remains the same.

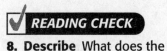

READING CHECK

8. Describe What does the law of conservation of energy state?

_____

_____

LOOKING CLOSER

9. Identify What are two kinds of energy that the chemical energy in fireworks changes into?

_____

_____

Energy also cannot be created from nothing. The total energy in a system can increase only if energy enters the system. Energy can enter a system by doing work on a system.

Imagine a boy bouncing on a trampoline. His second bounce is higher than his first bounce. How could his second bounce be bigger? Because energy cannot just appear from nowhere, he must have added energy by doing work with his legs.

SECTION 4 Conservation of Energy *continued*

Critical Thinking

10. Explain Why is it impossible to consider all the energy in the universe when doing energy calculations?

_____

_____

_____

Talk About It

Brainstorm In a small group, think of different processes or events that scientists may study. For each case, identify an appropriate system for a scientist to use. What objects or processes should be within the system? What objects or processes do not have to be included?

READING CHECK

11. Compare How is a closed system different from an isolated system?

_____

_____

_____

_____

OPEN AND CLOSED SYSTEMS

If we had to include all the energy in the universe during energy calculations, the calculations would be impossible. Therefore, to make studying a process easier, scientists often limit their view of the world. They may decide to study only a small area or small number of objects. Scientists call such small parts of the universe *systems*.

System   **Boundary**

Surroundings

A system is the object or group of objects that are being studied. A system is separated from its surroundings by a boundary.

A system might include a gas burner and a beaker of water. A scientist could study the flow of energy from the burner to the beaker of water. There is also energy in the room from the lights and heat. However, the scientist can ignore this energy because she has defined her system as the burner and the beaker.

Scientists describe systems based on whether matter and energy can flow across their boundaries. An *open system* is a system that can exchange both matter and energy with its surroundings. A *closed system* is a system that can exchange energy, but not matter, with its surroundings. An *isolated system* is a system that cannot exchange matter or energy with its surroundings. ☑

THERMODYNAMICS AND ENERGY CONSERVATION

Thermodynamics is the study of how energy moves during different processes. The process may be bouncing a ball, sanding wood, riding a roller coaster, or a plant converting sunlight into food. Thermodynamics can describe the movements of energy in each of these situations. ☑

Remember that work can transfer energy from one object to another. When you lift a ball, you do work on it. The ball gains potential energy.

Energy can also be transferred as heat. For example, when you place a piece of bread in a toaster, energy moves from the toaster to the bread. The energy causes the bread to heat up.

In any closed system, a change in energy must be caused by work or heat being gained or lost. When no energy is transferred as work or heat, energy is conserved. This form of the law of energy conservation is called the *first law of thermodynamics*.

What Is Useful Work?

We use machines to make work easier, but only part of the work done by any machine is useful work. *Useful work* is work that a machine is designed to do. ☑

For example, suppose you want to raise the sail on a sailboat. You can raise the sail with a pulley, but you must do work against the force of friction in the pulley. You also must lift the added weight of the rope and hook connected to the sail. As a result, only some of the energy that you transfer to the pulley is available to raise the sail. Therefore, only some of the work the pulley does to lift the sail is useful work.

The pulleys on a sailboat can do work. However, like all machines, not all the work they do is useful work.

READING CHECK

12. Define What is thermodynamics?

_____

_____

READING CHECK

13. Define What is useful work?

_____

_____

LOOKING CLOSER

14. Identify What happens to the energy you put into the pulley that is not used to raise the sail?

_____

_____

What Is Incidental Work?

Work that a machine does that does not serve its intended purpose is *incidental work*. Think again of the pulley on the sailboat. There is friction between the rope and the pulley. This friction causes some of the work you put into the rope to change into heat. The heat does not help to raise the sail, so it is incidental work. In addition, some of the energy in the pulley causes air to vibrate, producing sound. This is another form of incidental work.

Because of friction and other factors, only some of the work of any machine is applied to its intended purpose. The useful work done by a machine is always less than the total work put into it. ☑

EFFICIENCY

The **efficiency** of a machine is a measure of how much useful work the machine can do. Efficiency is the ratio of useful work output to total work input. The mathematical equation for efficiency is:

$$efficiency = \frac{useful\ work\ output}{work\ input}$$

Efficiency is usually expressed as a percentage. You can use the equation below to calculate percent efficiency:

$$\%\ efficiency = \frac{useful\ work\ output}{work\ input} \times 100$$

A machine that is 100% efficient would produce exactly as much useful work as the work done on the machine. However, every machine has some friction, so no machine is 100% efficient. Because no machine is 100% efficient, all machines need at least a small amount of energy input to keep going. ☑

People use machines to make work easier. Because of this, we must always put more energy into a machine than the machine can produce. The more efficient a machine is, the less extra energy we have to put into it. Therefore, scientists and engineers are always trying to design more efficient machines.

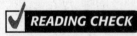
READING CHECK

15. Explain Why is the work done by a machine always less than the work put into it?

_____

_____

_____

READING CHECK

16. Describe If a machine were 100% efficient, how much work could you get out of it?

_____

_____

SECTION 4 Conservation of Energy *continued*

CALCULATING EFFICIENCY

A student uses a ramp to lift a 150 N box to a height of 2 m. The student uses 400 J of energy to push the box up the ramp. What is the percent efficiency of the ramp?

The useful work output of the ramp is the work done on the box. You can calculate the work done on the box using the work equation.

Step 1: List the given and unknown values.	Given: weight, $w = 150$ N height, $h = 2$ m work input, $= 400$ J	Unknown: efficiency
Step 2: Write the equations.	$W = Fd$ $efficiency = \dfrac{useful\ work\ output}{work\ input}$	
Step 3: Insert the known values and solve for the unknown values.	$W = (150\ N) \times (2\ m)$ $W = 300\ J = $ useful work output $efficiency = \dfrac{300\ J}{400\ J}$ $efficiency = 0.75$	

To convert the decimal efficiency to a percent, multiply by 100. This gives the percent efficiency of the ramp: 75%.

PERPETUAL MOTION MACHINES

Many clever inventors have tried to design machines that will keep going forever without any input of energy. Such a machine is called a *perpetual motion machine*. However, even with a lot of time and effort, no inventor will ever create a perpetual motion machine. This is because a perpetual motion machine can only work in the absence of friction and air resistance. These conditions are not found in our universe.

In theory, a perpetual motion machine is 100% efficient. However, in our universe, perpetual motion machines cannot exist.

Math *Skills*

17. Calculate A sailor uses a rope and an old, squeaky pulley to raise a sail. It takes 140 J of work to lift the sail 1 m. Using the pulley, he must do 180 J of work to raise the sail. What is the percent efficiency of the pulley? Show your work.

LOOKING CLOSER

18. Explain Why are perpetual motion machines impossible?

_____

_____

Section 4 Review

SECTION VOCABULARY

efficiency a quantity, usually expressed as a percentage, that measures the ratio of work output to work input	

1. Describe State the law of conservation of energy in your own words.

_____

_____

2. Calculate John uses a pulley to lift the sail on his sailboat. The sail weighs 150 N, and he must lift it 4.0 m. The pulley is 50% efficient. How much work must be done to lift the sail? How much work must John do on the rope to lift the sail? Show your work.

3. Calculate A student does 100 J of work on the handle of a bicycle pump. The pump does 40 J of work pushing the air into the tire. What is the efficiency of the pump? Show your work.

4. Apply Concepts Imagine a bouncing ball that does not lose any energy as it bounces. Could it ever bounce to a greater height than it was dropped from? Explain your answer.

_____

_____

5. Explain Why are machines never 100% efficient?

_____

_____

_____

6. Apply Concepts Are living things open or closed systems? Explain your answer.

_____

_____

CHAPTER 14 Heat and Temperature
SECTION 1 Temperature

> ## KEY IDEAS
>
> **As you read this section, keep these questions in mind:**
> - How are temperature and energy related?
> - What are the three common temperature scales?
> - Why do objects feel hot or cold?

What Is Temperature?

When you touch the hood of a car, you can feel if it is hot or cold. If someone asks you to describe the temperature of the car, you may use those words to describe it. However, the words *hot* and *cold* are not very precise terms. In science, we need to describe temperature in a more precise way.

To describe temperature precisely, you must first know what temperature is. Temperature is closely related to energy. Remember that matter is made up of particles, such as atoms and molecules. These particles are constantly moving, so they have kinetic energy. **Temperature** is a measure of the average kinetic energy of all of the particles in an object. ☑

People take temperature readings every day. In most cases, people use a thermometer to measure the temperature of an object. A **thermometer** is a tool that measures temperature. However, thermometers do not directly measure the average kinetic energy of particles. Instead, most thermometers measure the effects of changes in the kinetic energy of particles.

READING TOOLBOX

Ask Questions As you read this section, write down any questions you have. When you finish reading, try to figure out the answers to your questions by discussing them with a partner.

☑ READING CHECK

1. Identify Relationships How is temperature related to kinetic energy?

_____

_____

_____

Talk About It

Discuss In a small group, talk about why it is important to know the temperatures of certain things.

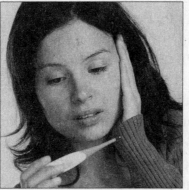

People use different kinds of thermometers to measure the temperatures of different things. For example, we use a different kind of thermometer to measure the temperature outside than to measure our body temperatures.

SECTION 1 Temperature *continued*

How Do Thermometers Work?

The particles in an object with a high temperature have a great deal of kinetic energy. Remember that the kinetic energy of an object is related to its speed. The faster the object is moving, the higher its kinetic energy. Therefore, the particles in a hot object are moving quickly. However, we can't measure the kinetic energy of every particle in an object. How, then, can we measure temperature? ☑

To measure temperature using a thermometer, we rely on the fact that most substances expand when their temperature increases. This is because the particles are moving faster and have more kinetic energy. Therefore, when the particles collide, they move farther away from one another. As the particles move apart, the substance expands.

A common thermometer contains a hollow tube with some liquid, such as mercury or colored alcohol, in it. On the outside of the tube, there are markings for different temperatures. If the kinetic energy of the particles in the liquid increases, the liquid expands. It rises up the tube. The liquid reaches a higher temperature marking. In this way, we can measure the temperature of a material.

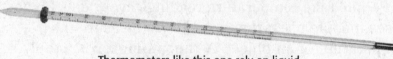

Thermometers like this one rely on liquid expansion to measure temperature.

READING CHECK

2. Review What happens to temperature as kinetic energy increases?

_____

_____

_____

Critical Thinking

3. Predict Consequences Imagine a liquid that contracts when its temperature increases. If that liquid were used in a thermometer, what would happen to the liquid level when temperature increased?

_____

_____

_____

METAL EXPANSION IN THERMOSTATS

Most metals also expand when they are heated and contract when they are cooled. This property of metals is used in a thermostat. A *thermostat* measures and controls the temperature inside a house, building, or machine. ☑

A thermostat contains a coil made of strips of two different types of metal. These two metals expand and contract by different amounts. As the temperature falls, the metal coil unwinds. This moves the pointer on the thermostat to a lower temperature reading. When the temperature rises, the coil winds up. This moves the pointer on the thermostat in the opposite direction, to a higher temperature reading.

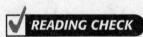

READING CHECK

4. Describe What does a thermostat do?

_____

_____

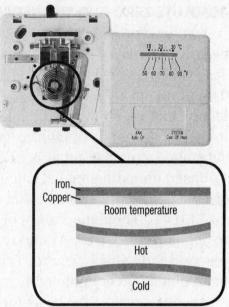

The coil inside a thermostat is made of two different metals. The metals expand at different rates when the temperature changes. This causes the coil to tighten or loosen. As the coil moves, the pointer moves to a different temperature reading.

LOOKING CLOSER

5. Explain What causes the pointer on a thermostat to move to a different temperature reading?

_____

_____

_____

_____

What Are the Three Temperature Scales?

If you hear someone say that it is 37 degrees outside, would you think that it is hot or cold? Would you wear a sweater or a T-shirt? It depends on which scale the person is using to measure temperature. There are three different temperature scales that are commonly used. They are the Fahrenheit, Celsius, and Kelvin scales. ☑

People in the United States mainly use the Fahrenheit scale to measure temperature. The units on the Fahrenheit scale are called *degrees Fahrenheit* (°F). Water freezes at 32 °F and boils at 212 °F.

Most countries other than the United States use the Celsius scale to measure temperature. Many scientists also use this scale. The units on the Celsius scale are called *degrees Celsius* (°C). Water freezes at 0 °C and boils at 100 °C.

You can *convert*, or change, temperature measurements in degrees Fahrenheit to measurements in degrees Celsius. To do this, use the equations below.

READING CHECK

6. Identify What are the three main temperature scales?

_____

_____

_____

Fahrenheit temperature = (1.8 × Celsius temperature) + 32.0

$$T_F = 1.8 T_C + 32.0$$

Celsius temperature = $\dfrac{\text{Fahrenheit temperature} - 32.0}{1.8}$

$$T_C = \dfrac{T_F - 32.0}{1.8}$$

Math *Skills*

7. Convert People sometimes write the "1.8" in the equations to the left as a fraction instead of a decimal. What is 1.8 written as a fraction?

_____

ABSOLUTE ZERO AND THE KELVIN SCALE

You have probably heard people give temperatures in negative degrees Celsius or negative degrees Fahrenheit. This is because even below temperatures of 0 °C or 0 °F, particles are still moving. These particles still have kinetic energy, so they still have a temperature. However, in theory, there is a point at which all of the particles in a substance stop moving. It is called **absolute zero**. ☑

Based on mathematical calculations and experiments, scientists have determined that absolute zero is equal to −273.16 °C. The temperature of outer space is very close to absolute zero. However, in reality, an object can never reach exactly absolute zero. This is because the particles in an object never completely stop moving.

Absolute zero is the basis for the Kelvin temperature scale. Many scientists use the Kelvin scale to measure temperature. The units for the Kelvin scale are called *kelvins* (K). On this scale, absolute zero is 0 K. Temperature measurements on the Kelvin scale do not use the degree sign (°).

There are no negative temperature values on the Kelvin scale. This is because absolute zero is the lowest possible temperature. Remember that absolute zero is equal to 0 K and −273.16 °C. Therefore, you can convert between the Kelvin and Celsius scales using the equation below: ☑

Kelvin temperature = Celsius temperature + 273.16

$$T_K = T_C + 273.16$$

Some recent scientific experiments have reached temperatures near absolute zero. Scientists have found that matter behaves in very unusual ways at such low temperatures. For example, friction seems to disappear between many surfaces near absolute zero.

The table below summarizes the main differences between the three main temperature scales. The figure at the top of the next page shows some common temperatures on all three scales.

READING CHECK

8. Describe In theory, what would happen to the particles in a substance at absolute zero?

_____

_____

_____

_____

READING CHECK

9. Explain Why can't there be negative temperatures on the Kelvin scale?

_____

_____

_____

_____

Scale	Temperature at which water freezes	Temperature at which water boils	Absolute zero temperature
Fahrenheit	32 °F	212 °F	−459.69 °F
Celsius	0 °C	100 °C	−273.16 °C
Kelvin	273.16 K	373.16 K	0 K

SECTION 1 Temperature *continued*

Common Temperatures on Three Temperature Scales

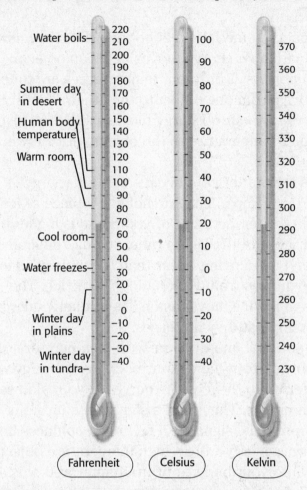

Water boils—
Summer day in desert
Human body temperature
Warm room
Cool room—
Water freezes—
Winter day in plains
Winter day in tundra—

Fahrenheit   Celsius   Kelvin

LOOKING CLOSER

10. Identify What is average human body temperature in degrees Celsius?

_____

11. Identify At what temperature on the Kelvin scale does water boil?

_____

CONVERTING BETWEEN TEMPERATURE SCALES

Let's try a problem converting between the different temperature scales. The highest temperature recorded on Earth was 57.8 °C, in Libya. What is this same temperature in degrees Fahrenheit and in kelvins?

Step 1: List the given and unknown values.	Given: Celsius temperature, $T_C = 57.8$ °C	Unknown: Fahrenheit temperature, T_F Kelvin temperature, T_K
Step 2: Write the equations.	$T_F = 1.8T_C + 32.0$ $T_K = T_C + 273.16$	
Step 3: Insert the known values and solve for the unknown values.	$T_F = 1.8 \times 57.8$ °C $+ 32.0$ $T_F = 136$ °F $T_K = 57.8$ °C $+ 237.16$ $T_K = 331$ K	

Math *Skills*

12. Convert The melting point of gold is 1,064 °C. What is its melting point in degrees Fahrenheit? Show your work.

So, 57.8 °C is the same as 136 °F and 331 K.

How Are Temperature and Energy Transfer Related?

What makes something feel hot or cold? The answer has to do with how energy moves between objects. When two objects at different temperatures are touching, energy moves from one object to the other. This is called *energy transfer*. Energy moves from the object with a higher temperature to the object with a lower temperature. ☑

Objects feel hot or cold because of this energy transfer. For example, imagine holding a piece of ice in your hand. The temperature of your hand is higher than the temperature of the ice. In other words, the molecules in your hand are moving faster than the molecules in the ice. Energy moves from your hand into the ice. The molecules in the ice move faster. Their kinetic energy— and their temperature—increases.

Where does the energy to raise the temperature of the ice come from? Your hand. Your body loses energy when it is transferred to the ice. The nerves in your skin sense this loss of energy. They send a signal to your brain. Your brain interprets the signal as a feeling of coldness. In a similar way, energy from a high-temperature object will move into your body. Your brain interprets this as a feeling of heat. ☑

READING CHECK

13. Identify When two objects touch, in which direction does energy move?

_____

_____

_____

READING CHECK

14. Describe If you are holding a hot object, does energy flow into or out of your hand?

_____

LOOKING CLOSER

15. Illustrate On the figure, draw arrows in each picture to show the direction in which heat moves.

Glass of ice water

Cup of hot tea

Energy flows from objects at high temperatures to objects at lower temperatures.

SECTION 1 Temperature *continued*

HEAT

The energy that is transferred between objects at different temperatures is called **heat**. Heat always moves from an object at a higher temperature to an object at a lower temperature. If two objects are at the same temperature, no heat will move between them. Heat moves between two objects until their temperatures are equal. At that point, the particles in both objects have the same amount of kinetic energy.

RATE OF ENERGY TRANSFER

The difference in temperature between two objects can tell you the direction in which heat will flow. The difference in temperature between two objects can also tell you how fast heat will flow. The greater the temperature difference, the faster heat flows.

For example, imagine two containers of water. The water in one container has a temperature of 60 °C. The water in the other container has a temperature of 40 °C. Both containers are in a room. The air in the room has a temperature of 10 °C, as shown below.

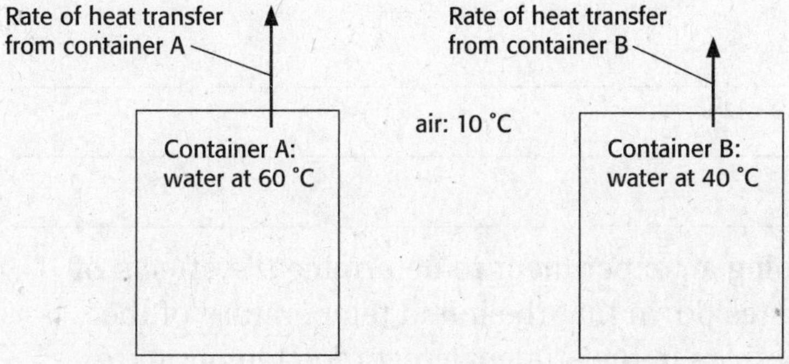

Rate of heat transfer from container A

Rate of heat transfer from container B

air: 10 °C

Container A: water at 60 °C

Container B: water at 40 °C

Heat will flow from the water in the containers into the air in the room. As heat flows, the temperature of the water will decrease, and the temperature of the air will increase. Heat will flow out of the warmer water faster than out of the cooler water. As the temperature of the water gets close to the temperature of the air, heat flows more slowly.

Critical Thinking

16. Apply Concepts A student places a cup of cold water on a counter in a warm room. The student measures the temperature of the water every minute until it stops changing. The water's final temperature is 28 °C. What is the final temperature of the room?

_____

LOOKING CLOSER

17. Identify Which container of water will lose heat the fastest? Explain your answer.

_____

_____

_____

Section 1 Review

SECTION VOCABULARY

absolute zero the temperature at which molecular energy is at a minimum (0 K on the Kelvin scale or −273.16 °C on the Celsius scale)	**temperature** a measure of how hot (or cold) something is; specifically, a measure of the average kinetic energy of the particles in an object
heat the energy transferred between objects that are at different temperatures; energy is always transferred from higher-temperature objects to lower-temperature objects until thermal equilibrium is reached	**thermometer** an instrument that measures and indicates temperature

1. Compare How is temperature related to heat?

_____

_____

2. Calculate The thermometer in an air-conditioned room reads 20.0 °C. What is the temperature of the room in degrees Fahrenheit and in kelvins? Show your work.

3. Compare Which atoms are moving faster: those in a spoon at 0 °F or those in a fork at 0 °C? Explain your answer. (Hint: Which is the higher temperature, 0 °F or 0 °C?)

_____

_____

_____

4. Identify Problems A student is doing an experiment to determine the effects of temperature on an object. He writes down that the initial temperature of the object was –3.5 °K. Identify two errors in the student's recorded temperature.

_____

_____

5. Calculate A sample of liquid nitrogen has a temperature of –320.8 °F. What is its temperature in degrees Celsius and in kelvins? Show your work. (Hint: Use the temperature in degrees Celsius to calculate the temperature in kelvins.)

CHAPTER 14 Heat and Temperature
SECTION 2 **Energy Transfer**

KEY IDEAS

As you read this section, keep these questions in mind:
- What are three kinds of energy transfer?
- What are conductors and insulators?
- What makes something a good conductor of heat?

How Can Energy Be Transferred?

In the morning, you might turn on the shower and wait for the water to warm up. Outside your home, the dew on the grass evaporates when sunlight hits it. In your freezer, the water in ice trays becomes solid after the water cools to 0 °C. None of these things could happen without energy transfer. There are three different ways that energy can be transferred between objects: conduction, convection, and radiation. ☑

The figure below shows an example of a situation in which all three kinds of energy transfer are occurring. Heat moves through the metal wire in the girl's hand by conduction. Convection in the air carries heat away from the fire. The light from the flames moves by radiation.

READING TOOLBOX

Compare As you read this section, make a table comparing convection, conduction, and radiation. In the table, define each term and give examples of it.

READING CHECK
1. Identify What are the three ways that energy can be transferred?

_____

_____

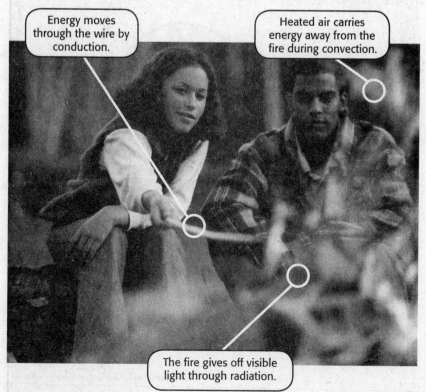

Energy moves through the wire by conduction.

Heated air carries energy away from the fire during convection.

The fire gives off visible light through radiation.

LOOKING CLOSER
2. Identify How is visible light transferred from the fire?

_____

SECTION 2 Energy Transfer *continued*

ENERGY TRANSFER BY CONDUCTION

One way that energy transfers between objects is by conduction. **Thermal conduction** is the transfer of energy through the collisions of particles. Heat can move by conduction between two objects that are touching one another. Conduction also happens within the particles of a substance. ☑

Imagine that you put a marshmallow on one end of a metal coat hanger. Then, you hold the marshmallow over a campfire flame. The wire absorbs heat from the fire and warms up. Then, the end of the wire that you are holding gets warmer. Energy moves from the wire to your hand as heat. This energy transfer through the wire and from the wire to your hand are examples of thermal conduction.

Conduction happens when particles collide with one another. For example, the wire nearest the flame is warmer than the wire farther away. Therefore, the particles in the wire near the flame are moving quickly. They collide with other particles further from the flame. Energy moves from the fast-moving particles to the slower-moving particles. The slower particles begin to move faster. In this way, heat moves from one end of the wire to the other.

✓ **READING CHECK**

3. Describe How is energy transferred during thermal conduction?

_____

_____

Critical Thinking

4. Apply Concepts Could conduction happen between two objects that were not touching? Explain your answer.

_____

_____

_____

_____

_____

_____

_____

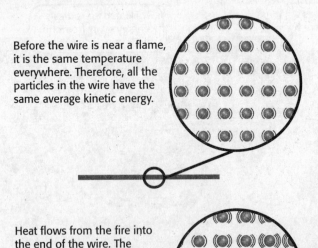

Before the wire is near a flame, it is the same temperature everywhere. Therefore, all the particles in the wire have the same average kinetic energy.

Heat flows from the fire into the end of the wire. The particles in the wire near the fire move more quickly. They collide with other particles in the wire. This transfers energy from the warmer parts of the wire to the cooler parts.

LOOKING CLOSER

5. Infer In the bottom image, which side of the wire is hottest?

_____

_____

308 Heat and Temperature

SECTION 2 Energy Transfer *continued*

ENERGY TRANSFER BY CONVECTION

Above a campfire, hot air expands and moves upward, carrying energy with it. This movement of energy through the movement of matter is called **convection**. ☑

Convection is possible only in fluids. Most fluids are liquids or gases. During convection, the density of a portion of a fluid changes. In most cases, a fluid's density changes because its temperature changes. The denser fluid sinks below the less dense fluid.

Convecting fluids often form convection currents. A **convection current** forms when density differences cause a fluid to flow along a circular path. Convection currents can form in any fluid that is not the same density everywhere. An example of how convection currents form in air is shown in the figure below.

✓ **READING CHECK**

6. Define What is convection?

_____

_____

_____

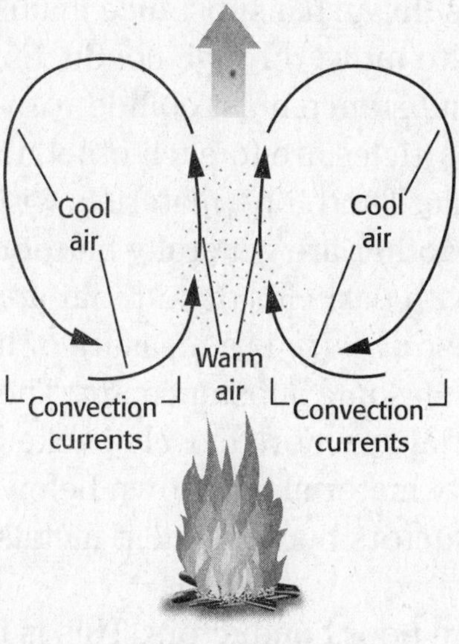

Cool air   Cool air

Warm air

Convection currents   Convection currents

ENERGY TRANSFER BY RADIATION

If you stand next to a campfire, you may feel its warmth. The fire gives off energy in the form of *electromagnetic waves*. These include infrared radiation, visible light, and ultraviolet rays. **Radiation** is energy that is transferred as electromagnetic waves.

Radiation is different from conduction and convection because it can transfer energy through a vacuum such as outer space. Almost all of the energy that we get from the sun is transferred by radiation. ☑

LOOKING CLOSER

7. Explain Why does the air directly above the flame rise?

_____

_____

✓ **READING CHECK**

8. Compare How is radiation different from convection or conduction?

_____

_____

_____

SECTION 2 Energy Transfer *continued*

What Are Conductors and Insulators?

If you toast a marshmallow using a metal wire, the wire gets hot quickly. If you used a wooden stick instead, it would not heat up as fast. This is because metal is a good conductor of heat, but wood is not. A *conductor* is a type of material through which heat can move easily. Most cooking pans are made of metal because most metals are good conductors. ☑

Heat does not move through the wooden stick very easily because wood is an insulator. An *insulator* is a material that transfers energy poorly. Insulation is often used in attics and walls of houses to keep heat from leaving the house. Insulation can also be part of clothing.

CHARACTERISTICS OF CONDUCTORS

Energy moves through a substance mainly by conduction. For energy to move through conduction, the particles in the substance must collide with each other. The closer the particles are to each other, the more likely they are to collide. Therefore, materials with particles that are close together are generally better conductors than materials with particles that are far apart. ☑

Remember that *density* is a measure of how closely packed the particles in a substance are. The particles in a dense material are more closely packed than those in a lower-density material, as shown below. Metals tend to be good conductors because most metals have high densities.

Most gases are poor conductors. This is because the particles in a gas are much farther apart than the particles in a solid or liquid. The particles in a gas do not collide with each other very often.

✔ **READING CHECK**

9. Describe Why does metal get hot quickly when it is placed near a heat source?

_____

_____

✔ **READING CHECK**

10. Identify What is the main way that energy moves through a substance?

_____

LOOKING CLOSER

11. Infer Which of the two materials in the figure is most likely a gas? Explain your answer.

_____

_____

_____

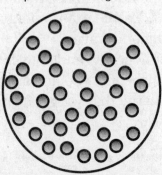

Dense material:
particles close together

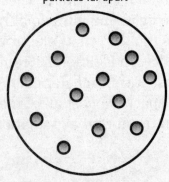

Less-dense material:
particles far apart

What Is Specific Heat?

If you place a metal spoon into a cup of hot tea, the spoon will become warm. The tea will become cooler, because the spoon absorbs heat from the tea. How much will the temperatures of the tea and the spoon change? That depends on three things:

- the mass of the tea and of the spoon
- the temperature of the tea and of the spoon
- the specific heat of the tea and of the spoon

Specific heat (c) describes how much heat a substance must absorb in order for its temperature to change by a certain amount. Specifically, it is the amount of heat required to increase the temperature of 1 kg of the substance by 1 K. The higher a substance's specific heat, the more energy it must absorb before its temperature will change.

The specific heat of a substance does not depend on how much of the substance is present. For example, 100 kg of water has the same specific heat as 1 kg of water: 4,186 J/kg•K. The tables below give the specific heats of different substances at 25 °C.

Substance	Specific heat at 25 °C (J/kg•K)
Liquid water	4,186
Liquid ethanol	2,440
Gaseous ammonia	2,060
Gaseous water vapor	1,870
Solid aluminum	897
Solid carbon (graphite)	709

Substance	Specific heat at 25 °C (J/kg•K)
Solid copper	385
Solid iron	449
Solid silver	234
Liquid mercury	140
Solid gold	129
Solid lead	129

Different substances have different specific heats. The particles in some substances need to absorb only a small amount of energy in order to move faster. The particles in other substances must absorb much more energy before they can move that fast. A substance with a high specific heat must absorb more heat than a substance with a lower specific heat before its particles begin to move faster.

Critical Thinking

12. Apply Concepts If the spoon was the same temperature as the tea, would the spoon heat up when it was placed in the tea? Explain your answer.

_____

_____

_____

_____

_____

_____

_____

LOOKING CLOSER

13. Identify Which substance would require the most heat to produce a temperature change: liquid water or gaseous water vapor?

_____

SECTION 2 Energy Transfer *continued*

USING SPECIFIC HEAT

It takes 4,186 J of energy to raise the temperature of 1 kg of water by 1 K. If you had 2 kg of water, it would take twice as much energy to raise the temperature by 1 K. It would also take twice as much energy to raise the temperature of 1 kg of water by 2 K. The equation below shows how to use specific heat to relate mass, temperature change, and energy:

$$energy = \text{specific heat} \times \text{mass} \times \text{temperature change}$$
$$energy = cm\Delta T$$

In this equation, the "delta" symbol (Δ) represents "change in." To calculate the change in temperature of a substance, use the following equation:

$$\Delta T = \text{final temperature} - \text{initial temperature}$$
$$\Delta T = T_f - T_i$$

Now, let's look at an example of how to use specific heat to solve problems involving heat and temperature. How much energy is required to increase the temperature of 200 kg of water from 25 °C to 37 °C?

Step 1: List the known and unknown values.	**Known:** mass of water, $m = 200$ kg initial temperature of water, $T_i = 25$ °C final temperature of water, $T_f = 37$ °C specific heat of water, $c = 4{,}186$ J/kg·K	**Unknown:** energy
Step 2: Write the equations.	$T_K = T_C + 273.16$ $energy = cm\Delta T$ $\Delta T = T_f - T_i$	
Step 3: Insert the known values and solve for the unknown values. Remember to convert all measurements to proper units.	$T_i = 25$ °C + 273.16 $T_i = 298.16$ K $T_f = 37$ °C + 273.16 $T_f = 310.16$ K $\Delta T = 12$ K $energy = (4{,}186$ J/kg·K$) \times (200$ kg$) \times (12$ K$)$ $energy = 10{,}000{,}000$ J $= 1.0 \times 10^4$ kJ	

So, it takes about 1.0×10^4 kJ of energy to increase the water's temperature.

Math Skills

14. Describe Relationships How is mass related to the amount of energy needed to raise a substance's temperature?

_____

_____

_____

Math Skills

15. Calculate How much energy is required to raise the temperature of 755 g of solid iron from 283 K to 403 K? Show your work. (Hint: Use the information in the table on the previous page.)

What Can Happen When a Substance Absorbs Heat?

Imagine placing a pot of cold water on a hot stove burner. The water absorbs heat from the burner. If you put a thermometer in the water, you would see the temperature of the water increase. When the water's temperature reached 100 °C, the water would start to boil. Many people think that the temperature of the water continues to rise as it boils. However, this is not the case.

If you watched the thermometer in the boiling water, you would see that the water's temperature would not rise. To understand why this is, you need to know what can happen to a substance when it absorbs heat.

Heat moving into a substance can cause the particles in the substance to move faster. If the particles move faster, the substance's temperature increases. This happens if the substance is far from its melting or boiling point. If the substance is at its melting or boiling point, however, the absorbed energy causes the substance to change in state.

When a substance is near its boiling point, it still absorbs energy. However, none of the energy is used to increase the kinetic energy of its particles. The energy is used to change the substance from a liquid to a gas. The same is true for a substance near its melting point. The energy it absorbs makes it change from a solid to a liquid.

The graph below shows an example of how temperature changes when energy is added to a substance. Notice that absorbing energy can cause the substance's temperature to increase, or it can cause the substance to change state. However, absorbing heat cannot cause both a temperature change and a change in state.

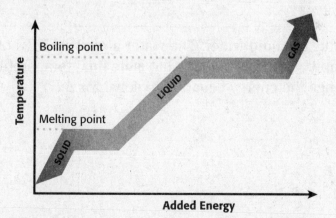

Copyright © by Holt, Rinehart and Winston. All rights reserved.

Critical Thinking

16. Apply Concepts What type of energy transfer causes heat to move from the side of a metal pan into the water inside the pan? What kind of energy transfer occurs when the heated water rises toward the top of the pan?

_____

_____

_____

_____

LOOKING CLOSER

17. Interpret What is happening during the times that the temperature of the substance doesn't change?

_____

_____

Section 2 Review

SECTION VOCABULARY

convection the movement of matter due to differences in density that are caused by temperature variations; can result in the transfer of energy as heat	**specific heat** the quantity of heat required to raise a unit mass of homogeneous material 1 K or 1 °C in a specified way given constant pressure and volume
convection current the vertical movement of air currents due to temperature variations	**thermal conduction** the transfer of energy as heat through a material
radiation the energy that is transferred as electromagnetic waves, such as visible light and infrared waves	

1. Explain Why are most cooking pots and pans made from metal?

_____

_____

2. Identify Fill in the blanks in the table below.

Example	Type of energy transfer
The moon's surface has a higher temperature on the side facing the sun.	radiation
When cold water is poured into a glass, the glass becomes colder.	
Warm ocean water carries heat from the equator toward the poles.	
The pavement in a parking lot becomes hot on a sunny day.	

3. Draw Conclusions Convection occurs within the rock in Earth's mantle. What can you conclude about the rock in the mantle based on this information? (Hint: In what kind of matter can convection occur?)

4. Infer Why can energy move through outer space by radiation, but not by convection or conduction?

_____

_____

5. Calculate A container holds 2.0 kg of liquid water. The water absorbs 477 kJ of energy. If the water's initial temperature was 298 K, what is its final temperature? Show your work. (Hint: Rearrange the energy equation to solve for ΔT.)

CHAPTER 14 Heat and Temperature
SECTION
3 **Using Heat**

KEY IDEAS

As you read this section, keep these questions in mind:
- What is thermodynamics?
- What are the first and second laws of thermodynamics?
- What is a heat engine?

What Is Thermodynamics?

People use many machines, such as air conditioners and automobile engines, to move energy from place to place. Scientists use the laws of thermodynamics to describe how energy moves. *Thermodynamics* is the study of how energy moves and changes in different situations.

THE FIRST LAW OF THERMODYNAMICS

The *first law of thermodynamics* states that the total energy in any process always remains the same. Another way to say this is that energy cannot be created or destroyed. ☑

Remember that work is the transfer of energy from one object to another. In many cases, work increases the kinetic energy of an object. For example, if you pick up and throw a baseball, you have done work on the baseball. The figure below shows how chemical energy in your body is transferred to kinetic energy in the baseball. Processes, such as throwing a baseball, in which energy is transferred as work are called *mechanical processes*.

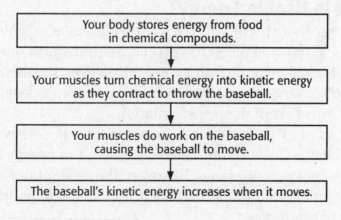

| Your body stores energy from food in chemical compounds. |
| Your muscles turn chemical energy into kinetic energy as they contract to throw the baseball. |
| Your muscles do work on the baseball, causing the baseball to move. |
| The baseball's kinetic energy increases when it moves. |

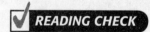

READING TOOLBOX

Find Examples As you read, make a list of examples of the first and second laws of thermodynamics.

✓ **READING CHECK**

1. Describe What is the first law of thermodynamics?

_____

_____

LOOKING CLOSER

2. Review Concepts If you hold the baseball up but do not throw it, what kind of energy does the baseball have?

_____

SECTION 3 Using Heat *continued*

Critical Thinking

3. Apply Concepts If the entropy of one part of the universe decreases, what must happen to the entropy of the rest of the universe?

_____

_____

LOOKING CLOSER

4. Describe What happens to the entropy of the cards when they are knocked over?

_____

_____

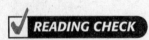

READING CHECK

5. Explain How can you decrease the entropy of a low-energy system?

_____

_____

THE SECOND LAW OF THERMODYNAMICS

The *second law of thermodynamics* states that the entropy of the universe is always increasing. **Entropy** is a measure of how disordered a system is. The more well-ordered a system is, the lower its entropy. For example, look at the house of playing cards in the left-hand figure below. The cards are very well-ordered. They are neatly stacked and carefully balanced. The entropy of the system (the house of cards) is low.

This house of cards is a low-entropy system.

When the cards fall into a random pile, they are less well-ordered. The entropy of the system is higher.

Now, look at the photo on the right. The house of cards has been knocked down. The cards are more disordered. Therefore, the entropy of the system has increased.

In many cases, highly ordered systems are also high in energy. Remember that you can transfer energy to a system by doing work on it. Therefore, you can often do work on a system to decrease its entropy. For example, you can do work on the playing cards to create a house of cards. However, the entropy of a larger system—such as the universe—must increase when this happens. ☑

What Is Usable Energy?

Energy that can be used to do work is called *usable energy*. Many machines that people use transform one form of usable energy into another. However, the amount of usable energy after a transformation is always less than it was before the transformation.

For example, air conditioners use electrical energy to move heat out of a room. The total amount of energy in the system stays the same. However, the amount of heat energy an air conditioner moves is less than the amount of electricity it uses.

What Is a Heat Engine?

A **heat engine** is a machine that uses heat to do work. It changes chemical energy into kinetic energy. This happens by a process called combustion. During *combustion*, fuel is burned to produce energy. ☑

There are two main types of heat engines. If an engine burns fuel outside the engine, it is called an *external-combustion* engine. A steam engine is an example of an external-combustion engine. If a heat engine burns fuel inside the engine, it is an *internal-combustion engine*. This is the type of engine found in most cars and trucks. The figure below shows how an internal-combustion engine works.

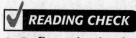

READING CHECK

6. Define What is a heat engine?

_____

_____

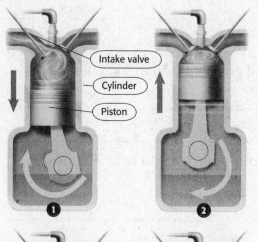

❶ During the intake stroke, the piston moves downward. Air and fuel move into the cylinder.

Intake valve
Cylinder
Piston

❷ During the compression stroke, the piston moves upward. This compresses the mixture of fuel and air in the cylinder.

❸ During the power stroke, the spark plug creates a spark, which causes the fuel and air to burn. This produces pressure inside the cylinder, causing the piston to move downward.

Spark plug

❹ During the exhaust stroke, the piston moves up again. This forces the waste gases to move out of the cylinder. Then, the piston moves down, and the cycle starts over.

Exhaust valve

Crankshaft

LOOKING CLOSER
7. Identify What causes the pistons in an internal-combustion engine to move?

_____

8. Describe What happens during the power stroke?

_____

_____

_____

_____

_____

In an internal-combustion engine, not all of the chemical potential energy in the fuel is changed into kinetic energy. Much of the energy becomes heat, which moves into the air. The heat cannot be used to do work. Therefore, it is not usable energy.

Section 3 Review

SECTION VOCABULARY

entropy a measure of the randomness or disorder of a system	**heat engine** a machine that transforms heat into mechanical energy, or work

1. Identify Give two examples of high-entropy systems and describe how you could decrease the entropy of each system.

_____

_____

_____

2. Define Write the second law of thermodynamics in your own words.

_____

_____

3. Explain How do heat engines change chemical energy into kinetic energy?

_____

_____

4. Compare In terms of using energy, how are your muscles and heat engines similar?

_____

_____

5. Apply Concepts A heat engine has an energy input of 300 J. Its output of useful energy is 150 J. What is the total output of non-useful energy from the heat engine? Explain how you know.

_____

_____

_____

6. Describe What happens during each of the four strokes in the cycle of an internal-combustion engine?

_____

_____

_____

_____

Name _____ Class _____ Date _____

SECTION
1 # Types of Waves

KEY IDEAS

As you read this section, keep these questions in mind:
- What is a wave?
- How do waves form?
- How are transverse and longitudinal waves different?

What Is a Wave?

Imagine a leaf floating on water when a wave passes by. First, the leaf bobs up. Then, it drops back to its original position, as shown in the figure below. In the same way, the water molecules in the pond rise up and fall back as the wave passes. Both the leaf and the molecules end in nearly their original positions. In other words, their displacement is almost zero.

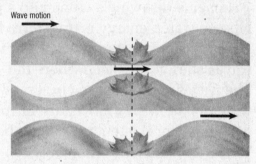

Wave motion

As the wave moves through the water, the water and the leaf move up and down.

If the wave does not move any matter, what does move with the wave? The answer is energy. A *wave* is a disturbance that carries energy though matter or space. Waves in a pond are disturbances that carry energy through water. Sounds are disturbances that carry energy through the air. The energy released by an earthquake is carried by waves within Earth.

Many waves, such as water waves, sound waves, and earthquake waves, can travel only through matter. The matter through which the wave travels is called the **medium**. Water is the medium for water waves. Earth is the medium for earthquake waves.

Waves that can travel only through a medium are called **mechanical waves**. Most waves, including water waves, sound waves, and earthquake waves, are mechanical waves. Electromagnetic waves are the most common kind of nonmechanical waves.

READING TOOLBOX

Compare After you read this section, make a chart comparing transverse and longitudinal waves. Include the characteristics of each kind of wave and examples of each kind of wave.

LOOKING CLOSER
1. Describe What is the displacement of the leaf?

_____

_____

Critical Thinking
2. Apply Concepts What is the medium that sound waves travel through?

_____

_____

SECTION 1 Types of Waves *continued*

What Are Electromagnetic Waves?

Electromagnetic waves consist of changing electric and magnetic fields in space. Light is an electromagnetic wave. Electromagnetic waves can travel through a medium, but they do not have to travel through a medium. For example, light from the sun travels to Earth through empty space, and can also travel through the air. ☑

There are many different kinds of electromagnetic waves. Visible light is one kind. Ultraviolet rays, X rays, and radio waves are also electromagnetic waves.

What Happens to Energy as a Wave Travels?

If you stand next to the speakers at a rock concert, the sound waves may damage your ears. However, if you stand 100 m away, the sound will cause no harm. This is because the energy of a wave spreads out as the wave travels.

Imagine throwing a stone into a pond. When the stone hits the water, energy is transferred from the stone to the water. The energy produces water waves in the pond. The waves start at the place where the stone hits the water. The waves spread out in circles, or *wave fronts*, that get wider as the waves move farther from the center. ☑

Remember that energy cannot be created or destroyed. Therefore, no matter how big each wave front gets, it has the same amount of energy. In the larger circles, the energy is spread out over a larger area. Therefore, the energy at each point in the wave gets smaller as the wave fronts get larger.

Wave front

Each wave front has the same amount of energy. The bigger the wave front, the more spread out the energy is.

When sound waves travel in air, they spread out in spheres. As the waves move outward, the spherical wave fronts get bigger. The energy spreads out over a larger volume. This is why noises sound fainter when you move farther from their source.

READING CHECK

3. Identify What kind of wave is visible light?

_____

_____

READING CHECK

4. Explain Why does dropping a stone in the water produce waves in the water?

_____

_____

LOOKING CLOSER

5. Describe How does the energy of the largest wave front compare to the energy of the smallest wave front?

_____

_____

SECTION 1 Types of Waves *continued*

What Produces Waves?

When a singer sings a note, the vocal chords in the singer's throat move back and forth. That motion makes the air in his throat vibrate. These vibrations travel through the air as sound waves and eventually reach your ears. Vibration of the air in your ears causes your eardrums to vibrate. The motion of your eardrums produces signals that travel through your nerves to your brain.

Waves are related to vibrations. Most mechanical waves, such as sound waves, are produced by vibrating objects. For example, the singer's vibrating vocal chords create sound waves. As a mechanical wave travels through a medium, the particles in the medium vibrate. Vibrations can also produce electromagnetic waves: vibrating charged particles can produce electromagnetic waves.

VIBRATING MASSES ON SPRINGS

Look at the mass hanging on a spring in the figure below. If you pull the mass down and let it go, it will move up and down around its original position. The spring exerts a force that causes the mass to vibrate up and down. The movements involve different types of energy.

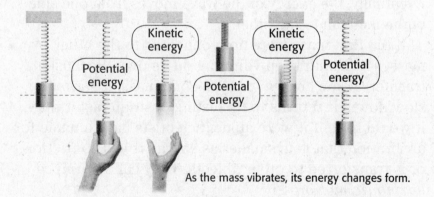

As the mass vibrates, its energy changes form.

When you pull the mass down, the mass and spring gain potential energy. As the spring pulls the mass up to its original position, the potential energy becomes kinetic energy. When the spring rises above its original position, kinetic energy again becomes potential energy. However, the total amount of mechanical energy does not change, except for energy that is lost to friction. This type of vibration is called *simple harmonic motion.*

Talk About It

Discuss In a small group, think of 10 different kinds of waves. For each wave, identify what vibrations produce the wave.

LOOKING CLOSER

6. Identify Name three kinds of energy that the spring can have as it vibrates.

_____

_____

_____

How Do Waves Transfer Energy?

The figure below shows a series of masses and springs tied together in a row. If you pull down on the mass at the end of the row and then let go, that mass will start to vibrate. As it vibrates, it pulls on the mass next to it. It causes that mass to vibrate. Each mass in the row vibrates in turn as the mass next to it pulls on it.

LOOKING CLOSER
7. Predict Consequences
Suppose the five masses in the figure were not connected by the small springs. What would happen to the other four springs when the person pulled on the first spring?

_____

_____

Because these masses are linked together, pulling on one of them causes the others to move.

The connected masses in the figure show how energy can move through a medium. Each mass is connected to the next mass. Therefore, energy can move from one mass to the next. Over time, the energy from the first mass moves to other masses in the line. In a similar way, energy moves from one particle to another in a medium. Eventually, the energy of the wave moves from one side of the medium to the other.

If the first mass were not connected to the other masses, it would keep vibrating on its own. Because it transfers some energy to the second mass, it starts to slow down. It returns to its resting position faster than it would have if it were alone. Scientists have a name for a vibration that gets smaller as energy is lost to friction or is transferred to other objects. They call it *damped harmonic motion.* ☑

READING CHECK

8. Define What is damped harmonic motion?

_____

_____

_____

Type of motion	Description
Simple harmonic motion	• masses move independently • masses do not lose energy
Damped harmonic motion	• masses are linked together • masses lose energy to other masses or to friction

Name _____ Class _____ Date _____

In What Ways Do Waves Move Particles?

When a mechanical wave travels through a medium, the particles in the medium vibrate. Different kinds of waves cause the particles to vibrate in different ways. Scientists classify mechanical waves based on how the waves cause the particles to move. ☑

TRANSVERSE WAVES

Look at the rope in the figure below. As the person moves the end of the rope, energy travels through the rope as a wave. The energy (and the wave) moves from left to right in the rope. However, the particles in the rope move up and down. The direction of motion of the rope is perpendicular to the direction of motion of the wave. The rope is an example of a transverse wave. In a **transverse wave**, the particles in the medium move perpendicular to the direction the wave is traveling.

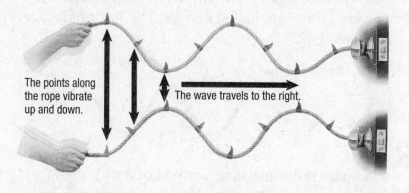

The points along the rope vibrate up and down.

The wave travels to the right.

In a transverse wave, particles vibrate perpendicular to the direction the wave travels.

LONGITUDINAL WAVES

Imagine stretching out a long, flexible spring, such as the one shown on the next page. If you move one end forward and backward, you will see a wave move along the spring. The coils in the spring move forward and backward, just like the wave. In other words, the particles in the medium vibrate parallel to the direction in which the wave moves. This is an example of a **longitudinal wave**.

Sound waves are longitudinal waves. As a sound wave moves through the air, air molecules move closer together and farther apart.

READING CHECK

9. Describe How do scientists classify mechanical waves?

_____
_____
_____

LOOKING CLOSER

10. Apply Concepts If the wave in the rope were traveling from right to left, which way could the particles vibrate?

_____
_____

SECTION 1 Types of Waves *continued*

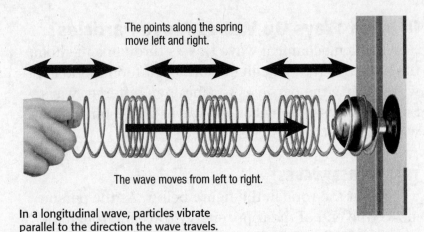

The points along the spring move left and right.

The wave moves from left to right.

In a longitudinal wave, particles vibrate parallel to the direction the wave travels.

LOOKING CLOSER
11. Compare How does the direction of motion of the particles in the spring compare with the direction of motion of the wave?

_____

_____

DESCRIBING WAVES

Scientists use different words to describe the parts of transverse and longitudinal waves. The figure below shows a transverse wave. Notice that parts of the wave are higher than the rest of the wave. Other parts are lower than the rest of the wave. The high points in a transverse wave are called **crests**. The low points are called **troughs**.

LOOKING CLOSER
12. Describe Draw and label arrows on the figure to show the directions of motion of the wave and of the particles in the medium the wave is traveling through.

Transverse wave

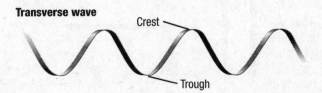

Crest

Trough

Compare the transverse wave above with the longitudinal wave in the figure below. The longitudinal wave does not have crests and troughs. As the wave moves through the medium, the particles in some areas move closer together. The particles in other areas move farther apart. Places where the particles are closer together are called *compressions*. Places where the particles are farther apart are called *rarefactions*.

LOOKING CLOSER
13. Identify What happens to particles in a medium when a rarefaction moves through them?

_____

_____

_____

Longitudinal wave

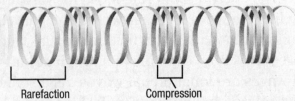

Rarefaction

Compression

SECTION 1 Types of Waves *continued*

What Are Surface Waves?

Waves on the ocean or a swimming pool are not simple transverse or longitudinal waves. Instead, they cause particles to move both parallel and perpendicular to the direction the wave is moving. These waves are surface waves. *Surface waves* form at the boundary between two different mediums, such as air and water. ☑

Look at the movements of the beach ball below as a surface wave passes it. The ball starts in a trough, or low point. As the crest, or high point, approaches, the ball moves to the left, parallel to the wave. It also moves up, perpendicular to the wave. When the ball is near the crest, it starts to move to the right. When the crest has passed, the ball starts to fall back downward and then to the left. The up-and-down motions combine with the side-to-side motions to give the ball a circular motion overall. ☑

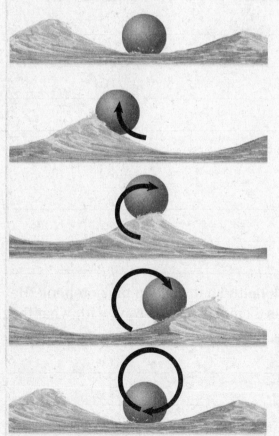

Ocean waves are surface waves that form at the boundary between air and water. Surface waves move particles along circular paths.

Particles in surface waves move just like the beach ball, in an ellipse. (A circle is a special type of ellipse.) The motion of the beach ball shows the motion of the water molecules that are particles in surface waves.

READING CHECK

14. Identify Where do surface waves form?

_____

_____

READING CHECK

15. Describe In what way do surface waves move particles?

_____

_____

LOOKING CLOSER

16. Compare How are surface waves similar to transverse waves?

_____

_____

_____

_____

_____

Section 1 Review

SECTION VOCABULARY

crest the highest point of a wave	**mechanical wave** a wave that requires a medium through which to travel
electromagnetic wave a wave that consists of oscillating electric and magnetic fields, which radiate outward at the speed of light	**medium** a physical environment in which phenomena occur
longitudinal wave a wave in which the particles of the medium vibrate parallel to the direction of wave motion	**transverse wave** a wave in which the particles of the medium move perpendicularly to the direction the wave is traveling
	trough the lowest point of a wave

1. Compare Give two similarities and one difference between mechanical waves and electromagnetic waves.

_____

_____

_____

2. Apply Concepts Why can light travel through outer space, but sound cannot?

_____

_____

_____

3. Compare What is the difference between how transverse waves and longitudinal waves move particles?

_____

_____

_____

4. Identify Problems A student is describing a longitudinal wave in his notebook. He writes down "The distance between crests is 3 cm." What is wrong with what the student recorded?

_____

_____

5. Explain Why does a noise sound fainter as you move away from its source?

_____

_____

CHAPTER 15 Waves

SECTION 2 Characteristics of Waves

As you read this section, keep these questions in mind:

• What are some ways to measure and compare waves?

• How can you calculate the speed of a wave?

• What is the Doppler effect?

How Can You Describe a Wave's Properties?

If you have spent time at the beach or on a boat, you have probably noticed many properties of waves. Sometimes the waves are very large. At other times they are smaller. Sometimes they arrive close together. Other times they come farther apart. Scientists use special terms to describe these properties of waves.

AMPLITUDE

One property of a wave is how much it moves particles as it passes them. The largest distance that a wave displaces particles from their resting position is called the **amplitude** of the wave. In a transverse wave, for example, the amplitude is the distance between the resting position and the wave's crest or trough. The figure below illustrates the amplitude of a transverse wave.

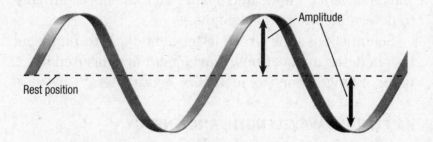

Amplitude

Rest position

Simple transverse waves have similar shapes, no matter how large they are or what medium they travel through. These waves are shaped like a sine curve. A *sine curve* looks like an S lying on its side. Waves with the shape of sine curves, like the one above, are called *sine waves*. Although many waves are not perfect sine waves, a sine curve is a good estimate of their shapes.

READING TOOLBOX

Describe After you read this section, make a chart comparing amplitude, frequency, wavelength, and period. In your chart, define each quantity and give the units used to measure it.

LOOKING CLOSER

1. Compare How does the distance between the resting position and the crest compare with the distance between the resting position and the trough?

WAVELENGTH

The crests of ocean waves lapping up on the beach may be several meters apart. In contrast, ripples on a pond may be separated by only a few centimeters. In transverse waves, the distance between one crest and the next, or one trough and the next, is the **wavelength**. In a longitudinal wave, the wavelength is the distance between two neighboring compressions or rarefactions. ☑

Generally, the wavelength is the distance between any two neighboring identical parts of a wave. The figure below shows the wavelengths of a transverse wave and a longitudinal wave.

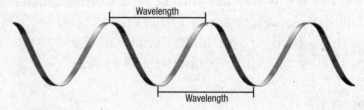

Transverse wave

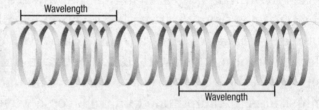

Longitudinal wave

Not all waves have an obvious wavelength. Most sound waves have a complicated shape. That makes it difficult to determine their wavelengths.

Scientists use the Greek letter lambda, λ, to represent wavelengths in equations. Wavelength is measured in units of length, such as meters or centimeters.

AMPLITUDE, WAVELENGTH, AND ENERGY

Remember that waves carry energy. There is a relationship between the amplitude of a wave and the amount of energy it carries. A wave with a large amplitude carries more energy than the same kind of wave with a smaller amplitude.

There is also a relationship between wavelength and energy. A wave with a large wavelength carries less energy than the same kind of wave with a smaller wavelength.

<hr>

READING CHECK

2. Define What is the wavelength of a longitudinal wave?

_____

_____

_____

LOOKING CLOSER

3. Review On the figure, label a crest, a trough, a compression, and a rarefaction.

Critical Thinking

4. Infer Wave A and wave B are the same kind of wave. Wave A has a smaller amplitude and longer wavelength than wave B. Which wave carries the most energy?

_____

PERIOD

Imagine floating in an inner tube away from the shore of the ocean, as shown below. As waves pass you on their way to the shore, your body rises and falls. If you had a stopwatch, you could count the number of seconds between one crest or trough and the next. You would be measuring the period of the wave. The **period** of a wave is the time it takes for one full wavelength of the wave to pass a specific point.

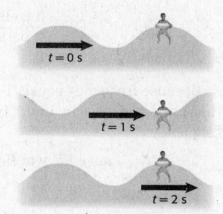

It takes 2 s for a full wavelength of this wave to pass the person. Therefore, the wave's period is 2 s.

LOOKING CLOSER
5. Apply Concepts If it took 3.5 s for the person to move up and down once on the wave, what would be the wave's period?

_____

Scientists use the letter T to represent the period in equations. Period is measured in units of time, such as seconds.

FREQUENCY

The period of a wave is how long it takes for a full wavelength of the wave to pass a point. Suppose you were to measure the number of wavelengths that passed the point in a certain amount of time. Then, you would be measuring the **frequency** of the wave.

The symbol for frequency is f. Its SI unit is the hertz (Hz). Hertz units measure the number of vibrations per second. One vibration per second is 1 Hz, and two vibrations per second is 2 Hz. The average person can hear sounds with frequencies as low as 20 Hz and as high as 20,000 Hz.

There is a relationship between the frequency of a wave and its period. The equation below describes this relationship:

$$\text{frequency} = \frac{1}{\text{period}}$$

$$f = \frac{1}{T}$$

Math Skills
6. Identify What is the relationship between period and frequency?

_____

_____

How Can You Measure Wave Speed?

Remember that you can describe the speed of a moving object using units such as meters per second. The speed describes how long it takes the object to move a certain distance. In a similar way, you can describe the speed of a wave. The speed of a wave is the time it takes for one part of the wave to travel a certain distance. ☑

You can calculate the speed of a wave in two different ways. One way is divide the wave's wavelength by its period:

$$\text{speed} = \frac{\text{wavelength}}{\text{period}}$$

$$v = \frac{\lambda}{T}$$

Because frequency equals $1 \div T$, you can also calculate the speed of a wave by multiplying its wavelength by its frequency:

$$\text{speed} = \text{wavelength} \times \text{frequency}$$

$$v = \lambda f$$

Let's look at an example of calculating the speed of a wave. A piano string vibrates to produce a note. The sound waves the string produces have a frequency of 262 Hz and a wavelength of 1.30 m. What is the speed of the sound waves?

Step 1: List the given and unknown values.	**Given:** frequency, $f = 262$ Hz wavelength, $\lambda = 1.30$ m	**Unknown:** speed, v
Step 2: Write the equation.	$v = f\lambda$	
Step 3: Insert the known values and solve for the unknown value.	$v = (262 \text{ Hz}) \times (1.30 \text{ m})$ $v = 341$ m/s	

So, the wave's speed is 341 m/s. This means that, in one second, a certain point on the wave travels 341 m.

Do Waves Travel at the Same Speed in Every Medium?

A wave's speed depends on the medium through which the wave travels. In any particular medium, however, the speed of waves stays the same. The speed does not depend on the waves' frequencies. The table on the next page shows the speed of sound in different mediums.

READING CHECK

7. Define What is the speed of a wave?

_____

_____

_____

Math Skills

8. Calculate An ocean wave has a wavelength of 15.0 m. Its period is 10 s. What is the speed of the wave? Show your work.

SECTION 2 Characteristics of Waves *continued*

Speed of Sound in Different Mediums	
Medium	**Speed of sound (m/s)**
Air at 25 °C	3.46×10^2
Water at 25 °C	1.49×10^3
Gold	3×10^3

LOOKING CLOSER
9. Identify In which substance does sound move the fastest?
_____
_____

DIFFERENCES IN WAVE SPEED

The arrangement of molecules in a medium determines how quickly waves travel through the medium. In gases, the molecules are far apart and move randomly. In a gas, a molecule must travel through a lot of empty space before it bumps into another molecule. As a result, gas molecules have few chances to transfer energy to other molecules. Therefore, waves generally travel slowly in gases.

In liquids such as water, the molecules are much closer than they are in gases. They can easily collide with each other and transfer their energy. Molecules in liquids act like masses on springs. They transfer vibrations from one molecule to the next. As a result, waves travel faster in liquids than in gases.

Molecules in solids are even closer to each other. They are also bound tightly to each other. You can imagine molecules in solids as masses that are glued together. When one mass starts to vibrate, all the others start to vibrate almost immediately. As a result, waves travel very quickly through most solids.

Critical Thinking
10. Infer The speed of a wave in a medium changes depending on the temperature of the medium. What do you think is the reason for this? (Hint: Remember what temperature describes.)

_____
_____
_____
_____
_____
_____
_____
_____

How Fast Do Light Waves Travel?

When you flip a light switch, light seems to fill the room instantly. However, like all waves, light waves take time to travel from place to place. All electromagnetic waves travel at the same speed in a given medium. In a vacuum, this speed is 3.00×10^8 m/s, or 186,000 miles per second. This value of the speed of light in empty space is a constant. Scientists give it the symbol c.

Light doesn't always travel at the speed that c represents. When light travels through a medium, such as air or water, it moves more slowly than in empty space. For example, light travels at 2.25×10^8 m/s in water.

SECTION 2 Characteristics of Waves *continued*

THE ELECTROMAGNETIC SPECTRUM

Remember that visible light is just one kind of electromagnetic wave. There are many different forms of electromagnetic waves. All travel at the same speed, but they have different wavelengths. For example, the wavelength of visible light varies from about 7.0×10^{-7} m to about 4.0×10^{-7} m. The different wavelengths of visible light correspond to the different colors we see.

LOOKING CLOSER

11. Identify Which color of light has the shortest wavelength?

_____

_____

Color of visible light	Wavelength (m)
Blue	4.75×10^{-7}
Yellow	5.70×10^{-7}
Red	6.80×10^{-7}

Some forms of electromagnetic radiation, such as gamma rays and X rays, have shorter wavelengths than visible light. Other forms, such as radio waves and microwaves, have longer wavelengths than visible light. The full range of wavelengths of all electromagnetic waves is called the *electromagnetic spectrum*.

Critical Thinking

12. Apply Concepts Name two forms of electromagnetic radiation that carry more energy than visible light waves. (Hint: What is the relationship between wavelength and energy?)

_____

_____

How Can Motion Affect the Properties of Waves?

Imagine that you are standing on a corner as an ambulance rushes by. As the ambulance passes, the sound of its siren changes. This happens because the ambulance is moving.

The *pitch* of a sound describes how high or low the sound is. High sounds, such as a bird singing, have a high pitch. Pitch is determined by the frequency or wavelength of a sound. The higher the frequency of a sound, the higher the pitch. ☑

READING CHECK

13. Infer Which sound has a lower pitch, a bass guitar or a flute?

_____

Suppose you could see the sound waves from the ambulance, as in the figure on the next page. When the ambulance stands still, sound waves from its siren spread out evenly in all directions. The pitch of the sound is the same no matter where you stand.

As the ambulance travels toward you, the waves are squeezed into a smaller space. When it is moving away, the waves are stretched. This squeezing and stretching affects the pitch of the sound you hear. If the ambulance is moving toward you, the pitch sounds higher. If it is moving away from you, the pitch sounds lower.

SECTION 2 Characteristics of Waves *continued*

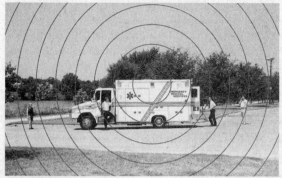

When the ambulance is not moving, the sound waves have the same frequency everywhere. No matter where you stand, the siren sounds the same.

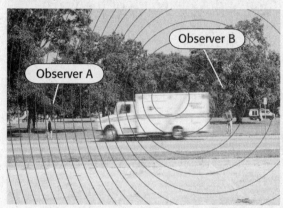

Observer B

Observer A

When the ambulance is moving, the sound waves are stretched or compressed. Observer A hears a higher-pitched siren than Observer B.

LOOKING CLOSER
14. Identify In the bottom image, circle the waves with the highest frequency.

Consider the situation in which the ambulance is moving toward you. Between the time when the siren emits one sound wave and the next one, the ambulance moves forward. The movement shortens the distance between wave fronts. As a result, the sound waves reach your ear at a higher frequency than normal. They sound higher-pitched than they would if the ambulance were parked.

The opposite happens if the ambulance is moving away from you. The movement lengthens the distance between wave fronts. The sound waves reach your ear at a lower than normal frequency. So, you hear the siren at a lower pitch than you would if the ambulance stayed still.

This change in the observed wavelength of a wave when the source and observer are moving relative to one another is called the **Doppler effect**. The Doppler effect happens any time the source and the observer are moving relative to each other. The effect occurs for all types of waves, including light and radio waves.

Scientists use the Doppler effect in several different ways. For example, meteorologists use the effect to help them track storms. Astronomers rely on the Doppler effect to measure the speeds at which galaxies are moving away from Earth.

Critical Thinking
15. Infer If you were riding in the ambulance, would the pitch of its siren seem to change? Explain your answer.

_____
_____
_____
_____
_____
_____
_____

Section 2 Review

SECTION VOCABULARY

amplitude the maximum distance that the particles of a wave's medium vibrate from their rest position	**frequency** the number of cycles or vibrations per unit of time; also the number of waves produced in a given amount of time
Doppler effect an observed change in the frequency of a wave when the source or observer is moving	**period** in physics, the time that it takes a complete cycle or wave oscillation to occur
	wavelength the distance from any point on a wave to an identical point on the next wave

1. Identify On the figure below, label the amplitude and wavelength of the wave.

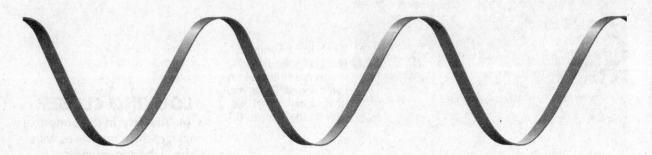

2. Calculate Green light has a wavelength of 5.20×10^{-7} m. The speed of light is 3.00×10^8 m/s. What is the frequency of green light waves? Show your work. (Hint: 1 m/s ÷ 1 m = 1 Hz.)

3. Explain A scientist strikes a long metal bar with a hammer. The energy produces waves that travel through the bar and through the air. Which will reach the end of the bar first, the wave traveling through the bar or the one traveling through the air? Explain your answer.

_____

_____

4. Describe As the frequency of a wave increases, what happens to its period and wavelength if its speed stays the same?

_____

_____

CHAPTER 15 Waves

SECTION 3

Wave Interactions

KEY IDEAS

As you read this section, keep these questions in mind:

• How do waves behave when they interact with objects?

• What happens when two waves meet?

• How do standing waves form?

How Do Waves Interact with Objects?

Think about a pebble dropped into a pond. The waves that form when the pebble hits the water travel out in circles from the center. What happens when the waves reach the shore, or hit an object in the middle of the pond?

Waves behave in different ways when they interact with different objects. When a wave meets a surface or boundary, the wave can bounce back. When a wave passes the edge of an object or passes through an opening, the wave bends. A wave can also bend when it passes from one medium into another. ☑

REFLECTION

The image below shows an example of water waves hitting a surface, such as a dock or pier. When the waves hit such a surface, they reflect. During **reflection**, a wave bounces back when it meets a surface or boundary.

Reflection occurs when waves bounce off a surface.

All kinds of waves can reflect when they hit a surface. For example, visible light reflects off of objects it strikes. The reflected light travels to your eyes, allowing you to see the objects. Echoes are another example of reflection. If you shout into a large, empty space, the sound waves reflect off the walls, ceiling, and floor. They travel back to your ears, producing an echo.

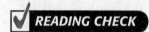
READING TOOLBOX

Compare After you read this section, make a chart comparing reflection, refraction, diffraction, and interference.

✓ READING CHECK

1. Describe What happens when a wave passes the edge of an object?

_____

_____

LOOKING CLOSER

2. Define What happens to a wave during reflection?

_____

_____

SECTION 3 Wave Interactions *continued*

DIFFRACTION

If you stand outside the doorway of a classroom, you may be able to hear voices inside the room. Sound waves cannot travel in a straight line through the wall to your ears. How can you hear the voices?

When waves pass the edge of an object, they bend and spread out on the other side. The same effect occurs if waves pass through an opening, such as an open door or window. The waves bend around the corner or opening.

Think back to the waves in the pond. What would happen if the waves passed through a gap between two objects? You might see something like the figure below. The waves bend around the two edges and spread out as they pass through the gap. Scientists call this effect **diffraction**. The amount of diffraction of a wave depends on its wavelength and the size of the barrier or opening. ☑

Diffraction occurs when waves pass through an opening or around a corner. The waves bend as they pass the corners.

Sound waves behave the same way when they pass through a door. As the waves pass through the door, they bend and travel into the space near the door. Because they spread out into the space beyond the door, a person near the doorway can hear sounds from inside the room.

REFRACTION

Imagine a spoon in a glass of water, such as the one shown at the top of the next page. The spoon looks like it is broken into two pieces where it enters the water. This occurs because light waves bend as they enter and leave the water. Scientists call this effect **refraction**.

✓ **READING CHECK**

3. Identify What are two things that can affect the amount of diffraction of a wave?

_____

_____

_____

LOOKING CLOSER

4. Label On the figure, label the diffracted wave.

SECTION 3 Wave Interactions *continued*

When waves move from one medium to another, they refract, or bend. The refraction of light waves makes this spoon look broken.

LOOKING CLOSER
5. Infer Would the spoon look broken if it was completely under the water?

_____

_____

Light waves that reflect off the top of the spoon pass through only air before reaching your eyes. Waves that reflect off the bottom of the spoon travel through water, glass, and air before reaching your eyes. The waves bend slightly each time they enter a new medium, because their speed changes. Because of refraction, light reflected from the top and from the bottom of the spoon reach your eyes at different angles. That's why the spoon seems to be broken.

What Happens When Waves Combine?

Imagine two people trying to walk through a narrow doorway at the same time. They will run into each other. Material objects, such as human bodies, cannot take up exactly the same space at the same time.

Waves are different. When two or more waves occupy the same space, they combine to form a single new wave. The process is called **interference**. An example of interference is shown in the photo below. ☑

Critical Thinking
6. Infer Light bends more when it moves from air into oil than from air into water. Will an object placed in a container of oil look more bent or less bent than it would in a container of water? (Hint: If there is no refraction, the object won't look bent.)

_____

_____

Interference happens when two waves pass through each other and combine.

READING CHECK

7. Define What is interference?

_____

_____

_____

_____

A new wave produced by interference differs from the original waves. When the waves have passed through each other, they return to their original shapes.

SECTION 3 Wave Interactions *continued*

CONSTRUCTIVE AND DESTRUCTIVE INTERFERENCE

There are two main types of wave interference: constructive interference and destructive interference. **Constructive interference** happens when the amplitude of the combined waves is larger than the amplitudes of the single waves. This can occur when the crests of two transverse waves overlap, as in the figure below.

LOOKING CLOSER

8. Calculate The amplitudes of the two waves are 4 cm and 3 cm. What is the amplitude of the combined wave?

_____

_____

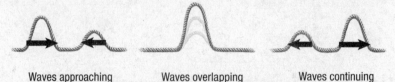

Waves approaching   Waves overlapping   Waves continuing

In constructive interference, the amplitude of the combined wave is the sum of the amplitudes of the two overlapping waves.

Destructive interference happens when the amplitude of the combined waves is smaller than the amplitudes of the single waves. This can occur when the crest of one transverse wave overlaps the trough of another. If both waves have the same amplitude, they may cancel out each other completely, as shown below.

LOOKING CLOSER

9. Infer The amplitude of the combined wave is zero. What must the relative amplitudes of the two waves be?

_____

_____

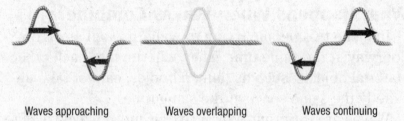

Waves approaching   Waves overlapping   Waves continuing

In destructive interference, the amplitude of the combined wave is the difference of the amplitudes of the two overlapping waves.

INTERFERENCE IN LIGHT AND SOUND WAVES

If you look at a soap bubble, you may see swirling colors on its surface. These colors are produced by interference of light waves reflecting off of different parts of the bubble.

Interference can also affect sound waves. For example, the notes from two different tuning forks can interfere with each other. This interference can produce a pattern of loud and soft sounds called *beats*. Piano tuners often compare the sound of a piano string with that from a tuning fork. When there are no beats, the piano string and the tuning fork are vibrating at the same frequency. This means the piano string is in tune.

SECTION 3 Wave Interactions *continued*

What Are Standing Waves?

Suppose you send a wave through a rope that has one end tied to a wall. The wave reflects from the wall and travels back along the rope. As you send more waves down the rope, they will interfere with the reflected waves. When a wave interferes with its reflection, it can form a **standing wave**. Two examples of standing waves are shown in the figures below. ☑

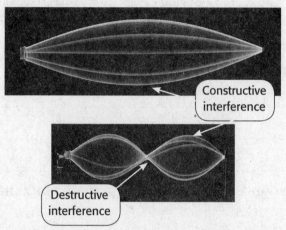

Constructive interference

Destructive interference

Standing waves can form when a wave interferes with its reflection.

A standing wave causes the medium to vibrate as if it is staying still. It appears that the wave is a single, stationary one. However, a standing wave really consists of two waves traveling in opposite directions. ☑

NODES AND ANTINODES

Standing waves form loops, as shown in the images above. Certain points that have no vibration, called *nodes*, separate the loops. Nodes lie at the points where the crests of the original waves meet the troughs of the reflected waves. In other words, nodes are points of complete destructive interference. The top wave above has a node at each end. The bottom wave has three nodes: two at the end and one in the middle.

Midway between two nodes, the crests of the original and reflected waves combine in complete constructive interference. These points are called *antinodes*. The top wave above has a single antinode in the middle. The bottom wave has two antinodes, one on the left and one on the right.

✓ READING CHECK

10. Define What is a standing wave?

_____

_____

_____

✓ READING CHECK

11. Describe What does a standing wave look like?

_____

_____

Critical Thinking

12. Compare How is a node different from an antinode?

_____

_____

_____

_____

_____

Section 3 Review

SECTION VOCABULARY

constructive interference a superposition of two or more waves whose intensity is greater than the sum of the intensities of the individual waves	**interference** the combination of two or more waves that results in a single wave
	reflection the bouncing back of a ray of light, sound, or heat when the ray hits a surface that it does not go through
destructive interference a superposition of two or more waves whose intensity is less than the sum of the intensities of the individual waves	**refraction** the bending of a wavefront as the wavefront passes between two substances in which the speed of the wave differs
diffraction a change in the direction of a wave when the wave finds an obstacle or an edge, such as an opening	**standing wave** a pattern of vibration that simulates a wave that is standing still

1. Compare Give one difference and one similarity between constructive interference and destructive interference.

_____

_____

_____

2. Identify What allows you to hear sounds in a room when you are standing outside the door? Explain how this effect works.

_____

_____

_____

3. Compare How is refraction different from diffraction?

_____

_____

4. Infer The crest of wave A has an amplitude of 5 cm. The trough of wave B has an amplitude of 2 cm. If the crest of wave A combines with the trough of wave B, what will be the amplitude of the resulting wave? Will the waves form a crest or a trough when they combine?

_____

5. Draw Conclusions A student ties a rope to a doorknob. The student moves the rope to create a standing wave with two nodes and one antinode. In the space below, draw what the standing wave looks like.

CHAPTER 16 Sound and Light

SECTION 1 **Sound**

As you read this section, keep these questions in mind:

• What are the characteristics of sound waves?

• How do musical instruments make sound?

• How do human ears work?

• How can the reflections of sound waves be used?

What Are The Properties of Sound?

When you listen to your favorite music, you hear many sounds. These sounds may come from many different sources, but they are all produced in the same way. All sounds are produced by vibrations.

For example, suppose you are listening to music from a drum. The figure below shows how the vibrations of the top of the drum produce sound.

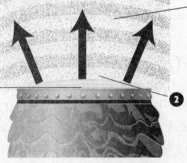

❸ The sound waves travel away from the drum in all directions.

❶ The top of the drum vibrates up and down when the player hits it.

❷ As the top of the drum vibrates, it causes the air near it to vibrate. The movements of the air particles are sound waves.

As you can see in the figure, the particles of air in sound waves vibrate in the same direction the waves travel. Therefore, **sound waves** are longitudinal waves. Like all longitudinal waves, sound waves consist of compressions and rarefactions. *Compressions* occur where particles are closer together. *Rarefactions* occur where they are farther apart. ☑

Sound waves are mechanical waves. In other words, they can travel only through a medium. Sound can travel through air, water, metal, and other matter. Sound cannot travel in a *vacuum*, or a space that does not contain matter. In a vacuum, there are no particles to transmit energy.

Summarize As you read this section, create a Concept Map with the following terms: sound, sound wave, pitch, loudness, intensity, amplitude, frequency, decibel, hertz, vibrations, medium.

LOOKING CLOSER

1. Apply Concepts Label a compression and a rarefaction on the figure.

READING CHECK

2. Identify What type of wave is a sound wave?

_____

_____

SECTION 1 Sound *continued*

THE SPEED OF SOUND

Sound waves travel through the air in order to reach your ears. Sound travels quickly in air, but it still takes time for the waves to travel. If you stand close to the drum, the time it takes for the sound to travel is small. Therefore, it seems as if you hear the sound at the same time the drummer hits the drum. However, if you stand far from the drum, you may be able to notice the difference in time.

As with all waves, the speed of a sound wave depends on the material through which it travels. The table below gives the speed of sound in different materials.

Medium	Speed of sound (m/s)	Medium	Speed of sound (m/s)
Gases		Liquids at 25 °C	
Air (0 °C)	331	Water	1,490
Air (25 °C)	346	Sea water	1,530
Air (100 °C)	386	Solids	
Helium (0 °C)	972	Copper	3,813
Hydrogen (0 °C)	1,290	Iron	5,000
Oxygen (0 °C)	317	Rubber	54

LOOKING CLOSER
3. Compare In which material does sound travel faster, cold air or rubber?

_____

_____

Why does sound travel at different speeds in different mediums? The speed of sound depends on how quickly the particles in a medium transmit the motion of the sound waves. In a gas, particles are farther apart than the particles in a solid or liquid. Therefore, sound waves generally travel more slowly in gases than in solids or liquids. For example, sound travels more slowly in air than in water.

The particles in solids and in liquids are generally closely packed. Therefore, most solids and liquids can transmit vibrations easily. However, some solids—such as rubber—absorb or reduce vibrations. As a result, sound does not travel well through them. ☑

READING CHECK
4. Explain Why is the speed of sound in rubber so low?

_____

_____

_____

Temperature also affects how quickly sound travels. Remember that particles in a warm material are moving faster than those in a cooler material. When molecules move faster, they collide with one another more often. Therefore, energy moves more quickly through the material. Therefore, in general, the warmer the medium, the faster the speed of sound. For example, sound moves more quickly through 100 °C air than through 0 °C air.

SECTION 1 Sound *continued*

LOUDNESS AND INTENSITY

Think back to the sounds from the drum. Imagine the drummer tapping the drum gently with her hand. The sound could be difficult to hear. Now, imagine that she strikes the drum harder. The sound would be louder. *Loudness*, how loud or soft a sound seems to be, depends partly on the energy contained in the sound waves. ☑

The loudness of a sound is determined by the intensity of the sound wave. The *intensity* of a sound wave describes how much energy a wave transmits through a given area. The greater the intensity of a sound is, the louder the sound will seem.

Intensity depends on the amplitude of the sound wave. Remember that the *amplitude* of a wave is the distance the wave moves particles from their rest positions. The amplitude of the wave is related to the amount of energy in the wave.

If the drummer hits the drum harder, she transmits more energy to the drum, and the drum top moves more. If the drum top moves more, the air particles above it also move more. The amplitude of the sound wave increases.

Intensity also depends on how far you are from the source of the sound. Remember that waves travel away from their source in all directions. As the waves travel farther away, the same energy is spread out into a larger space. Therefore, the amount of energy in the wave in a given area—the intensity—decreases. As a result, the sound is softer.

Factor	How it affects intensity (loudness)
Amplitude	Higher-amplitude waves sound louder than lower-amplitude waves that are the same distance away.
Distance	Waves that come from close by sound louder than waves from far away that started with the same amplitude.

You may think that a sound that has twice the intensity of another sound should seem twice as loud. However, this is not the case. In fact, the intensity of a sound must be 10 times greater before it sounds twice as loud. ☑

Scientists measure intensity in units called *decibels* (dB). When a sound's intensity increases by 10 dB, it seems twice as loud.

READING CHECK

5. Identify What is one thing that affects the loudness of a sound?

_____

_____

Critical Thinking

6. Explain Why does hitting a drum more gently produce a softer sound? Use the words energy, amplitude, and intensity in your answer.

_____

_____

_____

_____

_____

_____

_____

_____

READING CHECK

7. Describe How much higher must the intensity of a sound wave be before the sound seems twice as loud?

_____

_____

How Loud Are Common Sounds?

You can see the loudness of some common sounds in the figure below. The quietest sound an average human can hear, the *threshold of hearing*, is 0 dB. Sounds louder than 120 dB, the *threshold of pain*, can hurt your ears and give you headaches. If you hear too many sounds above 120 dB, they can cause permanent deafness.

LOOKING CLOSER
8. Apply Concepts About how many times louder does a vacuum cleaner sound than normal conversation?

_____
_____

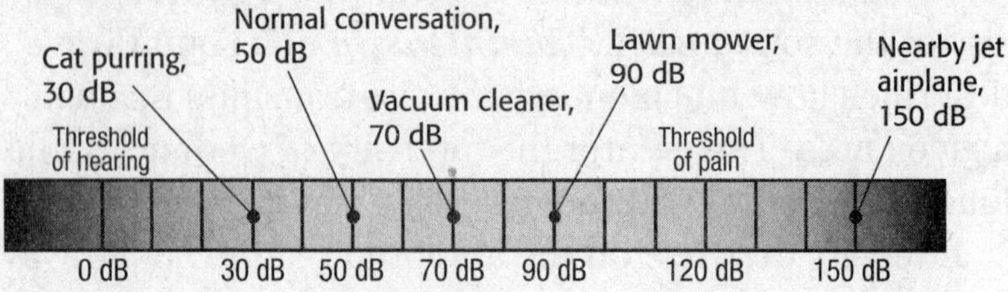

Cat purring, 30 dB — Normal conversation, 50 dB — Vacuum cleaner, 70 dB — Lawn mower, 90 dB — Nearby jet airplane, 150 dB

Threshold of hearing — Threshold of pain

0 dB | 30 dB | 50 dB | 70 dB | 90 dB | 120 dB | 150 dB

How Does the Frequency of a Sound Wave Affect the Sound?

The sound of a trumpet and the sound of a tuba are very different. In everyday speech, we may say that the trumpet has a "high" sound and the tuba has a "low" sound. Scientists use the term **pitch** to describe how high or low a sound is.

The pitch of a sound depends on the frequency of the sound wave. Remember that frequency is the number of waves produced in a specific amount of time. Frequency is expressed in *hertz* (Hz). One hertz is one wave per second.

A high-pitched sound is made by something vibrating rapidly, such as a violin string or air in a trumpet. A low-pitched sound is made by something vibrating slowly, such as a cello string or the air in a tuba. In other words, high-pitched sounds have high frequencies, and low-pitched sounds have low frequencies.

Most people can hear sounds with frequencies between 20 Hz and 20,000 Hz. The frequencies below the range of human hearing are called **infrasound**. The frequencies above the range of human hearing are called **ultrasound**.

Many animals can hear frequencies of sound outside the range of human hearing. For example, you may see someone blow a dog whistle, but you will not hear it. The frequency of the sound wave coming from the whistle is in the ultrasound range. Dogs can hear this high pitch, but humans cannot.

Critical Thinking
9. Infer Which instrument generally produces sounds with higher frequencies, a trumpet or a trombone? Explain your answer.

_____
_____
_____
_____
_____

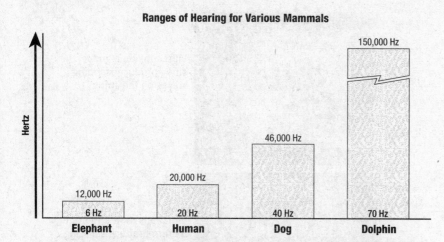

Ranges of Hearing for Various Mammals

How Do Musical Instruments Make Sounds?

Musical instruments are many different shapes and sizes. They produce a wide variety of sounds. However, all musical instruments make sounds by producing vibrations. Most musical instruments produce sound through the vibrations of strings, air, or membranes.

STANDING WAVES

The sound of a musical instrument is produced by standing waves. For example, when you pluck the string of a guitar, the string vibrates. The vibrations travel out to the ends of the string and then reflect back toward the middle. These vibrations form a standing wave on the string. The two ends of the string are nodes. In general, the middle of the string is an antinode. ☑

You can change the pitch by placing your finger firmly on the string anywhere on the guitar's neck. A shorter length of string vibrates more rapidly, and the standing wave has a higher frequency. The resulting sound has a higher pitch.

Standing waves can exist only at certain wavelengths on a string. The wavelength of the main standing wave on a vibrating string is twice the length of the string. The frequency of this wave—and of the string's vibrations—is the string's *fundamental frequency*. ☑

Standing waves also form in other instruments. For example, standing waves form on the head of a drum. In a flute, standing waves form in the *air column*, or body of air, inside the flute. Opening or closing holes in the flute body changes the length of the air column. This changes the frequency of the standing waves in the flute.

LOOKING CLOSER
10. Identify Which of the mammals shown has the highest range of hearing?

_____

_____

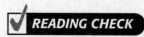 **READING CHECK**
11. Identify What produces the sound of a musical instrument?

_____

_____

READING CHECK
12. Define What is the fundamental frequency of a string?

_____

_____

_____

Vibrations on a guitar string produce standing waves on the string.

Vibrations on the top of a drum produce standing waves in the membrane on the drum.

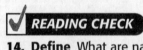

LOOKING CLOSER

13. Identify Where do standing waves form on a drum?

_____

_____

14. Define What are natural frequencies?

_____

_____

_____

READING CHECK

15. Explain Why does the body of a guitar transfer vibrations to the air better than the guitar's strings?

_____

_____

_____

AMPLIFYING SOUND

When you pluck a guitar string, you can feel the body of the guitar vibrate. These vibrations, which are a response to the vibrating string, are called *forced vibrations*. Some vibrations produce louder sounds than others. This is because the body of the guitar has certain natural frequencies. *Natural frequencies* are the frequencies at which an object is most likely to vibrate. ☑

A guitar's sound is loudest when forced vibrations have the same frequency as one of the guitar's natural frequencies. When one object vibrating at a natural frequency of a second object causes the second object to vibrate, **resonance** occurs. Resonance causes both the string and the guitar body to vibrate at the same frequency.

The guitar body has a larger area than the string and is in contact with more molecules in the air. Therefore, the guitar body is better at transferring the vibrations to the air than the string is. The guitar body *amplifies* the sound, or makes it louder. ☑

An object's natural frequencies depend on the object's shape, size, and mass. They also depend on the material from which the object is made. Complex objects, such as guitars, have many natural frequencies, so they resonate well at many pitches. However, some musical instruments, such as electric guitars, do not resonate well and must be amplified electronically.

How Do Humans Hear Sound?

The human ear is a sensitive organ. It senses vibrations in the air, amplifies them, and then transmits signals to the brain. In some ways, the process of hearing is the reverse of the process by which a drum makes a sound. In a drum, vibrations in the membrane of the drum produce sound waves. In the ear, sound waves produce vibrations in the membranes of the ear. The figure below shows the different parts of a human ear.

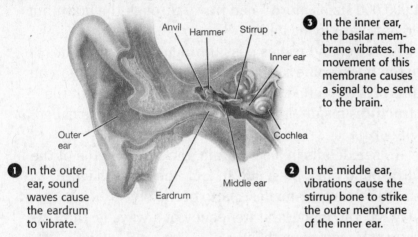

Anvil Hammer Stirrup

Inner ear

3 In the inner ear, the basilar membrane vibrates. The movement of this membrane causes a signal to be sent to the brain.

Outer ear

Cochlea

1 In the outer ear, sound waves cause the eardrum to vibrate.

Eardrum

Middle ear

2 In the middle ear, vibrations cause the stirrup bone to strike the outer membrane of the inner ear.

LOOKING CLOSER

16. Describe How do sound waves enter the ear?

_____

_____

Your ear has three main regions: the outer ear, the middle ear, and the inner ear. Sound waves travel through the fleshy part of your outer ear and down the ear canal. The ear canal ends at the *eardrum*, a thin membrane. ☑

The eardrum transmits the vibrations to the three small bones of the middle ear—the hammer, anvil, and stirrup. The vibrations cause the stirrup to strike a membrane at the opening of the inner ear. The vibrations of this membrane send waves through the spiral-shaped *cochlea* in the inner ear.

The cochlea contains a long, flexible membrane called the *basilar membrane*. Different parts of this membrane vibrate at different natural frequencies. Therefore, a wave of a particular frequency causes a specific part of the basilar membrane to vibrate. The cochlea also contains many tiny hairs. When the basilar membrane vibrates, the hairs move. The louder the sound, the more the hairs move. ☑

The movements of the hairs produce signals in the nerves in the ear. These signals travel to the brain. The brain interprets the signals as sounds of a specific frequency and intensity.

READING CHECK

17. Identify What are the three main regions of the ear?

_____

_____

_____

READING CHECK

18. Describe What is the basilar membrane?

_____

_____

How Do People Use Reflected Sounds?

Like all waves, sound waves can reflect when they strike a barrier. People use reflected sound waves for different purposes.

ULTRASOUND AND SONOGRAMS

Remember that ultrasound waves have frequencies greater than 20,000 Hz. People can use ultrasound waves to see inside the human body. High-frequency waves—1,000,000 Hz or more—can travel through the body, but do not harm living cells.

As the sound waves pass through different tissues in the body, some of the waves reflect. A computer can interpret the reflections and produce an image of the structures inside the body. This type of image is called a *sonogram.*

To see details in a sonogram, the wavelengths of the ultrasound must be small. In fact, they must slightly smaller than the smallest parts of the object being viewed. The higher the frequency of a wave is, the shorter its wavelength is.

Sound waves with frequencies of 15,000,000 Hz have wavelengths of less than 1 mm when they pass through soft tissue. Therefore, a sonogram produced using sound waves with this frequency could show details that are 1 mm or larger in size. ☑

Using sonograms, doctors can view organs inside the body without having to perform surgery. Sonograms can be used to diagnose problems and guide surgical procedures. Sonograms are also commonly used to check the progress of pregnancies because ultrasound does not harm the mother or the fetus.

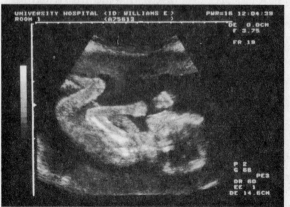
This sonogram of a developing fetus was produced using ultrasound waves.

Critical Thinking

19. Infer What do you think is the reason that ultrasound waves are useful for seeing inside the body?

_____

_____

READING CHECK

20. Describe Could sound waves with frequencies of 15,000,000 Hz be used to show objects that are 0.5 mm in size?

_____

LOOKING CLOSER

21. Infer What do you think is the reason that images like this one are sometimes called "ultrasounds?"

_____

_____

_____

SECTION 1 Sound *continued*

SONAR

Scientists can use reflected sound waves to map the ocean floor. **Sonar** is a tool that uses reflected sound waves to make measurements. The deepest parts of the ocean floor are thousands of meters below the surface. Sonar can measure large distances, so it is useful in mapping the floors of very deep oceans. ☑

Ultrasound is used in many sonar systems because the waves can be focused into narrow beams. They also can be directed more easily than other sound waves.

In a depth-finding sonar system, a device on a ship sends out a pulse of sound into the water. The sound travels through the water to the ocean floor. Then, it reflects off the ocean floor and travels back up to the ship. Computers on the ship record how long it takes the sound to travel from the ship to the ocean floor and back.

The computers can calculate the distance the sound wave traveled using the equation $d = vt$. In this equation, v is the speed of sound in ocean water and t is the time it took the wave to travel to the ocean floor. Using sonar, scientists can determine how deep the ocean floor is at different places. They can use this information to make a map of the ocean floor.

> ✔ **READING CHECK**
>
> 22. **Define** What is sonar?
>
> _____
> _____
> _____

Sonar equipment is carried on a ship. The equipment sends out a pulse of sound. The sound bounces off of the ocean floor and travels back to the ship. By timing how long it takes for the signal to bounce back, scientists can determine the distance to the ocean floor.

LOOKING CLOSER
23. **Identify** On the figure, circle the part of the ocean floor that the sound waves will arrive at soonest.

People can also use sonar to detect fish or other objects, as well as to measure ocean currents. Bats use reflected ultrasound to navigate in flight and to locate insects for food. This natural form of sonar is called *echolocation*.

Section 1 Review

SECTION VOCABULARY

infrasound slow vibrations of frequencies lower than 20 Hz

pitch a measure of how high or low a sound is perceived to be, depending on the frequency of the sound wave

resonance a phenomenon that occurs when two objects naturally vibrate at the same frequency; the sound produced by one object causes the other object to vibrate

sonar sound navigation and ranging, a system that uses acoustic signals and returned echoes to determine the location of objects or to communicate

sound wave a longitudinal wave that is caused by vibrations and that travels through a material medium

ultrasound any sound wave with frequencies higher that 20,000 Hz

1. Compare Give one similarity and one difference between infrasound and ultrasound.

_____

_____

2. Identify What are two factors that affect the intensity of sound?

_____

_____

3. Describe A flute player plays two notes. The second note is louder and has a higher pitch than the first note. Describe how the frequencies and amplitudes of the two notes are different.

_____

_____

_____

4. Describe Fill in the blanks in the boxes below to show how the human ear works.

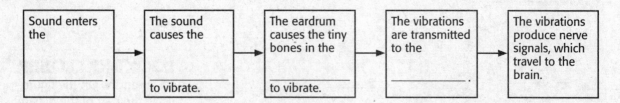

| Sound enters the _____. | The sound causes the _____ to vibrate. | The eardrum causes the tiny bones in the _____ to vibrate. | The vibrations are transmitted to the _____. | The vibrations produce nerve signals, which travel to the brain. |

5. Compare Give one similarity and one difference between sonograms and sonar.

_____

_____

_____

CHAPTER 16 Sound and Light

SECTION 2 The Nature of Light

As you read this section, keep these questions in mind:
- What two models do scientists use to describe light?
- What is the electromagnetic spectrum?
- How can electromagnetic waves be used?

What Is Light?

Most of us see and feel light almost every moment of our lives. We even feel the warmth of the sun on our skin, which is an effect of infrared light. We are very familiar with light, but how much do we understand about what light really is?

Like sound, light is a type of energy. Experiments with light show that it sometimes behaves in unexpected ways. Therefore, it is difficult to describe all of the properties of light with a single model. The two most common models describe light either as a wave or as a stream of particles.

EXPERIMENTING WITH LIGHT

In 1801, the English scientist Thomas Young devised an experiment to test the nature of light. He passed a narrow beam of red light through two small openings. The light was focused onto a screen on the other side of the openings. He found that the light produced a striped pattern of light and dark bands on the screen. This striped pattern is an *interference pattern*. Interference patterns form when waves interfere with each other.

READING TOOLBOX

Summarize After you read this section, make a chart describing the different types of electromagnetic waves and giving examples of how they are used.

❷ The light waves diffract as they pass through the slits.

❸ The diffracted light waves interfere both constructively and destructively.

❹ An interference pattern is created. The constructive interference results in the bright bands of light, and the destructive interference results in the dark bands.

❶ Red light of a single wavelength passes through two tiny slits.

LOOKING CLOSER
1. Describe What happens to light waves when they pass through slits in a barrier?

_____

_____

SECTION 2 The Nature of Light *continued*

THE WAVE MODEL OF LIGHT

Because the light in Young's experiment produced interference patterns, Young concluded that light consists of waves. This model, called the *wave model*, describes light as transverse waves. ☑

Light waves, like all transverse waves, can be described by their amplitude, wavelength, and frequency. Light waves are also called *electromagnetic waves* because they consist of changing electric and magnetic fields.

The wave model of light explains how light waves interfere with one another. It also explains other behaviors of light, such as reflection, refraction, and diffraction. The wave model of light is still used to explain many of the basic properties of light and light's behavior. However, the wave model cannot explain all of light's behavior. ☑

By the early 1900s, physicists were making observations that could not be explained with the wave model of light. For example, when light strikes a piece of metal, electrons may fly off the metal's surface. Scientists found that in some experiments, dim blue light could cause electrons to fly off the metal plate. Scientists also found that very bright red light could not cause electrons to leave the plate.

According to the wave model, bright light has more energy than dim light. This is because the waves in bright light have greater amplitude than the waves in dim light. Therefore, dim light should not be able to knock electrons off the plate, but bright light should. The wave model cannot explain the observations in the metal plate experiment.

READING CHECK

2. Identify According to the wave model of light, what does light consist of?

_____

_____

READING CHECK

3. Describe What are three behaviors of light that the wave model can explain?

_____

_____

_____

LOOKING CLOSER

4. Describe According to the wave model of light, which of the lights should cause electrons to fly off the plate?

_____

Bright red light cannot cause electrons to fly off this metal plate.

Dim blue light can cause electrons to fly off this metal plate.

PARTICLE MODEL OF LIGHT

Scientists proposed a new model of light to explain the effects of light striking a metal plate. According to this model, the energy in light is contained in individual particles called **photons**. This model of light is called the *particle model.* ☑

Photons of different colors of light have different amounts of energy. A photon of blue light carries more energy than a photon of red light. Therefore, blue light can cause electrons to fly off a metal plate, but red light cannot.

Photons are considered particles, but they are not like particles of matter. Photons do not have mass. Instead, they contain only energy. Unlike the energy in a wave, the energy in a photon is located in a specific area. A beam of light is a stream of photons. The more photons in the beam, the brighter the light appears.

Which Model of Light Is Correct?

Some scientists think that light has a *dual nature*. This means that light can behave both as waves and as particles. Some effects, such as the interference of light, are more easily explained with the wave model. In contrast, the particle model better explains how light can knock electrons off metal plates. It also explains why light can travel across empty space without a medium.

Most scientists currently accept both the wave model and the particle model of light. The model they use depends on the situation they are studying. In many cases, using either the wave model or the particle model of light gives good results.

✓ **READING CHECK**

5. Describe According to the particle model, what does light consist of?

_____

_____

Critical Thinking

6. Infer Which beam of light contains more photons, a dim blue beam or a bright red beam? Explain your answer.

_____

_____

_____

_____

_____

Property of light	Model that best explains the property
Light can reflect, refract, and diffract when it interacts with matter.	
Light can travel through a vacuum.	
Light produces interference patterns.	
Light can cause electrons to fly off of pieces of metal.	

LOOKING CLOSER

7. Identify Fill in the blank spaces in the table.

SECTION 2 The Nature of Light *continued*

How Can We Describe the Properties of Light?

Whether modeled as a particle or as a wave, light is a form of energy. Like all waves, light waves carry energy. In the particle model of light, each photon of light carries a specific, small amount of energy. The amount of energy in a photon of light is related to the frequency of the light waves. ☑

For example, ultraviolet photons have about twice as much energy as red light photons. Therefore, the frequency of ultraviolet waves is about twice the frequency of red light waves. The table below gives examples of the wavelengths, wave frequencies, and photon energies of different types of electromagnetic waves.

8. Identify According to the particle model, what carries the energy in light?

_____

_____

LOOKING CLOSER

9. Compare Which type of electromagnetic wave in the table has the greatest amount of energy?

_____

_____

Type of electromagnetic wave	Wavelength (m)	Wave frequency (Hz)	Photon energy (J)
Infrared	1.33×10^{-6}	2.25×10^{14}	1.5×10^{-19}
Visible light	6.67×10^{-7}	4.5×10^{14}	3.0×10^{-19}
Ultraviolet	3.33×10^{-7}	9.0×10^{14}	6.0×10^{-19}

Remember that all forms of electromagnetic radiation, including visible light, travel at the same speed in a vacuum. This speed, the speed of light, is represented by the letter c. The speed of light is about 3×10^8 m/s.

Light can travel through a vacuum, but it can also travel through mediums such as air, water, and glass. However, light travels more slowly in a medium than in a vacuum. The table below shows the approximate speed of light in different mediums.

LOOKING CLOSER

10. Identify In which of the mediums in the table does light travel the fastest?

_____

_____

Medium	Speed of light (m/s)
Air	2.997047×10^8
Ice	2.29×10^8
Water	2.25×10^8
Glass	1.97×10^8
Diamond	1.24×10^8

BRIGHTNESS AND INTENSITY

Remember that **intensity** is the rate at which the energy in a wave travels through a specific area of space. For sound waves, the intensity of the wave affects how loud a sound is. For visible light waves, the intensity of the wave affects how bright a light looks. The higher the intensity, the brighter the light.

SECTION 2 The Nature of Light *continued*

INTENSITY AND DISTANCE

Intensity depends on the number of photons per second that pass through a certain area of space. The intensity of light decreases as distance from the light source increases. This is because the light spreads out as it travels. ☑

The image below shows why intensity decreases as distance increases. The light from a light bulb travels outward in all directions. The light waves spread out into spheres that move away from the bulb. Each sphere is called a *wave front*. The total amount of energy in each wave front is the same. However, as the wave front gets bigger, that energy is spread out over a larger area. As a result, the intensity decreases.

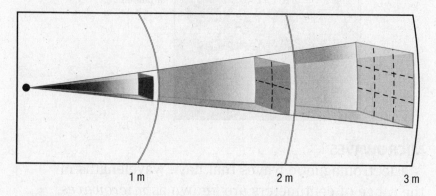

1 m   2 m   3 m

READING CHECK

11. Explain Why does the intensity of a light decrease as the distance to the light increases?

_____

_____

LOOKING CLOSER
12. Identify On the figure, circle the area at which intensity is lowest.

What Is the Electromagnetic Spectrum?

There are many different types of electromagnetic radiation. Each type has a different set of wavelengths. Humans eyes can detect only *visible light*, which has wavelengths between about 4×10^{-7} and 7×10^{-7} m. Visible light is only one kind of electromagnetic radiation.

The *electromagnetic spectrum* is all of the different wavelengths of electromagnetic radiation. Although all electromagnetic waves have some similarities, each type of radiation also has unique properties.

Electromagnetic Spectrum

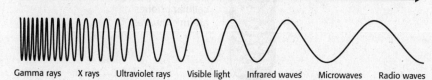

Shorter wavelengths ← ——————————→ Longer wavelengths

Gamma rays   X rays   Ultraviolet rays   Visible light   Infrared waves   Microwaves   Radio waves

LOOKING CLOSER
13. Compare Which type of electromagnetic radiation has the shortest wavelengths?

_____

_____

RADIO WAVES

Radio waves have the longest wavelengths of any kind of electromagnetic radiation. The wavelength of a radio wave may be several kilometers. This part of the electromagnetic spectrum includes TV signals and AM and FM radio signals. ☑

Radar is a system that uses radio waves to find the locations of objects. Police use radar to monitor the speed of vehicles. Air traffic control towers at airports use radar to find the locations of aircraft. Antennas at the control tower emit radio waves. The waves bounce off the aircraft and return to a receiver at the tower.

✓ READING CHECK

14. Identify Which kind of electromagnetic radiation has the longest wavelengths?

_____

Airports use radar to track the locations of airplanes.

LOOKING CLOSER

15. Define What is radar?

_____

_____

MICROWAVES

Electromagnetic waves that have wavelengths in the range of centimeters are known as *microwaves*. Microwaves are used to carry communication signals over long distances. Space probes use microwaves to transmit signals back to Earth. ☑

Microwaves are also used in cooking. Microwaves are easily transmitted through air, glass, paper, and plastic. However, the water, fat, and sugar molecules in food all absorb microwaves. The absorbed microwaves can cook food. The energy from the absorbed waves causes water and other molecules to vibrate. The energy of these vibrations spreads throughout the food and warms it.

✓ READING CHECK

16. Describe How long are the wavelengths of microwaves?

_____

LOOKING CLOSER

17. Compare Which type of signal has a shorter wavelength, a phone signal or a radio signal?

_____

The signals from cellular phones are microwaves.

SECTION 2 The Nature of Light *continued*

INFRARED AND ULTRAVIOLET LIGHT

Electromagnetic waves that have wavelengths slightly longer than wavelengths of red visible light are *infrared* waves. You cannot see it, but infrared light from the sun warms you. Devices that are sensitive to infrared light can produce images of objects that emit infrared waves. For example, remote infrared sensors on weather satellites can record temperature changes in the atmosphere and track cloud movements. ☑

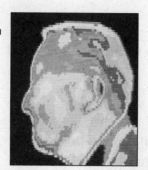

This photo of a person was taken with a camera that can detect infrared radiation. The different shades show different temperatures of the person's skin.

☑ READING CHECK

18. Describe What do weather satellites record using infrared waves?

_____

_____

_____

_____

The invisible light that lies just beyond violet light makes up the *ultraviolet* (UV) part of the spectrum. Nine percent of the energy emitted by the sun is ultraviolet light. UV light has higher energy and shorter wavelengths than visible light does. It has enough energy to pass through clouds and give you a sunburn. Sunscreens absorb or block UV light and can prevent sunburns. UV light also kills germs and can be used to disinfect objects. ☑

☑ READING CHECK

19. Compare Does ultraviolet light have more or less energy than visible light?

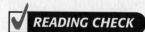

X RAYS AND GAMMA RAYS

Beyond the ultraviolet part of the spectrum are waves called *X rays* and *gamma rays*. X rays have wavelengths less than 10^{-8} m. Gamma rays have the highest energies and have wavelengths as short as 10^{-14} m.

Passing X rays through the body makes an X-ray image of bones. Most X rays pass right through, but bones and other tissues absorb a few. The X rays that pass through the body to a photographic plate produce an image.

X rays are useful tools for doctors, but they can also be dangerous. Both X rays and gamma rays have very high energies. Exposure to X rays and gamma rays may kill or damage living cells, which can cause cancer. However, gamma rays can also be used to treat cancer by killing the diseased cells.

Section 2 Review

SECTION VOCABULARY

intensity in physical science, the rate at which energy flows through a given area of space **photon** a unit or quantum of light; a particle of electromagnetic radiation that has zero rest mass and carries a quantum of energy	**radar** radio detection and ranging, a system that uses reflected radio waves to determine the velocity and location of objects

1. List Give two examples of how radar is used.

_____

_____

2. Explain Why do scientists use two different models of light?

_____

_____

3. Describe Give one observation that supports the wave model of light and one observation that supports the particle model of light.

_____

_____

_____

4. Identify Which photons have more energy, photons of radio waves or photons of visible light? Explain your answer.

_____

_____

5. Apply Concepts Why should you use sunscreen even on cloudy days?

_____

_____

6. Identify List the seven main kinds of electromagnetic radiation in order from highest frequency to lowest frequency.

_____

_____

CHAPTER 16 Sound and Light

SECTION 3 Reflection and Color

As you read this section, keep these questions in mind:
- What happens to light when it hits an object?
- Why can you see an image in a mirror?
- Why do we see colors?

What Happens When Light Hits an Object?

You may think of light bulbs, candles, and the sun as objects that send light to your eyes. However, all of the other objects that you see, including this book, also send light to your eyes. Otherwise, you would not see them. In order for you to see an object, light must travel from the object to your eyes.

There are two main ways that light can get from an object to your eyes. Some objects, such as the sun or a light bulb, produce light. However, most objects, including this book, only reflect light from other sources.

LIGHT AS A RAY

It can be hard to imagine how light waves travel. To make it easier to understand and predict how light waves behave during reflection, refraction, and other processes, scientists use light rays.

A **light ray** is an imaginary line that shows the direction in which light travels. The light ray's direction is the same as the direction the light wave travels. It is also the same as the path the photons of light take. When scientists draw light rays, they use single-headed arrows, like the ones shown below. ☑

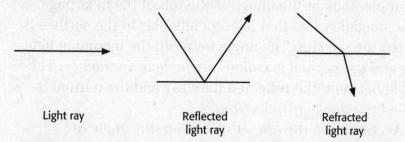

| Light ray | Reflected light ray | Refracted light ray |

Light rays cannot be used to model all the properties of light. However, they can be useful for showing how light behaves in many situations.

READING TOOLBOX

Compare After you read this section, make a chart comparing the images created when light is reflected from flat, concave, and convex mirrors.

READING CHECK

1. Define What is a light ray?

_____

_____

_____

Name _____ Class _____ Date _____

REFLECTION OF LIGHT

Remember that waves can *reflect*, or bounce off, surfaces. All objects that you can see reflect at least some of the light that hits them. The way the light reflects affects what the surface looks like.

Many surfaces, such as paper and skin, look dull. This is because light scatters off of them in many different directions, as shown in the figure below. This reflection of light into random directions is called *diffuse reflection*.

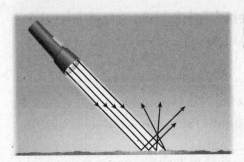

During diffuse reflection, light rays reflect in many different directions.

LOOKING CLOSER

2. Describe Would the surface in the figure look dull or shiny?

_____

_____

Smooth, polished surfaces, such as mirrors, look shiny. Instead of scattering, the light rays that hit smooth surfaces from a single direction all reflect in the same direction. You can see this in the figure below.

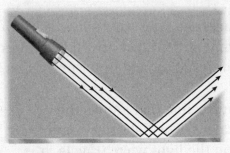

Light rays that reflect off a smooth surface all travel in the same direction.

THE LAW OF REFLECTION

Scientists describe reflection using angles. For example, look at the image at the top of the next page. The imaginary line that is perpendicular to the surface is called the *normal*. The angle between the incoming light ray and the normal is called the *angle of incidence*. The angle between the reflected light ray and the normal is called the *angle of reflection*.

According to the *law of reflection*, the angle of incidence is equal to the angle of reflection. You can use this law to predict the direction of a light ray that reflects off a smooth surface. ☑

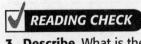

3. Describe What is the law of reflection?

_____

_____

_____

SECTION 3 Reflection and Color *continued*

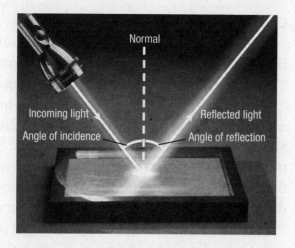

According to the law of reflection, the angle of incidence is equal to the angle of reflection.

Normal

Incoming light

Reflected light

Angle of incidence

Angle of reflection

LOOKING CLOSER

4. Apply Concepts On the figure, draw an incoming light ray that has a smaller angle of incidence. Then, draw the reflected light ray for that incoming ray.

Why Can You See Yourself in a Mirror?

When you look into a flat mirror, you see an image of yourself standing behind the mirror. Of course, there is not really a copy of you behind the mirror. The light rays that form the image seem to come from behind the mirror, but they actually don't. Therefore, the image you see in the mirror is a **virtual image**. ☑

The ray diagram in the figure below shows the paths of light rays striking a flat mirror. When a light ray reflects off a flat mirror, the light ray obeys the law of reflection. The angle of reflection equals the angle of incidence.

When the reflected rays reach your eyes, your brain interprets the light as if it traveled in straight lines. So, you see an image of yourself behind the mirror. In other words, flat mirrors "fool" you into seeing objects that aren't actually there.

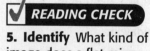

READING CHECK

5. Identify What kind of image does a flat mirror produce?

_____

_____

The man sees a virtual image behind the mirror. However, no light rays actually traveled from behind the mirror to the man's eyes.

This light ray reflects off the mirror and travels to the man's eyes. His brain perceives the light as if it had traveled in a straight line.

Visually, it appears that the reflected light ray traveled in a straight line from behind the mirror.

LOOKING CLOSER

6. Explain Why does the man see an image of himself in the mirror?

_____

_____

_____

_____

SECTION 3 Reflection and Color *continued*

CURVED MIRRORS

You are probably most familiar with flat mirrors. However, people sometimes also use curved mirrors. Curved mirrors *distort*, or change, images they reflect. ☑

Like flat mirrors, light reflects off of curved mirrors according to the angle of reflection. However, the surface of a curved mirror is not flat. Therefore, the normal to the mirror points in different directions at different places on the mirror. This results in the distorted images we see in curved mirrors.

There are two main kinds of curved mirrors: convex mirrors and concave mirrors. Mirrors that bulge out are called *convex mirrors*. Convex mirrors produce virtual images that are smaller than the actual object. People use convex mirrors to see large areas easily. For example, the mirror on the passenger side of a car is a convex mirror. This mirror allows the driver to see a larger area of the road behind the car.

Mirrors that curve inward are called *concave mirrors*. People use concave mirrors to focus reflected light onto a single point.

A concave mirror can form one of two kinds of images. It may form a virtual image behind the mirror or a real image in front of the mirror. Remember that light rays do not actually pass through a virtual image. A **real image** is an image that light rays pass through. The type of image that forms depends on the location of the object relative to the mirror.

Talk About It

Think Critically In a small group, think of situations in which a curved mirror would be more useful than a flat mirror. Try to identify examples, other than the examples given here, of the uses of curved mirrors in everyday life.

Critical Thinking

8. Compare How is a real image different from a virtual image?

_____

_____

_____

_____

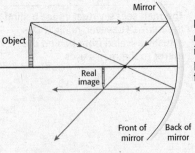

Light rays pass through a real image. Therefore, a real image would appear on a piece of paper placed in front of the mirror.

LOOKING CLOSER

9. Identify What determines whether the image produced by a concave mirror is virtual or real?

_____

_____

_____

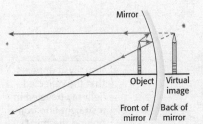

Light rays do not pass through a virtual image. If you placed a piece of paper behind the mirror, no image would form on the paper.

SECTION 3 Reflection and Color *continued*

How Do We See Colors?

White light from the sun contains all of the different wavelengths of visible light. What color an object appears to be depends on the wavelengths of light that come from it and enter your eyes. Your brain interprets different wavelengths of light as different colors. ☑

For example, when white light strikes a leaf, the leaf reflects only visible light with a wavelength of about 550 nm. The leaf absorbs light with other wavelengths. When the light reflected from the leaf enters your eyes, your brain interprets the light as green. Therefore, the leaf looks green. If you shine only red light on the leaf, the leaf looks black. This is because there is no green light for the leaf to reflect.

MIXTURES OF COLORS

Most of the colors that we see are not pure colors. They are mixtures of colors created by combining light or pigments. The *additive primary colors of light* are red, green, and blue. Mixing light of two of these colors can produce the secondary colors yellow, cyan, and magenta. Mixing light of the three additive primary colors makes white light. ☑

Filters and *pigments*, or dyes, absorb light. Therefore, mixing pigments or filters has a different effect on color than mixing light. The *subtractive primary colors*—yellow, cyan, and magenta—can be combined to create red, green, and blue. If pigments or filters of all three colors are combined in equal proportions, all visible light is absorbed. No light gets to your eyes, so you see black. Black is the absence of color.

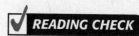

✓ READING CHECK

10. Identify What determines what color an object appears to be?

_____

_____

✓ READING CHECK

11. Describe What color of light is produced by mixing red, green, and blue light?

_____

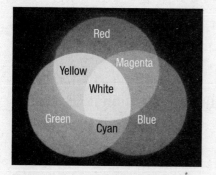

Red, green, and blue light can combine to produce yellow, magenta, cyan, or white light.

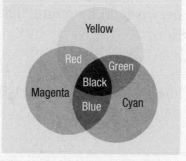

Cyan, magenta, and yellow filters or pigments can combine to produce red, green, blue, or black.

LOOKING CLOSER

12. Explain Why does a mixture of yellow, cyan, and magenta pigments look black?

_____

_____

Section 3 Review

SECTION VOCABULARY

light ray a line in space that matches the direction of the flow of radiant energy	**virtual image** an image that forms at a point from which light rays appear to come but do not actually come
real image an image of an object that forms when rays of light go through a lens and intersect at a single point	

1. Explain Why do scientists use light rays to represent light waves?

_____

_____

2. Identify Give three examples of objects that produce diffuse reflection. Explain how you know these objects produce diffuse reflection.

_____

_____

_____

3. Identify Label the normal, angle of incidence, and angle of reflection in the diagram below.

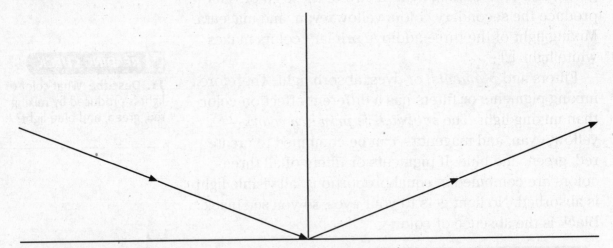

4. Apply Concepts The angle between an incoming light ray and the normal is 25°. What is the angle of reflection?

_____

5. Infer What color would a blue object look if you shined red light on it? Explain your answer.

_____

_____

_____

SECTION 4 | Refraction, Lenses, and Prisms

KEY IDEAS

As you read this section, keep these questions in mind:

- What happens to light when it passes from one medium to another?
- How do lenses work?
- How can a prism separate white light into colors?

What Happens When Light Passes from One Medium to Another?

Light, like all waves, travels in a straight line in a single medium. However, remember that waves *refract*, or bend, when they move from one medium to another. Like all waves, light bends when it moves from one medium to another. It does this because the speed of light is different in each medium.

The amount a light wave bends depends on the relative speeds of light in each medium. If light slows down when it enters a new medium, the light ray bends toward the normal. If it speeds up when it enters a new medium, it bends away from the normal. ☑

For example, the speed of light is higher in air than in glass. When light moves from air to glass, the ray bends toward the normal. When light moves from glass to air, the ray bends away from the normal, as shown below.

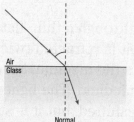

When light moves from air into glass, the light slows down. The light ray bends toward the normal.

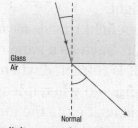

When light moves from glass into air, the light speeds up. The light ray bends away from the normal.

REFRACTION AND VIRTUAL IMAGES

Remember that a *virtual image* is an image that light rays do not pass through. Refraction of light, like reflection off of a flat mirror, can produce virtual images. The figure at the top of the next page shows an example of this.

READING TOOLBOX

Compare and Contrast As you read this section, make a chart to compare and contrast how light interacts with mirrors, lenses, and prisms.

☑ READING CHECK

1. Explain Why does light refract when it moves into a different medium?

_____

_____

LOOKING CLOSER

2. Describe What happens to the speed of light when light moves from air into glass?

_____

_____

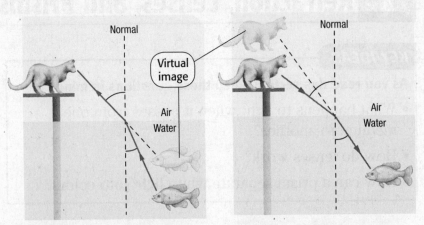

Light bends away from the normal when it moves from the water into the air. Therefore, the cat sees a virtual image of the fish that is higher in the water than the fish actually is.

Light bends toward the normal when it moves from the air into the water. Therefore, the fish sees a virtual image of the cat that is higher above the water than the cat actually is.

LOOKING CLOSER

3. Apply Concepts In which substance is the speed of light greater, air or water?

_____

_____

Critical Thinking

4. Explain If you look into a body of water, such as a lake, from a dock or boat, the water may look shallower than it actually is. What do you think is the reason for this?

_____

_____

_____

_____

_____

The images that the cat and the fish see are virtual images. Light bends away from the normal when it passes from the water to the air. The cat's brain interprets the light as if it traveled in a straight line. Thus, the cat sees a virtual image of the fish. Similarly, light bends toward the normal as it passes from the air into the water. Thus, the fish sees a virtual image of the cat.

How Do Lenses Work?

You may not realize it, but you use the refraction of light every day. Human eyes, as well as cameras, contact lenses, eyeglasses, and microscopes, contain parts that bend light.

When light travels at an angle through a thin, flat medium, such as a pane of glass, it is refracted twice. First, it is refracted when it enters the medium. Second, it is refracted when it leaves the medium. The light ray's position as it exits the medium is shifted, but it is still parallel to the original light ray.

If the medium has a curved surface, the exiting rays will not be parallel to the original ray. The light will be traveling in a different direction after it leaves the medium. Therefore, a curved piece of a transparent medium, such as glass, can change the direction in which light travels. Such curved mediums are called **lenses**.

SECTION 4 Refraction, Lenses, and Prisms *continued*

TYPES OF LENSES

There are two main kinds of lenses: converging lenses and diverging lenses. A *converging lens*, which is thicker in the middle than at the edges, bends light inward. This type of lens can create either a virtual image or a real image. The type of image depends on the distance from the lens to the object.

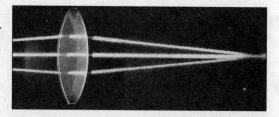

A converging lens focuses light inward. The light rays focus to a point called the focal point of the lens.

A magnifying glass is an example of a converging lens. If you hold the lens near the object, you see a larger image of the object through the lens. If you hold the lens farther from the object, you see a smaller image of the object.

A converging lens, such as a magnifying glass, can produce different magnifications. **Magnification** is any difference between the size of an image and the size of the object. A magnification of an object can be smaller or larger than the object.

A *diverging lens* is thinner in the middle than at the edges. It bends light outward and can create only a virtual image.

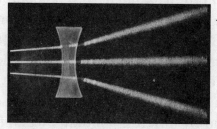

A diverging lens bends light outward. It can produce only virtual images.

LOOKING CLOSER
5. Identify On the figure, circle the focal point of the lens.

Talk About It
Identify Relationships Look up the words *converge* and *diverge* in a dictionary. In a small group, talk about why different lenses are called convergent lenses or divergent lenses.

LOOKING CLOSER
6. Describe What type of image can a diverging lens produce?

_____

_____

MICROSCOPES

A compound light microscope uses multiple lenses to provide greater magnification than a single magnifying glass can. The *objective lens* is close to an object and forms a large, real image of the object. The *ocular lens* in the eyepiece acts like a magnifying glass. It magnifies the real image from the objective lens. This creates the large, virtual image you see when you look through the microscope.

How Do Human Eyes Work?

Think about a camera that uses film. Light enters the camera through a large lens. The lens focuses the light into an image on the film at the back of the camera. Parts of the human eye work in very similar ways to these parts of a camera. The figure below shows how the different parts of the eye affect light.

How the Eye Works

❸ The light is refracted again by the lens. Muscles around the lens can change its shape to affect how much the light is refracted.

❷ After it passes through the cornea, the light passes through the pupil. The pupil is the dark hole in the center of the colored part of the eye.

❹ The refracted light is focused onto the back surface of the inside of the eye, which is called the retina.

❺ Special structures on the retina called rods and cones detect the light. Cones detect colors, but respond only to bright light. Rods detect dim light, but cannot resolve details well.

❶ The cornea is a transparent membrane that covers the eye. The cornea refracts light.

❻ The signals from the rods and cones are carried to the brain by the optic nerve. The brain interprets the signals to determine what you are looking at.

How Do Prisms Separate White Light Into Colors?

Remember that white light contains many different wavelengths, or colors, of visible light. A prism can separate white light into its component colors. A **prism** is a transparent solid that is generally made of glass.

Remember that light waves refract because their speed changes when they move into a new medium. The different wavelengths of light travel at different speeds in a medium, such as the glass in a prism. Therefore, they bend by different amounts when they pass through the prism, as shown below.

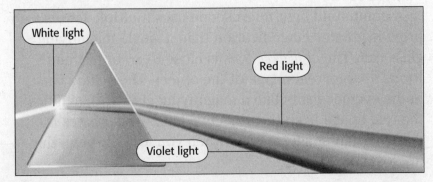

White light

Red light

Violet light

DISPERSION

From longest to shortest wavelength, the colors in the visible spectrum are red, orange, yellow, green, blue, and violet. Violet light has the shortest wavelength and travels the most slowly through a medium, such as glass. Red light has the longest wavelength and travels the most quickly. Therefore, violet light bends more than red light when they pass from one medium to another. ☑

Thus, when white light passes from air into a glass prism, violet bends the most and red bends the least. The other colors are bent by an amount between violet and red. When the light exits the prism, the light is separated into the colors in the visible spectrum. The separation of light into different colors because of differences in wave speed is called **dispersion**. ☑

How Do Rainbows Form?

Water droplets in the air can act like prisms. Sunlight that strikes a water droplet is dispersed into different colors as it passes from the air into the water. The refracted light rays strike the back surface of the water droplet at an angle.

If the angle is small enough, the rays can reflect off the back of the droplet. Some of the light will then travel through the droplet. The light is dispersed again as it passes out of the water droplet back into the air.

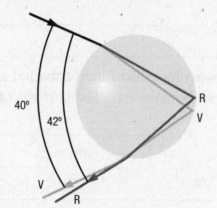

Rainbows form through a combination of dispersion and reflection.

LOOKING CLOSER

11. Describe What two effects combine to produce rainbows?

_____

_____

When light finally leaves the droplet, violet light emerges at an angle of 40°. Red light emerges at an angle of 42°. The other colors of visible light are in between these angles. We see light from many droplets as arcs of color, which form a rainbow.

Section 4 Review

SECTION VOCABULARY

dispersion in optics, the process of separating a wave (such as white light) of different frequencies into its individual component waves (the different colors)	**magnification** the increase of an object's apparent size by using lenses or mirrors
lens a transparent object that refracts light waves such that they converge or diverge to create an image	**prism** in optics, a system that consists of two or more plane surfaces of a transparent solid at an angle with each other

1. Identify Relationships How is dispersion related to refraction?

_____

_____

2. Describe Fill in the blanks in the flowchart below to describe how the human eye works.

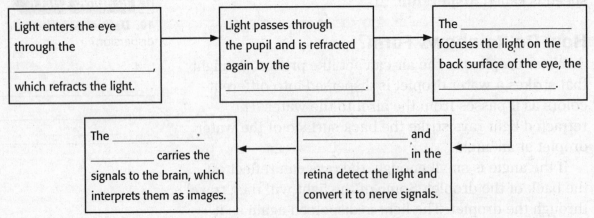

3. List Give three examples of objects that use converging lenses.

_____

_____

4. Predict Consequences If all wavelengths of light traveled at the same speed in different mediums, would rainbows occur? Explain your answer.

_____

_____

_____

5. Identify Which type of lens can produce both real and virtual images?

_____

6. Apply Concepts Green light travels more slowly in a medium than yellow light. Which color of light is bent more when it passes through a prism?

CHAPTER 17 Electricity
SECTION 1

Electric Charge and Force

As you read this section, keep these questions in mind:

• What are the different kinds of electric charge?

• How do materials become electrically charged?

• How do objects behave in an electric field?

What Is Electric Charge?

Have you ever reached for a doorknob or other metal object and received a shock? You may even have seen a flash of light that looked like a spark. This happens when electricity flows between your body and the metal object. This happens because your body and the metal object have different electric charges.

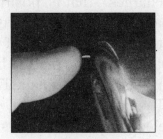

You may get a shock when you touch a doorknob because electricity flows between your body and the doorknob.

Electric charge is a property of an object that has a different number of protons than electrons. If the object has more electrons than protons, we say it has a *negative charge*. If it has more protons than electrons, we say it has a *positive charge*. If it has an equal number of protons and electrons, it has no electric charge, or a *neutral charge*. Most objects that you are familiar with have a neutral charge most of the time.

Electrons can carry electric charge from one object to another. When you walk across a carpet, electrons move from the carpet into your body. Therefore, your body no longer has a neutral charge. When you reach for the doorknob, electrons flow from your body to the doorknob. The moving electrons produce the shock and light. ☑

Like energy and matter, electric charge cannot be created or destroyed by ordinary chemical processes. In other words, electric charge is *conserved*. If one object loses electrons, another object must gain the same number of electrons.

READING TOOLBOX

Ask Questions As you read this section, write down questions that you have about the material you read. When you finish reading, work with a partner to figure out the answers to your questions.

Critical Thinking

1. Apply Concepts A particle contains 25 protons and 23 electrons. What type of electric charge does the particle have?

_____

_____

 **READING CHECK**

2. Identify What carries electric charge between your body and a carpet?

_____

_____

SECTION 1 Electric Charge and Force *continued*

How Do Electric Charges Behave?

Look at the girl in the picture below. She rubbed the balloon against her hair. When she moves the balloon away from her hair, some of her hair sticks to the balloon. This attraction occurs because electrons have moved from her hair to the balloon. As a result, her hair has a positive charge and the balloon has a negative charge.

The opposite charges in the girl's hair and the balloon cause her hair and the balloon to attract each other.

The behavior of the girl's hair and the balloon shows one way that two charged objects can interact. Opposite electric charges—that is, positive and negative charges—attract each other. The positive charge in the girl's hair attracts the negative charge of the balloon.

The balloons in the picture below have both been rubbed against the girl's hair. They both have a negative charge. They *repel* each other, or push each other away. Similar electric charges always repel each other.

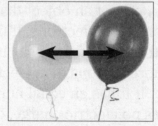

The similar charges in the two balloons cause them to repel each other.

MEASURING ELECTRIC CHARGE

The SI unit of electric charge is the *coulomb* (C). A proton has a charge of $+1.6 \times 10^{-19}$ C. An electron has a charge of -1.6×10^{-19} C. Notice that protons and electrons have the same size electric charge. However, the electron has a negative charge and the proton has a positive charge.

The charge on an electron or proton is very small. For an object to have a noticeable electric charge, it must have a large number of extra protons or electrons. For example, an object with a charge of -1.0 C has about 6.25×10^{18} extra electrons.

How Can Electrons Move Between Objects?

Remember that protons and neutrons are in the nucleus of an atom. Because they are inside the atom and are bound tightly together, they usually do not move out of the atom. However, electrons are located outside the nucleus of an atom. In many cases, electrons can easily move from one atom to another. Electrons can move more easily in some materials than in other materials. ☑

ELECTRICAL CONDUCTORS AND INSULATORS

You have probably noticed that the cords on electric appliances, such as toasters, are plastic on the outside. However, the cord is not plastic all the way through. The wire inside the cord contains copper metal.

Why is the inside of the cord made of a different material than the outside of the cord? The answer has to do with how electrons flow in different materials. Electrons can flow easily through some materials. These materials are called **electrical conductors**. Copper, like most metals, is a good electrical conductor. The electricity that flows to the toaster moves through the copper easily.

Electrons cannot easily move through the plastic on the outside of the wire. Therefore, the plastic is an **electrical insulator**. The plastic prevents electrons from moving out of the wire and into objects other than the toaster.

Copper is used in wires because it is a good electrical conductor. Plastic is used on the outside of the cord because it is a good electrical insulator.

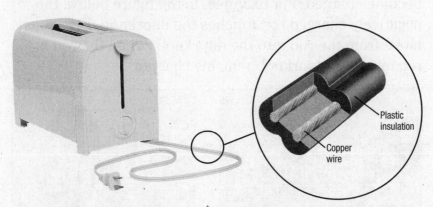

Plastic insulation

Copper wire

Whether a material is an electrical conductor or an electrical insulator affects what people use it for. As you've just seen, one of the reasons that people use metal for wires is because metals are electrical conductors.

✔ **READING CHECK**

6. Explain Why can electrons move between atoms more easily than protons?

_____

_____

_____

Talk About It

Brainstorm Make a list of five substances that you think are electrical conductors and five substances that you think are electrical insulators. Share your list with a small group. Explain why you think each substance is an electrical conductor or insulator.

LOOKING CLOSER

7. Predict Would the toaster work if the entire cord was made of plastic? Explain your answer.

_____

_____

_____

_____

_____

SECTION 1 Electric Charge and Force *continued*

INDUCED CHARGES IN CONDUCTORS

If an object gains or loses electrons, it will have an electric charge. However, sometimes part of an object can have an electric charge, even if the whole object does not.

For example, the end of the rod in the figure below has a negative electric charge. The negative electric charge on the rod repels electrons in the doorknob. The electrons in the doorknob move away from the rod. Therefore, part of the doorknob has a slight negative charge. The other part has a slight positive charge. However, the whole doorknob does not have an electric charge, because it has not gained or lost electrons. ☑

8. Explain How can the whole doorknob have a neutral charge, even though part of the doorknob has a positive charge and part has a negative charge?

_____

_____

_____

The charged rod can *induce*, or cause, parts of the doorknob to become charged.

If you moved the rod away from the doorknob, the charges on the doorknob would disappear. The charges are only there when the rod is near the doorknob. In other words, they are *induced charges*.

CHARGES MOVING THROUGH CONTACT

If a charged object touches a neutral object, electrons can move between the objects. The neutral object can become charged. For example, in the figure below, the negatively charged rod touches the doorknob. Electrons move from the rod into the doorknob. When the rod is removed, the doorknob remains charged.

LOOKING CLOSER

9. Describe After the rod touches it, does the doorknob have more electrons than protons or more protons than electrons? Explain your answer.

_____

_____

_____

When the negatively charged rod touches the doorknob, electrons move from the rod to the doorknob. The doorknob ends up with a negative charge.

CHARGING OBJECTS BY FRICTION

When two neutrally charged objects rub together, electrons can move from one object to the other. The direction the electrons move depends on the kinds of materials that are rubbing together. One material gains electrons and becomes negatively charged. The other material loses electrons and becomes positively charged. This is an example of *charging by friction*. Friction causes electrons to move between the objects. ☑

Have you ever pulled clothes out of the dryer and seen them stick together? They stick together because of *static electricity*. Your clothes are charged by friction when they rub against each other in the dryer. Electric charges build up on the clothes. These charges cause the clothes to stick together.

SURFACE CHARGES ON INSULATORS

Remember that you can induce a charge in a conductor by bringing it near a charged object. It is possible for insulators to become charged, too. However, because electrons cannot move easily through an insulator, only its surface becomes charged. ☑

When a charged object is brought near an insulator, the electrons in the molecules of the insulator move slightly. One side of a molecule becomes slightly positively charged. The other side becomes slightly negatively charged. Then, the molecule is *polarized*.

For example, the balloon in the figure below has been rubbed with wool. It has become negatively charged through friction. The negative charge on the balloon induces a positive surface charge on the stream of water. The water molecules become polarized. The positive and negative charges attract each other, causing the water to bend toward the balloon.

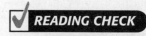
READING CHECK

10. Identify What causes electrons to move between objects that are rubbed together?

_____

_____

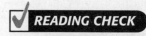
READING CHECK

11. Explain Why does only the surface of an insulator become charged when a charged object is near it?

_____

_____

_____

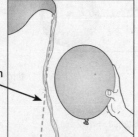

Path of water if balloon was not charged.

This balloon has been charged by friction with wool. The charge on its surface induces a surface charge on the water molecules, causing the stream of water to bend.

LOOKING CLOSER

12. Describe What type of electric charge does the surface of the water molecules nearest the balloon have?

_____

_____

What Is an Electric Force?

Pushing or pulling on an object—that is, applying a force to it—can cause the object's motion to change. In a similar way, electric forces can change the motions of charged particles. An **electric force** is a force that a charged object experiences when it interacts with other charged objects. ☑

READING CHECK

13. Define What is an electric force?

Electric forces cause many things that we see every day. For example, friction is produced by electric forces between the molecules on the surfaces of objects that are touching.

Electric forces also affect things that are too small for us to see. For example, atoms bond to each other and form molecules because of electric forces. Electric forces help proteins and other molecules in our bodies interact with one another. Without electric forces, life on Earth would be impossible.

EFFECTS OF CHARGE AND DISTANCE ON ELECTRIC FORCE

The electric force between two charged objects depends on two things. They are:

- the amount of charge each object has
- the distance between the objects ☑

READING CHECK

14. Identify What are two factors that affect the electric force between two charged objects?

The electric force between two objects is directly proportional to the charges of the objects. In other words, the greater the charges on the objects, the stronger the electric force between them.

The electric force is inversely related to the square of the distance between the objects. If the distance between the objects triples, the electric force between the object decreases by $3^2 = 9$ times. If the distance doubles, the force decreases by $2^2 = 4$ times, as shown below.

LOOKING CLOSER

15. Apply Concepts If both objects in the figure were negatively charged, in which directions would the arrows point?

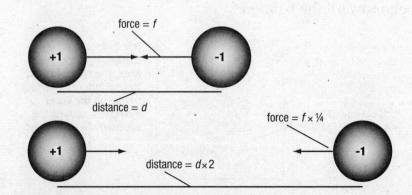

SECTION 1 Electric Charge and Force *continued*

ELECTRIC FIELDS

Remember that some forces can only act between objects that are touching. Other forces, such as gravity, are *field forces*—that is, they can affect objects without touching them. Electric forces are field forces. Charged objects do not have to be touching in order to produce electric forces on one another. ☑

Every charged object produces an electric field. An **electric field** is the space around a charged object that will produce an electric force on another charged object that moves into the space. We cannot see electric fields, but we can observe their effects on charged particles.

Although we cannot see electric fields, we can describe them in drawings by using electric field lines. *Electric field lines* are lines that show the effects of an electric field on a positively charged object. For example, the figures below show electric field lines around two differently charged objects.

16. Define What is a field force?

_____

_____

_____

Electric field lines point away from positive charges because a positively charged object will repel another positively charged object.

Electric field lines point toward negative charges because a negatively charged object will attract a positively charged object.

The electric field lines in the figures above show the electric fields around single charges. You can also draw electric field lines around groups of charges, as shown below.

LOOKING CLOSER

17. Explain Why do electric field lines point away from a positively charged object?

_____

_____

_____

_____

LOOKING CLOSER

18. Explain Why do all of the electric field lines in the image of two positively charged particles point away from the particles?

_____

_____

_____

_____

The electric field lines around these two positively charged objects show that the objects repel each other.

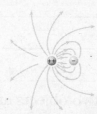

The positive charge is twice as strong as the negative charge. Therefore, half the field lines that start at the positive charge end at the negative charge.

When drawing field lines, remember these rules:
- Electric field lines can never cross one another.
- Electric field lines point in the direction a positive charge would move.

Section 1 Review

SECTION VOCABULARY

electrical conductor a material in which charges can move freely	**electric field** the space around a charged object in which another charged object experiences an electric force
electrical insulator a material in which charges cannot move freely	**electric force** the force of attraction or repulsion on a charged particle that is due to an electric field
electric charge an electrical property of matter that creates electric and magnetic forces and interactions	

1. **Compare** Explain how the movements of electrons in electrical conductors and electrical insulators affect the properties of the materials.

_____

_____

_____

_____

2. **Explain** More electrons move into your body when you walk across a carpeted floor than when you walk across a smooth floor. What is the most likely explanation for this? (Hint: What causes electrons to move between objects when they rub together?)

_____

_____

_____

_____

3. **Infer** Student A walks across a carpeted floor. Student B walks across a smooth floor. Which student is most likely to get an electric shock from a metal doorknob? Explain your answer. (Hint: The greater the difference in electric charge between two objects, the more likely a shock is.)

_____

_____

_____

4. **Describe** How do the charges on two objects affect the electric force between the objects?

_____

5. **Identify** Which way do electric field lines around a single, negatively charged object point?

CHAPTER 17 Electricity

SECTION 2 **Current**

As you read this section, keep these questions in mind:

- How are electrical potential energy and gravitational potential energy similar?

- What causes electrical resistance?

What Is Electrical Potential Energy?

When you turn on a light, the bulb lights up because electrons flow through it. The electrons get to the bulb by flowing through wires. What causes the electrons to flow through the wire and into the bulb? The answer has to do with potential energy.

Remember that *gravitational potential energy* is energy that objects have because of gravity. Similarly, charged objects have a type of potential energy that depends on their location in an electric field. This type of potential energy is called **electrical potential energy**. ☑

Remember that similar electric charges repel each other. For example, a negatively charged object will move away from another negatively charged object. The objects move apart because their electric fields produce forces on the objects. The forces cause the objects to move. As the objects move, their electrical potential energy decreases.

If you push a ball up a hill, you do work on the ball. This increases the ball's gravitational potential energy. Similarly, it is possible to increase an object's electrical potential energy by exerting a force on the object. For example, if two negatively charged objects are forced closer together, their electrical potential energy will increase. This is shown in the graph below.

As two similarly charged particles move closer together, their electrical potential energy increases.

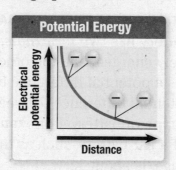

Potential Energy

Electrical potential energy

Distance

READING TOOLBOX

Compare After you read, make a chart comparing the SI units used to describe current, voltage, and resistance.

READING CHECK

1. Define What is electrical potential energy?

_____

_____

_____

_____

LOOKING CLOSER

2. Describe What happens to electrical potential energy when two similarly charged particles move apart?

_____

_____

_____

SECTION 2 Current *continued*

How Is Electrical Potential Energy Measured?

As you can see from in the figure below, electrical potential energy depends on the distance between two charges. When two similar charges move closer to each other, electrical potential energy increases. When two different charges move closer to each other, electrical potential energy decreases.

	Similarly charged particles	Oppositely charged particles
Small distance between particles	high electrical potential energy 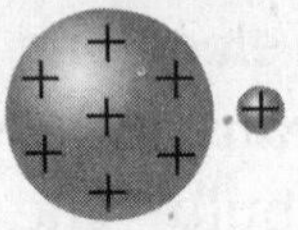	low electrical potential energy 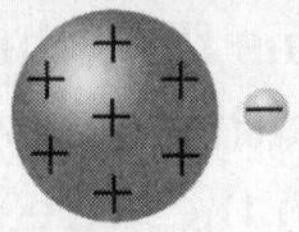
Large distance between particles	low electrical potential energy 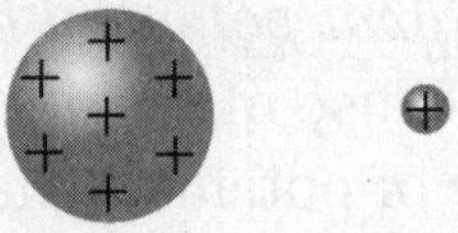	high electrical potential energy 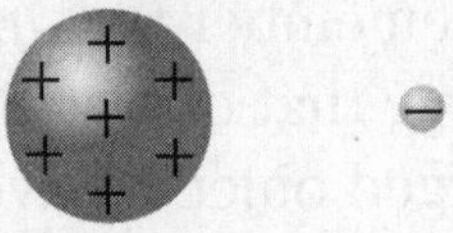

LOOKING CLOSER

3. Infer How would electrical potential energy in the top left-hand box change if the amount of charge on the two objects decreased?

_____

_____

A charged particle at a certain point in an electric field has a certain amount of electrical potential energy. The ratio of this energy to the particle's charge is called the *potential* of that point in the electric field. The SI unit for potential is the volt (V). One *volt* is equal to one joule per coulomb (1 J/C).

Different places in an electric field have different potentials. Because scientists generally study charged particles that are moving, they usually refer to potential difference instead of potential. The **potential difference** between two points is equal to the potential at one point minus the potential at the other. Because the SI unit for potential difference is the volt, potential difference is often called *voltage.* ☑

✓ READING CHECK

4. Identify What is another word for potential difference?

_____

POTENTIAL DIFFERENCE IN A BATTERY

A battery has two *terminals*, or ends. One terminal is positively charged, and the other is negatively charged. There is a potential difference between the two terminals. The potential difference between the terminals depends on the type of battery. For example, the potential difference of a car battery, such as the one at the top of the next page, is about 12 V.

SECTION 2 Current *continued*

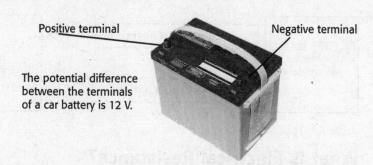

Positive terminal

Negative terminal

The potential difference between the terminals of a car battery is 12 V.

LOOKING CLOSER
5. Identify What is the voltage between the terminals of a car battery?

_____

Most batteries are electrochemical cells. A **cell** is a device that changes chemical energy into electrical energy. Some batteries, called *wet cells*, contain liquids that conduct electricity. Other batteries, called *dry cells*, contain solids or paste-like materials that conduct electricity.

What Causes Charged Particles to Move?

A voltage can cause charged particles to move. Positively charged particles move from areas of high potential to areas of low potential. Negatively charged particles move from areas of low potential to areas of high potential. ☑

✓ READING CHECK

6. Describe In which direction do positively charged particles move in response to a voltage?

_____

_____

ELECTRIC CURRENT

An **electric current** is the rate at which charged particles move in response to a voltage difference. The SI unit of current is the *ampere* (A). One ampere is equal to one coulomb per second (1 C/s).

Current can be produced by the movements of positively charged particles, negatively charged particles, or both kinds of particles. In solids, moving electrons generally produce current. In gases and many chemical solutions, both positively charged particles and negatively charged particles can move to produce current. ☑

A negative charge moving in one direction has the same effect as a positive charge moving in the opposite direction. However, scientists always describe current as if it were produced by positive charges.

Because electrons are negative, the direction of a conventional current is opposite to the movement of electrons. If electrons are flowing in a wire from left to right, the current in the wire is moving from right to left. The figure at the top of the next page shows this.

✓ READING CHECK

7. Identify What kind of particle generally produces currents in solids?

_____

Critical Thinking

8. Apply Concepts In a particular liquid, positive ions are moving because of a voltage. The ions are moving from left to right through the liquid. In which direction is the current in the liquid flowing?

_____

_____

9. Define What is resistance?

_____

_____

_____

_____

10. Identify What causes electrical devices to become warm when they are used?

_____

_____

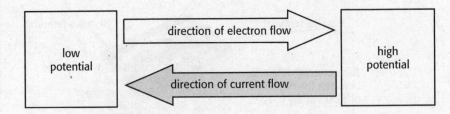

direction of electron flow

low potential

high potential

direction of current flow

What Is Electrical Resistance?

Imagine two flashlights that use the same kind of battery. Each has a different bulb. One bulb is very bright. The other is very dim. Because both flashlights use the same battery, the voltage of the bulbs is the same. One bulb is brighter because a different amount of current flows through each bulb. This is because the bulbs have different resistances. **Resistance** is the slowing of the movement of charged particles through a substance. ☑

Imagine pushing a heavy box of books across a carpeted floor. Now, imagine pushing the same box of books across a slippery tile floor. Friction causes the box to resist motion. Different surfaces produce different amounts of friction. Resistance in a material is like friction between the box and the floor. Different materials produce different amounts of resistance.

You have probably noticed that electrical devices become warm after they have been on for a while. Resistance within the devices produces this heat. This is similar to the way that friction can cause kinetic energy to change into heat energy. ☑

As electrons flow through a conductor, the electrons collide with the atoms in the conductor. These collisions cause kinetic energy to move from the electrons to the atoms of the conductor. As the atoms gain kinetic energy, the temperature of the conductor increases.

A light bulb, such as the one shown at the top of the next page, has a metal filament in it. The resistance of the metal in the filament determines how bright the light bulb glows. As electrons flow through the filament, the metal heats up and begins to glow. The higher the resistance, the dimmer the bulb.

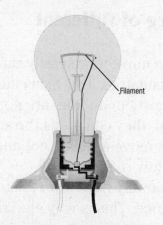

Resistance within the filament of a light bulb causes the filament to glow when electricity flows through it. Within the filament, electrical energy changes into heat and light energy.

Filament

DETERMINING RESISTANCE

It is difficult to measure the resistance of a material directly. Instead, scientists usually determine resistance by measuring the current and voltage in a material. Then, they can calculate the resistance of the material using the equation ☑.

$$resistance = \frac{voltage}{current}$$

$$R = \frac{V}{I}$$

This equation is commonly called *Ohm's law*. The SI unit of resistance is the ohm (Ω). One ohm is equal to one volt per ampere (1 V/A).

You can use Ohm's law to calculate voltage and current. To do this, you must rearrange the resistance equation.

Let's look at an example of how to calculate the resistance in a conductor. A light bulb is connected to a 12 V battery. The current through the light bulb is 3.0 A. What is the resistance of the light bulb?

READING CHECK

12. Describe How do scientists usually determine the resistance of a substance?

_____

_____

Step 1: List the given and unknown values.	Given: voltage, $V = 12$ V current, $I = 3.0$ A	Unknown: resistance, R
Step 2: Write the equation.	$R = \dfrac{V}{I}$	
Step 3: Insert the known values and solve for the unknown value.	$R = \dfrac{12 \text{ V}}{3.0 \text{ A}}$ $R = 4.0 \ \Omega$	

Math *Skills*

13. Calculate The current in a device is 0.50 A. The resistance of the device is 12 Ω. What is the voltage of the battery in the device? Show your work.

So, the resistance of the light bulb is 4.0 Ω.

What Is the Resistance of Different Materials?

Remember that electrons move more easily through conductors than through insulators. This is because the electrons in the atoms of most conductors are not tightly bound to the atoms. Instead, they can move through the material. Because electrons move easily in conductors, conductors generally have low resistance. ☑

Although conductors generally have low resistance, they still have some resistance. This is why electricity flowing through a wire can make the wire heat up. The resistance of the wire changes electrical energy into heat energy.

RESISTANCE IN INSULATORS

Electrons do not flow through insulators easily. Therefore, most insulators have high resistance. For this reason, insulators are used to stop the flow of electric current. The plastic coating around a copper wire is an insulator. The plastic keeps current from moving into the floor or into your body.

RESISTANCE IN SEMICONDUCTORS

Semiconductors have properties similar to both insulators and conductors. In its natural form, a semiconductor is an insulator. However, people add other materials to semiconductors to change how they behave. These materials are *impurities*. The impurities help semiconductors conduct current. This lowers the resistance of the semiconductor.

People may use semiconductors, conductors, and insulators in the same device. Each type of material helps the device do what it is designed to do. For example, computer boards, such as the one in the figure below, contain semiconductors, conductors, and insulators.

Circuit boards like this one contain semiconductors, conductors, and insulators.

✓ **READING CHECK**

14. Explain Why do conductors generally have low resistance?

_____

_____

Critical Thinking

15. Apply Concepts Which probably has lower resistance, a metal fork or a plastic fork? Explain your answer.

_____

_____

_____

_____

_____

LOOKING CLOSER

16. Infer What do you think is the reason that devices like this one contain conductors?

_____

_____

SECTION 2 Current *continued*

RESISTANCE IN SUPERCONDUCTORS

At very low temperatures, some compounds have no resistance. These types of materials are *superconductors*. Superconductors have zero resistance below a certain temperature, called the *critical temperature*. ☑

The critical temperature depends on the material. It can be as low as –272 °C (–458 °F) or as high as –123 °C (–189 °F). Currently, scientists are looking for materials that have even higher critical temperatures. These materials could be superconductors at room temperature.

When current starts to flow in a superconductor, it doesn't stop. This is true even when the voltage difference is removed. Current has been observed to flow for many years in superconducting material. This makes superconductors very useful for many different things. ☑

One use for these materials is superconducting magnets. These magnets are strong enough to float commuter trains, such as the one in the figure below, above their tracks. This removes any friction between the train and the tracks. These magnets may also one day be used to store energy.

Superconducting magnets allow this commuter train to float above its tracks.

✔ **READING CHECK**

17. Define What is a superconductor?

_____

_____

_____

✔ **READING CHECK**

18. Describe What happens to current in a superconductor when voltage is removed?

_____

_____

LOOKING CLOSER

19. Infer Is there probably more or less friction between this train and its tracks than between a regular train and its tracks?
(Hint: Is there friction between two objects that do not touch?)

_____

Superconductors could also be useful for transmitting electricity to people. Electricity we use today loses a great deal of energy to the resistance in the wires. If the wires were superconductors, no energy would be lost when electricity flowed through them. This would allow people to transmit electricity more efficiently.

Type of material	Resistance	Properties
Conductor	low	conducts current easily
Insulator	high	does not conduct current easily
Semiconductor	moderate	has properties of both conductors and insulators
Superconductor	zero	has no electrical resistance

Section 2 Review

SECTION VOCABULARY

cell in electricity, a device that produces an electric current by converting chemical or radiant energy into electrical energy	**electric current** the rate at which charges pass through a given point; measured in amperes
electrical potential energy the ability to move an electric charge from one point to another	**potential difference** the voltage difference in potential between two points in a circuit
	resistance in physical science, the opposition presented to the current by a material or device

1. Describe According to Ohm's law, how are current, voltage, and resistance related?

_____

_____

2. Classify Fill in the blank spaces in the table below.

Material	Conductor or insulator?	High resistance or low resistance?
Copper		
Plastic		
Air	insulator	
Silver		low resistance
Concrete		high resistance

3. Calculate A portable lantern uses a 24 V power supply. The current in the lantern is 0.80 A. What is the resistance of the lantern? Show your work.

4. Calculate A light bulb is connected to a battery. The battery has a voltage of 1.5 V. The light bulb has a resistance of 3.5 Ω. What is the current in the light bulb? Show your work.

CHAPTER 17 Electricity
SECTION 3 Circuits

As you read this section, keep these questions in mind:
- What is a closed circuit?
- How can devices be connected in a circuit?
- What happens to energy in a circuit?
- What can happen if too much power flows through a circuit?

What Are Circuits?

Have you ever plugged a string of light bulbs into an electrical outlet? The outlet provides a voltage to the circuit. The voltage makes electrons move through the wire and bulbs from one side of the outlet to the other. The electric charges in the string of bulbs have a complete path to follow. In other words, electrons can move in a loop through the system. A system in which electrons can move in a closed loop is called an **electric circuit**.

There are two main kinds of electric circuits: closed circuits and open circuits. The string of lights in the figure below is an example of a closed circuit. A *closed circuit* is a circuit in which current can flow along a complete path due to a voltage.

This string of bulbs and the outlet it is connected to is an example of a closed circuit. Electrons flow in a loop from one side of the outlet, through the bulbs, to the other side of the outlet.

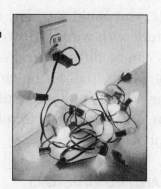

If the path is interrupted or there is no voltage, then no charge can flow through the circuit. Therefore, the circuit becomes an *open circuit*.

If a bulb is connected to a battery, the inside of the battery is part of the circuit. Current can flow through the battery. The source of the voltage is always part of the conducting path of a closed circuit.

READING TOOLBOX

Describe Relationships
After you read this section, create a chart showing how current, resistance, and voltage affect power in a circuit.

LOOKING CLOSER
1. Define What is a closed circuit?

_____

_____

SECTION 3 Circuits *continued*

USING SWITCHES IN A CIRCUIT

In many cases, we need to be able to change a closed circuit into an open circuit and back again. For example, we do not need to leave the lights on in an empty room. To change a circuit from open to closed, we use a switch. A *switch* is a device in a circuit that allows the circuit to be changed from open to closed and back again. The figure below shows a circuit that contains a switch.

2. Describe How can you tell that the switch in the image is closed?

_____

_____

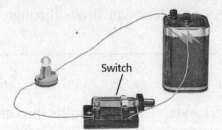

Switch

When the switch is closed, the circuit is also closed. Electrons can flow, and the bulb lights up.

Many switches work by breaking the path that electrons flow through in a circuit. For example, a switch may have metal bars on it that can touch part of the wire. When the switch is open, the metal bars do not touch the wire. Electrons cannot flow through the circuit if the bars are not touching the wire. Then, the circuit is open. When the bars touch the wire, electrons can flow, and the circuit is closed.

How Can You Draw a Circuit?

It is easy to describe a simple circuit in words. For example, you could say "The light bulb is connected to the battery with wires." However, more complicated circuits can be difficult to describe in words. Instead of using words to describe circuits, scientists often use drawings called **schematic diagrams**. In a schematic diagram, each part of a circuit is represented by a different symbol. ☑

✓ READING CHECK

3. Explain Why do scientists use schematic diagrams?

_____

_____

_____

WIRES AND CONDUCTORS

In a schematic diagram, wires and other simple conductors are represented by straight lines and right angles, as shown below.

Straight lines and right angles represent wires in a schematic diagram.

RESISTORS

Remember that different materials have different resistances. *Resistors* are devices that are used in circuits to control the amount of current flowing through the circuit. Each resistor has a specific resistance. For example, a resistor may be a 10 Ω resistor. In schematic diagrams, resistors are shown as bent lines. ☑

Multiple bends in a wire represents a resistor. ──∿∿∿──

LIGHT BULBS

Remember that resistance is what makes light bulbs glow. Light bulbs are a special kind of resistor. Therefore, a light bulb is shown as a resistor with a circle around it.

A resistor with a circle around it represents a light bulb.

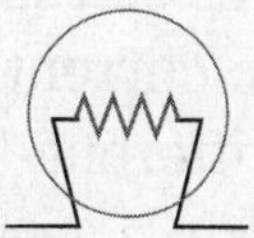

BATTERIES

Every circuit must have a source of voltage. In many circuits, this source is a battery. Batteries are represented by two lines.

Two lines with different heights represent a battery. The longer line represents the positive terminal of the battery.

SWITCHES

Switches can be represented by two different symbols. One symbol represents an open switch. The other represents a closed switch.

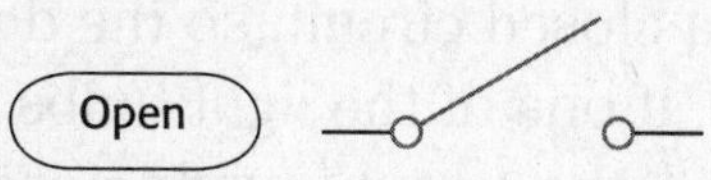

Open

Different symbols represent open and closed switches.

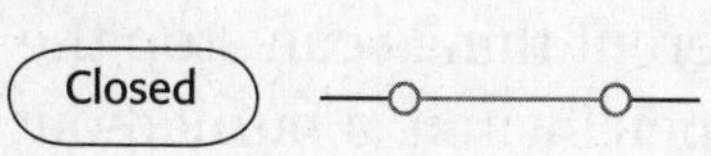

Closed

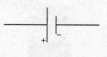

READING CHECK

4. Define What is a resistor?

_____

_____

LOOKING CLOSER

5. Describe What does the symbol in the center of the circle represent?

_____

LOOKING CLOSER

6. Identify On the figure, circle the line that represents the positive terminal of the battery.

What Are Two Ways of Connecting the Components of a Circuit?

Most circuits that we use every day contain more than one *component*, or part. For example, a circuit may contain a battery, a light bulb, and a switch. There are two main ways of connecting these elements in a circuit: in parallel or in series. The type of connection in a circuit affects how much voltage each component receives.

SERIES CIRCUITS

In a **series circuit**, the voltage of the battery is divided between the different components in the circuit. The current must flow through all of the components in order to complete the circuit. All of the current flows along the same path. Therefore, the current in each component of a series circuit is the same.

Even though the current is the same, the resistance in each device is different. That means that the voltage across each device in a series circuit may be different. You can see a series circuit in the figure below.

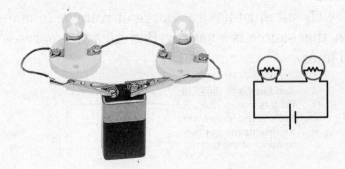

In a series circuit, all of the current flows along the same path. It must flow through each device in the circuit.

If one device along the path of the series circuit is removed, it will cause a break in the circuit. The circuit is no longer a closed circuit, so the devices will not work. For example, if one of the light bulbs in the figure above were removed, the current could not follow a complete path. Therefore, the circuit would be open, and the remaining light bulb would not work.

Many different things can stop the current in a series circuit. An open switch, a burned-out light bulb, or a cut wire may prevent the whole series circuit from working.

Critical Thinking

7. Infer The voltage source for a series circuit is a 9 V battery. Does each component of the circuit have a higher or a lower voltage than the battery? Explain your answer.

_____

_____

_____

_____

_____

LOOKING CLOSER

8. Identify What is the same in all components of a series circuit?

_____

SECTION 3 Circuits *continued*

PARALLEL CIRCUITS

In a **parallel circuit**, the voltage across each part of the circuit is the same. However, the current in each device can differ. The current can follow several different paths through the circuit. This is different than in a series circuit. The figure below shows an example of a parallel circuit.

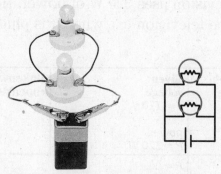

In a parallel circuit, the current can flow through different paths. The voltage in each device is the same.

In a parallel circuit, one or more of the devices can be removed and there will still be current in the circuit. For example, if you were to remove one of the light bulbs in the circuit above, the other light bulb would still light. Electrons would flow from the battery through the other light bulb.

How Is the Power of a Circuit Determined?

Many appliances and devices that you use every day use electrical energy. This energy may come from a battery or from a power plant miles away. The amount of work the device can do depends on how much power it uses. For example, a 1,200 W microwave oven can heat food faster than an 800 W microwave oven. (Remember that the watt, W, is the SI unit of power.)

As a charge moves in a circuit, the charge loses energy. Some energy turns into useful work. However, remember that no machine is 100% efficient. The same is true for electronic devices. As current moves through a circuit, some of the energy is lost to the surroundings as heat. The rate at which electrical energy is turned into other forms of energy is called **electric power**.

Remember that *power* is the rate at which work is done. This is also true for electric power. Electric power is the rate at which electrical work is done.

LOOKING CLOSER
9. Identify Circle the symbol in the schematic diagram that represents the battery.

Critical Thinking
10. Apply Concepts Which type of light bulb uses more power, a 100 W light bulb or a 50 W light bulb?

_____

Critical Thinking

11. Describe What happens to power as the current in a circuit increases?

_____

_____

12. Calculate A hairdryer is plugged into a 120 V outlet. The current in the hair dryer is 9.1 A. How much power is the hair dryer using? Show your work.

DETERMINING ELECTRIC POWER

You can calculate electric power by multiplying the current, *I*, by the voltage difference, *V*, in a circuit. The equation below shows this relationship.

$$power = current \times voltage$$
$$P = IV$$

Let's look at an example of how to use the power equation. A television uses 320 W of power. How much current does the television use when it is plugged into a 120 V outlet?

Step 1: List the given and unknown values.	Given: voltage, $V = 120$ V power, $P = 320$ W	Unknown: current, *I*
Step 2: Write the equation and rearrange to solve for the correct variable.	$P = IV$ $I = \dfrac{P}{V}$	
Step 3: Insert the known values and solve for the unknown value.	$I = \dfrac{320 \text{ W}}{120 \text{ V}}$ $I = 2.67$ A	

So, the television uses 2.67 A of current.

POWER LOST IN A RESISTOR

You can combine the electric power equation with Ohm's law. This allows you to calculate the power that is lost when current flows through a resistor. For example, if voltage difference is constant, you can use the equation below to calculate power loss:

$$P = I^2 R$$

Remember that one watt (W) is equal to one joule per second (1 J/s). From the power equation, you can see that one watt is also equal to one volt times one ampere (1 V•A). ☑

READING CHECK

13. Identify Give two units that are the same as one watt.

_____

_____

POWER AND ENERGY

If you have ever seen an electricity bill, you may have noticed that the electric company charges by the kilowatt-hour (kW•h). Kilowatt-hours are units of energy. One kilowatt-hour is equal to 3.6×10^6 J.

How Do Fuses And Circuit Breakers Work?

If you plug many devices into an electrical outlet, the total resistance of the circuit decreases. This can increase the current in the circuit. If the electrical wires carry more current than is safe, the circuit is *overloaded*. An overloaded circuit can cause fires. ☑

If the insulation around an electrical wire is worn, two wires may touch. This creates another path for current to travel, which is a *short circuit*. A short circuit can also cause fires. Fuses and circuit breakers, seen in the figure below, lower the danger in short and overloaded circuits.

A **fuse** is a ribbon of wire with a low melting point. When the current in a circuit reaches a certain temperature, the fuse melts, or *blows*. This opens the circuit and the current stops For example, a 20 A fuse will melt if the current in the circuit is more than 20 A. A blown fuse is a sign that a short circuit or a circuit overload is present.

Once a fuse has blown, it must be replaced before the circuit will function. The image below shows examples of a normal fuse and a blown fuse.

Blown fuse   Normal fuse

When the current in a fuse gets too high, the metal in the fuse melts. This opens the circuit and can prevent overloads and short circuits.

Many homes have circuit breakers instead of fuses. A **circuit breaker** acts like a switch. It opens when there is a current overload. If you fix the circuit so there is no overload, you can reset the switch in the circuit breaker. Then, the circuit will work again.

A *ground fault circuit interrupter* (GFCI) is a special kind of electrical outlet. It acts like a small circuit breaker. GFCI outlets may be found where water is used near electricity, such as in bathrooms and kitchens.

☑ READING CHECK

14. Define What is an overloaded circuit?

_____

_____

_____

Critical Thinking

15. Apply Concepts Can a fuse prevent an overloaded circuit if it is connected in parallel with the devices in the circuit? Explain your answer.

_____

_____

_____

_____

_____

_____

_____

_____

_____

Name _____ Class _____ Date _____

Section 3 Review

SECTION VOCABULARY

circuit breaker a switch that opens a circuit automatically when the current exceeds a certain value

electric circuit a set of electrical components connected such that they provide one or more complete paths for the movement of charges

electric power the rate at which electrical energy is converted into other forms of energy

fuse an electrical device that contains a metal strip that melts when current in the circuit becomes too great

parallel circuit a circuit in which the parts are joined in branches such that the potential difference across each part is the same

schematic diagram a graphical representation of a circuit that uses lines to represent wires and different symbols to represent components

series circuit a circuit in which the parts are joined one after another such that the current in each part is the same

1. **Compare** What is the difference between an open circuit and a closed circuit?

_____

2. **Apply Concepts** Label each component in the circuit shown in the schematic diagram below.

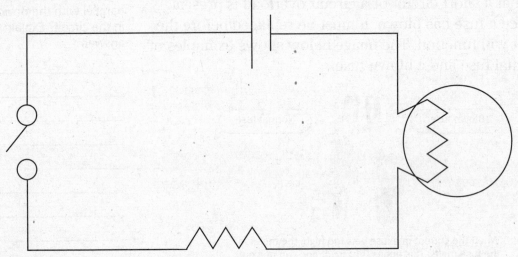

3. **Identify** Are the components in the circuit above connected in series or in parallel?

_____

4. **Describe** Will the light bulb in the circuit above light up? Explain your answer.

_____

_____

5. **Compare** How is a circuit breaker different from a fuse? How are they similar?

_____

_____

_____

CHAPTER 18 | Magnetism
SECTION 1

Magnets and Magnetic Fields

As you read this section, keep these questions in mind:

• What happens when the poles of two magnets come close together?

• What causes a magnet to attract or repel another magnet?

• How is Earth's magnetic field oriented?

What Are Some Properties of Magnets?

Magnets get their name from Magnesia, now a part of present-day Greece. Almost 3,000 years ago, people there first found naturally magnetic rocks. These rocks are called *lodestones*. An example of a lodestone is shown in the figure below.

Lodestones are naturally magnetic rocks. They attract other magnets and objects made of iron.

Sailors first used magnets as compasses for navigation. Today, magnets play roles in many aspects of our lives. Motors, VCRs, medical imaging machines, and many home alarm systems all rely on magnets.

MAGNETIC POLES

Recall that like electric charges repel each other and unlike charges attract. A similar situation occurs for **magnetic poles**, or points that have opposite magnetic properties. ☑

All magnets have at least one pair of poles, a north magnetic pole and a south magnetic pole. A north magnetic pole attracts a south magnetic pole on another magnet. In addition, a north magnetic pole always repels another north magnetic pole.

Magnetic poles always exist in pairs. If you cut a magnet in half, each part will have a north pole and a south pole. Even the tiniest magnets have two poles.

READING TOOLBOX

Compare and Contrast
After you read this section, make a chart showing the similarities and differences between Earth's geographic and magnetic poles.

LOOKING CLOSER
1. Identify What is a lodestone?

_____

_____

READING CHECK

2. Define What are magnetic poles?

_____

_____

_____

What Are Permanent Magnets?

Some substances, such as lodestones, stay magnetic all the time. Scientists call them *permanent magnets*. You can use a permanent magnet to make other objects magnetic. For example, if you place an iron nail near a magnet, the nail will become magnetized. If you take away the magnet, the nail will stay magnetic for a time. ☑

Even though they are called permanent magnets, the magnetism of permanent magnets isn't really permanent. Heating or hammering a permanent magnet can make it less magnetic, or even remove its magnetism completely.

MAGNETIC FORCES

Imagine placing a magnet into a bucket filled with iron nails. As you pull the magnet out of the bucket, nails stick to the magnet and to other nails. That happens because each nail that touches the magnet becomes magnetized. The magnetized nails exert magnetic forces on nails below them and pick them up. A *magnetic force* is a force that one magnet exerts on another.

How long is the chain of nails that the magnet can pull from the bucket? That depends on the strength of the magnet and the ability of the nails to become magnetized. The greater the distance between a nail and the magnet, the weaker the magnetic force holding the nail up. Far from the magnet, the magnetic force is weaker than the force of gravity on a nail in the bucket. Therefore, no more nails can be lifted out of the bucket.

✓ **READING CHECK**

3. Identify What is a permanent magnet?

_____

_____

Critical Thinking

4. Predict Consequences Magnet A is a stronger magnet than magnet B. Which magnet would be able to lift more nails from the bucket?

_____

LOOKING CLOSER

5. Explain Why are nails far from the magnet less able to magnetize other nails?

_____

_____

_____

The magnet magnetizes the nails it touches. Those nails, in turn, magnetize nails they touch. The farther a nail is from the magnet, the less magnetic it is. Therefore, nails far from the magnet are less able to magnetize other nails.

SECTION 1 Magnets and Magnetic Fields *continued*

What Are Magnetic Fields?

Try holding a magnet and moving its south pole toward the south pole of a magnet that can move freely. Do not let the magnets touch. You will see the free magnet move away from the one in your hand. It moves because the two magnets exert magnetic forces on each other, even though they never touch.

Because it acts at a distance, a magnetic force is a field force. Remember that every electrically charged object produces an electric field. In a similar way, every magnet produces a magnetic field. A **magnetic field** is the space around a magnet in which another magnet experiences a magnetic force. The strength of a magnetic field depends on the magnetic material and how much it is magnetized.

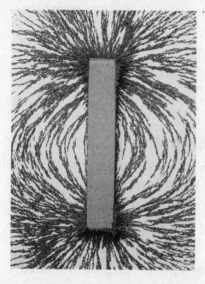

The small shavings of iron show the shape of this magnet's magnetic field.

What Produces Magnetic Fields?

Moving electric charges produce magnetic fields. Atoms have magnetic properties because of the movements of the electrons in the atoms. The magnetic fields of individual atoms balance one another in most materials. Those materials, such as copper and aluminum, are not magnetic. ☑

In some materials, including iron, nickel, and cobalt, atoms form larger groups called *magnetic domains*. The magnetic fields of all the atoms in a magnetic domain line up in the same direction. This forms small magnetized regions in the material. If there is another magnetic field nearby, the small regions align with each other. That increases the material's magnetic field.

Critical Thinking

6. Apply Concepts What would happen if you held the south pole of one magnet near the north pole of a magnet that could move freely?

_____

_____

_____

LOOKING CLOSER

7. Describe What is the shape of the magnetic field around the center of the magnet?

_____

_____

✔ **READING CHECK**

8. Explain Why are most materials not magnetic?

_____

_____

_____

How Can You Draw Magnetic Fields?

Remember that you can use electric field lines to show the shape of the electric field around a charged object. In a similar way, you can use *magnetic field lines* to show the magnetic field of a magnet.

Magnetic field lines start at the north pole of a magnet and end at its south pole. They always form closed loops. The field lines actually continue inside the magnet itself to form the loops.

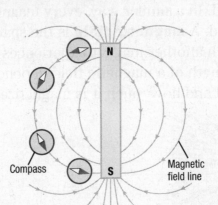

Magnetic field lines show the shape of a magnetic field. You can use a compass to determine how to draw magnetic field lines.

Compass

Magnetic field line

LOOKING CLOSER
9. Describe In which direction do the arrowheads on the magnetic field lines point?

_____

_____

Where Are Earth's Magnetic Poles?

Earth has a magnetic field. A *compass* is a device that can show the direction of Earth's magnetic field. The needle of a compass lines up with Earth's magnetic field. The compass points along Earth's magnetic field lines at any particular point.

Earth has two *geographic poles*, or points where Earth's axis of rotation meets Earth's surface. Earth also has two magnetic poles. However, Earth's magnetic poles are not in the same places as its geographic poles.

A compass needle is a small magnet. Like all magnets, it has a north pole and a south pole. Remember that north and south magnetic poles attract each other. Therefore, a compass needle's north pole must be attracted to Earth's south magnetic pole. ☑

The north pole of a compass needle points toward Earth's north geographic pole. Therefore, the magnetic pole in Earth's northern hemisphere is actually a south magnetic pole. The magnetic pole in the southern hemisphere is a magnetic north pole. In other words, Earth's magnetic and geographic poles are opposite one another. This is shown in the figure at the top of the next page.

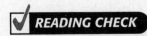

READING CHECK
10. Identify Which of Earth's magnetic poles is the north pole of a magnet attracted to?

_____

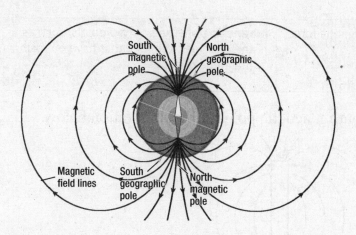

Earth's north geographic pole is closest to Earth's south magnetic pole.

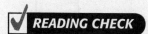

LOOKING CLOSER
11. Identify Which of Earth's magnetic poles is located in the northern hemisphere?

_____

_____

FINDING THE MAGNETIC POLES

To find the exact locations of the magnetic north and magnetic south poles, scientists use a *magnetic dip needle*. This is a compass needle that can point up and down. The needle points in the direction of the Earth's magnetic field at its location. In most parts of the world, the needle points slightly down. At the south and north magnetic poles, however, a dip needle points straight down. ☑

What Produces Earth's Magnetic Field?

Scientists do not know for certain what makes Earth magnetic. They know that Earth's core consists mostly of iron. However, the core is too hot for the iron to retain any magnetic properties.

Many scientists think that ions or electrons moving in the liquid layer of Earth's core cause Earth's magnetism. Others think that several different factors produce Earth's magnetic field.

The sun has its own magnetic field, and ejects charged particles into space. Earth's magnetic field deflects most of those particles. If Earth did not have a magnetic field, these particles could strike Earth. They could harm living things.

Many scientists think that some living things use Earth's magnetic field to guide them as they migrate. They have found magnetic particles in the tissues of migrating animals such as birds, bees, and fish.

☑ READING CHECK

12. Describe In which direction does a magnetic dip needle point at Earth's north magnetic pole?

_____

_____

_____

Section 1 Review

SECTION VOCABULARY

magnetic field a region where a magnetic force can be detected	**magnetic pole** one of two points, such as the ends of a magnet, that have opposing magnetic qualities

1. Draw Label the north and south magnetic poles in the illustration below.

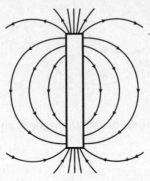

2. Apply Concepts Which pair of magnets below will move toward each other? Explain your answer.

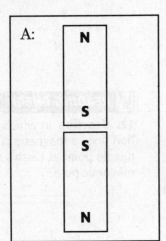

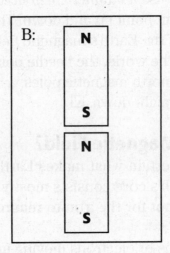

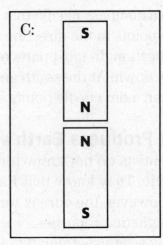

_____

_____

_____

3. Identify What produces magnetic fields?

_____

_____

4. Explain A student places a magnet into a box of paper clips. When she lifts the magnet, some of the paper clips are pulled out of the box. However, some of the clips remain in the box. Why can't the student pull all of the paper clips out of the box?

_____

_____

_____

CHAPTER 18 | Magnetism

SECTION 2

Magnetism from Electric Currents

As you read this section, keep these questions in mind:

• What happens to a compass near a wire that is carrying current?

• How do electric motors work?

How Are Electricity and Magnetism Related?

During the 1700s, people noticed that lightning can cause a compass needle to move. They also noticed that iron pans sometimes become magnetized during lightning storms. These observations show that there is a relationship between electricity and magnetism. However, this relationship was not understood until the 1800s.

In 1820, Danish science teacher Hans Christian Oersted first studied the effects of electric current on compass needles. He discovered that, when charged objects move, they produce magnetic fields. A compass needle brought close to a wire carrying a current moves from its usual north-south orientation. ☑

If no current is in the wire, the compass needle lines up with Earth's magnetic field. This shows that the magnetic field around a wire comes from the current in the wire, and not from properties of the wire itself.

The figure below shows a group of compasses placed around a current-carrying wire. Each compass needle points in a different direction. Together, the compasses show that the magnetic field around a current-carrying wire is a circle around the wire.

The magnetic field around a wire with a current in it is a series of *concentric*, or nested, circles.

READING TOOLBOX

Define As you read, underline words you don't know. When you figure out what they mean, write the words and their definitions in your notebook.

✔ READING CHECK

1. Describe What did Hans Christian Oersted discover?

_____

_____

_____

LOOKING CLOSER

2. Draw On the figure, draw magnetic field lines that show the shape of the magnetic field around the wire. Do not include arrowheads showing the direction of the field.

SECTION 2 Magnetism from Electric Currents *continued*

THE RIGHT-HAND RULE

Remember that there are arrows on magnetic field lines that show the direction of the magnetic field. You can use the right-hand rule to determine whether a magnetic field around a wire is clockwise or counterclockwise.

To use the *right-hand rule*, point the thumb of your right hand in the direction of the current in the wire. Then, curl your fingers as if you were going to grasp the wire. Your fingers curl in the direction of the magnetic field. For example, in the figure below, the magnetic field is counterclockwise. **Caution:** You should never touch an uninsulated wire connected to a power source. If you do, you could be electrocuted.

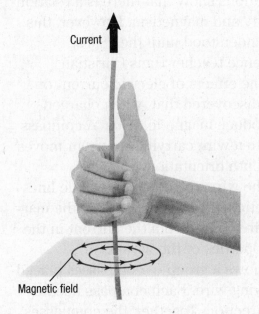

Current

You can use the right-hand rule to determine the direction of a magnetic field around a wire.

Magnetic field

Critical Thinking

3. Explain Can you use the right-hand rule to find the direction of a magnetic field around a wire that is not carrying a current? Explain your answer.

_____

_____

_____

_____

LOOKING CLOSER

4. Infer If the magnetic field around the wire was in the opposite direction, in which direction would the person's thumb point?

_____

How Can You Increase the Magnetic Field Around a Wire?

When current is in a wire, a magnetic field forms around the wire. This field is very weak for small currents. To increase the strength of the field, you could increase the amount of current in the wire. However, large currents can cause fires or other dangers.

There is another, safer way to create a stronger magnetic field around a wire. It involves wrapping the wire into a coil, as shown in the figure at the top of the next page. The device produced this way is called a **solenoid**.

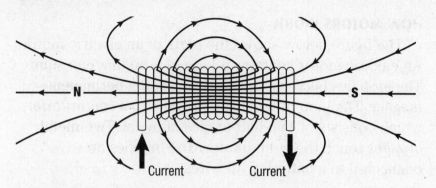

Wrapping a current-carrying wire into a coil increases the magnetic field around the wire.

5. Compare How is the magnetic field around a solenoid similar to the field around a bar magnet?

_____

_____

The magnetic field of each loop in a solenoid adds to the strength of the magnetic field of neighboring loops. The magnetic fields of all the loops add up. They produce a strong magnetic field for the whole solenoid.

The magnetic field of a solenoid acts in a similar way to the magnetic field of a bar magnet. Like a bar magnet, a solenoid has a north pole and a south pole.

You can increase the strength of a solenoid's magnetic field in three main ways. One way is to increase the current in the wire. Another way is to add more loops to the solenoid. You can also increase a solenoid's magnetic field by inserting a rod of magnetic material inside the coils. That produces a device called an **electromagnet**. For example, you could insert an iron rod into a solenoid to produce an electromagnet. ☑

The solenoid's magnetic field causes the rod to become magnetized. The rod's magnetic field adds to the coil's magnetic field. The result is a magnet that is stronger than the solenoid alone.

What Are Electric Motors?

Many devices rely on magnetic fields that are produced by currents in wires. Most of these devices use electric motors.

Electric motors are machines that convert electrical energy into mechanical energy. They can perform work when attached to an external device. In your home, large electric motors drive washing machines and clothes dryers. Simple motors make electric fans work.

✓ READING CHECK

6. Identify Describe three ways to increase the magnetic field of a solenoid.

_____

_____

_____

_____

_____

SECTION 2 Magnetism from Electric Currents *continued*

HOW MOTORS WORK

The figure below shows the parts of an electric motor. An electric motor contains a loop of wire that can spin. The loop lies between opposite poles of a permanent magnet. The loop of wire is connected to a *commutator*, which consists of two half-circles of metal. Two metal *brushes* touch the commutator. The brushes are connected to a battery with wires.

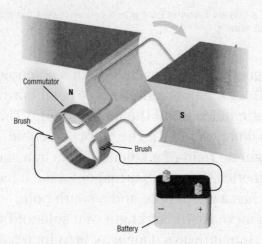

LOOKING CLOSER

7. Describe On the figure, draw arrows showing the direction of the current in the wire loop.

Current flows from the battery, through one brush, to half of the commutator. Then, it flows through the wire, to the other half of the commutator, through the other brush, to the battery. The current flows from the positive terminal of the battery to the negative terminal. Therefore, it flows from the right side of the loop, across the top, to the left side of the loop.

The current produces a magnetic field around the loop of wire. As a result, the poles of the permanent magnet repel the long sides of the loop. They produce a magnetic force on the loop, causing it to spin in the direction shown by the arrow.

Talk About It

Identify In a small group, think of some everyday devices that use electric motors. What do the motors in the devices do?

When the loop has spun halfway around, the brushes touch opposite sides of the commutator. The current still flows from the positive terminal to the negative terminal. However, now the current flows from the left side of the loop, over the top, to the right side. This produces an opposite magnetic field.

When the magnetic field reverses, the poles of the magnet again repel the loop of wire. However, because the wire is facing a different direction, it continues to spin in the same direction.

SECTION 2 Magnetism from Electric Currents *continued*

MEASURING ELECTRIC CURRENTS

Scientists use a tool called a **galvanometer** to measure current. The galvanometer shown below consists of a coil of insulated wire wrapped around an iron core. The core can rotate between the poles of a permanent magnet. ☑

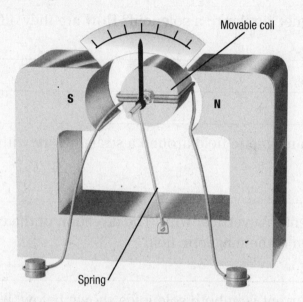

Movable coil

S   N

Spring

When there is a current in the coil, the coil produces a magnetic field. The magnetic fields of the coil and the magnet interact, causing the coil to turn.

When the galvanometer is attached to a circuit, a current is in the coil of wire. The coil and the iron core become an electromagnet and produce a magnetic field. The magnetic field interacts with the magnetic field of the surrounding permanent magnet. The interaction of the fields produces a force on the core. This causes the core to turn.

There is a needle attached to the core of the galvanometer. As the core turns, the needle moves left or right. It points to a different place on the dial, which shows how much current or voltage is in the circuit.

Scientists call a galvanometer an *ammeter* when it measures current. Because current and voltage are related, a galvanometer can also be used to measure voltage. Then, it is called a *voltmeter*.

✓ READING CHECK

8. Define What is a galvanometer?

_____

_____

_____

LOOKING CLOSER

9. Infer If more current flows through the galvanometer, will the coil turn more or less? Explain your answer.

_____

_____

_____

_____

Critical Thinking

10. Apply Concepts If there were no iron core inside the coil of wire in the galvanometer, what type of device would the coil be?

_____

_____

Section 2 Review

SECTION VOCABULARY

electric motor a device that converts electrical energy into mechanical energy **electromagnet** a coil that has a soft iron core and that acts as a magnet when an electric current is in the coil	**galvanometer** an instrument that detects, measures, and determines the direction of a small electric current **solenoid** a coil of wire with an electric current in it

1. Compare How is an electromagnet similar to a solenoid? How are they different?

_____

_____

_____

2. Describe What is the shape of a magnetic field around a straight wire with a current in it?

_____

3. Apply Concepts There is a current in a vertical wire. The direction of the current is downward. In which direction is the magnetic field?

_____

4. Identify The same amount of current is in both solenoids shown below. Which one has a stronger magnetic field? Explain your answer.

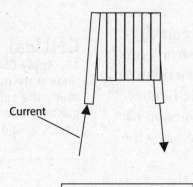

Current

Solenoid A: 8 coils

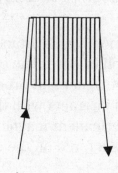

Solenoid B: 16 coils

_____

_____

5. Compare What is the difference between an ammeter and a voltmeter? How are they similar?

_____

_____

CHAPTER 18 | Magnetism)

SECTION 3
Electric Currents from Magnetism

As you read this section, keep these questions in mind:

• What is electromagnetic induction?

• How are electricity and magnetism related?

• What are the basic parts of a transformer?

What Is Electromagnetic Induction?

Remember that electric motors use magnetism to convert electric energy into mechanical energy. In contrast, electrical power plants use magnetism to convert mechanical energy into electricity. They use technology discovered by British physicist Michael Faraday in 1831.

Faraday produced a current by pushing a magnet through a coil of wire. The movement of the magnet into and out of the coil causes electrons in the wire to move. The moving electrons produce a current. This process is called **electromagnetic induction**. ☑

Look at the loop of wire moving between two magnets in the figure below. As the wire moves into and out of the magnetic field, the magnetic field induces a current in the loop. Rotating the loop or changing the strength of the magnetic field also induces a current in the loop. In each case, a changing magnetic field passes through the loop.

In general, a current is induced in a circuit if the magnetic field passing through the circuit changes. This is known as *Faraday's law*.

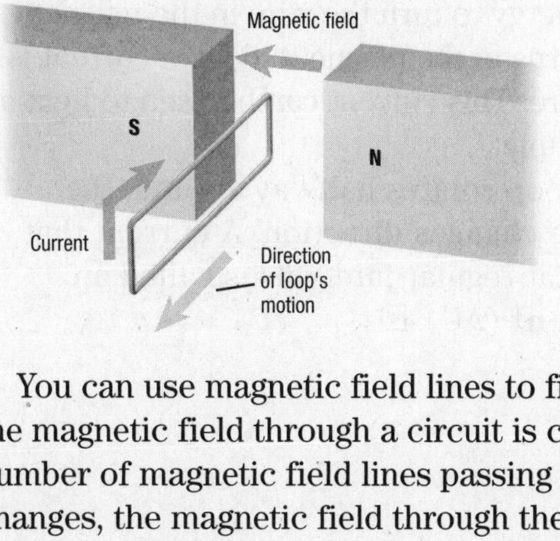

READING TOOLBOX

Compare After you read this section, make a table showing the features of step-up and step-down transformers.

☑ READING CHECK

1. Describe What is electromagnetic induction?

_____

_____

_____

_____

Magnetic field

S

N

When the loop moves in the magnetic field, a current is induced in the wire.

Current

Direction of loop's motion

LOOKING CLOSER

2. Infer If you held the wire still and moved the magnets forward and backward, would there be a current in the wire?

_____

_____

You can use magnetic field lines to figure out whether the magnetic field through a circuit is changing. If the number of magnetic field lines passing through the circuit changes, the magnetic field through the circuit changes.

What Happens to Energy During Induction?

Electromagnetic induction does not break the law of conservation of energy. It does not create energy from nothing. Actually, induction requires energy. Pushing a loop through a magnetic field requires work. The stronger the magnetic field, the more force you need to push the loop. The energy needed for that task comes from an outside source, such as your muscles. ☑

What Do Generators Do?

Remember that electric motors convert electrical energy into mechanical energy. **Generators** have the opposite effect. They convert mechanical energy into electrical energy. For example, look at the simple generator shown in the figure below. Notice that it is similar in structure to an electric motor. ☑

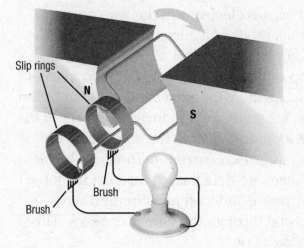

A generator converts the mechanical energy used to turn the wire into electrical energy.

Slip rings

Brush

Brush

You must use energy to turn the wire in the magnetic field. As the coil turns in the magnetic field, a current is produced in the wire. This current can be used to light a light bulb, for example,

Each time the loop rotates halfway around, the current in the wire changes direction. A current that changes direction at regular intervals is called an **alternating current** (AC). ☑

READING CHECK

3. Explain Why doesn't electromagnetic induction break the law of conservation of energy?

_____

_____

_____

READING CHECK

4. Define What is a generator?

_____

_____

_____

LOOKING CLOSER

5. Compare How is a generator similar to an electric motor?

_____

_____

_____

READING CHECK

6. Identify What is an alternating current?

_____

_____

_____

SECTION 3 Electric Currents from Magnetism *continued*

GENERATORS AND AC CURRENT

The diagram below shows the amount of current an AC generator produces as the loop rotates. Before the loop begins to rotate, it is perpendicular to the magnetic field. There is no current in the loop. When the loop has rotated 90°, it is parallel to the magnetic field. Then, the current is at its maximum.

When the loop rotates another 90°, to 180°, it is again perpendicular to the magnetic field. Therefore, the current is zero. At 270°, the loop is parallel to the magnetic field. The current is at its maximum. However, because the sides of the loop are in opposite locations, the current in the loop is in the opposite direction. As the loop continues to rotate, the current continues to change direction. ☑

Position of loop	Amount of current	Graph of current versus angle of rotation
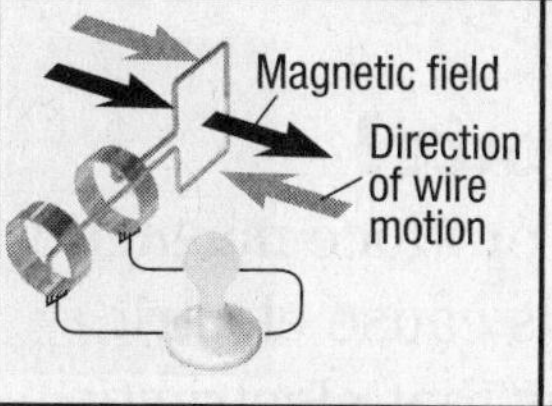 Magnetic field / Direction of wire motion	zero current	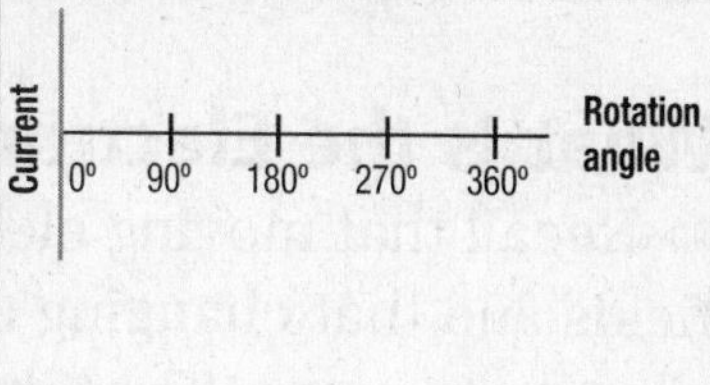
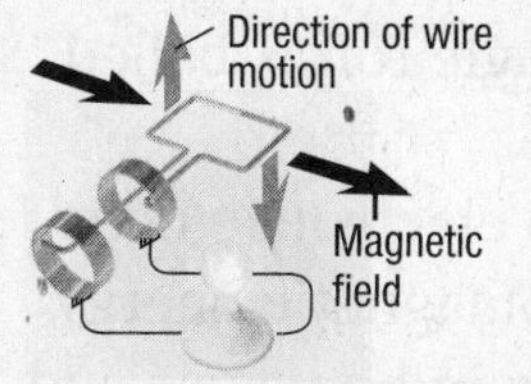 Direction of wire motion / Magnetic field	maximum current	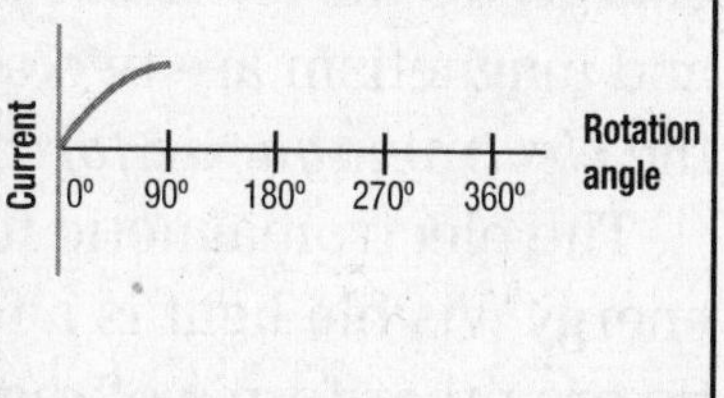
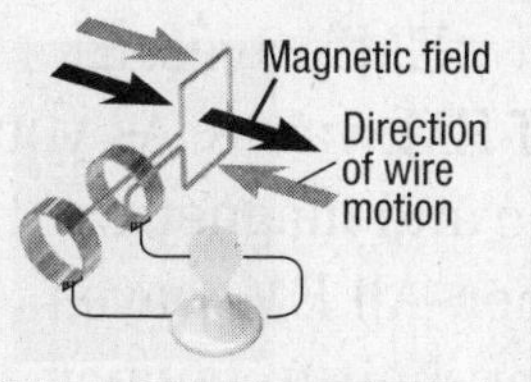 Magnetic field / Direction of wire motion	zero current	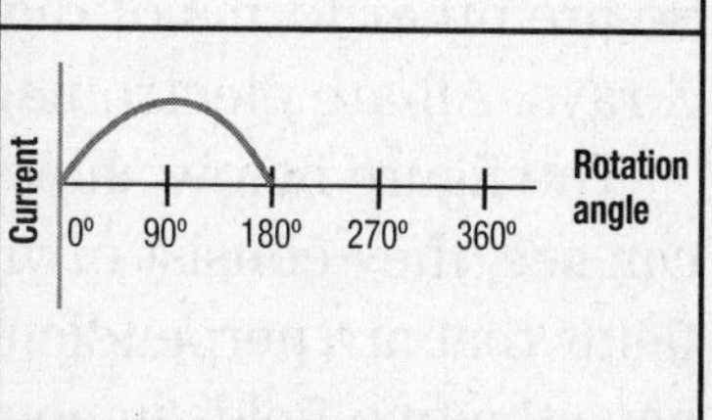
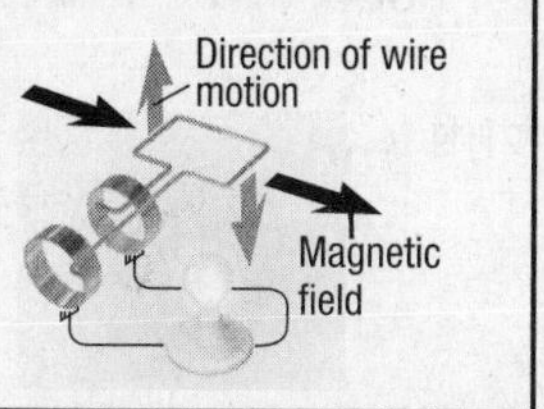 Direction of wire motion / Magnetic field	maximum current (opposite direction)	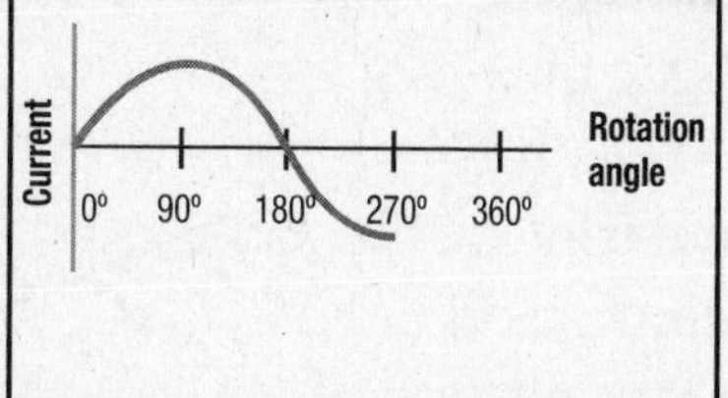
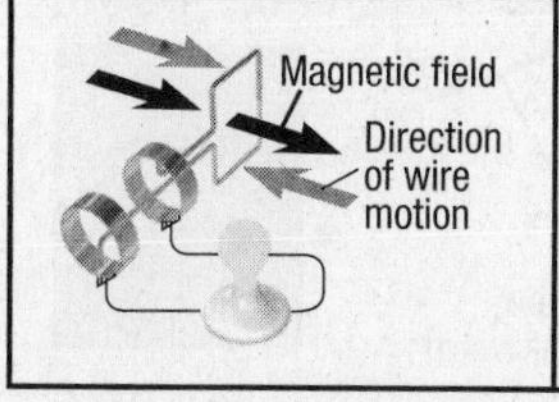 Magnetic field / Direction of wire motion	zero current	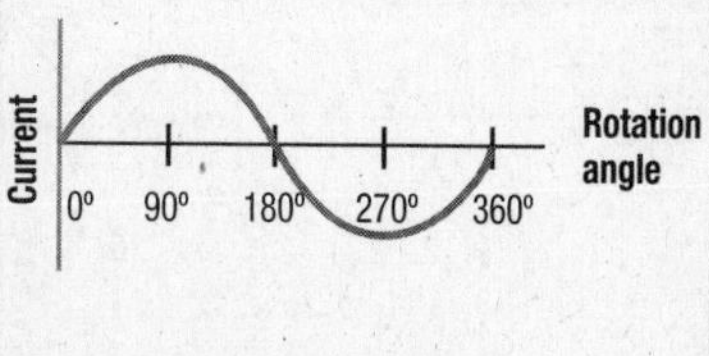

READING CHECK

7. **Explain** Why does the direction of the current change as the loop rotates?

_____

_____

_____

LOOKING CLOSER

8. **Identify** At which three angles of rotation is the current zero?

_____

_____

_____

AC CURRENT IN THE HOME

Remember that batteries produce direct current. That is, the current from a battery does not change with time. In contrast, most electrical outlets supply alternating current. This is why many battery-powered devices, such as radios, require special adaptors to use power from an outlet.

The electrical energy supplied through electrical outlets comes from generators at power plants. The mechanical energy needed to turn these generators can come from many sources.

Some sources, such as wind, turn the generators directly. Other sources, such as coal and oil, are burned to release heat energy. The heat energy is used to boil water and produce steam. The steam turns special fans called *turbines*. The turbines are connected to the generator. As the steam turns the turbines, the generator produces electricity.

What Is the Electromagnetic Force?

Recall that moving electric charges produce magnetic fields and that changing magnetic fields cause electric charges to move. Those two facts show that electricity and magnetism are two aspects of a single force, called the *electromagnetic force*.

The electromagnetic force produces electromagnetic energy. Visible light is a form of electromagnetic energy. So are other forms of radiation, such as radio waves and X rays. All are electromagnetic waves, or EM waves. ☑

The figure below shows the nature of EM waves. As you can see, they consist of vibrating electric and magnetic fields that are perpendicular to each other. All EM waves have the two fields in common, whatever their frequency.

Critical Thinking

9. Explain Why is the current from a power plant an alternating current? (Hint: What type of current do generators produce?)

_____

_____

_____

_____

✓ READING CHECK

10. Identify What are three forms of energy that are produced by the electromagnetic force?

_____

_____

_____

LOOKING CLOSER

11. Describe How do the vibration directions of the electric and magnetic fields in an electromagnetic wave compare?

_____

_____

_____

_____

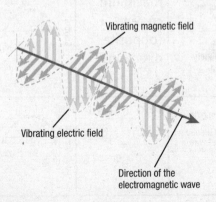

Vibrating magnetic field

Vibrating electric field

Direction of the electromagnetic wave

GENERATING AND REGENERATING

An EM wave's electric and magnetic fields are both perpendicular to the direction in which the wave travels. Therefore, EM waves are transverse waves.

As an EM wave travels, the changing electric field generates the magnetic field. At the same time, the changing magnetic field generates the electric field. Because each field generates the other, EM waves have a special property: they can travel through a vacuum. Without that property, light from the sun would not be able to reach Earth. ☑

What Are Transformers?

You have probably seen metal cylinders on power line poles. These cylinders contain devices called **transformers** that increase or decrease the voltage of alternating current. The simplest type of transformer consists of two coils of wire wrapped around opposite sides of a closed iron loop. ☑

In the transformer shown below, one wire is attached to a source of alternating current, such as a power outlet. This wire is called the *primary coil*. The other wire is attached to an appliance, such as a lamp. This is the *secondary coil*.

Current in the primary coil creates a changing magnetic field. This, in turn, magnetizes the transformer's iron core. The changing magnetic field of the iron core then induces a current in the secondary coil. That current's direction changes every time the direction of the current in the primary coil changes.

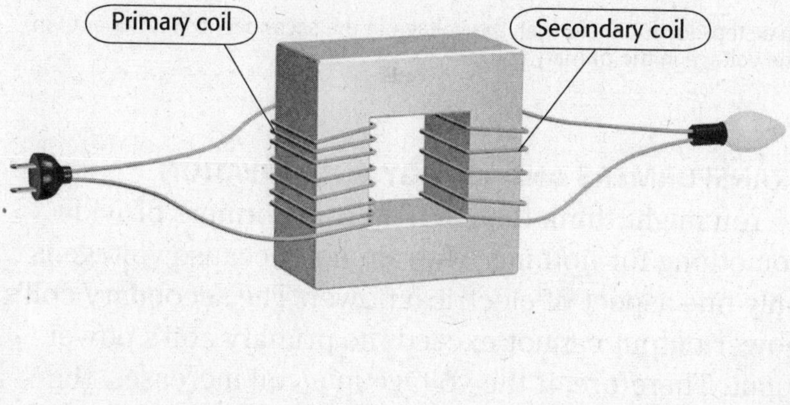

✓ READING CHECK

12. Explain Why can EM waves travel through a vacuum?

_____

_____

_____

✓ READING CHECK

13. Define What is a transformer?

_____

_____

_____

Primary coil

Secondary coil

LOOKING CLOSER
14. Identify Label the core of the transformer in the figure.

STEP-UP AND STEP-DOWN TRANSFORMERS

The voltage induced in a transformer's secondary coil depends on the number of loops, or turns, in the coil. If the secondary coil has more turns than the primary coil, the voltage in the secondary coil is higher. Then, the transformer is called a *step-up transformer*, shown at the top of the figure below.

If the secondary coil has fewer turns than the primary coil, the voltage in the secondary coil is lower. Then, the transformer is a *step-down transformer*, shown at the bottom of the figure below.

Critical Thinking

15. **Apply Concepts** A transformer has 10 turns in its primary coil and 15 turns in its secondary coil. Is it a step-up or step-down transformer?

_____

_____

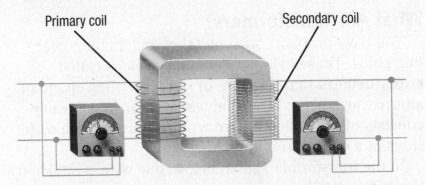

Primary coil   Secondary coil

In a step-up transformer, the voltage in the secondary coil is higher than the voltage in the primary coil.

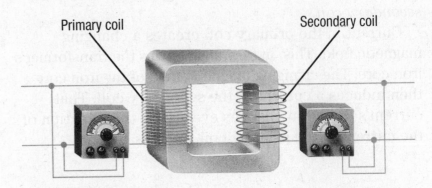

Primary coil   Secondary coil

In a step-down transformer, the voltage in the secondary coil is lower than the voltage in the primary coil.

LOOKING CLOSER

16. **Identify** Circle the side of each transformer that has the higher voltage.

TRANSFORMERS AND ENERGY CONSERVATION

You might think that step-up transformers provide something for nothing. They do not, because voltage is only one aspect of electrical power. The secondary coil's power output cannot exceed the primary coil's power input. Therefore, if the voltage in a coil increases, the current in the coil must decrease. ☑

✓ **READING CHECK**

17. **Describe** How does the current in the secondary coil of a step-up transformer compare to the current in the primary coil?

SECTION 3 Electric Currents from Magnetism *continued*

TRANSFORMERS ON POWER LINES

Real transformers are not perfectly efficient. Because of resistance in the coils, they lose some of the energy put into them as heat. The power loss increases as the current increases. ☑

Power companies want to decrease loss to maximize the amount of energy they transmit. Therefore, they use high voltages and low currents in their long-distance power lines. However, it is safer for appliances in the home to use lower voltage. Therefore, there are transformers on power lines.

Step-up and step-down transformers help to transmit electrical energy from power plants to homes and businesses. Step-up transformers near power plants increase the voltage to about 120,000 V. Then, near homes, step-down transformers reduce the voltage to the 120 V that is safe to use in the home.

Step-down transformers like the ones shown here are used to reduce the voltage across power lines when they enter people's homes.

☑ **READING CHECK**

18. Identify What causes energy loss in transformers?

_____

_____

Critical Thinking

19. Compare How does the current in power lines compare to the current in wires in the home? Explain your answer.

_____

_____

_____

_____

_____

_____

_____

_____

_____

Section 3 Review

SECTION VOCABULARY

alternating current an electric current that changes direction at regular intervals (abbreviation, AC)	**generator** a machine that converts mechanical energy into electrical energy
electromagnetic induction the process of creating a current in a circuit by changing a magnetic field	**transformer** a device that increases or decreases the voltage of alternating current

1. Compare Describe how the current produced by a battery is different from the current produced by a generator.

_____

_____

_____

2. Identify What is Faraday's law?

_____

_____

3. Describe How can you use magnetic field lines to determine whether a magnetic field will induce a current in a circuit?

_____

_____

_____

_____

4. Explain How can the chemical energy in oil be used to produce electrical energy?

_____

_____

_____

_____

5. Describe The primary coil of a transformer has 1,000 turns of wire. The secondary coil has 500 turns of wire. Identify what type of transformer this is, and describe how the voltage in the two coils will be different.

_____

_____

_____

6. Compare How is a generator different from an electric motor?

_____

_____

_____

_____

The Periodic Table of the Elements

☐ Hydrogen

▨ Semiconductors
(also known as metalloids)

☐ Metals

☐ Nonmetals

Group 18

2
He
Helium
4.002 602

Group 13	Group 14	Group 15	Group 16	Group 17
5 **B** Boron 10.811	6 **C** Carbon 12.0107	7 **N** Nitrogen 14.0067	8 **O** Oxygen 15.9994	9 **F** Fluorine 18.998 4032

10
Ne
Neon
20.1797

			13 **Al** Aluminum 26.981 5386	14 **Si** Silicon 28.0855	15 **P** Phosphorus 30.973 762	16 **S** Sulfur 32.065	17 **Cl** Chlorine 35.453	18 **Ar** Argon 39.948

Group 10	Group 11	Group 12						
28 **Ni** Nickel 58.6934	29 **Cu** Copper 63.546	30 **Zn** Zinc 65.409	31 **Ga** Gallium 69.723	32 **Ge** Germanium 72.64	33 **As** Arsenic 74.921 60	34 **Se** Selenium 78.96	35 **Br** Bromine 79.904	36 **Kr** Krypton 83.798
46 **Pd** Palladium 106.42	47 **Ag** Silver 107.8682	48 **Cd** Cadmium 112.411	49 **In** Indium 114.818	50 **Sn** Tin 118.710	51 **Sb** Antimony 121.760	52 **Te** Tellurium 127.60	53 **I** Iodine 126.904 47	54 **Xe** Xenon 131.293
78 **Pt** Platinum 195.084	79 **Au** Gold 196.966 569	80 **Hg** Mercury 200.59	81 **Tl** Thallium 204.3833	82 **Pb** Lead 207.2	83 **Bi** Bismuth 208.980 40	84 **Po** Polonium (209)	85 **At** Astatine (210)	86 **Rn** Radon (222)
110 **Ds** Darmstadtium (271)	111 **Rg** Roentgenium (272)	112 **Uub*** Ununbium (285)		114 **Uuq*** Ununquadium (289)		116 **Uuh*** Ununhexium (292)		

The discoveries of elements with atomic numbers 112, 114, and 116 have been reported but not fully confirmed.

63 **Eu** Europium 151.964	64 **Gd** Gadolinium 157.25	65 **Tb** Terbium 158.925 35	66 **Dy** Dysprosium 162.500	67 **Ho** Holmium 164.930 32	68 **Er** Erbium 167.259	69 **Tm** Thulium 168.934 21	70 **Yb** Ytterbium 173.04	71 **Lu** Lutetium 174.967
95 **Am** Americium (243)	96 **Cm** Curium (247)	97 **Bk** Berkelium (247)	98 **Cf** Californium (251)	99 **Es** Einsteinium (252)	100 **Fm** Fermium (257)	101 **Md** Mendelevium (258)	102 **No** Nobelium (259)	103 **Lr** Lawrencium (262)

The atomic masses listed in this table reflect the precision of current measurements. (The value listed in parentheses is the mass number of a radioactive element's most stable or most common isotope.)